Political Philosophy and the God of Abraham

THE JOHNS HOPKINS UNIVERSITY PRESS

Political Philosophy and the God of Abraham

THOMAS L. PANGLE

THE JOHNS HOPKINS UNIVERSITY PRESS
Baltimore and London

© 2003 The Johns Hopkins University Press
All rights reserved. Published 2003
Printed in the United States of America on acid-free paper

Johns Hopkins Paperback edition, 2007
2 4 6 8 9 7 5 3 1

The Johns Hopkins University Press
2715 North Charles Street
Baltimore, Maryland 21218-4363
www.press.jhu.edu

*The Library of Congress has catalogued the hardcover edition of
this book as follows:*
Pangle, Thomas L.
Political philosophy and the God of Abraham / Thomas L. Pangle.
p.   cm.
Includes bibliographical references and index.
ISBN 0-8018-7328-2 (alk. paper)
1. Politics in the Bible. 2. Bible. O.T. Genesis—Criticism, interpretation, etc.
I. Title.
BS1199.P6 P36 2003
222'.110832—dc21
2002013973

ISBN 13: 978-0-8018-8761-1
ISBN 10: 0-8018-8761-5

A catalog record for this book is available from the British Library.

Frontispiece: Rembrandt van Rijn. *Abraham and Isaac.* Etching and burin, 1645.
Rosenwald Collection. Photograph © 2002 Board of Trustees, National Gallery of
Art, Washington.

To Lorraine.

You who consider that you understand a book that is the guide of the first and the last men while glancing through it as you would glance through a historical work or a piece of poetry: collect yourselves and reflect, for things are not as you thought.

Maimonides *Guide of the Perplexed* 1.2

> So We commanded you to follow
> The way of Abraham the upright;
> Call them to the path,
> And reason with them in the best way possible.

Al-Qur'an 16.123–25

The human being is only a reed, the most feeble in nature; but this is a thinking reed. It isn't necessary for the entire universe to arm itself in order to crush him; a whiff of vapor, a taste of water, suffices to kill him. But when the universe crushes him, the human being becomes still more noble than that which kills him, because he knows that he is dying, and the advantage that the universe has over him. The universe, it does not have a clue.

All our dignity consists, then, in thought. This is the basis on which we must raise ourselves, and not space and time, which we would not know how to fill. Let us make it our task, then, to think well: here is the principle of morality.

Pascal, *Pensées,* #200

Contents

Acknowledgments

FOR FINANCIAL SUPPORT DURING THE YEARS WHEN I WORKED ON THIS book, I wish to express my gratitude to the Lynde and Harry Bradley Foundation, the Connaught Fund of the University of Toronto, the Social Sciences and Humanities Research Council of Canada, the National Endowment for the Humanities, and the Carl Friedrich von Siemens Institute in Munich, where I spent a very profitable year as Fellow.

An earlier version of parts of chapters 1 and 2 appears as "Political Philosophy's Response to the Challenge of Creation: An Essay in Honor of Wilson Carey McWilliams," in *Friends and Citizens: Essays in Honor of Wilson Carey McWilliams,* edited by Peter Dennis Bathory and Nancy L. Schwartz (Lanham, Md.: Rowman and Littlefield, 2000), 13–43.

Political Philosophy and the God of Abraham

Introduction

THIS BOOK SEEKS TO REINVIGORATE THE ENCOUNTER BETWEEN POLITI-
cal philosophy and the Bible. I remain at the beginning in almost every
sense. My focus is on that portion of Genesis that treats (with amazing
compression) by far the longest period of human history, stretching from
the Creation through the initial patriarchal establishment of the chosen
people. It is here that the foundation is laid for everything that follows;
and accordingly, this has been the portion of Scripture that has received by
far the most attention from commentators.[1] In these chapters of Genesis
are to be found the most basic presuppositions of a reflective life that roots
itself finally in obedience to the mysterious God Who reveals Himself in
the Scriptures. I provide a close reading of these chapters, animated by the
concerns and questions and doubts of the philosophic enterprise as it was
refounded by Socrates—and then once again refounded, with a dramatically altered but not wholly new agenda, by Machiavelli, Hobbes, and
Spinoza in the early modern period. I aim to show how the meaning of
the Bible, and of the way of life that it demands, and, by way of contrast,
the meaning of political philosophy (and of the way of life that it defends)
can be mutually illuminated when the Scripture is thus addressed and
interpreted.

Political philosophy in the strict sense aspires to be unqualifiedly normative rationalism: political philosophy claims to show how human beings, led by the wisest among them, can discover the fixed truth about
their situation in the universe, about the good, about justice, and even
about the revelations of divinity, by using reason as their "only Star and
compass" (John Locke, *Two Treatises of Government*, 1.58). As St. Augustine critically observes, Socrates and the philosophers who follow in
his wake seek the "attainment of happiness" by "relying on the human
senses and human reasoning."[2] Or as Plato's Socrates himself declares, in
his most famous public statement about the meaning of his life (*Apology of
Socrates* 37e–38a),

Perhaps someone would say: "Socrates, can you not go away from us and live in quiet, remaining silent?" In regard to this it is most difficult of all to persuade some of you. For if I say that this is to disobey the god, and on account of this it is impossible to live in quiet, you will not believe me on the grounds that I am being ironically deceptive. But if on the other hand I say that this happens to be the greatest good for a human being—each day to make rational arguments about virtue and also about the other matters concerning which you hear me carrying on dialogues and examining both myself and others; and the unexamined life is not worth living for a human being—you will believe me still less when I say these things. But so it is, as I affirm, men—though to persuade of it is not easy.

Socrates' reference here to his proclaimed obedience to the god, taken together with his previous invocations of his famous personal experience of the *daimonion,* or "demonic voice," suffices to indicate that he (and the authentic heirs to the enterprise of political philosophy that he initiated)[3] does not by any means discount divine revelation or inspiration as an experienced source of guidance that may be beyond what reason and the evidence of the senses manifestly provide. Socrates himself went so far as to proclaim that his peculiar refutative activity had been "given him as a commandment by the god, even from prophecies and from dreams and in every manner in which any divine dispensation has ever been afforded any human being as a commandment to do anything" (ibid., 33c4–7). But the Socratic way is to bow to such guidance solely insofar as it can be recognized as delivered by an intelligibly wise and benevolent deity—supplementing (especially for educational purposes), but not contradicting, reason. Accordingly, we hear from Xenophon of at least one momentous occasion on which Socrates repeatedly refused to obey a commandment delivered by his demonic voice; Socrates had evidently not yet grasped the reasonableness, and therefore or thereby the truly divine authorization, of the audible injunction that he finally came to accept as from "the gods."[4] Near the beginning of the private conversation that Plato allows us to overhear in his *Symposium,* Socrates declares that he has "scientific knowledge of nothing else except things pertaining to *eros* [love]" (177d; see also *Theages* 128b and ff.); subsequently in the same dialogue, Socrates reports that Diotima showed him that he understood Eros to be a (or the) "Great *Daimon,*" and that "all the *daimonic* is in-between god and mortal," having the power to "interpret and transmit to gods the things from humans, and to humans the things from gods—from the former, the imploring prayers and sacrifices; from the latter, the commandments and reciprocations" (*Symposium* 202d–e). Thus according to Socrates, erotic love—at once devotional and needy, and deeply linked to righteousness or justice—is *the* avenue to the divine; but if love is to conduct the soul to the truly divine, to the truth about the divine, then love must be purified in the fire of severely self-critical rational investigation of both love itself and its primary or apparent objects.

We may surmise that it is as a consequence of such purifying investigation that Aristotle, in his treatise on prophecy through dreams, while proving the regular existence of such prophecy and demonstrating the probable causes, nonetheless doubts the claim that such prophetic power comes from God rather than nature ("which is *daimonic,* but not divine"), on the grounds that "it would be strange to send the prophecies not to the best and most prudent but to simply anyone"; since "if it were God who sent them, they would occur also in the daytime, and to the wise."[5] Speaking in a similar spirit, as regards divine will, Averroës insists that "the philosophers do not deny the will of God, nor do they admit that He has a human will, for the human will implies a deficiency in the willer"; "the philosophers only attribute a will to God in the sense that the acts which proceed from Him proceed through knowledge, and everything which proceeds through knowledge and wisdom proceeds through the will of the agent"—"not, however, necessarily and naturally" (Averroës hastens to add), "since the nature of knowledge does not imply the proceeding of the act." This is clear from the knowledge of contraries, Averroës explains: the fact that only one of two known contrary options is realized by God "shows that there is another attribute present besides knowledge, namely will."[6]

As these bold but puzzling asseverations make manifest, the classical and medieval political philosophers' conceptions of divinity put them at dangerous odds with popular, lawfully enforced, pious belief. We cannot too often recall that Socrates himself was executed for impiety and corruption of the young by one of the most permissive of the classical republics. Yet the same Socrates managed to postpone the calamity until his seventieth year. In the pages of Plato and Xenophon we see Socrates portrayed as at pains to disguise the extent of his unorthodoxy, through the weaving of a designedly ambiguous and even deceptive self-presentation. Xenophon and Plato manifestly carry further this benevolently deceptive, responsibly prudential rhetoric—adding major new dimensions to a longstanding poetic tradition of concealment.[7] Clement of Alexandria, the Church Father most steeped in classical philosophy, advises that "those taught in theology by these prophets, the poets—I mean Orpheus, Linus, Musaeus, Homer and Hesiod and the ones wise in this way—philosophize concerning many things by way of a hidden sense (ὑπονοία). The poetic leading of souls is for them a veil with a view to the multitude." To the multitude, "all things that appear through a certain veil show the truth grander and more exalted." Once the veil is removed, "the enveloping rays of light are refutative, in addition to the fact that things made evident are understood by the mind unambiguously." "With reason then," Clement concludes, "Plato too, in the *Letters,* treating of God, says: 'you ought to speak through enigmas; that should the writing-tablet be carried by any mischance either by sea or by land or winds, he who reads may not understand.' " And this is why "Plato also says, in the second book of the *Republic* [378a], 'It is those that sacrifice not a sow, but some grand and difficult sacrifice,' who thus ought to inquire respecting God."[8] Locke makes more pointed the reasons for, and therefore the precise character of, specifically philosophic (as opposed to priestly) self-concealment. In concluding his argument for the "reasonableness of Christianity," Locke looks back to his classical philosophic forebears and remarks that as regards the truth about the nature of God Himself, it is the case that prior to the advent of Christ, and without any knowledge of the Bible, "the Rational and thinking part of Mankind, 'tis true,"

> when they sought after him, found the One Supream Invisible God: But if they acknowledged and worshipped him, it was only in their own minds. They kept this Truth locked up in their own breasts as a Secret, nor ever durst venture it amongst the People; much less amongst the Priests, those wary Guardians of their own Creeds and Profitable Inventions. Hence we see that *Reason,* speaking never so clearly to the Wise and Virtuous, had never Authority enough to prevail on the Multitude; and to perswade the Societies of Men, that there was but One God, that alone was to be owned and worshipped. The Belief and Worship of One God was the National Religion of the *Israelites* alone: And if we will consider it, it was introduced and supported amongst that People by *Revelation.* . . . Whatsoever *Plato,* and the soberest of the Philosophers thought of the Nature and Being of the One God, they were fain, in their outward Professions and Worship, to go with the Herd, and keep to the Religion established by Law.[9]

The role assigned here to revelation implies that the philosophers understand genuine revelation as the prudent instructional and political rhetoric attributable to a wisely benevolent deity. As Locke, again, observes of his classical forerunners, "The Philosophers who spoke from Reason, made not much mention of the Deity, in their *Ethicks*. They depended on Reason and her Oracles; which contain nothing but Truth. But yet some parts of that Truth lye too deep for our Natural Powers easily to reach, and make plain and visible to mankind, without some Light from above to direct them." Because "the greatest part cannot know," it follows that they "must believe":

> And I ask, whether one coming from Heaven in the Power of God, in full and clear Evidence and Demonstration of Miracles, giving plain and direct Rules of *Morality* and Obedience, be not likelier to enlighten the bulk of Mankind, and set them right in their Duties, and bring them to do them, than by Reasoning with them from general Notions and Principles of Humane Reason? And were all the Duties of Humane Life clearly demonstrated; yet I conclude, when well considered, that Method of teaching men their Duties would be thought proper only for a few, who had much Leisure, improved Understandings, and were used to abstract Reasonings. But the Instruction of the People were best still to be left to the Precepts and Principles of the Gospel.[10]

It is true that the character of the divinity that unassisted reason is held to disclose is in serious dispute between the ancient and the modern rationalists. We may circumscribe the dispute by employing the classic categories that have come down to us from Marcus Varro through Augustine (*City of God* 6.5–7): the ancient rationalists are much less serious than are the moderns about promulgating a "civil theology" (*theologia civilis*) and, by the same token, more serious about elaborating a "natural theology" (*theologia naturalis*)—which they expect to be only barely tolerated in society, and which will provide a map of the path toward constructive fundamental questions. Thus the speculations of Plato and Aristotle culminate in a pure and eternally active mind, disembodied but manifest in the visible universe, especially in the stars, which appear to be the bodies of lesser divinities. Given the premise of the "special blessedness and happiness of the gods," would it not be "absurd," Aristotle asks, "for them to manifest themselves as entering into covenants and returning deposits and other things of this kind?"[11] Hobbes, in contrast (anticipating Locke in some but not all crucial respects), teaches of a divinity that is the first efficient cause, and hence part, of the material universe; this divinity exercises a "kingdom by nature" over humanity, on the basis of "power irresistible." The "precepts" for which this deity known by nature has "propounded rewards and punishments to mankind" are "the natural dictates of right reason."[12] Hobbes insists that there is no contradiction between this conception of deity and that of the Scriptures, so long as the Scriptures are reinterpreted in strict accordance with the principle that "though there be many things in God's word above reason (that is to say, which cannot by natural reason be either demonstrated or confuted), yet there is nothing contrary to it; but when it seemeth so, the fault is either in our unskillful interpretation or erroneous ratiocination" (*Leviathan,* chap. 32, para. 2). Hobbes proceeds to a synoptic if selective commentary on the Bible, claiming to prove that from the text, "by wise and learned interpretation, and careful ratiocination, all rules and precepts necessary to the knowledge of our duty both to God and man, without enthusiasm or supernatural inspiration, may easily be deduced." For, Hobbes insists, "our Saviour Christ hath not given us new laws, but counsel to observe those we are subject to; that is to say, the laws of nature, and the laws of our several sovereigns: nor did he make any new law to the Jews in his sermon on the Mount, but only expounded the laws of Moses, to which they were subject before. The laws of God therefore are none but the laws of nature, whereof the principal is, that we should not violate our faith, that is, a commandment to obey our civil sovereigns, which we constituted over us, by mutual pact one with another" (ibid., chap. 43, para. 5).

It can surely be doubted whether Scripture, candidly interpreted on its own terms, truly subordinates itself to reasonableness in the manner claimed by Hobbes and Locke and their modern comrades-in-arms. Discerning study of the texts of the modern philosophic rationalists discloses that this contention of theirs is in fact a key dimension of a titanic strategy of propaganda, whereby Holy Writ is to be reconceived and in a sense rewritten so as to be subsumed in a vast secular cultural revolution.[13] The Bible is to be reinterpreted so as to serve a merely civil religion that will support, or at least in no important way challenge, the requirements of rational, secular political prudence—guided by a new teaching on human nature that deliberately and drastically lowers the conception of human ends taught by classical rationalism. The deepest goal of this vast cultural experiment is the erosion of humanity's awareness of and testimony to precisely that core of the biblical revelation that manifestly chastises reason's pretensions to self-sufficiency, and that demands the transcendence and subordination of the concern for worldly prosperity and security.

The encounter with Genesis that is elaborated in the pages that follow springs from the conviction that this chastisement, this stern biblical call for what Pascal calls "la simple soumission de la raison,"[14] must be squarely faced. The gravity of this challenge will not be recognized so long as it is mistakenly regarded as the call of a "faith" that understands itself as mere "belief." Biblical faith at its most challenging understands itself to be rooted in experiential *knowledge*—of a kind superior to that available to unassisted reason, or to human experience not yet illuminated by grace:

> Profane men think that religion rests only on opinion, and, therefore, in order that they may not believe foolishly, or on slight grounds, they desire and insist that it be proved by reason that Moses and the prophets were divinely inspired. But I answer, that the testimony of the Spirit is superior to reason. For as God alone can properly bear witness to His own words, so these words will not obtain full credit in the hearts of men, until these words are sealed by the inward testimony of the Spirit. The same Spirit, therefore, who spoke by the mouths of the prophets, must enter into our hearts, in order to convince us. [Calvin, *Institutes* 1.7.4; see also 1.7.5, 1.8.1, 1.8.13]

In the lapidary words of Augustine,

> Not with a doubtful, but with *certain consciousness* do I love Thee, Lord [*Non dubia, sed* certa conscientia, *domine, amo te*]. To be sure, heaven and earth and all that is in them—behold!—on every side they say to me that I should love Thee; nor do they cease to say it to all, so that they may be inexcusable. More profoundly, however, Thou shalt have mercy, on whom Thou shalt have mercy, and shalt show compassion, to whom Thou will show compassion—without which, heaven and earth speak Your praises to the deaf! What is it then that I love, when I love Thee? . . . I love a distinct light and a distinct voice . . . an embrace of my inner humanity, where my soul is illumined by a light no place can contain, and where there speaks what time cannot steal. . . . The whole world, . . . manifesting itself in the same way everywhere, is mute to that man, speaks to this man: always, in truth, it speaks to all; but those who understand it are the ones who compare the voice received from outside with the

Truth that is within. It is Truth that says to me, "your God is not heaven and earth or any body."[15]

On the basis of a return to this crux witness of Augustine, Karl Barth, the deepest Christian dogmatist of the twentieth century, took sharp issue with "the extremely disturbing" dogmatics of his liberal nineteenth-century predecessors. Those predecessors, in a desperate attempt to deflect the shattering impact of modern evolutionary science and historical scholarship on faith in the Creation, had come to conceive of Creation as a "hypothesis" or "postulate," a "conception of man" derived from a so-called "religious consciousness" of "dependence." Such a teaching, Barth protested, falsifies the meaning of faith in the Creation. What is properly "presupposed" in authentic biblical faith is "the certain knowledge of God in His word." That is to say, "The question is not: How do we come to be justified in supposing this? What premonitions and feelings, what outward and inward probabilities, testify to us that it may be the case? Nor is it: What logical necessities support the view that it must be so?" "No," Barth rejoins, "the question is, How do we arrive at the position where we can simply say that we know that it is so?" For "we are in a sorry case," he deploringly observes, "if we are compelled to think and finally to live and die on the ground of . . . a mere opinion and hypothesis." The full experience of faith is that of "giving an answer to the divine self-witness, and therefore confessing a faith which puts an end once and for all to all other contradictory conjectures. We can only pray that this may be so. But it is a great and special thing to have and to confess the belief." For "if the universe is not actually silent, it is still silent to those who are not participators in the truth, i.e., in the *direct self-revelation* of God."[16] To be sure, the essential mediating role of (a) tradition is implicit in every such affirmation of direct religious experience. We learn from Gershom Scholem that, for understandable reasons, self-conscious faithful reflection upon this dimension of the individual's "reception" of revelation seems to have reached a kind of high point in some of the writings of the mature rabbinic Kabbalah. Granted that there was in the distant past a supremely authoritative original revelation (e.g., to Moses, on Mount Sinai), "every religious experience" after that revelation "is a mediated one." It is "the experience of the *voice* of God rather than the experience of God." The "unique event" of the original revelation is "juxtaposed to the *continuity* of the voice." In the words of the influential Kabbalist Isaiah

Horovitz, "It thus follows that while we say of God that 'He *has* given the Torah,' He can also be designated at the same time as 'the One Who gives the Torah.' At every hour and at every time the fountain gushes forth without interruption and what He gives at any time was potentially contained in what He gave." Thus "all the words of the wise men" recorded in the Talmud "are words of the living God." The later Kabbalah, Scholem tells us, "formulated a widely accepted dictum: that the Torah turns a special face to every single Jew, meant only for him and apprehensible only by him, and that a Jew therefore fulfills his true purpose only when he comes to see this face and is able to incorporate it into the tradition."[17]

Now, philosophy in the strict Socratic sense wholly agrees with Augustine and Milton and Barth and the Rabbis that a fully human life can and ought to be guided solely by the manifest Truth. But Socratic philosophy springs from truthful knowledge of its own ignorance. In particular and above all, Socratic philosophy confesses that it has experienced only in ambiguous and dubious forms the suprarational illumination to which these apparently privileged witnesses testify with supreme confidence. Socratic philosophy is therefore obliged to look upon its own religious experiences, and upon testimony such as that submitted by Augustine and the Kabbalah, with good-willed but deeply uneasy skepticism. But this skepticism (a condition through which Augustine himself and others like him claim to have passed) is not a lastingly tenable philosophic position— though it may remain an inescapable personal fate. For undogmatic philosophy (and dogmatic philosophy is, strictly speaking, a contradiction in terms) cannot ignore, while skepticism cannot dispose of, the claimed human experience of a reportedly certain divine call to submit and even to sacrifice one's intellect—a call accompanied by a warning of what we have seen Augustine declare to be the "inexcusable" guilt and hence eternal punishment incurred by failure to kneel.[18] The situation in which this apparently leaves the rational skeptic has been stated as follows by Pascal, speaking of those whom he sees "combating" the claims of revelation: "Let them be honest people if they cannot be Christians, and recognize that there are only two kinds of people that can be called reasonable: either those who serve God with all their heart because they have knowledge of him, or those who search for him with all their heart because they do not have knowledge of him" (*Pensées,* #427 [= Brunschvicg #194]). Still, if the search (and the submission) is to be genuine and not pro forma, if it is to be a search that entertains submission of the conscious spirit or mind and not merely of the lips and knees, one must consciously know (as much as one can) who and what it is to which one is called to submit. Pascal again: "*Authority.* So far is it from being the case that having heard something ought to be the rule of your believing, that you ought not to believe anything without first putting yourself in a condition as if you had never heard it. It is the consent of yourself to yourself and the constant voice of your reason, and not others, which ought to make you believe" (*Pensées,* #505 = B. #260). At the very least, those compelled to attempt to be philosophic find it a matter of utmost urgency to inquire with precision into what is at stake—into all that is promised, and into all that we are called upon to sacrifice—in this bowing of the intellect to the claim of the superior knowledge vouchsafed by revelation. As the full implications are laid out, the philosophically minded cannot help but inquire of Scripture, and of its most cogent theological explicators, as to the extent to which this humbling demand is made intelligible, to the open-minded, through the Bible's teaching as to what is evidently right and good as well as through its account of what is historically and empirically plausible. And charity would seem to demand that the exponents of Scripture accept, in good faith, this invitation to dialogue. Now, it is in regard to the right and the good—that is, in regard to justice or righteousness—that political philosophy and scriptural piety have the fullest basis for a conversation that may well be mutually illuminating. For righteousness, or justice in the fullest sense, is *the* theme of political philosophy, *the* cynosure of its meditations, even as righteousness (or justice in the full sense) is among the highest and most essential themes of Scripture.

In our effort of retrieval or renewal of this perennial dialogue, we will find some significant assistance from those uncompromising modern rationalists, beginning preeminently with Hobbes, Spinoza, and Locke, who commented extensively upon the Scriptures—and in particular upon key passages in Genesis. To be sure, what is most valuable about the modern philosophers' interpretative observations is to some extent obscured by their impishly ironic conspiracy to make the Scriptures appear to conform to, and to support, their revolutionary, secularizing project of "enlightenment." But it is not too difficult to discern this strategy, and then to begin to recognize the truly serious and troubling questions these thinkers raise (often implicitly or quietly) about the coherence, sophistication, and provenance of the original biblical message. The closer one looks, the more one recognizes that the modern rationalists' critiques or revisions of the Bible—even when apparently crude and hostile or derisive—are rooted in a searching prior attempt to grasp as clearly as possible the biblical challenge to their rationalist independence. But the strategic priority of the modern philosophers, as teachers, is not to put in the foreground this deepest level of their exegesis. They do not characteristically make it their business to set forth the most plausible and coherent interpretation of the Bible's teaching on the basis of its own premises. Instead, they tend to foist on the Scripture deliberately bogus "reasonable" readings that, when well considered, often place the actual words of the Holy Writ in an absurd or lurid light. The modern rationalists do not devote their didactic energies to eliciting, and then to wrestling with, powerful scriptural-based retorts to their exegetical impositions or their penetrating doubts. That is a task and a challenge to which they may point their most thoughtful readers; but they consciously prepare a world mesmerized by the rewards of secular progress, in which fewer and fewer, even or especially among the thoughtful, will recognize that it is worthwhile to make the effort to confront in a sustained way the challenge posed to reason, and its secular progress, by Scripture. The ultimate cultural aim of the modern theologico-political treatises is to reduce religious reflection and argument (along with reflection on and argument about virtue, as it was aspired to in ancient republicanism) to the status of a birdlike cacophony of merely private and personal, shallow and shifting, opinions.

The success of the cultural revolution that these modern rationalists launched and carried out has been big enough to bring about a condition in which it is more and more the case that discussion not only of theology but of humanity's spiritual fulfillment and destiny has become radically "relativized" and thus increasingly rendered unserious. A civilizational perimeter has been constructed from within whose ever-higher walls there is practically no access to genuine encounter with the texts that make possible a passionate and intense quest for final answers to the fundamental and abiding questions of the eternal truth about divinity and human excellence. Now, a reversal of the *sociopolitical* achievement of liberation and reconstruction effected by the Enlightenment is as unlikely in the foreseeable future as it would be deleterious. But on the level of serious and meditative *thought,* and for the sake of authentic self-understanding, we must break out of this cultural amusement park that more or less benevolently confines us like etiolated adolescents. If we are fully to assess and to appreciate our being shaped by the great project of the modern rationalists, in their achievement and in their failing, we need to recover their own *radical* perspective on the fundamental challenge from revelation that they confronted and sought to dispose of through their cultural revolution. What we are seeking, then, in trying to win our way back to the truest and fullest dialogue between political philosophy and biblical revelation is nothing less than a provisional escape, on the level of thought, from the apparently successful modern cultural revolution. We are embarking, one might say, on a theologico-political investigation that proceeds directly against the current set in motion by the project of the theologico-political treatises that launched modernity.[19]

This book's enterprise, insofar as it is a response to the present historical context, is related to what has been called "the revival of political theology in our generation"—a revival closely linked to "the strong inclination which our generation has evinced to question the presuppositions of modern society, and to think through our present situation afresh with a more critical perspective on 'modernity.'"[20] But the acute concern that animates the present book is the revival not of political theology but rather of rationalism in its classic form—that is, of political *philosophy,* understood as the essential dialectical partner/antagonist of political theology. In this regard what is so deeply troubling about the current scene is the degree to which what is called contemporary "philosophy" represents the explicit abandonment of rationalism. "Postmodernism," in the hands of its highest priests, is more and more clearly visible as a vindication of amorphous quasi-religious faith(s) over and against the supposedly exploded pretensions of autonomous reason.[21] The time is ripe, and over-ripe, for political philosophy in the strict or genuine sense, political philosophy as the foundation of rationalism, to be brought back from its late-modern exile. Such a repatriation ought to be welcomed especially by political theologians; for ever since the time of Augustine, truly profound and authentic political theology has owed its vitality in part to the perhaps providential challenge of this its most challenging adversary or questioner.

We want, in short, to recover the possibility of a philosophic interrogation of the Bible, in unqualified openness to eliciting and hearing its message—a message whose supremely troubling challenge to philosophy we want to wrestle with in all essentials. The dialogue we seek to enter into with Scripture is thus both less polemical and less presumptive than that carried on by the leading modern political philosophers. We will seriously entertain the modern rationalists' exegetical suggestions, reinterpretative contentions, implicit and explicit critiques; but in every case we will turn back to the Scripture to seek a rejoinder, to elaborate a dialogue that looks to find in the mutual challenges and replies a way to illumine more fully what we can gather of the integral intelligible teaching of the Bible—and of philosophic rationalism's response to that integral intelligible teaching.

In this endeavor we are not as utterly without help from the original Socratics as might at first seem to be the case. It is indeed true, as Locke stresses in the passage quoted earlier, that Plato and Aristotle confronted, with their philosophic monotheism, a pagan polytheism—that they did not, so far as we know, ever themselves encounter the more profound challenge of biblical monotheism.[22] Yet the medieval Platonists and Aristotelians contended that the original vindication of classical rationalism— carried out in the face of the challenge posed by popular and poetic claims of contrarational polytheistic revelation—remained valid when rethought or reenacted in a confrontation with the challenge posed to philosophic rationalism by the more awesome Holy Scriptures. The medieval rationalists insisted at the same time that a dialogue between Socratic philosophy and informed spokesmen for revelation led to an otherwise unavailable deepening of the humanly comprehensible meaning of Scripture. Our commentary will attempt to exhibit something of what the medieval Platonists seem to have had in mind. For if these latter do not themselves offer commentaries on Genesis, they do give some guidance as to what would or should be the foci of a classically rationalist interrogation of the Bible. They indicate that the cynosure ought to be, in the first place, Creation and the divine attributes; and then in the second place, and most decisively, the meaning of divine law and right as delivered through prophecy—the principles of justice and nobility underlying and animating the divine law, and also animating the providence and the prophecy that bring this law from God to humanity. According to Maimonides, the focus on Creation and the divine attributes clarifies and deepens the meaning of the philosophy of *nature* (including, of course, human nature) which is the heart of the enterprise that political philosophy comes into being to defend (consider Plato *Theaetetus* 173c7–177c2). And then the philosophic inquiry into divine law and lawgiving—into the foundation or vindication of law as such, in its majesty or in its most complete self-expression—is the authentic expression of classical *political* philosophy, that is, of the only adequate philosophic grounding for or justification of the philosophic study of nature.

We can understand Maimonides to suggest that there persists some crucial degree of probative validity in the "midwifing" activity that constitutes the original core Socratic meaning of political philosophy. For we must never overlook the indirect but profound consequences for religious experience and belief of this Socratic "midwifing." This characteristic Socratic "dialectic" activity leads, in the very few best cases, to the "conversion" of the young—through an initially painful refutational purification of the authoritative opinions concerning justice and nobility with which they have been imbued by the divinely inspired written and unwritten law. Plato indicates that the purgation of the understanding of justice and nobility has as its sequel a catharsis of the understanding of the divinity that the purified ones previously believed in and believed that they had been experiencing in some fashion. And in the opening pages of the sub-Socratic *Laws,* Plato shows how a Socratic political philosopher can bring about, even in certain elderly and altogether subphilosophic statesmen, a partial but telling version of such refutative purification, as the basis for winning acceptance of a thorough reformulation of the truth about divine law.[23] Maimonides may give us a glimpse of his own attempted reenactment of something like Socratic refutational conversion when, in his *Guide of the Perplexed,* he takes his "honored pupil Rabbi Joseph" through an analysis of prophecy, providence, and the law, an analysis that includes a notable reflection on Abraham's binding of Isaac as exhibiting the principle that is "the final end of the whole of the Torah" (*Guide* 3.24).

Socrates and those who follow his lead insist that the divinity to which political philosophy thus conduces is already present, is dimly but decisively adumbrated, in the sacred traditions, texts, and beliefs whose authority everyone begins by acknowledging—even as, similarly, the truth about divine law is already lurking in the principles of the divine laws as those laws are known to everyone prior to any philosophic interrogation and purification.[24] What is required, and what is possible, is a dialectical ascent, wrenching but not discontinuous, from the primary experiences and opinions to their higher and truer inner meaning. In this book we can, of course, do no more than circumscribe the threshold of such an ascent.

To take Socrates seriously is to take seriously the possibility that he is right about the answer to the question, How ought one to live? But this means to entertain in all seriousness the thought that we ourselves ought to try—within the limits of our much lesser capacities and less fortunate circumstances—to partake in some degree of such a life as he led. What would that signify, here and now? How could or should we begin to conceive of a Socratic existence in our time? It is obviously necessary to study with the utmost care and with the fullest self-reflection the writings of Plato and Xenophon, in which the life of Socrates as a political philosopher is so richly and provocatively depicted. But that depiction provides no easily applicable guidance for a recapitulation of the Socratic activity of liberation and self-liberation. The most massive and obvious difficulty for us is that Socrates dwelled in a world in which the philosopher could say that "no one could be so mad" as to deny "that everything is full of gods."[25] For Socrates (and indeed for all the thinkers of the premodern centuries), authoritative, commanding divinity—and hence the undeniable, all-comprehensive challenge revelation poses to independent reason—was part of the very air one breathed as one grew to maturity. The spur to think one's way to the truth about the divine was ubiquitous. Our education, in contrast, places us at an enormous artificial distance from this starting point of the Socratic path to the "examined life." It thus becomes necessary to undertake enormously delicate, specifically contra-artificial, endeavors at retrieval—efforts that were not required by the original Socratic project. One such didactic effort or experiment is gingerly embarked upon in this present study. The Bible still lives, as an accessible, vivid, and intrinsically mighty revealed challenge to philosophic reason. To begin to do justice to the challenge we must, however, make laborious exertions of recovery and revival. We must disinter the original, strange, Protean (ambiguously unified but nonetheless uncompromising) message of the Bible from overlaying sediments of familiar routinization, of traditional homiletics and apologetics, and of modern scientific and philosophic criticism that tends or seeks to reduce the meaning of the text to its merely human, all-too-human, origins. We do indeed have something to learn from this last, so-called higher, criticism (rooted philosophically in Spinoza). We have even more to learn from the competing traditional commentators, orthodox and unorthodox, poetic and prosaic. But we must not lose sight of our own distinctive purpose, sketched in what has preceded. I have therefore introduced the preeminent traditional, as well as modern, commentators only when they make observations that arrest the attention of one studying the text with the philosophic purpose I have here set forth.

Of the hermeneutic that best enacts such an approach to the Scripture, I will have more to say shortly, once we have begun to taste the grave interpretative difficulties; but the most basic principle that has guided me was well formulated in the words with which Karl Barth opened his preface to the first (1919) edition of his classic *Letter to the Romans:*

Paul, as a son of his time, surely wrote for his contemporaries. But *much more important* than this truth is the other: that he spoke as a prophet and apostle of the kingdom of God to all men in all times. The distinction between then and now, between there and here, has to be borne in mind. But the goal of the meditation can be only the knowledge, that this distinction has *no* significance in the essence of things. The historical-critical method of biblical study has its justification: it makes a contribution, to the preparation for understanding, that is in no way superfluous. But if I had to choose between it and the old *Inspirationslehre,* I would decide to go with the latter: it has the greater, deeper, *more important* justification, because it aims at the work of understanding itself, without which every scaffolding is worthless. I am glad that I do not have to choose between the two. But my entire effort has been directed to seeing *through* the historical into the spirit of the Bible, which is the eternal spirit. What once existed, in the serious sense—*that* exists still today; and what today exists, in the serious sense—and is not simply contingency and fad—stands in unmediated connectedness with that which once existed, in the serious sense. Our questions are—when we understand ourselves correctly—the questions of Paul. . . . This is certain: that every age hungering and thirsting after justice is by nature situated next to Paul, and not in the position of being a mere observer of him. Maybe we are entering such an age. . . . But should I be mistaken in my friendly hope for a new common questioning and exploration of the biblical message, then this book will have to—wait. The Bible too, of course, will be waiting there for us.[26]

CHAPTER ONE

The Twofold Account of Creation: and the Hermeneutical Problem

TO APPROACH THE BIBLE FROM THE PERSPECTIVE OF THE HISTORY OF political philosophy is to be struck by the apparent lack of congruence between the concerns of political philosophy and the primary concerns of Scripture. Inquiry into "politics"—the art of ruling and being ruled in cities and in states; the meaning of statesmanship, of citizenship, of civic virtue and civil liberty; the clarification of civil society's common good—these are not, to say the least, the foreground themes of the Bible. The very terminology is of Greco-Roman, rather than biblical, provenance. Yet this massive first impression is misleading in a crucial respect. From the start, the Bible focuses on and teaches the character of God's rule—of what one may venture to call "God's politics."[1] The accounts of Creation and of the Fall, and of the latter's unfolding aftermath, initiate the reader into an understanding of what is revealed to be the character and aims of Him who is the Giver, through Moses, of those laws that are the heart of the Bible's teaching on the right way of life for humans on this earth, individually and collectively. Accordingly, an ancient Platonic exegete has plausibly characterized the scriptural account of Creation as an educative "prelude" to the laws of Moses, intended "to mold beforehand the minds of those who were to use the laws."[2] From the outset, then, the Bible means to enlighten the reader as to that Ruler and ruling that are the transcendent model and standard for all just rule and lawgiving; the Bible is at every moment educating the reader in the ultimate source of legitimation of all lawful or just human obedience—the obedience that constitutes the core of genuine human virtue and freedom. This enlightenment or teaching, we may say, takes the place of the inquiries characteristic of political philosophy.

As a work of education, lawful and translawful, "the Bible begins reasonably," for it begins "with *the* beginning" (Strauss, "Jerusalem and Athens," 152). The opening of Genesis lays the cornerstone for all that is to follow by elaborating a chronological, causal or quasi-causal explanation for the world as it is perceived and experienced in all times and all places, by all human beings regardless of their diverse faiths or lack of faith. The

Bible thus presupposes, as what is to be explained or accounted for, a foundation in universal experience, a foundation shared with philosophy. This foundation is "what we may call the phenomenal world, the given whole, the whole which is permanently given, as permanently as are human beings." "All human thought, even all thought human or divine, which is meant to be understood by human beings willy-nilly begins with this whole."[3] To be sure, this universally experienced whole is given a specific and controversial (if lucid) articulation by the Bible, and that specific articulation is a consequence of the revelation of the radically mysterious origin of the whole in the unfolding act of divine Creation: the "articulation of the visible universe is the unthematic presupposition of the biblical author"; "his theme is that the world has been created by God in these and these stages" (Strauss, "Interpretation of Genesis," 14).

What is more, the account of these stages splits into two different versions which, if taken literally, are mutually contradictory, or at any rate incompatible. According to the first account of Creation, vegetation and all the other animals were created prior to humanity, which was created simultaneously male and female, in the image of God (Gen. 1:11–12, 24–29). According to the second account, at least some vegetation and most if not all of the animals were created subsequently to the first man, and the human female (Eve) was created, as a "helper," from and for the human male (Adam)—and only after the animals had proved to be inadequate companions for him (Gen. 2:5–9, 18–24). The reasonable beginning thus soon becomes bewildering.[4]

It would appear to be impossible to take literally the two accounts of Creation without falling into incoherence. To be sure, it does not necessarily follow that we are not to take the two accounts literally. At the least, must we not recognize that Holy Writ may well intend to warn us, from the beginning, that we cannot avoid contradiction, and thus that we cannot achieve full intelligibility, when speaking or thinking of Creation—of the *enigma* of Creation? And it is only a short step from this chastising admonition to reflection on the serious possibility, or indeed likelihood, that the full or deepest meaning of each and every passage in the Bible depends on the prior or simultaneous reception by the reader of an illuminating divine grace. In other words, the Bible begins in a way that impresses upon us the recognition that this is not a book whose meaning is entirely available in the way of books known to be fully designed or concerted by human authors.[5]

18

Still, even if the Bible intends to impress upon us first and foremost this rather forbidding sort of admonition, the Scripture would also seem to indicate, as a second and more inviting impression, the somewhat parabolic or figurative, and hence nonliteral, character of its teaching. Does not the Bible at the very outset—by presenting two such literally inconsistent accounts one after the other—warn us against strict literalism? No doubt we must beware of the risk of anachronism here, as elsewhere. Simply because, in the light of modern scientific geology and archaeology, it is difficult (to say the least) for us today to read Genesis, and certainly its first twelve chapters, in the way that the text was read by many for centuries—as literal historical truth—we cannot conclude that the text was not so intended. On the other hand, however, perhaps our skepticism liberates us to recover a long-obscured key to a more ambiguous original outlook and intention working in and through the text. For especially in light of the manifest tensions between the two opening Creation accounts, we may justifiably doubt whether the text was originally understood and intended to be an exact chronicle; we may on textual grounds be justifiably inclined to surmise that the text was rather understood as something more like a theopneust but partially allegorical saga or series of sagas, unified most explicitly, though not most profoundly, by successive genealogies (at Gen. 2:4, 5:1, 6:9, 10:1, 11:10 and 27, 25:12 and 19, 36:1, 37:2). May not deeper teachings implicit in the beginning of Genesis emerge only or especially when we read the specific events and characters as meant to convey the truth about the human situation, its origins and decisive development, through something like inspired imaginative—and not *strictly* historical—archetypes or exemplars? It is relevant to note here that "we have no right to assume that" the accounts of Creation are presented as direct speeches of God, "for the Bible introduces God's sayings by expressions like 'God said,' " and this is not said at the beginning. "We may," therefore, "assume that the words were spoken by a nameless man." Yet "no man can have been an eyewitness of God's creating heaven and earth (Job 38:4)." And "the narrator does not claim to have heard the account from God."[6] On the other hand, it would be going too far—it would be bending the text to fit contemporary "respectable" opinion, it would be closing ourselves to the discomfiting challenge of the text—if we were simply to dismiss the manifest historical claims of the opening of Genesis.

Let us pause here to recall our guiding intention: we seek to articulate and to confront the fullest intelligible challenge posed to political philosophy by the Bible's claim to inspired wisdom. We will accordingly proceed by taking the stark apparent contradiction between the two Creation accounts at the very outset of Genesis—an apparent contradiction so glaring that it is hard to believe it ever escaped the notice of any compiler—as illustrative of the didactic wisdom of the Bible. The twin, competing narrations of Creation may be seen, precisely if they are *not* taken strictly literally—precisely if they are taken as requiring a strenuous effort of reflective, interpretative integration by the reader—to present two complementary, *because* contrasting, perspectives on the mystery of Creation.[7] The first of the two accounts, in order to survey the whole of Creation and to clarify the rank, and indicate the principle of the ranking, of all the various kinds of created beings, suppresses other essential and qualifying aspects of Creation—above all the momentous *limitations* of the human creature who is the peak of Creation. The initial abstraction from the deficiencies of the human creature is entirely corrected in the succeeding, alternative account; but the incompleteness, the need for supplement, of this second rendition is made palpable when it is viewed in contrast with the first—which teaches, in a less ambiguous fashion, divine omnipotence. The surface contradictions between the two narrations of Creation may be understood as intended to limn delicately the most profound—and deeply puzzling—tension within Creation: the tension between divine omnipotence and human capacity for evil. It would then be part of the Bible's educative intention to challenge us with the task of ascending, through intense interpretive questioning, from the surface contradictions between two incomplete presentations toward a properly ambiguous, perhaps never wholly consistent or intelligible, single lesson. For is it not likely that the successive compilers and redactors, feeling themselves to be the awed but responsibly thoughtful custodians of a manifold, providentially guided, and pregnantly mysterious literary heritage, were gripped by the conviction that the difficulties and inconsistencies in the tradition(s) led or pointed beyond their own—beyond any merely human—understanding?

Hermeneutics

This interpretive stance, which views Scripture as the product of a self-consciously didactic integration of long-maturing literary traditions—

carried out by succeeding compilers and redactors whose artful but pious intelligence never dared to presume itself simply the master of its materials or sources—does not require us to resolve every puzzling feature by finding behind it an intelligible authorial intention (though we are spurred, in the case of each major difficulty, to strive to do so). We need not and should not ever rule out the possibility that in any particular case of contradiction, obscurity, or apparent error, we are confronted by irresolvable unclarity caused *either* by reverent as well as humbly bewildered human equivocation and incompetence *or* by divine mystery (or by both). By the same token, as Strauss has shown, we may, in adopting this approach, accept the sensible results, and even some reasonable version of the principles, of modern "higher criticism"—without necessarily siding from the outset with the authority of scientific reason over and against that of faith: "For the Bible does not require us to believe in the miraculous character of events that the Bible does not present as miraculous. God's speaking to men may be described as miraculous, but the Bible does not claim that the putting together of those speeches was done miraculously" ("Jerusalem and Athens," 151–52). The deepest debt we owe to the "higher criticism" is that it has liberated us to take a critical stance toward the centuries-old dogmatic insistence that the Bible, or at the least the Pentateuch, can be understood to put forward an empirically verifiable historical account carried down to us through uninterrupted transmission from the prophets and above all from a holographic writing of Moses.[8]

It is beyond the present book's purpose adequately to explain, or even to survey, the manifold and longstanding debate over how the scriptural text ought to be interpreted. But it is appropriate and necessary to clarify and situate the perspective on the text that has here been adopted as that which seems most conducive to the fullest elaboration of the challenge the Bible poses to political philosophy.

The Higher Criticism

In the twentieth century, scholarly study of Genesis was dominated by the "documentary hypothesis," due above all to Julius Wellhausen, who in the late nineteenth century redeployed and cogently argued for this approach—doing so in the service of an Hegelian-Spinozistic deconstruction of all previous claims for the integrity and Mosaic authority of the

Pentateuch.[9] The intent and many of the specifics of Wellhausen's effort were modified or abandoned by his diverse successors, but usually only in order to try to strengthen the core of his thesis. That thesis is that the Pentateuch as we have it is the product of a late editorial splicing of four sharply diverse and readily distinguishable great sources or "documents," all of which date from long after the era of Moses, and three of which have been put together to make up what we have as the book of Genesis (the fourth and latest source is thought to find clearest expression in the book of Deuteronomy and is hence usually designated "D").[10]

More specifically, the first account of Creation (Gen. 1:1–2:3 or 1:1–2:4) is to be understood as the initial chunk of a "Priestly" document (usually designated "P"), which was intent to lay down God's laws and judgments, especially as regards the cult and the priesthood (e.g., in Exod. 25–31, all of Leviticus, and large sections of Numbers), but which also aimed to deliver God's intended teaching about Himself and about His Creation, including the genealogical facts of human descent. These aims were pursued with only occasional and spare dramatic narration (e.g., in Gen. 9:1–17 and—more of a challenge for the hypothesis of undramatic, priestly authors—Gen. 23 as a whole and 17:15–22). The document "P" has been generally characterized, since Wellhausen, as the latest of the three sources for Genesis, though it is admitted that much in "P" is very old. "P" is usually surmised to have received its final form, after centuries of slow accretions, only in the period after the return from the Babylonian exile—that is, circa 538–450 B.C.[11] The sections of Genesis ascribed to "P" are recognized as having been written with exceeding care. As a leading expositor of the documentary hypothesis has it, "Here everything is written after reflection; nothing is without theological relevance." Indeed, one may say that "nothing is here by chance"; that "everything must be considered carefully, deliberately, and precisely" (von Rad, *Genesis,* 26–27, 45; cf. 61–62).

The second account of Creation, in contrast, is viewed as the beginning of the grand narrative ascribed to the "Yahwist" ("J"), who unfolds the drama of God, as Yahweh, in His intense interaction with mankind and especially with His chosen ones.[12] Since the work of Hermann Gunkel at the beginning of the twentieth century, the tendency has been to consider "J" more a knitting together of previous diverse and originally oral folk legends or "sagas," and less as the work of an original author.[13] Despite this, "J" is authoritatively recognized as exhibiting an "artistic mastery" that constitutes "one of the greatest accomplishments of spiritual history of all times."[14] While the Yahwist, "in shaping the individual narrative, probably did not go beyond trimming of the archaic profiles and making definite fine accents," he could "act much more freely when joining originally independent narratives."[15] Many scholars used to follow von Rad in supposing the Yahwist source to have been put together, out of manifold sagas and traditions, around the middle of the tenth century B.C., at the time of the high Solomonic culture.

But the picture has always been complicated by the observation that (according to the higher criticism) the Yahwist document was at some disputed point in time interwoven with yet a third, less profound and artistically less brilliant narrative woof: the "Elohist" (usually designated "E"). This third hypothesized documentary source is most obviously distinguished by its conceiving of God's relationship to man as more mediated through dreams, angels, and prophets.

The interweaving of "J" and "E" is, however, recognized to be "so thorough that any separation can be made only with great damage to the text."[16] This concession may be said to be a most obvious crack in the dike protecting the plausibility of the entire hypothesis. For as von Rad also is compelled to concede, there is a difficulty even in the separation of the "P" and the "JE" documents—and this applies even to what has always been regarded as the most obvious instance, the two diverging Creation accounts. In von Rad's words, once we see that "such a carefully considered and often skillful intertwining of both great compositions is more than an obtuse archivist arrangement, then it also places its demands on the exegete. Surely a perceptible failure in our expositions to date is that they renounce every mutual reference from one source to the other by their separated interpretations of the three source documents. Must one not say, however, that the two Creation stories are in many respects open to each other?"[17] Indeed. Arrived at this point, however, we are on the verge of having to acknowledge the artistry of the final Redactor, "R"—which initial Franz Rosenzweig ("The Unity of the Bible," 23) somewhat archly suggested should be taken as designating not "the Redactor" but rather the traditional rabbinic honorific "Rabbenu" (our Master). If, like the composer of a well-wrought trio or quartet, "R" left evident the distinctiveness of His major instruments (sources), did He not orchestrate their contributions—precisely inasmuch as He did not blur and weaken but instead called successively into complementary play their distinctive strengths, as contributing to an inspired integral *oeuvre?*

But one can and must go even further, to question whether the three documents are in fact as distinguishable as has been claimed since Wellhausen, given the acknowledged heterogeneity of the traditional sources supposedly put together into each document. As Houtman says ("The Pentateuch," 192–93), "If the complex character of the tradition history of the material is consistently recognized, the question can be asked whether its allocation to the various sources is not to be regarded as arbitrary." Houtman goes on to observe, "Attempts to show that there are no tensions between Genesis 1 and Genesis 2–3 are unconvincing. Here two stories are combined. It is, however, important to note that, though chapters 1–3 are not a perfect unity, it appears that *they are intended as a unity.* In its context, Genesis 2:4 and following verses are not a second creation account but the story about what happened to human beings and the world when they had been created."[18] Houtman's own detailed and sympathetically critical examination of the pillars of the documentary hypothesis concludes as follows:

> The question is not so much whether, with respect to a few passages, one may suspect that the text is composed of or based upon a combination of elements from two or more parallel traditions, but whether such a phenomenon occurs frequently enough for one to argue justifiably that large parts of the Pentateuch are composed of two or more continuous narrative strands. In my judgment such is not the case. The examples I have given here are among the showpieces cited in support of the sources theory. Other passages present great problems.
>
> After the centuries in which the emphasis has been on the heterogeneity of the material in the Pentateuch, it has gradually become time to pay more attention to the coherence in the Pentateuch and to the fact that, because of the creative manner in which stories and laws of diverse origin have been used as components (components often still recognizable and sometimes apparently not fully blended together), these books have been combined into a new integral unity. This integral unity—not, as is still so often the case, the reconstructed layers—should be the object of exegesis.

Genesis in particular "is a well-constructed and integral unity," although or because, Houtman speculates, it may have "belonged originally to a larger writing (with its own prehistory) of which the writer(s) of the work extending through 2 Kings included only the beginning (i.e., the present book of Genesis)."[19]

Houtman is only one of a chorus of biblical scholars who in the latter part of the twentieth century voiced deepening reservations about the previously regnant documentary hypothesis. By 1987 Thomas Thompson could declare that "the documentary hypothesis has become a creed empty of substance, something which students learn in their early years of study. It is no longer a tool used by scholars to analyze or clarify a text."[20] "When one examines the narratives of Genesis 1–11," Thompson concludes, "one finds a continuous, coherent, meaningful narrative, constructed out of a large number of independent short and long tales and genealogical narratives which had been at the disposal of the author"; "the hypothesis of an extended Yahwistic document ['J'] with its own theology" has, in contrast, "little to support it" (*The Origin Tradition of Ancient Israel I,* 79). The transformation of the scholarly landscape is nowhere more visible than when the Anchor Bible Commentary on Genesis, published in 1964 (and republished in 1982), with its complacent assumption of the unquestionable truth of the documentary hypothesis, is placed alongside the sharply contrasting Anchor Bible Reference Library volume on Genesis, published in 1992. The latter declares that "there is no longer a consensus on the existence of identifiable, continuous narrative sources"; that "criticism of the standard paradigm has taken aim at the J source"—for which "von Rad's 'Solomonic enlightenment' seemed to be the right option at one time, but relatively few would endorse today"; that "much less attention has been paid in recent years to the other documents postulated by the hypothesis; . . . E has long been problematic, and there is no longer much enthusiasm for retaining it"; that "debate continues as to whether P stands for a distinct narrative source or a stage in the redaction of an existing narrative corpus"; and finally, that "the entire issue of the relation between law and narrative still remains to be clarified." This last remark refers to the anarchic fact that the source "D," once thought to have no role in Genesis, has now been recognized there, rendering dubious previously clear (and apparently crucial) lines of demarcation between late legal and earlier narrative sources.[21]

In the light of these scholarly developments, it would seem to become a question to what extent the unity of the Scripture as we now have it must be attributed solely to the *final* redaction, or whether this last is not better understood as the crowning culmination of a previous, richly reflective and self-consciously architectonic, theologico-literary development—in which the diverse source traditions were interactive and complementary, continuously building a synoptic synthesis. Confronting in the late 1970s the "dissolution of the broad European consensus in which [he] was trained," Brevard Childs contended that what was "fundamentally wrong with the foundations of the biblical discipline" was its failure to take into account the importance of a self-conscious concern with "canonization," centered on the concept of the law, entailing a dynamically unifying "process of theological reflection," at work *throughout* the historical process that generated the Scripture as we have it. "The issue," Childs submitted, "is not whether or not an Old Testament Introduction should be historical, but the nature of the historical categories being applied." The purported evidence for the traditional scholarly assumption, that "canonization" was a process limited to discrete and late moments in the historical process, has been shown to be flimsy at best and largely nonexistent. While it is likely that the Pentateuch achieved its present shape only in the time of Ezra, it is nonetheless reasonable to surmise that "the formation of the canon was not a late extrinsic validation of a corpus of writings, but involved a series of decisions deeply affecting the shape of the books." The "usual historical critical Introduction has failed to relate the nature of the literature to the community which treasured it as scripture." The higher criticism has tended to "assume the determining force on every biblical text to be political, social, or economic factors which it seeks to establish in disregard of the *religious* dynamic of the canon." But once this latter dynamic is given the decisive independence it deserves in our understanding of the historical process, it is no longer necessary to exaggerate the role and genius of the final redaction in order to make the final version of the text the cynosure of our respectful study: "Canonical analysis focuses its attention on the final form of the text itself," which "alone bears witness to the full history of revelation." Canonical analysis "treats the literature in its own integrity," in an effort "to do justice to a literature which Israel transmitted as a record of God's revelation to his people along with Israel's response," and this "requires the highest degree of exegetical skill in an intensive wrestling with the text." This is "not to lose the historical dimension, but it is rather to make a critical, theological judgment regarding the process."[22]

Accordingly, Childs looks with sympathy, as do Houtman, Blenkinsopp, and others, upon holistic literary interpretations such as have been exemplified most notably by Robert Alter. Alter has demonstrated, on the basis of sensitive literary readings, that key scriptural passages that have previously been treated by conventional historical scholarship as disjointed products of the gluing together of divergent sources are instead "manifestly the result not of some automatic mechanism of interpolating traditional materials but of careful splicing of sources by a brilliant literary artist" (*The Art of Biblical Narrative*, 10, 11–12). Alter provides an incisive running critique of the previously reigning historical scholarship's grave literary-hermeneutic lacunae.[23] Of equal importance for our purpose is Alter's appreciative but all the more telling critique of the attempts of his colleagues Menakhem Perry and Meir Sternberg to defend themselves against conventional scholarly criticism by isolating their object of concern—the "aesthetic" or "literary" dimension of the text—from other "purposes" or "tendencies." Alter aligns himself with Joel Rosenberg[24] when he protests that "rather than viewing the literary character of the Bible as one of several 'purposes' or 'tendencies,' I would prefer to insist on a complete interfusion of literary art with theological, moral, or historiosophical vision, the fullest perception of the latter dependent on the fullest grasp of the former."[25] Alter thus endorses, though he unfortunately does not always so clearly exhibit, Childs's insistence that we need to "understand the nature of the theological shape of the text rather than to recover an original literary or aesthetic unity." As Childs also judiciously remarks, we must bear in mind that "for theological reasons the biblical texts were often shaped in such a way that the original poetic forms were lost, or a unified narrative badly shattered" (*Introduction to the Old Testament as Scripture*, 74).

Alter (like Houtman) does indeed sensibly demur from the tendency "to write about biblical narrative as though it were a unitary production just like a modern novel that is entirely conceived and executed by a single independent writer who supervises his original work from first draft to page proofs."[26] In a similar vein, Blenkinsopp (*The Pentateuch*, 37–41) has criticized the arguments by Van Seters and Whybray suggesting that the Pentateuch may be not the end product of a long process of redaction but rather the work of a single magisterial historian who incorporated sources in a manner analogous to Herodotus.[27] These animadversions are akin to those of Strauss, insofar as he draws a sharp line of demarcation between his own hermeneutic hypothesis and that of Cassuto. Cassuto argues that a sophisticated literary reading of Genesis shows that the "final redactor" was "a writer in the true sense of the word," a "creator of a work of art by his own efforts," whose artistic command of his text is comparable to that of Dante or Titus Livy.[28] Strauss, schooled by the Greeks, has a much more stringent criterion for what a "book" in the strictest sense is, and for what an author or "poet" in the true sense of the word is. He accordingly questions whether the Bible—whether even the Pentateuch or any portion of it—can be said to constitute "a book in the strict sense":

> The author of a book in the strict sense excludes everything that is not necessary, that does not fulfill a function necessary for the purpose that his book is meant to fulfill. The compilers of the Bible as a whole and of the Torah in particular seem to have followed an *entirely* different rule. Confronted with a variety of pre-existing holy speeches, which as such had to be treated with the utmost respect, they excluded only what could not by any stretch of the imagination be rendered compatible with the fundamental and authoritative teaching; their very piety, aroused and fostered by the pre-existing holy speeches, led them to make such changes in those holy speeches as they did make.[29]

My own exploratory hermeneutic approach differs from that of Strauss only inasmuch as it seems to me that Strauss may go too far, or at any rate may give the wrong impression, when he repeatedly asserts that the compilers "excluded *only* what could not *by any stretch of the imagination* be rendered compatible with the fundamental and authoritative teaching." Does this do justice to the degree to which the writers more or less self-consciously accepted the responsibility of themselves reformulating or reconstituting (through their inspired selective editing) "the fundamental and authoritative teaching"? Moreover, at least as regards the book of Genesis, while I hesitantly concede (again in Strauss's words) that the compilers' "work may then *abound* in contradictions and repetitions that no one ever intended as such," I have striven to entertain seriously—in at least the substantively most important instances—the possibility that originally unintended contradictions and repetitions were later intentionally knit together so as to effect at least partial reconciliations, and thereby genuine enrichments of coherent meaning.

CHAPTER TWO

Creation and the Meaning of Divine Omnipotence

IN TEACHING US, AT THE OUTSET, ABOUT THE CREATURELY CHARACTER of the heavens and the earth and everything that they contain, the Bible ignores, or does without, what the Greek philosophers have taught us for centuries to speak of as "nature" (φύσις; *physis*). This silence signifies the denial of the very possibility of what philosophic science means by knowledge. Creation renders self-destructively delusive the life consumed in the love of such knowledge. For this life and love is constituted by the deeply gratifying, progressive discovery of the unaltering and unalterable attributes and causal relations that define the beings that make up our perceived world. But the opening of the Bible implies that all such apparent insight is not merely incomplete (as philosophic science readily admits) but superficial and unsteady; what is truly at work in every single thing we experience is the expression of an unfathomable and totally autonomous will:

> He therefore moves His whole creation by a hidden power, and all is subject to this movement: the angels carry out commands, the sidereal things revolve, the winds blow now this way, now that, a deep pool seethes with tumbling waterfalls and mists forming above them, meadows come to life as their seeds put forth the grass, animals are born and live their appropriate lives according to various appetites, the evil are permitted to try the just—God unfolds the ages which he laid up in creation when He first founded it; and they would not be unfolded to run their course if He who founded those things ceased to administer with His provident motion. [Augustine *Genesis XII* 5.20.41]

> In the entire scope of the Torah there are only miracles, and no nature or custom. . . . [A]ll the assurances of the Torah concerning those blessings [which will result from the observance of the law], and all the good fortune of the righteous ones because of their righteousness, as well as all the prayers of our king David [in the book of Psalms] and all our prayers, all are founded upon miracles and wonders, except that there is no heralded change in the nature of the world, as I have already mentioned, and I

will explain yet further, with the help of God. [Nachmanides *Commentary on Genesis* ad 46:15 (pp. 556–57)][1]

As Augustine and Nachmanides are well aware, philosophic science in general, and Socratic/Platonic science in particular, frames the fundamental issue in its classic form by asserting the eternity of nature or of the natural whole.[2] The deepest import of this insistence is suggested by the pregnant declaration of Averroës that "the philosophers only call the world eternal in order to safeguard themselves against the kind of creation which is from something, in time, and after a state of non-existence"; for once creation in this sense is accepted, "then anything whatever might proceed from anything whatever, and there would be no congruity between causes and effects."[3] Or in Pierre Bayle's acuminate words,

> Continue to assure yourself as much as you wish that, according to the notions that Logic gives us in the chapter *On Contraries,* a human is not a rock; only take care not to assure yourself, as Aristotle would have done, that it is impossible that a human be a rock. Would not Aristotle have assured himself that it is impossible that God be born of a woman; that God suffer cold and heat; that God die; that God, in a word, be man? And would he not have been mistaken in this assertion? Now, as soon as one knows that the contradiction between the concept of God and the concept of a human does not prevent one of these being truthfully predicated of the other, must one not say that nothing stands in the way of a human and a rock becoming, the one the subject, the other the attribute, of a very truthful affirmation?[4]

As Augustine stresses, "Since it was not impossible for God to institute whatever he wished, therefore it is not impossible for him to change, in whatever way he wishes, those natures that he instituted."[5] "Within the limits of our human weakness we can know what might be in the nature of a being we have observed by experience in so far as past time is concerned; but with regard to what the future might be, we are ignorant."[6] Augustine also makes crystal clear the humanly most gripping implication: "Why therefore cannot God make it so that the bodies of the dead are resurrected and the bodies of the damned are tortured in an eternal fire?"[7]

What is at stake here includes, moreover, a profound challenge to the philosophical/theological foundation of our liberal democratic politics.

For that foundation is the peculiarly modern version of the doctrine of immutable natural human rights and consequent natural law—"the transcendent law of nature and of *nature's* God" (*Federalist Papers*, #43)—and the peculiarly modern dedication to the project of the rational enlightenment of all mankind on the basis and by means of the intelligible lawfulness of things as discovered by mathematical natural science. Montesquieu is acknowledged by the authors of *The Federalist Papers,* and also even by the anti-federalists, as the most authoritative theorist of our modern constitutionalism and thus of our modern conception of law and lawfulness. He begins his *Spirit of the Laws* by laying down, as the necessary foundation of his liberal (or of any) political science the following theological principles: "The Creation, which would appear to be an arbitrary act, presupposes rules as invariable as the fatality of the atheists":

> God has a relation to the universe, as creator and as preserver: the laws *according to which he has created* are those according to which he preserves. He acts in accordance with these rules, because he knows them; he knows them because he has made them; he has made them, *because they have a relation with his wisdom and his power.*
>
> Since we see that the world, formed by the movement of matter, and lacking intelligence, subsists always, it is *necessary* that its movements have *invariable* laws; and, if one could imagine a world other than this one, it would have constant rules, or it would be destroyed.

"It would be absurd," Montesquieu concludes, "to say that the Creator, without these rules, could govern the world, since the world would not endure without them."[8]

Montesquieu states with unusual boldness what one is inclined to call the characteristically philosophic or rationalist teaching on "creation." Montesquieu's master in this crucial matter may be said to be Descartes, whose formulation is in some respects less radical:

> I pointed out what are the Laws of Nature; and without resting my reasons on any other principle, than the infinite perfections of God, I tried to demonstrate all those about which one could have any doubt, and to point out that even if God had created several worlds, there could not have been any in which they would fail to be observed. . . .
>
> [I]n this way, although He had not, in the beginning, given any other form than that of Chaos, provided that, after establishing the Laws of

Nature, he had lent his aid in order to act according to her custom, one can believe, without doing outrage to the miracle of the creation, that by this means alone all the things which are purely material would have been able, in course of time, to render themselves such as we observe them to be at present. And their nature is much easier to understand when one sees them being born little by little in this manner, than were one to consider them as all complete.[9]

Philosophic science in its classic form makes the issue sharper by stressing the eternity of "matter." Pierre Bayle correctly observes,

There was among the Natural Scientists of Paganism a great diversity of opinions on the origin of the World, and on the nature of the element or the elements from which they claimed that particular bodies had been formed . . . : but they all agreed on this point—that the matter of the World was not a product. There was no dispute among them on the question of whether something was made out of nothing, but they all agreed that this was impossible. . . . [A]ccording to the system of all the pagan philosophers who believed in God, there was an eternal and uncreated Being distinct from God: this was matter. This Being owed its existence solely to its own nature. It depended on no other cause either as regards its essence, or as regards its attributes and properties.[10]

As is obvious from Plato's *Timaeus,* it is not only the "materialist" philosophers, it is also the "spiritualists," who stress the eternity of "matter." Hippolytus of Rome (A.D. 170–236), engaging in polemics against the Platonist Christian heretic Hermogenes, is especially scornful of his opponent's attempt to appear original in his exegesis of the opening of Genesis: "Imagining that he was thinking something new, a certain Hermogenes said that the god has made all things out of coeval and ungenerated matter, for it was impossible that the god could make generated things out of things that are not"; in fact, "this happens to be the Socratic myth, which is worked out better by Plato than by Hermogenes."[11]

The purport of the "Socratic" stress on the eternity of matter is illuminated by Averroës's comment on Aristotle's conception of "agency" and "creation." Aristotle's or the philosophic view is that "an agent *only* produces a composite of matter and form, and this *only* comes about by his moving *matter* and transforming it, until it proceeds from what was in it potentially." "The agent in Aristotle's view does not compose two things *really,* but draws forth what was in a potential state to actuality. Thus *as it were* he conjoins potency and actuality, i.e., 'matter' and 'form.' "[12]

More pointedly, the Platonic philosophers, by their stress on the eternity of "matter," in contrast to "form," mean to indicate (among other things) the ubiquitously observable limitations on the power and persistence of mind, of spirit or soul, of life, in all its forms: the perceptible qualities of every individual living being of whom we have direct experience reveal each to be formed as a composite generated out of the encounter of locomotive tangibles that eventually disperse so as to dissolve into elements that no longer preserve the form (soul) of the being in question.[13]

Now, all these attempted philosophic strictures on creation limn, by way of contrast, the infinitely more mysterious Creation presented in the Bible. Formulations such as that of Descartes and Montesquieu provoke the remonstrance that the Bible means to say that God is omnipotent in the unlimited sense that no prior law, no "necessary relationship" of Him to beings within His Creation, governs Him or His action in any way: "For is anything too marvelous for the power [היפלא] of the Lord?"[14] The critical significance of the biblical rejection of the philosophic conception of an eternal though formless "matter" is seen in Grotius's insistence that it is the corporeal resurrection of Jesus that is *the* proof, and test, of the unique truth of Christianity (*The Truth of the Christian Religion,* 2.7, 10; 4.8; 6.5). For as St. Paul declares (1 Cor. 15:13ff.), "How can some of you say that there is no resurrection of the dead? If there is no resurrection of the dead," then "our preaching is useless and so is your faith!" This most acute existential implication of the opposition to the philosophic conception of matter is limned in the comment on Gen. 2:17 by Nachmanides (see also Maimonides *Guide* 2.27):

In the opinion of men versed in the sciences of nature, man was destined to die from the beginning of his formation, on account of his being a composite. . . . [T]here was bound to be depletion in his body, and he was subject to the cause of existence and destruction.

But in the opinion of our Rabbis, if Adam had not sinned he would have never died, since the higher soul bestows life forever, and the will of God which is in him at the time of his formation would always cleave to him and he would exist forever, as I have explained in the verse, "and God saw that it was good."

Know that composition entails destruction only in the opinion of those wanting in faith, who hold that creation came by necessity. But in the opinion of men of faith who say that the world was created by the simple will of God, its existence will also continue forever as long as it is His desire. This is clear truth.

Still, though biblical Creation seems unlimited by any preexisting matter, that Creation does not seem totally unlimited by intelligible necessity. To begin with, the Bible conspicuously employs number without indicating God's creation of number. "We should call to mind," Augustine comments,

> what Scripture says elsewhere: "Thou hast ordered all things in measure and number and weight" [Wisd. of Sol. 11:20]. And let the soul that has the capacity, reflect on this, calling for help on God, the source of its strength and inspiration; and let it consider whether these three things—measure, number, and weight—in which, according to Scripture, God ordered all things, existed somewhere before the Creation of every creature, or whether even they too are created; and if they existed before, where were they? Before the creatures nothing existed except the Creator. Therefore these were in Him. But how? . . .
>
> Now if anyone says that the measure, number, and weight—by which, as Scripture testifies, God ordered everything—are created, and if by them He ordered everything, by what did He order these themselves? If it was by others, how did He then order everything by them, since they would be ordered by others? There is no doubt, then, that those things by which everything has been ordered are outside of the things so ordered.[15]

It would appear that for Augustine omnipotence is bounded or in part defined by unalterable mathematical necessity. Similarly, we find Rashi contrasting (ad Gen. 2:2) human ignorance of the exact temporal intervals with the meticulous knowledge possessed by God, Who can discern the precise hairsbreadth of time when the Sabbath begins; Rashi thus at least verges on the suggestion that the mathematical nature of time intervals is fixed a priori even or especially for the Creator. On the other hand, Bonhoeffer protests, in the face of twentieth-century mathematical physics, that "although man knows number and its secret he no longer knows that even number, which determines days, years, and seasons, is not self-contained, that it too rests only upon the Word and command of God. . . .

We have forgotten this connection. . . . What we comprehend is the godless language we speak ourselves, the language of an eternal law of the world resting in itself, silent about the Creator and boasting about the creature" (*Creation and Fall*, 27–28).

Of greater obvious significance than number, the *goodness* of Creation seems to be recognized, or even discovered, by God—rather than willed or created ("and God *saw* that the light was good"; Gen. 1:4). In reaction, we find Nachmanides designating as "incorrect" the interpretations of both of his two great predecessors, Rashi and Ibn Ezra, inasmuch as they both take "saw" here in its most evident or usual sense: "If they were correct, it would appear that there was on the part of God a change of mind and a new counsel, as if to say that after God said, ' "Let there be light," and there was light,' He saw that it was good, and therefore He divided between it and darkness, just as a human being who does not know the nature of something until it comes into existence! . . . The purport of the word 'seeing' is thus to indicate that their continuing existence is at His will, and if that will should for a second depart from them, they will turn into nought" (*Commentary on Genesis*, pp. 29–30; see similarly ad 1:10, 1:12, and 1:31). Would it not perhaps keep us closer to the direct meaning of the words if we were to take the Scripture as meaning "God *saw to it*" that His Creation was enduringly good? Philo, we note, is willing to say that in God as ruler "there is the power to do either, but He wills only the good things"; yet this implies that the *meaning* of good and evil is not created by God. The same Philo declares in his account of Creation that "God guides everything as he wishes, *in accordance with* law and justice."[16] In no case is it suggested that God could have put the stamp of "good," or "just," on anything whatsoever.

In the specifically Christian revelation we encounter a third perimeter of divine Creation. The Godhead revealed to be the Trinity, and thus not only the Father but simultaneously the Son, who is the Word or Reason (*logos*) by Whom "all things were created" (John 1:1–14) and Who is yet also somehow "the firstborn of all creation" (Col. 1:16), introduces an enormous additional complication. For this implies that prior to Creation "there is a real pre-existence of man," namely, "a pre-existence in the counsel of God, and to that extent, in God Himself," insofar as "the Son is the uncreated prototype of the humanity which is to be linked with God" (Barth, *Church Dogmatics*, 3:2, p. 155). Does this not mean that something like the Platonic form or idea of man is uncreated, existing somehow

35

within, and defining, limiting, the Godhead?[17] While from the post-apostolic period Christian theologians have insisted on Creation *ex nihilo,* they have evinced a remarkable continuing openness to speculation that the Platonic ideas, or something akin to such ideas, exist, uncreated or eternally, within the mind of God:

> From an early date the explanation was added that, though all created things did not yet exist in the counsel and being of God before they came into being, yet their archetypes did. . . . It was particularly Augustine who (not without express allusion to the Platonic doctrine of ideas) laid emphasis on this point. . . . Since we cannot suppose that God did not know things before He caused them to be, we must conclude that the *rationes omnium faciendarum rerum* were already previously existent in His wisdom and therefore in His being (*Ad Orosium* 8.9). . . . Hence the act of creation does not take place without a reference back to something preceding it, to the extent that in performing it God proceeds from Himself or from the plenitude of His ideas, and it is the act of *imitatio.*[18]

One may wonder whether this path of interpretation does not run the grave risk of reducing the divine will to mere intelligent agency responding to intelligibly unalterable inner necessities.[19]

The difficulty becomes palpable in Thomas Aquinas's doctrine. He declares that "Creation out of nothing" properly understood means exactly the same as what Aristotle or indeed "the philosophers" generally mean by the causality exercised by the first principle or cause of the universe. Temporal priority of cause to effect is not implied. There is no reason why God's Creation out of nothing could not have produced a universe coeval with the Creator. The sole feature of Creation unknowable to reason which revelation discloses and which the Bible adds is the fact that the first cause (God) "delayed" its (His) eternally "willed" causing of the universe; yet this "delay" is not temporal, except in our human imagination, since time depends on motion and God is immutable. But even this revealed fact is far from simply mysterious. To begin with, we can know that the nontemporal delay was due to wisdom, if to a "wisdom that is beyond our understanding." God delayed for an eternally good reason. Nay, we can even figure out a part of that reason: "If one should ask, why He wished it this way, the response should doubtless be": He wished that things "have not always existed, so that His self-sufficiency be manifested." We remark that in Thomas's elaboration of his teaching on the meaning of Creation *ex nihilo,* there are frequent respectful appeals to the authority of Aristotle, Avicenna, and Averroës, but hardly a reference to the Scripture. The more one considers the trajectory of the Thomistic analysis, the more one can understand why Martin Luther warns near the start of his *Lectures on Genesis* that "whoever desires to be saved and to be safe when he deals with such great matters, let him simply hold to the form, the signs, and the coverings of the Godhead, such as His Word and His works."[20] Yet can Luther deny that in crucial respects, scriptural Creation is intelligible only within some defining limits or bounds on even, or precisely, an intelligibly omnipotent Creator?[21]

We are compelled, however, to go further—or to reconsider. For we must agree with Ibn Ezra and Rashi and Rashbam, as well as Milton, that (*pace* Cassuto) the content as well as the syntax of the opening sentences of the Bible does not convey unambiguously or even most obviously the idea of what philosophers, and theologians deeply informed by philosophy, have taught us to think of as "Creation *ex nihilo.*" The opening words may well be taken to mean "When God began to create"; and this becomes more likely with the immediately following or accompanying characterization of the earth as if it preexisted "Creation," in a "formless and empty" condition (Septuagint: "invisible and unformed"), along with a "Deep," or "Abyss," and "Waters"—as if they too were present as uncreated substances upon which God's "spirit was moving." In this light, one is forced to wonder if the opening of the Bible is so radically different, in this crucial respect, from the opening of Ovid's *Metamorphoses.* As even Tertullian must concede (*Against Hermogenes* 21), the text fails to foreclose the preexistence of an uncreated, as yet formless, but essential "matter" in chaos.[22] Ibn Ezra permits himself to comment, on Gen. 1:1, "The meaning of ברא [the verb usually translated as "create"] is to cut or to set a boundary. The intelligent person will understand what I am alluding to."[23] We find ourselves forced to conclude that the beginning of Genesis does not address squarely the question whether or not God has to work with, and within the limits imposed by, a "matter" that He did not create and whose fundamental nature He therefore cannot alter.[24]

The scriptural text that has traditionally been taken to be the first explicit statement of the notion of Creation *ex nihilo* is in the late[25] and Hellenistic second book of Maccabees—in a context in which (by no accident, it would seem) for the first time martyrdom is introduced as a major theme into biblical literature. There we find a mother, who, with

her seven sons, is horribly martyred by Hellenizing tyrants (written originally in Greek, the book characterizes Greeks as "the barbarians"), testifying that God "made heaven and earth and everything in them," including humanity, *"not from beings."*[26] These same martyrs, in this same
context, are among the first in Scripture to articulate unambiguously the
doctrine of corporeal resurrection[27]—that is, the doctrine that depends
most acutely on God's capacity utterly to overcome the resistance of what
the philosophers teach us is "matter." Yet even here in the crux passage of
2 Maccabees (*pace* the traditional commentators), while we discern a
passionate *reaching* for an adequate articulation of God's unqualified omnipotence rooted in His Creation, we nevertheless do not in fact yet find
an unambiguously clear statement of the idea of Creation *ex nihilo*—as was
already stressed by Milton (*Christian Doctrine*, 1.7, p. 306). For to say that
there were no "beings" prior to Creation does not rule out the possibility
that there was a substratum with a unalterably bounded potentiality that
had not yet been molded into "beings."[28] And indeed, the mother in this
context draws an analogy to the mysterious formation of her sons in her
womb, saying, "It was not I who set in order the elements within each of
you" (18:22)—obviously not referring to a creation *ex nihilo*.

The more or less contemporaneous and equally Hellenistic Wisdom of
Solomon (11:17) unambiguously attributes to God a creation of the world
"out of formless matter."[29] While it is clear from Rom. 4:17 that in the
mind of St. Paul, the two articles of faith—resurrection and Creation—are
closely conjoined, the scriptural text does not make it clear that Paul sees
the necessity for Creation *ex nihilo* (see similarly 2 Pet. 3:5).[30] But it has
come to be assumed that Paul's words do connote Creation *ex nihilo*.
Bonhoeffer goes so far as to say, "It is because we know of the Resurrection that we know of God's Creation in the beginning, of God's creation
out of nothing" (*Creation and Fall*, 16).

The historical evidence indicates, however, that the meaning of Creation as *ex nihilo* was finally grasped with clarity only in the face of
the challenge from Platonic/Socratic philosophy, and—especially among
Christians—from Gnostic heretics, such as Basilides, Hermogenes, and
Marcion, who were profoundly shaped by Platonism and Stoicism, and
were so understood by their orthodox antagonists.[31] The earliest surviving articulation by a Christian of the idea of Creation *ex nihilo* is probably
that of Tatian the Assyrian (A.D. 110–172) in his *Address to the Greeks*, secs.
5–6 (precise date uncertain). There, immediately after a harsh attack on

"your" philosophers, including Plato (in his polemic Tatian snidely re-marks to his audience, "I am trying to reduce to order the unarranged matter in your minds"), Tatian declares that "the Logos, begotten in the beginning, begat in turn our world, having first created for Himself the necessary matter." "For," he continues, "matter is not, like God, without beginning." And "on this account we believe that there will be a resurrec-tion of bodies." Tatian goes on subsequently (sec. 13) to stress the close link between the faith in bodily resurrection and the faith in the immor-tality of the soul, conceived as a consequence not of the soul's "nature" (as the Platonists claimed) but rather of divine omnipotence exercising justice and punishment: "The soul is not in itself immortal, Oh Greeks! but mortal! But it is possible for it not to die."[32] Still more pointedly anti-Platonic are the statements in the second book of *To Autolycus* (2.4, 10, 13; but contrast 1.8) of Bishop Theophilus of Antioch (written after A.D. 170):

> But if matter also is not generated, then the God is not any longer, accord-ing to the Platonists, the maker of the wholes, nor is God's monarchy demonstrated insofar as they are concerned. Moreover if, even as God, being ungenerated, is unalterable, so, if also matter were ungenerated, then it too would be unalterable and equal to God. For what is generated is mutable and alterable, but what is ungenerated is immutable and un-alterable. What is so great, if God merely made the cosmos from material substance? . . . But the power of God is made evident in this, so that he might make what he wished from things that are not, even as the bestowal of living soul and motion belongs to no one else except God alone.

Eventually, in the third century, we find the absolute sort of pronounce-ment epitomized in the following words of Hippolytus of Rome (written after A.D. 222): "One God, the first and only and maker and Lord of all things, had nothing coeval: not infinite chaos, not measureless water or solid earth, not dense air, not hot fire, not light spirit, not the blue canopy of the great heaven. But He was one, alone in Himself. By an exercise of His will He made the beings, which antecedently had no being, except when he willed to make."[33]

It would appear that the full, true, meaning of God as Creator is not available until or unless the Bible and its believers come into confronta-tion with Plato and the challenge of the philosophic science discovered first by the Greeks. For only then does the believer grasp what is neces-sarily entailed in speaking intelligibly about divine omnipotence.[34] Is this not perhaps one of the most important meanings of Maimonides' strange insistence that the import of the biblical account of Creation becomes clear only to one who has learned from the study of the Greek philosophers to recognize that this account is identical to the true natural science or physics—which is an essential prerequisite of the true science or knowledge of God, which in turn is a prerequisite of the most authentic faith in and love of God—since insofar as one does not have an accurate conception of what one claims to believe and love, one cannot really be said to believe in it or love it for what it is?[35] Could this be the radical implication of the introduction, into the Midrash, of a challenging, nonbelieving "philosopher" whose presence prompts the following remarkable dialogue?

> A certain philosopher asked R. Gamaliel [ca. 100 C.E., grandfather of the Judah who edited the Mishna], saying to him:
> "Your God was indeed a great artist, but surely He found good materials, which assisted Him?"
> "What are they?" said R. Gamaliel to the philosopher.
> "Tohu, Bohu, darkness, water, wind, and the deep [Gen. 1:2]," replied the philosopher.
> "Woe to this man!" R. Gamaliel exclaimed: "The term, *Creation,* is used by Scripture in connection with all of them!—With *Tohu* and *Bohu* it is said, 'I make peace and create evil' [Isa. 45:7]; with darkness it is said, 'I form the light and create darkness' [ibid.]; with water it is said, 'Praise Him, ye heavens of heavens, and ye waters that are above the heavens' [Ps. 148:4]; Why are they to praise Him? 'Because He commanded and they were created' [ibid. 148:5]. With wind it is said, 'he formeth the mountains and createth the wind' [Amos 4:13]; with the deeps it is said, 'When there were no depths I (Wisdom) was brought forth' [Prov. 8:24]." [*Midrash Rabbah* on Gen. 1:9; see also 1:5]

Nachmanides reveals a similar deep indebtedness to Greek philosophy, by way of Maimonides, when he contends, with a free exegesis of the text (ad Gen. 1:1), that one must indeed interpret the account of Creation in terms of "what the Greeks call *hyly*" but must read the verses that treat the first day of Creation as explaining the Creation of this very matter. Though the "Holy One, blessed be He, created all things from absolute non-existence," still, everything that exists under the sun or above was not made from non-existence at the outset. Instead He brought forth from total and absolute nothing a very thin substance devoid of corporeality but having a power of potency, fit to assume form and to proceed from potentiality into reality. This was the primary matter created by God; it is called by the Greeks *hyly.* After the *hyly,* He did not create anything, but He formed and made things with it, and from this *hyly* He brought everything into existence and clothed the forms and put them into a finished condition. Know that the heavens and all that is in them consist of one substance, and the earth and everything that is in it is one substance. The Holy One, blessed be He, created these two substances from nothing; they alone were created, and everything else was constructed from them. This substance, which the Greeks called *hyly,* is called in the sacred language תהו (*tohu*). . . . The form which this substance finally takes on is called in the sacred language בהו (*bohu*). . . .

Now after saying that with one command God created at first the heavens and the earth and all their hosts, Scripture returns and explains that the earth after this creation was *tohu,* that is, matter without substance. It became *bohu* when He clothed it with form. Then Scripture explains that in this form was included the form of the four elements: fire, water, earth, and air. The word הארץ (earth) includes these four. . . . And the element air is here called "spirit." [Pp. 23ff.; see also 38, 43–44, 55, 61]

This Nachmanidean reading is akin to Augustine's exegesis, as expressed in passages such as the following: "Thou indeed, Lord, made the world from a matter without form, a thing almost nothing which you made from nothing."[36]

Yet even or precisely on this assumption, Augustine is forced to concede that the text remains ambiguous and puzzling (see esp. *Confessions* 12.22), and he concludes with the confession, "Behold how confidently I say that in Your immutable word You made all things, visible and invisible; but can I so confidently say that Moses intended nothing else but this when he wrote, 'in the beginning God made heaven and earth?'—No. Though I see this to be certain in Your truth, I do not thus see that he thought this in his mind, when he wrote this."[37]

The fundamental ambiguity and its consequences reappear vividly in Milton's divinely inspired poetic retelling of Creation. On the one hand, Milton informs us that according to the Holy Spirit's revelation to him, God's angel Raphael told Adam that

> one Almighty is, from whom
> All things proceed, and up to him return,
> If not deprav'd from good, created all
> Such to perfection, one first matter all,
> Indu'd with various forms. [*Paradise Lost,* 5.469–473]

And God Himself told His son,

> Boundless the Deep, because I am who fill
> Infinitude, nor vacuous the space
> Though I uncircumscrib'd myself retire,
> And put not forth my goodness, which is free
> To act or not, Necessity and Chance
> Approach not mee, and what I will is Fate. [Ibid.,7.168–73]

These pronouncements have to be considered, however, in light of what the Holy Spirit revealed directly to the inspired poet about the existence of the realm

> where eldest *Night*
> and *Chaos,* Ancestors of Nature, hold
> *Eternal* [my italics] Anarchy, amidst the noise
> Of *endless* [my italics] wars, and by confusion stand.
> For hot, cold, moist, and dry, four Champions fierce
> Strive here for Maistry, and to Battle bring
> Thir embryon Atoms; . . .
> *Chance* governs all. Into this wild Abyss,
> The Womb of nature and perhaps her Grave[38]
> Of neither Sea, nor Shore, nor Air, nor Fire,
> But all these in thir pregnant causes mixt
> Confus'dly, and which thus must ever fight,
> Unless th' Almighty Maker them ordain
> His dark materials to create more Worlds. [Ibid., 2.894ff.][39]

This makes more intelligible the fact that, according to the revelations Milton received, one out of every three angels in heaven joined Satan in his rebellion, based on their errant surmise that the divine claim to omnific omnipotence was a deception or self-delusion, rendering God and His Son unfit to rule—and legitimating rebellion against them, in the name of the just political principles of equality, liberty, and rule by the most meritorious, their authority recognized by the consent of the ruled.[40]

The political philosopher Spinoza, for his part, exploits the difficulty or ambiguity in the first two verses of Genesis as a key step in his attempted demolition of the intellectual authority of the Pentateuch. According to Spinoza, "Moses"—or, in truth (Spinoza claims), the simpleminded, prephilosophic, pious redactors of the traditional texts—simply lacked awareness of the fundamental issue between Creationism and the philosophic insistence on the eternity of nature. The biblical text evinces an ignorance of the meaning of omnipotence—a lack of perspicuous understanding of the basic distinction between the category of the possible and that of the impossible.[41] As for the attempt to save the authority of the Bible by following Ibn Ezra and Maimonides—that, Spinoza submits, would require adopting the incredible thesis that the Bible was written with a hidden or esoteric wisdom that is indecipherable without the help of that very Greek philosophy and science that is everywhere condemned by the biblical sages as idolatrous.[42] Yet how can Spinoza be confident that it was not part of the providential plan that the deepest meaning of Creation and omnipotence be disclosed late, and only through the encounter with the challenge of alien Greek philosophy?

Montesquieu, Bayle, Spinoza, and the other early modern rationalists, following in the path of the classical rationalists and the medieval Maimonides, self-consciously confront biblical Creationism as *the* most radical challenge and alternative to philosophy or science. But the battle lines, and thus the fundamental issue, become less accessible in the later, historical if not historicist, rationalism of Hegel. For Hegel, Genesis is the expression of what he calls (*Lectures on the Philosophy of Religion*, 2.561–79) "the Religion of Sublimity (*Erhabenheit*), or Jewish Religion," which is to be viewed as the antistrophe of "the Religion of Beauty (*Schönheit*), or Greek Religion" (these being *the* two primary articulations of religious elevation of the spiritual over the natural). According to Hegel, when we look back at the Bible from the vantage point of our historically perfected conception of spirituality (the "completed religion"), we can see that the Bible's teaching on Creation, by severing God or divinity (as Creator) from the world (as Creation), makes the world "prosaic." The Bible thus unknowingly takes the first giant step toward a conception of the world in terms of a concept of "nature" that is no longer understood (as it still is in the more ambiguous Greek outlook) as somehow divine:

Here then is what *we* call natural or necessary connectedness; here, for that reason, the category of "miracle" can emerge for the first time too, as opposed to the natural connection of things. In the Hindu religion, for example, there is no miracle; there, everything is crazy starting from your doorstep. Only in contrast with order, with the lawfulness of nature, with natural laws—*even though these laws are not recognized* and one finds only a consciousness of natural connectedness—only in that context does the category of "miracle" arise, represented in such a way, that God sporadically manifests Himself in singular events. [Ibid., 2.568; my italics]

But precisely because "miracle is grasped as a contingent manifestation of God," it transpires that the Bible's truest message (according to Hegel) is that "the true manifestation of God in the world is the absolute, the eternal;[43] and the mode and manner of this manifestation, its form, appears as what we call 'sublimity.'" Now what does Hegel mean by "sublimity"? Sublimity is *not* holiness, and therefore not an attribute of God in Himself: "The Infinite Subject in itself one cannot call sublime; That is the Absolute in and for Itself; It is holy." Sublimity emerges "only as the appearance, the *relation,* of this Infinite Subject *to* the world. The world is grasped as a manifestation of this Subject, but as a manifestation that is not affirmative; or, to the extent that it is indeed affirmative, it still has the chief character that the natural, the worldly, is negated, as incommensurable with the Subjective."

Unlike the early moderns, Hegel finds in biblical Creationism an important and distinctive contribution to our full, rational, present-day understanding of things. But he thereby subordinates the Bible, making it play a supporting role in an early act of the unfolding world-historical drama whose plot has become clear only as the end of the story has come into sight: the Bible's redactors unknowingly read from a script finally deciphered by Hegelian philosophy of history in the nineteenth century. The Bible thus loses altogether the appearance of being a critical and even dangerous challenge to rationalism. One may doubt whether the Hegelian embrace treats the Bible with as much respect as does, paradoxically, the Spinozistic spurning. Surely Hegel no less certainly, though less conspicuously, rejects what is truly radical in the Bible's self-understanding. In Hegel's reading, the true, not-fully-conscious depth of the Bible comes to sight only in a perspective through which the Bible appears as a "moment" in a historical scheme ultimately governed by a way of thinking that is less biblical than Greek—and not so much "religiously" Greek as philosophically or scientifically Greek. But Hegel's insistence on the biblical "contribution" runs the risk of blurring the historical truth that it was the Greek philosophers who were the first (of whom we have clear records) who attempted to orient human existence by a stable truth of "nature" discoverable by independent reason.

The most fundamental implication of the biblical text is surely that "heaven and earth," and all they contain, do *not* constitute a cosmos whose character is fixed, or whose roots are "invariable" elements, or forms, or matter, or atoms, or "laws" of "physics." All such apparently unvarying entities and principles, insofar as they do exist, are in truth, according to the Bible, the unnecessitated, and hence changeable or even extinguishable, products of a willing, thinking, impassioned, mysterious Being Whose perfect existence preceded and was independent of His Creation— and Whose being and consciousness are thus radically unlike our own (see Isa. 40:12–31 and Job 38:4ff.). In the light of the biblical teaching of Creation, the objects of science—"nature" as a whole, human "nature," "natural" law, "natural" rights—are so mutable as to afford only a provisional, an incomplete or essentially uncertain, semiknowledge.[44] The Bible will abound with marvels, portents, or powers (פלא or θαυμάσια) that we are inclined to call "miracles"—beginning with the greatest miracle, that of Creation. But just as the Hebrew Bible does not speak of "nature,"[45] so it does not speak of "miracles." To speak of the "miraculous" implies, as Hegel stresses, a natural order that is somehow suspended or interrupted; and despite the force of what Spinoza says about the biblical author's unclarity about the meaning of omnipotence, it would seem that the deepest, or at any rate the most profoundly challenging (if not univocal), teaching of the Bible is one that seeks to do without "nature," and hence without "miracles."[46]

While the Hebrew Bible does not refer to "nature," it does refer to the concomitant concept of "chance" or "accident."[47] The Bible quotes certain Philistine priests and diviners who carry out a test to see if widespread suffering said to be a providential punishment might not in fact be an "accident" (1 Sam. 6:9). The outcome of the test confirms that the suffering is providential. The general implication is less clear. Does the Bible leave any room for accident? If so, would this not entail some limitation either on God's power or on His caring justice? Must not the Bible mean to teach that, just as there is no "natural necessity" in Creation, so there is no "accident"? The same term that is used by the Philistine diviners in I Samuel (and also by the narrator of Ruth 2:3) to mean "accident" or "chance" is used by Ecclesiastes to mean God's iron decree.[48] Calvin applauds as "well put the retort of Basil the Great ['Homily of Psalm 32'], when he wrote that Fortune and Chance are pagan terms, the meaning of which ought not to enter a faithful heart." "We do not admit the vocabulary employed by the Stoics, that is, 'Fate.' " That term belongs to "the vocabularies which St. Paul teaches us to shun, as profane vanity (I Tim. 6:20)." The "Providence of God, as taught in Scripture, is opposed to fortune and to all fortuitous causes." Yet in his own concluding comments, Calvin finds himself compelled to have recourse to a distinction that "is needed to assist our sluggish minds": things admittedly "are as if fortuitous," because the true divine "order, reason, end, and necessity of events are, for the most part, hidden in the counsel of God and cannot be comprehended by human opinion."[49]

Let us sum up the most important suggestion that emerges from the confrontation between Greek philosophy and the initial biblical presentation of Creation. If "Creation" is to have the meaning that the Bible seems to intend to convey, then it seems that God's Creation must be understood as *ex nihilo* in the sense of being unlimited by any preexisting nature of His creatures or of a substratum that would impede His ability to transport us beyond mortal necessity, as is threatened and as is promised by His covenants and by the sanctions for His laws (see Nachmanides ad Gen. 1:1 beg.). But then it necessarily follows that faith in omnipotence *cannot* mean faith that "absolutely anything is possible." It is not intelligible that omnipotence be in any way impotent. Omnipotence, if it is to convey intelligible meaning, must be understood as bounded by a canon of the impossible and hence the possible. This canon presupposes and requires both the Aristotelian science of logic, linked to mathematics, and the Greek philosophers' discovery of the idea of nature as intelligible necessity. Yet what we can say or think of the Creator, in addition to or in explanation of His being the sole source and ground of all else, is almost entirely negative: what He *cannot* be. Creative omnipotence renders impossible the existence of nature, or even of "matter," in the sense of Greek philosophy; but therefore we remain ignorant of both the "how" and the "why" of Creation, and *a fortiori* of the being of the Creator Himself. Indeed, one's confidence that there must be some nonabsurd coherence at the core of the divine existence does not by any means imply that divinity will always or even usually manifest itself as consistent or coherent. Apt here are the words of the great Kabbalist Meir ben Gabbai: "The differences and contradictions do not originate out of different realms, but out of the one place in which no difference and no contradiction is possible. . . . [T]hese things appear contradictory and different to us, but only as seen from our own standpoint—for we are unable to penetrate to those points where the contradictions are resolved."[50] A vast cloud of mystery, or "negative attributes," and of apparent contradiction is nonetheless illumined from somewhere within by an emanating brilliance. As has already been indicated, and as will become steadily more apparent, the brightest part of this visible divine spectrum is divine justice.

CHAPTER THREE

The Ontological Implications of the Unfolding of Creation, for Creatures and Creator

THE HEAVENS ARE THE FIRST, AND IN SOME SENSE THE PREEMINENT,[1] part of Creation: "In the beginning God created the heavens and the earth." But by putting "the heavens" (השמים) first, the Bible would seem to be meaning to say most emphatically that the heavens too, even the heavens, are created by God; no beings, not even the visibly highest, are independent of God.[2] What is more, in one of the most arresting features of the account, the life-giving light and warmth of day are emphatically and very conspicuously not traced to the sun or to any heavenly body (cf. Rev. 21:23–26); light exists, day and night follow their order, vegetation flourishes on the earth, before the creation of the sun.[3] We note also that the second day is conspicuously missing any divine pronouncement that the thing created on that day—the "expanse" or "firmament" between the waters, which God named "the heavens"—was "good." As Barth remarks, "An accidental omission of these words is almost inexplicable in a passage where every word counts."[4] The demotion of the heavens and the heavenly bodies goes with a promotion of the earth and the earthly: on the third day, in striking contrast to the second day, God twice pronounces His day's work "good."

On the fourth day, God finally creates two heavenly "lights" or "lamps" (מארת),[5] to which He assigns specific functions. The two are to separate day and night, to mark seasons and days, to give light to the earth, and, finally, "to rule over" the day and the night respectively. He calls these two creatures, and the stars that accompany them, "good"—but only after He has emphasized the (admittedly elevated) function they perform for the beings on earth. Besides, "it is particularly to be noted that" in the case of the work of the fourth day, "and from now on right up to the sixth day, not excluding the creation of man," there "is no divine naming of what is created"; even or especially in the case of "Sun" and "Moon," "to give them their names is a matter for man."[6]

On all sides, and from the time of Abraham, the Hebrews seem to have found themselves surrounded—and all too often corrupted—by peoples practicing various forms of star-worship.[7] The Babylonian sages are por-

48

trayed in the Bible as having appealed to the sidereal order in the light of
the promise or hope that life could somehow be guided by a fatalistic but
predictive astrology (Dan. 1:20ff., Isa. 47:13). The Greek philosophers,
probably unknown to the authors of Genesis, became famous or notorious for appealing to the unvarying mathematical orderliness of the mo-
tions of the principal heavenly bodies for the decisive clue as to the
character of what they called the "cosmos."[8] Through its treatment of the
heavens and the heavenly bodies, the Bible, in its initial account of Creation, expresses its polemical stance toward all these varying pretensions
to wisdom based on insight into the ruling divinity of the heavens.

Even though the beings aloft are demoted, their splendor and allure are
not denied: "The heavens record the glory of God, the expanse of the sky
proclaims His handiwork" (Ps. 19:2; cf. 8:3–6). As we later learn, the
worship of the heavenly bodies among the gentiles, after the Fall, would
seem to be in accordance with the divine plan.[9]

Yet we note (*pace* Nachmanides, who follows Maimonides' *Guide* 1.40
and 2.30) the Bible's amazing silence on the all-important but invisible atmosphere—what the Greek philosophers refer to as the "air," or "ether"—
aloft; there is, indeed, not even a word in biblical Hebrew for "air" (or
for "ether"). Here at the beginning, not only is there no mention of the
creation of air, but the birds are conspicuously and surprisingly *not* said to
belong to the air, or to any element other than the land (Gen. 1:20–22;
contrast Aristophanes' *Birds*). For the Bible, the winged does not need the
support of air (Isa. 6:1–2). In the second account of Creation, God is said
to have "breathed into man's nostrils the breath of life" (Gen. 2:7)—again
without any reference to the atmosphere. The Bible knows that breathing
is of the essence of life, but (as is implicit in the attribution here of
breathing to God) it does not even hint that breathing has as its function
the intake and exhaust of a crucially necessary gaseous substance. Is this
silence studied, or is it ignorant? We note that in subsequent biblical
tradition, Satan is known as being especially "Lord of the Air" (thus
Milton has Satan address his Peers as follows: "O ancient Powers of Air
and this wide World / [For much more willingly I mention Air, / This
our old conquest, than remember Hell, / Our hated habitation]"; *Paradise
Regained,* 1.44–47). We observe that in Homeric or Hesiodic Greek there
is also no word for "air" (in Homer and Hesiod, ἀήρ always means "mist"
or "haze"). It seems to be the philosophers—above all Anaximenes, Socrates, and Diogenes of Apollonia—who recognized, exalted, and even

deified "Lord and Master, measureless Air" as the elemental medium whose constant circulation is essential to human, and all terrestrial, life (according to Aristotle, respiration "we see to be the sovereign cause of living and of dying").[10] Is it possible that piety recoils instinctively from an acknowledgment of the sole "power invisible" that the philosophers (in their irony) exalt?

However this may be, it is tempting to ascribe the most obvious peculiarities of the sequence of Creation to the Bible's intended polemic against sun-, moon-, and star-worship (a polemic that may even involve some deliberate exaggeration, here at the outset, in order to counter the all-too-human, as well as peculiarly philosophic, tendency to be overly impressed by the splendor of the heavens). Yet as Strauss has shown, this is far from sufficient. Governing the account more fundamentally and pervasively is an intelligible and even lucid, though complex, plan of ascent, an ascent that discloses the ontological ranking, and principles of ranking, of the creaturely beings that make up the experienced universe.

The initial clues to the first chapter are the pervasive stress on Creation as intimately involving "separation" or "distinction," and the fact that the account of the six days of Creation manifestly fall into two equal and parallel parts. The first triad of days begins with the creation of light and culminates, after the separation of the waters, in the dual creation and naming of the earth and its vegetation—the inseparability of the latter from the earth being underlined. The second triad begins with the creation of the heavenly lights and culminates, after the bringing forth of animals from the waters, in the second dual creation: that of the terrestrial animals and, as an obvious peak, of mankind in the image of God. The first triad of days stresses separation or distinction (so emphatically that Thomas Aquinas christens this triad "the work of distinction"; ST 1a qu. 65–69). We are thus prompted to ask, Is there not an additional principle manifested in the ordering of the creatures of the second triad of days? Thomas declares this to be the "work of adornment," on the basis of a misconstrual of the phrase ending Gen. 2:1.[11] Strauss more meticulously seeks a principle "based on, or which presupposes, separation or distinction but which is not reducible to separation or distinction" (even as "the sun presupposes light but is not light"). It transpires that the principle in question is that of local motion. In Strauss's words, "Local motion is separation of a higher order because it means not merely for a thing to be separated from other things but to be able to separate itself from its place" (see the similar remark of Thomas, ST 1a qu. 70 a. 1: "Distinction of certain things is made most evident by their local movement, as separating one from another"). In the second triad of days we ascend through the creation of creatures from those with lesser to those with greater latitude of locomotion, culminating in a latitude that presupposes but transcends even local motion. Sun and moon (fourth day) can change their place, but animals can change their course—beginning with those kinds of animals (fish, birds; fifth day) that do so in media that are removed from the earth. Then we ascend on the sixth day to animals that change their course as they move upon the earth, culminating in the telluric animal that is the only being created in the Creator's image—the meaning of which is here limned, then, by the fact that this creature alone can change not only its place and course but (finally transcending even the most free locomotion) its very way. As Strauss summarizes, "The sequence of creation in the first chapter of the Bible can be stated as follows: from the principle of separation, light; via something which separates, heaven; to something which is separated, earth and sea; to things which are productive of separated things, trees, for example; then things which can separate themselves from their places, heavenly bodies; then things which can separate themselves from their courses, brutes; and finally to a being which can separate itself from its way, the right way."[12] The order implicitly teaches that it is humanity's singular self-mutability that above all constitutes man and woman as being in the image of divinity. For as Creation massively indicates, biblical divinity is most evidently characterized by unfathomably radical spontaneity.[13] And we are subtly and most gracefully prepared for the second account of Creation, whose focus will be the use to which mankind puts its quasi-divine spontaneity. The first account of Creation is so little independent of the second that the full implication of its ordering principle foreshadows and becomes fully evident only in the light of the account of the Fall.

Precisely because providence, focused on terrestrial life, excludes both Babylonian-astrological fatalism and Greek-philosophic natural necessity, it entails orderly care. The absence of nature in the account of Creation does not entail the presence, let alone the predominance, of the monstrous or the chaotic. Indeed, with the exception of the "sea monsters," there is no reference, in the first account of Creation, to any creature unknown to us in common experience. In Herder's words, "Everything incomprehensible to man, and lying out of his sphere of vision, it excludes; and confines itself to what we can see with our eyes, and comprehend with our minds."[14] Even as regards the second account, Herder continues, "of all the miraculous things and romantic forms, with which the stories of all Asia have abundantly stored their Paradise of the primitive world, this tradition has only two marvelous trees, a speaking serpent, and a cherub. . . . Compare this narrative, considered merely as an allegory, with the tales of other nations; it is of all the most refined. . . . All the dragons and wondrous forms of the ancient fairyland stretching over the Asiatic mountains . . . disappear in the most ancient written tradition, and only a cherub keeps watch at the gate of Paradise." By the same token, however, and against Herder (*Ideas for a Philosophy of the History of Mankind,* 1.3), we must observe that the Bible gives no hint of an evolution of the species—of the species known to us—from some strange earlier species of which we have no direct experience, no nonhypothetical knowledge. The Bible joins Aristotle (in shared opposition to Lucretius: *On the Nature of Things* 5.855ff.) in teaching that the perceptible species are the only species. Yet as we shall see, the Bible departs radically from Aristotle insofar as it suggests that the character of those species has undergone over time a radical change—due not to any necessitated process such as "natural selection" but instead to sin, sin eventually so ubiquitous as to deserve and incur the punishment of global extermination.

The Distinctiveness of the Biblical God as Disclosed in His Act of Creation

This world—our world, the only world—is the product of divine will, not of divine passion that overpowers God or yokes God to another. Creation does not bespeak "Eros, He the most beautiful among the immortal gods, / Liberator of the limbs, Who overwhelms in all gods and humans / The mind and prudent counsel in their breasts" (Hesiod *Theogony* 120–22). God as Creator of the beings is emphatically not a procreator, and the earth and seas, though fertile, are also not procreative; so far are they from being maternal or paternal that they are not even alive. The utterly unerotic character of God and of His creating is particularly striking if we compare ancient Near Eastern cosmogonic accounts and the remains we possess of Canaanite Phoenician religion—as well as Greek cosmogony, poetic and philosophic.[15] The curious phrasing with which the second account of Creation begins—"these are the generations [תולדות] of the heavens and the earth"—may well, as Westermann suggests (*Genesis 1–11*, 16 and 26), "preserve the Superman-Babylonian tradition that the origin of heaven and earth was at one time understood as a succession of begettings." But what Westermann fails to note is the likelihood of a deeply self-conscious irony that is tantamount to mockery of these traditions. Humanity, as male and female, is created in the image of God, and this verse of the Scripture, read in isolation, could well suggest that God is somehow bisexual or even dual (as in the Egyptian and Mesopotamian precursors cited by Westermann, *Genesis 1–11*, 37). But the whole context warns us against taking the verse in this way, or supposing that eroticism is an aspect of biblical divinity.

The Bible's "first word" on eros is a conspicuous silence as regards divine eroticism. God's first permissive blessing and commandment, for the fish and birds, is, "Be fruitful and multiply" (Gen. 1:22).[16] God does not multiply. This commandment is then reiterated, not only for or before man and woman but "to them," and is then immediately conjoined with the commandment to subdue the earth and rule over the beasts (Gen. 1:28). The lawful injunction addressed to humans to engage in procreative sexual intercourse is coupled with a commandment to rule over, or to dominate (רדה), the animal. Sexual eros, the Bible implies, should be seen as obviously more akin to the animal than to the divine; sexual eros (though not the sexual difference—God is the Father) is that aspect of humanity that is most problematic for, or most qualifying of, man's being in the image of God.[17] The first consequence of the Fall is Adam and Eve's shame at the sight of their nakedness (Gen. 3:7). Procreation is the consequence of a divine law; it does not "come naturally"; when Eve bears her first child, she quite properly recognizes that what she has gained is due to the help of the Lord (Gen. 4:1).[18] After the Flood, God renews to Noah the divine commandment that permits and legitimates procreation (Gen. 9:1). Sexuality is encouraged and blessed by the Creator as a means to lawful procreation, not as an end or a pleasure good in itself; and procreation is an activity excluded from the being (one is tempted to say the nature) of the "Lord our God, who is One" (Deut. 6:4).[19] The transcendence of erotic need is a principal distinguishing feature of the holiness of God the Creator. The Scripture can dare to employ vivid erotic metaphors for God's relation to His people (e.g., Jer. 3:6–13, Ezek. 23, Song of Songs) only because the writers are confident that the metaphors will never be taken literally. A ritualized transcendence of eros through constant purification will be a principal feature of the "cleanliness" as well as "holiness" that God eventually demands of His people.[20]

We may add that while God's transcendence of sexual need is unambiguous from the outset; His strict or absolute incorporeity is less certain. Gunkel surely errs when he asserts that the creation of man in the image of God originally means that "the first human resembles God in form and appearance," a likeness that "relates first of all to the human body, although the spiritual aspect is not excluded." On the other hand, however, one cannot so easily reject Gunkel's further, if somewhat overstated, contention that "the notion of God's incorporeality requires a capacity for abstraction which would have been unfeasible in ancient Israel and which was first attained by Greek philosophy." For as Gunkel points out, "The Old Testament always speaks of God's form with great naiveté—of his ears, hands, and feet, of his tongue, his mouth, etc. God strolled in paradise. Moses saw him, if only his back, from behind." Doubtless, the divine countenance remains unseen, even for Moses; but this implies, of course, that there is in fact a divine countenance to be seen, a countenance that is visible, or *not* essentially invisible.[21]

God's making is deliberate, but, as creative, it is radically unlike human art. As we have had occasion to stress, almost as prominent as God's production in the opening verses is His intrusive activity of separation or distinction. Without God, there would be no distinction, no form. Formlessness, fluidity, precedes form; the only element whose character is established at the moment of its creation is water. But prior to any articulation, there is to be light, by which to make discernible even the pre-articulate confusion. God exists prior to light, without need for light, and yet He makes His Creation illuminated and hence intelligible.[22] God is the enshrouded, unilluminable source of the light, of the light that God sees to be good, of the light that illuminates Creation. Yet even light, once created, is in or of itself not distinct from darkness; even this distinction is an effect of the superimposing divine will. According to Isaiah, God creates the darkness—though He does not see it as good, though He associates it with woe (Isa. 45:7; cf. the Talmudic Tamid 32a, secs. 4–5). Darkness, it would seem, then, is not uncreated or simply given, even though it first hovered over the surface of the deep. Before Creation, we may venture to speculate, God existed in a state prior to darkness as well as to light;[23] unlike His creatures and Creation, God's "sight" would seem not to have presupposed light and darkness (cf. Ps. 139:11–12)—just as

His goodness, unlike the goodness we know, would seem not to have presupposed evil or woe.

On the seventh day, God rested; and because He rested, He did not only bless, He declared holy this seventh day. God had not declared holy any of His Creation, or any of the previous days—not even the sixth day, on which the Creation was completed and seen to be "very good." God, this would seem to suggest or to remind us, is not merely the Creator; He has a distinctive being, a being at rest, that transcends His creating. It is true that we later hear God Himself saying that "on the seventh day He rested, *and was refreshed*" (Exod. 31:17; cf. 20:11 and Cassuto, *Commentary on Genesis,* 1:63). But Augustine thought that it would verge on Manichean heresy to take this as implying that God was in need of recuperation—let alone that He hallowed the day because on it He recuperated (*Two Books on Genesis against the Manicheans* 1.22). Milton, characteristically dissenting, protested that "we ought not to imagine that God would have said anything or caused anything to be written about himself unless he intended that it should be a part of our conception of him." In particular, Milton declared, referring to this passage in Exodus on God's resting after the Creation, "let us believe that it is not beneath God to feel what grief he does feel, to be refreshed by what refreshes him, and to fear what he does fear" (*Christian Doctrine* 1.2, pp. 134–35).

A comment by Thomas Aquinas brings out another fundamental and controversial implication of the seventh day for divine omnipotence and for the biblical message about the Creator in relation to His Creation: "When all things were made He is not said to have rested *in* His works, as though needing them for His own happiness, but to have rested *from* them, as in fact resting in Himself, as He suffices for Himself and fulfills His own desire. And even though from all eternity He rested in Himself, yet the rest in Himself, which He took after He had finished His works, is that rest which belongs to the seventh day. And this, says Augustine (*Commentary on Genesis* ad loc., 4), is the meaning of God's resting from His works on that day."[24] God was not in need of Creation or of anything created. But this seems necessarily to entail that during the eternity in which God existed wholly without any creature or being other than Himself, He exercised no justice, loved nothing beyond Himself, and had no object to which to show mercy or compassion—all without any experience of incompleteness or deficiency in virtue or excellence. Maimonides leads us to surmise that divinity was, as Aristotle suggests, wholly absorbed in and satisfied by self-knowledge, by noetic self-contemplation (cf. *Guide* 1.2). The difficulty of this Maimonidean thought is indicated by the resistance it meets, especially as regards the implication for the status of divine love and justice. When Luther contemplated being asked what God was doing before the creation of the world, he answered that God was cutting canes to be used on those who would ask such useless questions. "This not only stopped the questioner short," Bonhoeffer acerbically observes, "but also implied that where God is not recognized as the merciful Creator he must needs be known only as the wrathful judge." The questions "why the world was created, about God's plans or about the necessity of creation" are "godless questions"; "God must remain the Creator in His rest, too."[25] But we must observe in response to Bonhoeffer that his response, and even more Luther's (no doubt partly tongue-in-cheek) response, has the troubling implication that God could never have been tranquil—that indeed He was eternally busy preparing just punishment for His enemies. Does this not bring us back to the dilemma posed by Bayle's evocation of Epicurean criticism of the biblical conception of the deity?

We may thus find less impious Hegel's silence, in his interpretation of the biblical doctrine of Creation, about the seventh day and its significance. Reading the first verses of Genesis retrospectively, from what he regards as the final triumph in history of Spirit as reason, Hegel tacitly jettisons—and thereby helps us to see the radical significance of—any biblical suggestion that the Divinity is characterized by an ineffable essence that transcends or is prior to His relation to the world:

> The attributes of God are God's relation to the world. . . . [This] is a bad expression if by it one means that we *only* know about this relation of God to the world but know nothing about Him. Instead that *is* God's own determinateness, and hence God's own attributes. The way in which one human is related to another—that is just what is human, that is its own nature. (The acid is nothing else than the mode and manner of its relation to the base—that is the nature of the acid itself.) When one knows how an object is related, then one knows its very nature. To distinguish between relatedness and nature is to make a bad distinction that collapses, because it is the production of an understanding that does not know what it is doing. (*Lectures on the Philosophy of Religion*, 2.566)

In rebuttal, one may protest that the Bible seeks to convey the experience of a living God Who as Creator and not merely first cause cannot be captured in or limited by the net of intelligible relatedness. Thus Bonhoeffer, whose interpretation of the opening of Genesis is explicitly opposed to Hegel, finds himself compelled to declare not only that "every use of a causal category for understanding the act of creation is ruled out" but that "*between* Creator and creature there is simply nothing: the void" (*Creation and Fall,* 14, my italics; on Hegel, see 10). Surely Hegel would counter by wondering whether Bonhoeffer understands what he is saying. For "nothing: the void" is void also of justice and mercy and love. Bonhoeffer would appear to land back on the side that he wants to refute. Perhaps Thomas Aquinas succeeds where Bonhoeffer fails when the former teaches that "when the creature is related to the Creator, the relation is really founded in the creature, but is in God as a mental construct only."[26] There seems to be a tension within the concept of Creation or omnipotence, inasmuch as the concept includes both unneedy or wholly self-sufficient will and, on the other hand, divine love, justice, and mercy. This tension became fertile ground, we learn from Gershom Scholem, for the leading Kabbalists—who thereby failed, however, to maintain monotheism as purely as did Maimonides and the philosophers.[27]

However this may be, God concludes His creating by giving the vegetation as a whole to mankind and to "all" the animals as food; the carnivorous, and thus the necessary shedding of blood, does not seem to be part of God's original, harmonious Creation.[28] If so, this would seem to be one of many reasons why God can survey His Creation as a whole and find it "very good." Yet this emphatic pronouncement draws our attention to the fact that God conspicuously failed to declare, after His Creation of man in His image, that man was "good." This faintly ominous omission is the sole hint of trouble in an otherwise blissful picture.

CHAPTER FOUR

Creation and Divine Solicitude
for Mankind

HUMANITY, MALE AND FEMALE, WAS CREATED IN GOD'S IMAGE, AND this means—as the principle underlying the ordering of the works of Creation suggests—that humanity is characterized above all by radical (spiritual) spontaneity. But the goodness of such latitude in the creature, we now learn, is inextricably interwoven with that creature's capacity for evil: a human creature's quasi-divine freedom entails its following the Creator or the Creator's plan through *voluntary* obedience, and hence with the possibility or capacity for willful disobedience—and even for the aspiration to some kind of autonomy. The second account of Creation supplements and completes the first by elaborating this fundamental lesson about the character and the consequences of humanity's being created in the image of God.

Still, what must be stressed to begin with is that the second account of Creation continues and reinforces the teaching, presented in the first account, to the effect that Creation, as it left God's hands, was immaculate.[1] Creation as we now know it is the product, the Bible here teaches, of a catastrophic change due not to God but to man. It is true that God actually effected most of the change, but He did so in His capacity as judge and as upholder and enforcer of justice, responding to and rectifying human injustice.

The Socratic political philosopher, reading the second account of Creation (including the Fall) with a view to the question why mankind exhibits such a powerful proclivity to mutual antagonism and injustice, will add the reflection that "the life of man as we know it, the life of most men, is that of tillers of the soil; their life is needy and harsh; they need rain which is not always forthcoming when they need it and they must work hard"; and if human life had been thus "needy and harsh from the very beginning, man would have been compelled or at least irresistibly tempted to be harsh, uncharitable, unjust; he would not have been fully responsible for his lack of charity or justice." The Bible therefore teaches that humanity is "fully responsible"—that "the harshness of human life" is entirely "due to man's fault."[2] Otherwise—if nature or the natural condition of humanity were from the beginning or essentially as it manifests itself to our experience, especially in international relations and wherever humans live without the rule of humanly contrived law and order—one would be compelled to wonder whether nature and nature's God sustains or coheres with justice, that is, whether there is natural right or natural law in an original or strict sense. For we cannot consistently maintain that justice is not ultimately good, good for those who act justly: "If there is to be justice among men, care must be taken that they are not compelled to think constantly of mere self-preservation and to act toward their fellows in the way in which men mostly act under such conditions. But such care cannot be human providence. The cause of justice is infinitely strengthened if the condition of man as man, and hence especially the condition of man in the beginning (when he could not yet have been corrupted by false opinions), was one of nonscarcity" (Strauss, *Natural Right and History*, 150 n. 24). Yet while this reflection arises inevitably, it is not explicitly provoked by Genesis, which says not a word about the intended society, about the mutual charity and justice, of humans had they persisted—after "being fruitful and multiplying"—in the garden of Eden.

Humanity's pollution of God's Creation is rendered all the more shocking by virtue of the fact that we now learn how assiduous and complete was God's original provision for mankind. This indeed would seem to be a key to at least some of the most important differences, or apparent inconsistencies, between the two accounts. The first account abstracted somewhat from God's meticulous solicitude for humans, and from humanity's needy dependence on God, in order to highlight the ruling rank of humanity within Creation—a rank based on humanity's relative freedom or godlike independence among the creatures; the second account stresses humanity's elevated rank somewhat less (nothing is said of man being created in the image of God), in order to bring into relief God's intimate care for humanity's needs—and the consequent outrageousness of humanity's heedlessness of or ingratitude for that care.

The Original Condition of Mankind

We now learn that while humanity—as male and female—may have been created in the image of God on high, the male ("Adam," presumably from *adamah,* meaning "ground") was created out of the lowly dust (cf. Gen. 2:7 with 3:19) and the female then out of, and for the sake of, the male.

The sexual differentiation now appears as the primary manifestation of mankind's human, all-too-human, social interdependency or neediness: God (not Adam; though contrast Ginzberg, *Legends of the Jews,* 1.65 and 77) recognized that "the man's being alone is not good." But God did not at once supply man with the companion he needed. God apparently wished to bring man to consciousness of his need and thereby to teach him about his unique relationship to the creature who would satisfy that need. (The narrator indicates both this didactic intention and its success by quoting, for the first time, Adam's own words in response to the creation of woman.) By bringing woman into being out of the flesh of man, and only after the wild beasts and birds have been formed out of earth and then found to be inadequate helpers for man, God taught Adam—and the Scripture teaches us—woman's unqualified sharing in full humanity, though in a status distinctly subordinate to man. This second account confirms our impression that when, in the first account, the declaration of man's being created in the image of God was immediately followed by the addendum "male and female He created them," the addendum was to be taken as a qualification (see *Midrash Rabbah* on Gen. 8:11 and Deut. 2:31). God, not being male as is Adam, never had need of a female helper or complement.

By quoting Adam's own words for the first time, the narrator signals the depth and fullness of the first man's satisfaction at the advent of the woman as his partner in the flesh. The narrator then does something even more remarkable. He adds, for the first and almost the only time in Genesis, his own judgment, linking Adam's recognition of the corporeally complementary character of his woman to the preeminence, in all times and places (and not only among the narrator's own, Hebrew, people), of marriage, as a union of the flesh between one man and one woman that takes precedence even over filial attachment—and that rules out incestuous union with one's mother.[3] The biblical account of Creation would seem to indicate that the separate patriarchal family, centered on the corporeal union of father and mother but oriented toward God—transfigured through its loving obedience to God—was, and in some sense always remains, the intended focal point of human sociability (cf. Tob. 6:18).

The full significance of this aspect of the Creation account—what is thus disregarded or demoted—becomes evident only when we place in juxtaposition the dramatically different conception of human sociability found in the classical philosophers (for what follows, see Isaac Abravanel's

Commentary on the Pentateuch ad Gen. 11:1–9). According to Aristotle's lapidary formulation, "The human is by nature a political animal."[4] In saying this, Aristotle indicates, he has in mind above all the participatory republican city as the locus of the fulfillment of the human capacity for rational self-government through collective deliberation issuing in the rule of man-made law. Aristotle does not mean to deny that the human being is also by nature a coupling or familial being, and indeed that man is in an important sense more naturally so—more necessarily, more universally, more spontaneously familial than civic (*Ethics* 1162a17–19). The family precedes, and perdures within, the city or civic association. But the economic security and the spiritual maturity of reason at which the family and its members ultimately aim can be fulfilled only when the family, like the individual, exists as a part of the greater whole that is the city under human law (*Politics* 1260b8–24; cf. Hegel, *Philosophy of Right,* secs. 156–57).

In the course of his argument in the *Politics* justifying the subordination of the familial to the political in his conception of human nature, Aristotle observes that the universal belief that providential and punitive monarchic rule characterizes divinity reflects the fact that the gods are images of those primitive forms of society—family, clan, nascent cities—that still knew only patriarchy: "Just as human beings assimilate the looks of the gods to themselves, so too do they assimilate the gods' ways of life to their own" (*Politics* 1252b27–28; contrast Thomas Aquinas's commentary ad loc.). From this amazingly bold remark, together with the rarity of his references to piety or to the gods in the rest of the *Politics* as well as the *Ethics,* one at first might be tempted to conclude that for Aristotle piety, rooted in the prepolitical family, is largely transcended by mature and therefore truly self-governing civic life. But in this very context Aristotle refers to purposive Nature with quasi-religious reverence, and by the end of the *Politics* he has made it clear that political life at its most self-conscious can find measure only by looking up to the divinity that presides over the whole (1325b16–31). Moreover, in the *Ethics* (1160a9–30) Aristotle shows his vivid awareness of the centrality of civic worship—through ancestral rituals and cults and holidays—in the communal life of the city; these ancestral cults, he indicates, are essential to the claim that the city is the complete association of which all other associations are subordinate parts. One is led, then, to wonder whether, despite the truncated character of his elaboration of the "best regime," Aristotle did not take the first decisive steps up the path followed to its end by Plato, whose dialogues elaborating the best, and second or third best, regimes include a theology that replaces or supplements the traditional conceptions of divinity with truer—and in a sense therefore older—conceptions that are compatible with (and even proven by) political science.

These rational or quasi-rational gods of the best city demand a radical subordination of many or most individual goods that are ordinarily associated with happiness, including above all the family and its private property. Even if the family is not abolished—as it is in the best case, among at least the rulers of the city that one ought to "pray for"—the goodness of the family is reinterpreted to consist chiefly of a participation in eternity that itself transcends (and does not strictly require every adult individual to participate in) the family or family life (*Laws* 721). The cult of the gods in the best regimes of the philosophers thus awakens the "guardian of the city" to his soul's natural hunger for a satisfaction and an object of concern that is purified of preoccupation with corporeal, familial, and mundane needs. But in the best city's divine worship, this yearning is always entwined with another yearning, with the longing to devote or to sacrifice oneself to something more aloof, more splendid, and more lasting than individual or familial existence. The philosophic civil religion thereby compels the guardian to confront, and may prompt him to wonder about, to start thinking critically through, this latter longing.

In elaborating their teachings on the moral and civic and ultimately intellectual virtues that call men beyond their families and familial attachments, the classical philosophers offer as a kind of consolation or enticement the prospect of passionate friendship, between two mature men. As Thomas Aquinas declares in his commentary on Aristotle's *Ethics,* "Aristotle shows that this friendship lacks nothing that belongs to the notion of what is perfect" (sec. 1578). Similarly, Cicero has his Laelius proclaim that "except for wisdom, nothing better has been given to humans by the immortal gods" than friendship—nay, more: "We have been given by the immortal gods nothing better or more delightful than friendship" (*On Friendship* 20, 47; cf. 103–4). This philosophic honoring of friendship, in explicit and emphatic contrast to the family, may be said to reach a crescendo in Montaigne's essay "Of Friendship." It is pertinent to add that, as is well known, Plato's Socrates endorses a kind of spiritualized pederastic attachment between teacher and student—and between fellow guardians of the best regime (*Republic* 402–3, 468b–c; *Laws* 835bff.). It goes without saying that this erotic male friendship has no place whatsoever in the biblical conception of the human good, though discipleship under prophets becomes a high calling.[5] But it does not go without saying—it arouses the puzzled astonishment of Augustine (*Genesis XII* 9.5)—that, just as there is no suggestion in the scriptural account of Creation that what man needs in order to find completion or fulfillment (in the perfect beginning or subsequently) is a city, fellow citizens, or a political community of any kind, so there is no indication that loving friendship with another male (such as Jonathan was to have for David; cf. *Mishnah,* Pirke Avoth, 5.16) was what Adam needed or what man as such needs for completion. Creation in its pristine state reserves no prized place for future intimate male friendship, and this will not be a theme of Scripture subsequently.[6]

The contrast deepens when we observe that it is in the context of his thematic teaching on friendship that Aristotle speaks at greatest and most revealing length about the proper or most complete relation between man and wife. Such a relationship, he contends, can entail a genuine spiritual friendship—but almost incidentally. The central and truest tie between husband and wife as such is their offspring, and the jointly owned household aimed at the collective preservation and appropriate education of all the members, slave and free, but especially the children (*Ethics* 1162a16–33; see again Augustine *Genesis XII* 9.5). Aristotle clearly teaches in this context that man's desire for spiritual kinship draws him away from wife and family toward a teacher of virtue and, at the fullest, toward an equal soul mate with whom he can perfect and enjoy the shared actualization of his and his "second self's" virtues—most purely in rich conversation. Yet Aristotle's very lengthy account of intimate friendship, as the culmination of the moral life and as a key support or expression of the intellectual life, is surrounded, so to speak, by an adumbration of the life of god, whose intellectual virtue apparently has little or no need for companionship. The moral life of the city transcends the family and is itself surpassed or at least crowned by intimate friendship, but even the latter is ultimately transcended, in and by an ascent toward the divine spiritual self-sufficiency that is the dimly beheld highest aspiration of the life of the city (*Politics* 1325b16–32).

Returning to the Bible in the light of this striking contrast, we caution ourselves that the account of Creation is of course far from being the Bible's last word on human sociability and society. We must watch to see how and in what contexts civic life makes its appearance and then develops in the Bible—and how this development affects and is affected by the deeper and primary familial tie. We note here only that biblical politics culminates in monarchy, not in republicanism. The Bible's political peak is the hereditary monarchy established by David, a monarch whose reign adumbrates the Messianic age (a republican constitution, strictly speaking, appears in Scripture only once, in the praise of the alien Roman Senatorial regime in 1 Macc. 8:14–16).[7]

The Fall as Necessary Education

No sooner are we told that Adam and his delightful "helper" experienced no shame at their nakedness than we are abruptly initiated into the drama of their fall into the deepest shame. Through that shameful drama it becomes clear that since woman is a full human being, her subordination to her husband by no means effaces her need and capacity to deliberate and to act as a free agent—as a being who can profoundly influence, and even wrest the lead from, her partner. Yet the story makes only more certain the teaching that the lead properly belongs to the male: just as it is to the man that God assigns the tilling of the garden, so it is to the man that God delivers the first momentous commandment. In fact, the prohibition, accompanied by the first threat of punishment, is delivered well before woman has come into existence. God implicitly assigns to Adam the grave responsibility for teaching his wife the decisive commandment and its terrible sanction.[8] God does not, however, announce, or draw Adam's attention to, or give him any guidance in the successful performance of, this very important duty.

So it is not altogether surprising that Adam's execution of this responsibility would appear to have been quite faulty. He certainly seems to have treated the woman like a child. On the one hand, Adam apparently "made a hedge about his words" (*Avoth of Rabbi Nathan,* chap. 1, pp. 8–10) by telling the woman that they were not only forbidden to eat but forbidden even to touch the fruit of what Adam referred to as "the tree in the midst of the garden." But, on the other hand, Adam failed to explain that the tree whose fruit they were prohibited from eating was the Tree of *Knowledge,* the knowledge of good and evil (or the knowledge of "the noble and the base," as the Septuagint has it: καλὸν καὶ πονηρόν).[9] It was the serpent who was thus allowed to be the first to call the woman's attention to the nature of the fruit, and the serpent did so in a most seductive and dazzling manner.

The serpent is a questioner and a reasoner; one is tempted to characterize him as a dialectician. His opening question very subtly introduces Eve to the possibility of passing judgment on God's commandment. For by suggesting that God may have imposed a total and severe prohibition, the serpent seduces Eve into a reply explaining the very limited prohibition God actually imposed. The serpent thus gently but insidiously introduces Eve to apologetics, and thereby to the beginning of an independent evaluation—initially only for purposes of defense, to be sure—of the reasonableness of God's commandments.[10] On this foundation, the serpent unfolds his refutation of the divine commandment, his demonstration of its absurdity. The serpent's expressed syllogism is as follows: *if* you eat of the fruit of the Tree of Knowledge, *then* on that day your eyes shall be opened, and *it follows* that you will be as gods, knowing good and evil; *therefore* (as God well knows, Who is thus lying to you out of anxious jealousy) you will *not* die as a consequence! Now, the implied premise of this syllogism would seem to be the conclusion of a prior reasoning, as follows: gods cannot die; but divinity is constituted above all by knowledge; therefore those creatures who become godlike in knowledge, since they thereby acquire what is constitutive of divinity, must share in divine immunity to death. If this is indeed the viper's foundational syllogism (perhaps based on his personal experience), then this presumption proves to be either seriously mistaken or seriously misleading. Or do not the later words of God at Gen. 3:22 indicate that the serpent rather bases his syllogism on a different, prior and unstated, reasoning with himself, to the effect that once the pair know good and evil fully, they will then see the full value of the Tree of *Life*, and as a consequence eat of *its* fruit, and thus gain for themselves immortality? In other words, doesn't the snake reason thus: while those who acquire the godlike wisdom about good and evil do not thereby *automatically* become immortal, they *are* thereby liberated and spurred to figure out how to secure immortality for themselves? If this latter is his thought, then the serpent fails, of course, to reckon with God's unpredictable and dramatic preventative intervention.

This much is certain: the serpent tempted the woman with the prospect of becoming godlike and thus immortal by the acquisition of a knowledge of tremendous significance, a knowledge that would open the hitherto closed or blinded eyes of her mind. The serpent evidently appealed to the woman's longing to become equal to God—that is, to her pride and to her fearful desire to escape the threat of death. But was it in fact either pride or fear that motivated her to eat the forbidden fruit? After all, until she tasted the fruit, the Bible subsequently stresses, her eyes were closed, in the sense that she (like Adam) did not know shame at her own nakedness. Can a being that has little sense of shame have much sense of pride? If we focus attentively on the few words that actually describe the woman's criminal act (Gen. 3:6), our strong impression is that the woman succumbed to the temptation because of her childlike response to the carnal goodness of the tree (for eating), to the visual beauty of the tree, and, above all, to the desirability of the tree as a source of wisdom. Wisdom, it would at first seem, the woman desired simply for its own sake. She appears to have been, for that moment, a "lover of wisdom," a *philo-sophos,* if in a childlike sense. To say the least, the Scripture suggests that succumbing to the charm of this love is childlike in the sense of being childish, and dangerously so. The woman seems, like a child playing at the edge of a cliff, to have sensed no abyss beneath her; it appears that she quite casually shared the fruit with her man, who with equally childlike insouciance accepted the fruit and ate of it. But then their eyes were opened; then both were brought, for the first time it seems, to the shameful self-consciousness that we associate with adulthood; then the childish, comparatively guiltless, love of wisdom evaporated.

If the woman appears childlike in her fascinated attraction to the tree, Adam appears puerile both in his conduct of his companion's instruction and in his disregard of the significance of the fruit itself that she offered to share with him. There seems at first sight to be no suggestion of prideful rebellion in Adam's acceptance of the fruit from his wife. Indeed, one is led to wonder whether Adam or Eve had grasped the real significance of the divine prohibition. After all, in their ignorance of good and evil, could they have understood the evil of disobedience? Or of punishment? Could they have interpreted the divine prohibition and threat as anything more than prudent counsel, as parental advice? Thus Nachmanides comments on Gen. 3:6, "She had thought that the fruit of the tree was bitter and poisonous and *that this was why* He admonished them against eating thereof, but now she saw that it was good and sweet food."

But did God as Father instill into Adam even such a modicum of fear as a sensible parent might instill in his child? Did God bring Adam to begin to grasp the significance of the harm against which he was being warned—did Adam (or Eve) comprehend at all adequately the meaning of death?[11] God's remarkable statement at Gen. 3:22 would seem to imply that at any time during the pair's sojourn in Eden, they could have eaten of the unprohibited Tree of Life, thus gaining immortality; they were not so moved.[12] Even in the period immediately after they ate the fruit of the Tree of Knowledge, they did not yet awaken to the opportunity to pick and to consume the fruit of the Tree of Life; they seem even then not yet to have fully grasped the (thus readily remediable) evil of their mortal condition. (One might add that the possibility of God's executing the capital punishment that He threatens might seem to depend, paradoxically, on the pair's not grasping the evil of the threat, for God's words at Gen. 3:22 suggest that the pair would have become immunized against death if they had eaten at any time of the fruit of the Tree of Life.) The couple's not apprehending their own mortality might seem to be further indicated by their not being moved to procreate. Only after the Fall does Adam "name his wife Eve, because she was the mother of all the living"; only after the expulsion does he "know his wife" so that she conceives (Gen. 3:20, 4:1; contrast Milton, *Paradise Lost,* 4.741ff.). In the creation of the woman and in her reception by Adam—whose own words, as we have noted, are here quoted for the first time—there is no reference to the woman's role as partner in procreation; and this silence is underlined by the narrator's own striking interruption, which does, by contrast, emphatically refer to procreation and parenthood in the narrator's own, much later, postlapsarian and thus mortal epoch (Gen. 2:24). After all, it was God, not Adam, Who recognized that it was not good (or "noble, fine, proper," as the Septuagint has it: καλόν) for Adam to be alone. Adam seems to have felt no explicit desire even for companionship; he seems to have had no conscious awareness of his own loneliness, neediness, or vulnerability (contrast Milton, *Paradise Lost,* 8.355ff.).

In sum, was not the situation in Eden prior to the Fall truly infantile in its innocent ignorance?[13] But does this not mean that the pair were lacking in the capacity for true responsibility? Is not the "Fall" in fact a *necessary* step on the way to maturity, to a capacity for understanding the meaning of commandment or law and obedience as well as disobedience? Is this not God's understanding, and does this not explain His intention? Are we not to understand that the whole story shows God's directing a kind of educational drama?[14] For was it not He who created the serpent and allowed or moved him to tempt the utterly naive newborn woman?

These reflections lead to the interpretative hypothesis that the drama of the "Fall" is in fact nothing more and nothing less than a means of educating, first, Adam and Eve (within the drama), and then, more seriously, the entire human race, who will subsequently come to hear their story or parable through the transmission of the Scriptures. The intended lesson would begin from the premise that humans cannot become fully human, or become complete as images of God, without knowing good and evil—as opposed to the merely pleasant and unpleasant, and the good and bad (or beneficial and harmful); but we may surmise that in order truly to know good and evil, creatures (unlike the Creator) must have begun to experience sin, as sinners. Shame, guilt, and moral fear of punishment (as opposed to the prudential fear of hurt) may be understood as necessary preconditions for aspiration to dignity—that is, to an eligibility, and an awareness of eligibility, for salvation at the hands of a God Who is perceived as an awesome though merciful judge and not merely as a benevolent parent or keeper. A true sense of dignity, a true striving after dignity, may be thought to presuppose a vivid experience of the conflict, uncertain in outcome, between what is tempting—what is apparently good for us in our own estimation—and what is rightfully commanded by the just God. Dignity consists in self-overcoming through obedience to divine law and deliberate denial of our own judgment as to what is best. Humans may have open to them the destiny of living in ultimate harmony with God, but that ultimate harmony, in order to be fully self-conscious, must (we may suppose) be a reconciliation won by a long climb, with God's help, from a prior alienation that is necessarily attendant on the emergence from the cocoon of innocence.

The hypothesis that the "Fall" is in fact such an education, planned by God from the beginning, not only makes intelligible the presence of the serpent in Eden, as an agent of God's benevolent educative drama. It helps us to understand, in a manner that does not call into question divine omnipotence and omniscience, how God tolerates what otherwise would seem to be a drastic overturning of His "original plan," and why He does not revert to that supposed plan after the Flood. God's abandonment of what is merely an *apparent* original plan is not a sign of any defect in His true, initially concealed, plan; nor does it imply that God had something to learn, or that He was compelled to revise His original plan in the light of hard-won experience.

A drastic further leap is taken, however, when the story is subjected to reinterpretation so as to become grist for the mill of modern rationalism, with its de facto excision from the Bible of "evil" or "sin." Hobbes begins this process, with a characteristically stunning proposal that the Fall be read as a parable teaching the denial of free will, thus rendering the Bible consistent with scientific determinism. Explaining how he would reply to the Bishop Bramhall's outraged question concerning the compatibility of Hobbes's materialistic determinism with the revealed truth of Scripture in its account of the Fall, Hobbes writes, "And whereas he asketh, 'Doth God reprehend [Adam] for doing that which he hath antecedently determined him that he must do?' I answer, no; but he convinceth and instructeth him, that though immortality was so easy to obtain, as it might be had for the abstinence from the fruit of only one tree, yet he could not obtain it but by pardon, and by the sacrifice of Jesus Christ; nor is there here any punishment, but only a reducing of Adam and Eve to their original mortality, where death was no punishment but a gift of God."[15]

Far more seductive have been the explicitly "progressive" historicist reinterpretations developed most prominently by Kant and Hegel on the basis of Rousseau's account of the human as by nature a "stupid beast" that has acquired its humanity entirely through historical "perfectibility." This transformation of the text finds perhaps its most attractive or eloquent formulation in the rendition of the Fall given in Herder's *Spirit of Hebrew Poetry*:

> He, Who knows the bounds of all things, foresaw also this error [*Verirrung*]; and since it would have been foolish to create a humankind so that in the first moment of its existence it went under, He put on the path of error a plant that, in the plan for humanity, both corresponded to His present aim and had to lead on in a manner to a subsequent condition. The fruit enflamed desire, aroused man's blood, put him in a state of fear, unease, horror, and astonishment. The Father made use of this state of their feelings, and showed his children the consequences of their first offense [*Vergehen*], for themselves and for their seducer. . . . [H]e prophesied for them a new scene of life brought about by their new experiences. The girl of Paradise must in the future become a mother. . . . For the quiet dweller in Paradise, who was to spend only the first period of his young life in this garden of his earliest education, there lay ahead more toilsome work, which however belonged to his destiny: finally, the hard word, "death," was announced to him—and he was also prepared in the gentlest way for this fate.

[Mankind's] first error [*Versehen*] was a fatherly advance in his condition; the punishment of God was (and how else can the all–Good punish?) a new, merely more severe, blessing. . . . [E]ven in the tone of the punishment, all is paternal and indulgent: for this is the progressive natural history of humanity [*fortgesetzte Naturgeschichte der Menschheit*].[16]

CHAPTER FIVE

Creation and the Meaning
of Good and Evil

IT IS NOT POSSIBLE TO SUSTAIN, ON THE BASIS OF THE ACTUAL TEXT OF the Scripture, the "didactic" interpretation in any of the versions set forth in the preceding chapter. The Fall indeed begins to afford an education, but the lesson is more problematic or less coherent than we have thus far admitted. For nothing that has been said up till now explains the single most important feature of the story: God's proclamation of terrible and genuinely retributive punishment.[1] As Luther stresses (LG, *Werke*, 42:136), "Nowhere else in Moses [the Pentateuch] does God speak in Person as extensively as he does here [3:9–22]," devoted "all to promising and threatening."

To the extent that Adam and Eve's misdeed was the result of childish or more than childish ignorance—to the extent that they acted prior to being given the decisive education—their misdeed would seem to deserve no more than a rebuke or mild chastisement suited to innocent children. To be sure, an *apparently* harsh judgment was perhaps in order, to give the "children" a vivid, if benevolently false, experience of consequence, responsibility, and guilt. But the onlooker, and, as the lesson sank in, Adam and Eve themselves, within the story, would recognize that whatever the pair suffered as a consequence of their failure to heed the commandment given in Eden was principally a means of helping them (and others) to understand the possibility and danger of *future,* no longer so innocent, sins, attended by *future* retributive, and not merely or chiefly educative, punishment. This kind of purely educative punishment is, of course, known to the Scriptures. The Hellenistic, deuterocanonical book of the Wisdom of Solomon argues that this is indeed the spirit in which God first chastised the pagan Canaanites, and the Egyptians—which peoples came only subsequently to deserve their eventual, crushing punishment, because they failed to heed the initial didactic discipline:

Those who lived long ago in Your holy land
You hated for their detestable practices. . . .

But even these You spared, since they were but human,
And judging them little by little, You gave them leeway to repent. . . .

Being just, You manage all things justly:
to condemn him who is not deserving of punishment
You regard as alien to Your power.
For Your strength is the source of justice,
and Your mastery over all makes You spare all. . . .

. . . it was as to children who do not reason that
You sent Your judgment, as a mocking jest.
But those who have not heeded the admonition of the playful punishment
will make trial of the deserved judgment of God.[2]

Now, this spirit of apparently stern but essentially playful, because educative, castigation is *not* what is conveyed by the lasting severity, and the sternly retributive character, of the punishments God in fact decrees—first and foremost for the serpent (whose retributive punishment is usually ignored in "progressive" readings; contrast *Midrash Rabbah* on Gen. 20:4–5), and then for the man and woman, in whose nemesis are somehow implicated all subsequent men and women (and serpents).[3]

At the heart of the horror, at the heart of the needy and dangerous struggle for survival with which man and woman are punished, is the alienation from the Tree of Life, entailing the condemnation of humanity to mortality—mortality that is thus clearly presented as an estrangement from, a contradiction of, life itself and in no way as a "natural" or necessary conclusion to human existence.[4] Indeed, it is not much of an exaggeration to say that when we reach Gen. 3:22–23, "it is now obvious that the whole story has really been about *this* tree [of life]" (Bonhoeffer, *Creation and Fall*, 92). The story of the Fall teaches that our mortality is not intrinsic to creaturely human existence but rather came about as the consequence of a punishment that cuts off access to our originally destined, everlasting earthly life. The genealogies in chapter 5 of the antediluvian generations in Seth's line, marking with precision the enormous lifespan that each father in succession enjoyed until, in every case but one, "then he died"—and also the subsequent still impressive lifespan of the patriarchs—constitute a lingering legacy of longevity that poignantly reminds the reader of the most terrible loss incurred by the awful divine punishment of the initial sin. One might go further and with Luther remark that "in this ordered sequence there shines forth like a star the most lovable light of immortality, in that which Moses commemorates regarding Enoch [who alone is said to have 'walked with God' while on earth]: he was no longer living among men and yet was not dead but taken up by God" (LG, *Werke*, 42:244, referring to Gen. 5:23). From the very outset Scripture is speaking to humans as to beings who see in their earthly mortality a horrible and unnecessary rupture of existence—and who thus hunger for subtle signs of hope that for the purified and godly, at any rate, the breach can somehow be healed.[5]

The Problematic Justice of the Punishment of Adam's Posterity

It is impossible, then, to escape the conclusion that the story of the Fall ascribes the most wretched miseries of the human condition, the miseries centering on the earthly mortality into which we all are now born, to divine punishment for sins committed by the original pair prior to all other humans' individual coming into being. And so the prophet Ezra expostulates, in an apocalyptic-prophetic conversation with an angel from the Lord,

> For the first Adam, burdened with an evil heart, transgressed and was overcome, as were also all who descended from him. Thus the disease became permanent: the law was in the hearts of the people along with the evil root; but what was good departed, and the evil remained. . . . O Adam, what have you done? For though it was you who sinned, the fall was not yours alone, but ours also who are your descendants. For what good is it to us, if an immortal time has been promised to us, but we have done deeds that bring death? And what good is it that an everlasting hope has been promised to us, but we have miserably failed? Or that safe and healthful habitations have been reserved for us, but we have lived wickedly? Or that the glory of the Most High will defend those who have led a pure life, but we have walked in the most wicked ways? Or that a paradise shall be revealed, whose fruit remains unspoiled and in which are abundance and healing, but we shall not enter it because we have lived in perverse ways? [2 Esd. 3:21–22 and 7:118–24; see also 7:48; cf. Sir. 25:24]

"But here" (to quote John Locke) "will occur the common Objection, that so many stumble at: 'How doth it consist with the Justice and Goodness of God, that the Posterity of *Adam* should suffer for his sin; the

Innocent be punished for the Guilty?'"—whom (our liberal political philosopher remarks, a bit earlier) "Millions had never heard of, and no one had authorized to transact for him, or be his Representative." To this grave question Locke himself responds that in fact there was no punishment of any of Adam's heirs involved in the punishment of Adam, because it cannot be called "punishment" merely to "keep one from what he has no right to"; and "the state of Immortality in Paradise is not due to the Posterity of Adam." "Therefore, though *all die in Adam*" (i.e., "by reason of his Transgression all Men are Mortal, and come to die") "yet none are truly *punished* but for their own deeds" (*Reasonableness of Christianity,* 5–10). Or as Locke says regarding the implications for womankind of the "Curse" that was Eve's punishment, in his parallel treatment of the Fall in the *Two Treatises of Government* (1.47), God "only foretells what should be the Woman's Lot, how by his Providence he should order it so." This Lockean exegesis seems calculated to arouse the subversive question, How is such a providence consistent with God's benevolence? And is such gratuitous injury or deprivation of life, even when inflicted on creatures by their Creator, not at some tension with justice?[6]

Little wonder that we find Thomas Aquinas insisting, on the contrary, that "since God watches over men's actions, so as to assign rewards to good deeds, and punishments to evil deeds,"

> we can conclude that where there is punishment, there has been sin. Now the whole human race suffers various punishments, both bodily and spiritual. Of bodily punishments the chief is death, to which all others are conducive and subordinate, such as hunger, thirst, and so on. Of spiritual punishments, the principal is weakness of reason, the result being that man encounters difficulty in acquiring knowledge of the truth, and easily falls into error; also that he is unable wholly to overcome his animal propensities, which sometimes even obscure his mental vision.

Thomas anticipates as a possible rejoinder an attempt at an alternative justification along philosophic lines: "Someone, however, might reply that these defects, whether of body or of soul, are not penalties but natural defects, and a necessary consequence of the conditions of matter." This response Thomas finds incompatible with divine omnipotence and mercy: "If we look at this rightly, it will appear sufficiently probable that, divine providence having fitted each perfection to that which is to be perfected, God has united a higher to a lower nature in order that the former might dominate the latter, and, should any obstacle to this dominion arise through a defect of nature, God by a special and supernatural act of kindness would remove it."[7] In other words, Thomas helps us to see that the second account of Creation, and what it implies about the meaning of the knowledge of good and evil, can truly be grasped only if we have first, with the help of philosophic science, comprehended the full meaning of omnipotence as expressed in the first account of Creation. One must understand the meaning and status of "matter" in order to grasp the necessary implications of the existence of evil.

Yet Thomas is certain that God's justice must conform to the principle of responsibility taught by Aristotle, and that therefore "the fact of having a defect by the way of origin seems to exclude the notion of guilt, which is essentially something voluntary. Wherefore, granted that the rational soul were transmitted, from the very fact that the stain on the child's soul is not in its will, it would cease to be a guilty stain binding its subject to punishment; for, as the Philosopher says (*Ethic.* iii, 5), 'no one reproaches a man born blind; one rather takes pity on him' " (ST 1a–2ae qu. 81 a.1). And for this teaching of reason Thomas finds clear revealed or scriptural authority: "One man's sin is not imputed to others: wherefore it is said (Ezek. 18:19): 'The son beareth not the iniquity of his father.' The reason for this is that we are neither praised nor blamed for that which is not in our power. Now those things are in our power, that we do freely. Therefore the sin of the first man is not imputed to all mankind."[8]

"We must therefore," Thomas submits, "explain the matter otherwise, by saying that all men born of Adam may be considered as one man, inasmuch as they have one common nature, which they receive from their first parents; even as in civil matters, all who are members of one community are reputed as one body, and the whole community as one man."[9] This seems to suggest that in order to become attuned to the moral perspective of Holy Writ, we have to abandon from the outset what may seem to us modern liberals to be the apparently obvious Lockean individualist premise. We must not conceive of humans as responsible only for those actions of others whom they have "authorized to transact for them" or whom they have formally made their "representatives." Humans should be understood as *essentially* members of the human race conceived of as an extended family or as a genuine *community*, analogous to a true monarchic political community—that is, a community not grounded in or presupposing individual contractual consent, but instead preceding and even constituting the person as a subordinate part of the larger whole. Thus the Lord Himself, even while proclaiming His mercy, informs Moses that He applies the lawlessness of the fathers to the children and the children's children, to the third and fourth generation.[10] In the deuterocanonical book of Baruch (3:2–8), the Babylonian captivity is understood to be a punishment for the sins of the ancestors, in which the present generation is somehow implicated—even as it pleads with God for mercy in light of the fact that "we have put away from our hearts all the injustice of our fathers who sinned against You." The prophet Jeremiah, in the book of that name (31:29–30), reports from the Lord the ambiguous revelation that a time *is coming* when children will *no longer* say they are suffering for their fathers' sins but "each will die for his own sin."

Yet does not the revelation delivered by Ezekiel definitively establish divine justice as assigning only individual responsibility?[11] And does not the invocation—even if only by analogy—of the Aristotelian conception of political community in order to draw from it strong conclusions about personal criminal responsibility of offspring for the crimes of their parents lead in a direction that contradicts the Aristotelian principle of retributive justice to which Thomas previously appealed? Thomas therefore hastens to rule out the possible implication that offspring are accountable for or tainted by any *other* sins of their parents or ancestors; *only* Adam could ever have been in a position to commit a crime in the name or with the authority of all his offspring.[12]

Augustine, in his most philosophic grappling with the issue (*On Free Choice of the Will* 3.20), does not let himself become drawn into the defense of the principle of collective responsibility. Having made a very brief appeal, in passing, to that principle, he focuses instead on the possibility that the "ignorance and difficulty" in which each soul born after Adam finds itself are "not the punishment of sin for souls as they are born" but instead are meant to constitute a challenge that offers each the opportunity to "educate itself with the help of the Creator," and thus, "by pious zeal, [to] acquire and possess all the virtues." The "ignorance and difficulty" would then be "the admonition for advancement and the prelude to perfection." What was "the first human's penalty of mortality" would "in this way" become for his progeny "not themselves sins except in the sense that the flesh, coming from the seed of the sinner, makes ignorance and difficulty for the entering soul—to which these faults are not to be attributed any more than to the Creator." This approach finds a certain support or echo in the deuterocanonical book of Judith. There the heroine eloquently repudiates the thesis embraced by the populace, according to which its present desperate straits constitute a divine punishment, not only for their own but also for their ancestors' sins. "In spite of all these things," she implores the elders, "let us give thanks to the Lord our God, Who is trying us even as He tried our fathers." "It is not the case," she continues, "that He has visited us with just retribution; He scourges those who are near Him for the sake of admonition" (Jth. 7:28, 8:25–27).

We are not altogether surprised, however, to learn from Augustine himself, in his *Retractions* (1.9.6), that his treatise on freedom of the will was exploited by Pelagian heretics, who simply denied that humans are born in a state of sin. Replying to the Pelagian abuse of his treatise on free will, Augustine asserts the orthodoxy of his conception of original sin, though he does not explain the argument of *On Free Will* further in detail, except to stress that he at no point failed to assert the need for the assistance of divine grace in overcoming any and all moral challenges (see also *City of God* 21.12).

Calvin, while accepting Ezekiel's teaching on individual responsibility, denies that from this teaching it follows that children cannot be regarded as justly implicated in the sins of their forebears. On the contrary, Ezekiel's revelation is to be understood as a *vindication* of the justice of God's punishing the descendants of sinners (see also Lev. 26:39–41): "What can be anticipated but that the father, being deprived of the spirit of God, will live most wickedly? That the son, being in like manner abandoned by God, because of his father's iniquity, will follow the same road to destruction? That the nephew, and the other descendants, go to the same ruin, being an execrable line of evil-doers?" God's withdrawing from the children "the light of his truth and other helps to salvation" is indeed a "curse" but not itself a punishment, since God does not owe this help to anyone. Now "all those on whom the Lord does not bestow the communication of his grace must be doomed to destruction; and nevertheless, they perish by their own iniquity, not by unjust hatred on the part of God." As for original sin, it "may be defined as a hereditary corruption and perversity of our nature":

One must not say that this liability is only another's fault. . . . For when it is said, that the sin of Adam has made us defaulted under the judgment of

God [*redevables au jugement de Dieu/obnoxios esse factos Dei judicio*], the meaning is not that we are innocent, and that without having deserved any punishment we bear the consequences of his sin; but because by his transgression we are all enveloped by confusion, it is said that we are all liable [*pource que par sa transgression nous sommes tous enveloppés de confusion* (Latin *maledictione*) *il est dit nous avoir tous obligez*]. From him, however, not only do we derive punishment, but from him we derive pollution that resides in us, for which punishment is justly due. . . . For this reason even infants are included in this condemnation, not solely for another's, but their own sin. . . . For if we were not guilty, we would not be included in the condemnation.[13]

Humans after the Fall thus sin "necessarily" but nonetheless "voluntarily." For necessity, Calvin contends, understood as the inescapably perverted "confusion" of one's will and inclination, making it impossible for one to "make a movement towards goodness," can and must be distinguished from "compulsion," which is force exerted upon a will from without. One is justly held responsible for whatever one wills without external compulsion, even or especially if one cannot will otherwise—as is proven by the example of divinity: "If the free will of God in doing good is not impeded, because he necessarily must do good; if the devil, who can do nothing but evil, nevertheless sins voluntarily; who will argue that sin is not done voluntarily by man because he is under a necessity of sinning?" "This necessity is always proclaimed by Augustine, who hesitated not to assert it . . . in the following terms: 'Man through liberty became a sinner, but corruption, ensuing as the penalty, has converted liberty into necessity' (*On Perfect Justice* [4.9]). And always and whenever he makes mention of the subject, he declares, without difficulty, that there is in us a necessary bondage of sin (*On Nature and Grace* [66.79], and elsewhere [see, e.g., *On Free Will* 1.11])."[14]

In their competing attempts to employ the fundamental concepts of classical political philosophy to make intelligibly just the scriptural teaching on the fateful consequences of the Fall, Thomas, Augustine, and Calvin share a fundamental premise, which is made fully explicit by Locke: the actions of God must conform to "the Notion we have of Justice," or to a rationally, humanly comprehensible notion of that "Goodness and other Attributes of the Supream Being, which he has declared of himself, and Reason as well as Revelation must acknowledge to be in him, unless we confound Good and Evil, God and Satan" (*Reasonableness of Christianity*, 10). For as Augustine writes, "Anyone who would doubt the omnipotence *or justice* of God is demented" (*On Free Choice of the Will* 3.18). Still, Augustine and other strict adherents to biblical revelation do oppose Locke's strict rationalism inasmuch as they insist that God's intelligible justice, His just reasons, often remain hidden from us on earth. Or as Calvin puts it, "Let it be our law of modesty and soberness to acquiesce in His sovereign Empire, regarding as our only rule of justice, and the most just cause of all things, His will—I do not mean that absolute will, indeed, of which sophists prate, when by a profane and impious divorce, they separate His justice from His power, as if he was capable of doing this or that against all equity; but that universal, overruling, Providence from which nothing flows that is not right, though the reasons thereof may be concealed from us" (*Institutes* 1.17.2 end). If we frequently cannot understand *how* it is that God's actions conform to intelligible justice, we cannot doubt that in some yet unseen way they *do* so conform: "Though someone may suffer some harm by the vice or error of another, and though a man sins who does some harm to another by ignorance or injustice, God nevertheless does not sin, Who allows this to be done through a just, though hidden, judgment" (Augustine *City of God* 21.13). Ibn Ezra dares to go still further. Indicating the narrow grounds on which he finds esoteric interpretation of the Bible permissible, he writes, "The fact of the matter is that the laws of the Torah do not disagree with what is right." Those "who invent secret explanations for everything in Scripture," believing "that the laws and the statutes of the Torah are riddles," are "correct in only one thing, viz., that every precept, be it minor or major, must be weighed in the scale of one's heart wherein the Eternal has planted some of His wisdom." Thus "if there appears something in the Torah that is intellectually impossible to accept or contrary to the evidence of our senses, then we must search for a hidden meaning."[15] It remains a far cry from this, of course, to the philosopher Rousseau's subversive pronouncement, overthrowing the authority of Scripture: "No one is more penetrated than am I by love and respect for the most sublime of all Books: it consoles me and instructs me every day, when the rest inspire in me only distaste: but I contend that if the Scripture itself were to give us some idea of God that is not worthy of him, it would be necessary to reject it in that regard, as you reject in Geometry demonstrations that lead to absurd conclusions; because whatever may be the authenticity of the Sacred text, it is more believable that the Bible has been altered, than that God is unjust or evildoing" (*Letter to D'Alembert*, in *Oeuvres complètes*, 5.12).

At the opposite pole to Rousseau, and resisting even the steps taken by Ibn Ezra, we have Pascal's insistence that human existence gains such comprehensibility as it can have, in this life, *only* if we accept original sin— that is, the "eternal damnation, of an infant incapable of willing, on account of a sin in which he *seems* to have *so little* share" (my italics)—as an "unintelligible mystery." The "mystery" does not consist in original sin's being a violation of "true justice." On the contrary, the mystery consists rather in the fact that original sin must be accepted as an exemplification of "true justice," and as a violation only of the "rules of our miserable justice." In other words, the doctrine of original sin confirms and even in some measure explains what we are vividly aware of prior to hearing of the doctrine—namely, the peculiar "doubleness" that pervades human existence and most acutely our experience of justice. Even prior to any supervening grace of revelation, we experience the revolting dispropor-tion between the actual meaning of human justice everywhere on earth— the domination of conflicting cultural conventions and of majority will, on account of the need to make justice enforceable—and the nature of that true justice, the "laws of nature," whose principles and character, unfailingly sanctioned by irresistible "force" without "violence," we can sense dimly and powerfully but cannot define precisely. Once one is in addition graced by the knowledge that justice is sanctioned by a God Who is the "single principle of all" and the "sole end of all—all by him, all for him," once one sees then that "the true religion must teach us to adore only him and to love only him," then the doctrine of original sin neces-sarily follows. For we know concerning ourselves that "we are born so contrary to that love of God that it is so necessary that it must be that we are born guilty—or else God would be unjust."[16]

Now, one may ask—we must watch to see—whether or to what extent the far-reaching basic premise shared by both the strict philosophic ra-tionalists and the adherents to biblical revelation has explicit scriptural authority. Or in other words, we must look to see whether the Bible supports the Platonic Socrates' contention that experience of divinity is inseparable from a conception of divinity as loving what is pious because it is pious, because it participates in the idea of piety, which is in turn inseparable from the idea of justice (*Euthyphro*). Might one not object that pure or true biblical faith entails, on the contrary, the experience of a demand for a sacrifice of the intellect precisely as regards knowledge of justice and injustice? Could that not be taken as a clear entailment of the original prohibition on eating of the fruit of the Tree of Knowledge of good and evil? Yet are we not now seeing that the sacrifice of the intellect demanded in and by the religious experience cannot be total, if the prohibition itself is to be intelligible, and hence accepted and obeyed, as lawful and obliging commandment—rather than as sheer incomprehensible fiat of an all-powerful and malevolently envious despot? Must there not be given primordially, as Calvin especially insists,[17] a manifestly coherent or fundamentally unmysterious awareness of goodness and righteousness, as divine attributes, essential to our recognizing God as God, even in or at least behind His most perplexing demands and interventions? Or does study of the Scripture lead us to see that faith requires us finally to let go of even this anchor in reason?

The Fall as Archetypical Sin

In whatever way we decide to interpret the consequences of the Fall for future generations, this much is clear: sin is ubiquitous in the human condition, and it is through the story of Adam and Eve that the Bible gives its archetypical portrait of what it means to sin—and then to suffer God's condign punishment, softened by unmerited mercy. To grasp the biblical teaching on what is meant by crime or sin and just punishment, we need therefore to narrow our focus back to the original drama.[18]

We seem compelled to revise our first—and, we now see, too easygoing—interpretation of the moral condition the story imputes to Adam and Eve prior to their tasting of the forbidden fruit. For if the couple genuinely disobeyed and thereby incurred genuine guilt, must they not have been capable of understanding the meaning of obedience and disobedience, and hence of good and evil, including the evil of capital punishment (and hence of death), prior to their tasting of the Tree of Knowledge? Their knowledge of evil may have been very incomplete, but it cannot have been nonexistent or even merely incipient. "You should know," Ibn Ezra teaches (ad loc.), "that the man was full of intelligence, for God would not command someone who is not intelligent. The man just did not know good and bad in one aspect." Similarly Augustine: "If, therefore, the human is so made that, although not yet wise, he is nonetheless able to accept a command which he obviously ought to obey," then he did "possess something by which he could have ascended to that which he did not yet have, if only he had rightly willed to do so."[19]

The original couple must never have been simply ignorant—as very young children may be (Deut. 1:39)—of the decisive difference between right and wrong. If Eve was deceived, she let herself be deceived (Thomas Aquinas ST 1a qu. 94 a. 4). Yet can this reasonable conclusion, drawn by almost every great theological commentator, be supported by the text of the Scripture? If we look again with more suspicious eyes, we may discern that Eve's answer to the serpent's opening question was not an expression of perfectly innocent obedience; for would not perfectly innocent obedience have dictated bemused or contemptuous refusal to enter into the discussion of what God had commanded? As Bonhoeffer comments, "Man cannot resist" such a question "except by saying ὕπαγε, Σατανᾶ [Satan, get thee hence]!"[20] But "she does become involved in this clever conversation; it has struck some spark in her" (*Creation and Fall*, 69). The serpent knew he could appeal to Eve's pride and desire to escape the threat of death because he discerned that although she lacked shame at her nakedness, she did not totally lack the capacity for envy, or the desire for autonomy.[21] Yet could one not retort that the slight degree of independent judgment expressed by Eve and manipulated by the serpent is no more than is necessarily consequent on a (rationally) innocent being? In order to respond to the serpent with the rejoinder Bonhoeffer demands, would not Eve have had to be suspicious of the serpent, bristling against him—that is, already having gained sophisticated or no longer innocent knowledge of good and evil?

Adam's sin is more incomprehensible than Eve's inasmuch as he did not hear, and Eve did not tell him of, the serpent's tempting promises. But in order to render intelligible Adam's sin as a sin—as the most terrible sin—it is understandable that the theological tradition has presumed that a covert, nascent longing for self-determination and rebellion against God's rule hid itself also beneath or within Adam's negligence and carelessness. As Luther puts it, "Uncorrupted nature, which had the true knowledge of God, nevertheless had a Word or command which was beyond Adam's understanding and had to be believed"; and it is precisely this fundamental demand of faith or trust that the devil tempts the human to violate, as the sin of sins: "This is the beginning and the head of *every* temptation, when reason on its own without the Word tries to judge about the Word and God" (LG, *Werke*, 42:116). "The reasons for the divine precepts are not to be inquired into. This is to judge the divine will, and to search out His ways, which are unsearchable" (ibid., 646–47; see also 669–73 and 43:77, 209). The fact that the couple's "eyes were opened" only *after* they ate the forbidden fruit could not then imply that they were previously altogether unaware of the potential for sin (i.e., for defiance of God's ordinance). Accordingly, the excuses that the pair offer to God, when He calls them to account, sound pathetically hollow; the excuses in fact betray the pair's own apprehension of their guilt (Gen. 2:12–13; Augustine *Genesis XII* 11.35).

The Scripture, then, prompts us to penetrate the love of knowledge with lynx eyes: that apparently pure or self-forgetting love is not divorced from a desire to govern one's own existence on the basis of one's own knowledge.[22] Lurking at the heart of Eve's apparently pure delight in the beauty of knowledge would be something akin to the serpent's cunning, and Cassuto plausibly suggests that this initially almost invisible vice is signaled, if almost invisibly, by the text's cunning play on the words for "naked" and "cunning": "Adam and his woman were naked [ערומים] but unashamed. The serpent was cunning [ערום]" (Gen. 2:25–3:1). Just the omission of a dagesh forte (or dot in the מ) would turn the word for "naked" into the word for "cunning" that was applied to the serpent and would make the first sentence read, "Adam and his woman were cunning [ערומים] but unashamed."[23]

That particular dimension of existence that the pair come to know for the first time, when their eyes are opened by the tasting of the forbidden fruit, is their sense of shame at their corporeal nakedness. But the previous lack of such shame need not necessarily imply a lack of all knowledge of the potential for evil; and the inception of the actual experience of sexual shame may be interpreted as meaning that the couple become rightly aware of the powerful temptation to *further* transgression implicit in their sexuality (Gen. 2:7; cf. Exod. 20:23). That awareness expresses itself in a shame-induced fear: "I was afraid because I was naked," says Adam (Gen. 3:10). This specific kind of fear is not simply or primarily a fear of punishment but is rather an awareness of actual and potential baseness, of a chosen and avoidable baseness that makes one feel oneself deserving of punishment. The sexual shame, as the immediate sequel to the violation of the divine commandment not to eat the forbidden fruit, may be taken to signal the fact that at the heart of human evil is humanity's perverse refusal to accept its proper rank: man experiences the temptation to degrade his holy, and austerely demanding, share in divinity by descending into the lascivious enjoyment of animal sexuality for its own sake; and this is not merely temptation to descend into sensual pleasure, for it is simultaneously and more profoundly an expression of perverse rebellion, and thus an expression of the temptation to free oneself from, to ascend in arrogant revolt against, tutelage to God. The appropriate awareness of mankind's fallen condition, beset and infected with this complex movement simultaneously toward debasement and arrogance—the awareness that constitutes the appropriately human, all-too-human, or sinful, knowledge of good and evil—is an awareness that expresses itself in the passion of shame (contrast Aristotle *Ethics* 1128b10–33). By the same token, the improper awareness, the actual succumbing to the temptations to violate the true ranking of things, expresses itself in the passions of pride and lust, followed by inevitable self-loathing. If the Fall had been avoided, we may venture to surmise, mankind would have felt dignified humility, and awe or reverence, but neither pride nor shame, let alone guilt.[24] Temptation would have been experienced as proffered but not as gripping—as something like a pleasure that a healthy person can imagine, at least by way of analogies, but only as the experience of a perverted appetite. Eve, admiring God, could readily have understand that it would be good, joyful, to be God; from this the serpent's suggestion could lead her to imagine, though with abhorrence—perhaps in a bad dream, spawned by fancy released from dormant reason (Milton, *Paradise Lost*, 5.31ff.)—the perverted outlook of one, human like herself, who sought to usurp God's place. According to Milton's *Paradise Regained*, it is such a posture toward evil that must be exhibited if mankind is to recover from the Fall.

Must we not understand, then, that God's original prohibition was not intended to provoke an eventually educative disobedience but was instead "meant merely as a medicine to make man's obedience strong" (Augustine *City of God* 14.15)? God, it may be suggested, permitted the serpent to tempt Eve because He wanted humans to *choose* to reject full autonomy, to *choose* to remain in what would then become a state of purity but no longer of innocence.[25] Inspired by the Holy Spirit, Milton puts the following words into God's mouth, in explanatory conversation with His only begotten Son:

> Not free, what proof could they have giv'n sincere
> Of true allegiance, constant Faith or Love,
> Where only what they needs must do, appear'd,
> Not what they would? what praise could they receive?
> What pleasure I from such obedience paid,
> When Will and Reason (Reason also is choice)
> Useless and vain, of freedom both despoiled,
> Made passive both, had serv'd necessity,
> Not mee. [*Paradise Lost,* 3.103–11]

This implies that there is or was a *superior,* purer knowledge of good and evil that would have been fully actualized through the dignified refusal to succumb to the proffered temptation to disobey. "He who has not been tried will know little" (Sir. 34:11). God wanted His human creatures to advance to a condition of knowledge that represented a deeper, truer awareness of sin than any that can be gained by sinning (cf. Plato *Republic* 409, 413c–414a). In Milton's arresting formulation, God wanted Adam and Eve to "know to know no more."[26] Augustine puts it this way:

A person who is pleased by the good without having any experience of evil—that is, a person who, before feeling the loss of the good, chooses to hold on to it so as not to lose it—is worthy of praise above all humans. Now if this were not a matter of singular merit, it would not be attributed to that child, of the race of Israel who, receiving the name Emmanuel, "God is with us," reconciled us to God. . . . How does He reject or choose what He does not know except that these two are known in one way by the prudent knowledge of good and in another way by the experience of evil? Through the prudent knowledge of good, evil is known, although it is not felt. . . . How could the human being, they ask, understand what was said to him about the tree of knowledge of good and evil when he was completely ignorant of the meaning of evil? Those who think this way do not notice how most unknown things are understood from their contraries which are known, so that even the names of nonexistent things can be used in conversation without bewildering the hearer. For instance, what is entirely nonexistent we call nothing [*nihil*]; and anyone who understands and speaks Latin comprehends these two syllables.[27]

Luther, following Thomas Aquinas, goes still further. When God says, after finishing His works, that they are "very good," it is "as if He wished to say, 'man is to have *knowledge* of God and, with the greatest security, *justice, wisdom,* he is to make use of the creatures even as he wishes.'" Luther deplores "the books of all the sophists" who "make foolish statements" in answer to the question, "What is original justice?" It suffices to reply that "if we follow Moses, we should take original justice to mean that man was just, truthful, upright not only in body but especially in mind, that he *knew* God, that he obeyed God with the utmost pleasure, and that he *understood* the works of God even without prompting." The sophists do not grasp the fact that "original sin really means" that "the intellect has become darkened"—"just as blindness is the deprivation of sight." So, Luther concludes, "if we wish to proclaim someone an outstanding philosopher, let us proclaim our first parents while they were still pure of sin."[28]

This idea that Adam and Eve were to actualize fully their wisdom by refusing the temptation to eat the fruit of the Tree of Knowledge helps make more sense of the retributive punishment—but at a price, for it diminishes drastically the special or additional knowledge of good and evil that is consequent to the eating of the fruit of the Tree of Knowledge. On this reading, it would seem that, contrary to what the serpent claimed would come to pass, what the pair's "eyes were opened" to cannot have been so significant. "Opened to nothing except to concupiscence for one another, in punishment for sin, born of the death of the flesh," says Augustine in contempt.[29] The Augustinian interpretation denudes the tree and its fruit of any important moral, spiritual, or intellectual content. Thus Thomas Aquinas declares (following Augustine), "Eating of the fruit of this tree was prohibited, not because it was evil in itself, but that at least in this *slight* matter man might have some precept to observe for the sole reason that it was so commanded by God. Hence eating of the fruit of this tree was evil because it was forbidden. The tree was called the tree of knowledge of good and evil, not because it had the power to cause knowledge, but because of the sequel: by eating of it man learned by experience the difference between the good of obedience and the evil of disobedience."[30] The Midrash (Tadshei) of R. Pinhas ben Yair (quoted with strong approval in Leibowitz, *Studies in the Book of Genesis,* 22–23, 54) goes still farther: "Before Adam partook of this tree, it was called simply 'tree,' just like all other trees. But as soon as he partook of it, thereby transgressing the decree of the Holy One blessed be He, it was called the tree 'of the knowledge of good and evil,' alluding to its future destiny." This Midrash might be taken to explain, and thus be verified by, the fact that when Eve responds to the serpent she reveals that Adam did not tell her any name of "the tree in the midst of the garden" from which they were forbidden to eat (Gen. 3:3).

In the same spirit, Luther suggests that there was probably a grove of trees ("in the fashion of Scripture, the singular is used for the plural") and the intention was that this "would have been the church at which Adam, together with his descendants, would have gathered on the Sabbath day." "Augustine and those who follow him state correctly that the Tree of the Knowledge of Good and Evil was so named from the event which lay in the future"; "the Tree was a good tree, it produced very fine fruit. But because the prohibition is added and man is disobedient, it becomes more injurious than any poison." Yet we note that Luther himself in this context also characterizes Adam's condition as that of "the innocence of a child," "because Adam could be deceived by Satan."[31]

Moreover, does this interpretation that demotes the significance of the knowledge gained by eating of the fruit of the Tree of Knowledge account for what God says just before He sends the pair out of the garden: "Behold, the man has become like one of us, knowing good and evil!" (Gen. 3:22)? Do not these words of God imply that the new knowledge the couple attained through the eating of the fruit of the Tree of Knowledge has the awesome power, or makes the tremendous difference, that was ascribed to it by the serpent?[32] Hegel protests that "this verse is usually overlooked, or else nothing is said about it." But in fact, Hegel argues, this verse must be the key to the intelligibility of the whole drama—which therefore can only metaphorically be a drama of sin or guilt. (Hegel ignores the possibility a Greek would pose: that this verse betrays, or is at least a relic of an understanding of, God as being like Zeus—a malevolently jealous, because not altogether secure, leader or king among other gods.) What "is expressed in this speech of God," Hegel continues, is the thought that the "cleavage" (*Entzweiung*) caused by the eating of the Tree of Knowledge is something that "ought to persist, insofar as it contains the source of its healing." This speech shows, Hegel notes with satisfaction, that "what the serpent said is no lie; on the contrary, even God Himself corroborated it." The "confirmation of the fact that the knowledge of good and evil belongs to the divinity of humanity is put in the mouth of God Himself." The human becomes divine only by breaking out of the "stupor" (*Dumpfheit*) caused by lack of that knowledge

(*Erkenntnis*) of good and evil that bestows autonomy: "We can say that this is the eternal story of the freedom of man, that he goes forth out of this stupor." "That is the true idea, as opposed to the simple representation of Paradise, this befogged, un-self-conscious, and will-less innocence. That man in the original condition had the highest understanding of goodness and of nature is certainly generally accepted; but it is utterly absurd."[33]

In response, we must remonstrate that Hegel is misinformed when he complains that this verse is overlooked or ignored by orthodox commentators. They in fact struggle with the verse. Augustine tries to interpret the words as ironic (as does Calvin, *Commentary on Genesis* ad 3:22), though Augustine expresses some bewilderment (*Genesis XII* 11.42 beg.; see also 11.39 end): "How are we to understand this except to say, that it is an example presented for the purpose of inspiring us with fear, because the man not only did not become what he wanted to be but did not even retain the condition in which he was created" (see also St. Chrysostom's uneasy discussion, *Homilies on Genesis* 18.6). Luther boldly explains (LG, *Werke* 42:166) that "this is sarcasm and very bitter derision" (*sarcasmus et acerbissima irrisio*), but he admits that such a reading leads to the question, "Why does God deal so harshly with wretched Adam? Why, after being deprived of all his glory and falling into sin and death, is he further vexed by his Creator with such bitter scorn?" Luther answers that it is a "bitter reminder" both for Adam and for all his descendants of the precise nature of the sin that is fundamental to all sinning: "He wanted to become like God."

Isaac Abravanel, taking the words of God seriously, concedes that the eating of the fruit of the Tree of Knowledge must indeed be interpreted as symbolizing the acquisition of a new kind of knowledge of good and evil—but, he insists, of an essentially deformed character. In Paradise God intended man to seek "for divine knowledge, since it was for this that he was created." Such divine knowledge is true knowledge of good and evil: "The knowledge of good and evil is the perfection of man." Indeed, "the *whole* perfection of man lay in his possession of the capacity to choose freely between evil and good." "How then could God have intended to withhold it from him?" In fact, the prohibition on eating the fruit of the Tree of Knowledge of good and evil, as a divine commandment, presupposed man's moral knowledge. So it follows that the knowledge prohibited to man must be a defective or merely apparent knowledge. In

eating of the prohibited Tree of Knowledge man sinned "in that he was
not satisfied with the natural things that God had placed before him, but
was attracted to the things of the appetite and the generally accepted
[conventionally approved] actions." Man's eating of the fruit of the tree—
as opposed to merely looking upon it and touching it—symbolizes mankind's embrace of knowledge perverted to luxury and vanity. It was the
same with "the sins of the generation of the Tower of Babel" and the sins
of "Cain and his sons": they all "placed the Tree of Knowledge as their
final end and abandoned the Tree of Life, which is the true end."[34] As
Nehama Leibowitz notes in severe disapproval (*Studies in the Book of
Genesis*, 21–22), Abravanel's uncompromising reading implies that in the
light of biblical revelation, almost everything that Hegel would regard as a
mark of "advanced civilization" is to be viewed as a perversion. This
applies not least, paradoxically, to Abravanel's own "entire life as a politi-
cian and statesman in the courts of kings and princes." Abravanel "found
support for this from the rabbinic dictum (Pirke Avoth 1.11): 'Hate public
office and do not be familiar with authority.' "

Yet it is hard to dispute Abravanel's insistence that the divine knowledge of good and evil that Hegel and the serpent regard as a wonderful
acquisition for mankind, the biblical God views as a most dubious acquisition; and the reason is evident in the serpentine words we have quoted
above from Hegel. Insofar as the Bible presents the knowledge of good
and evil as demonic, it does so out of a recognition that to seek to know
adequately what is good and evil necessarily entails a quest for an autonomy that is not compatible with obedience in any strict sense. To a being
that knows, or believes that it knows, by itself what is good and what is
evil, the good is no longer good because it is commanded, but rather,
what is commanded is good if and inasmuch as it conforms to what is
known to be good, independently of the command (see the words of Eve
in Milton's *Paradise Lost*, 9.758–60). Adam and Eve may not have in-
stantaneously obtained full divine wisdom about good and evil by eating
of the fruit of the Tree of Knowledge, but they surely took the decisive
first enormous step along the path to such knowledge; and, the Bible as a
whole teaches, mankind's great struggle is to find its way back from this
path, or up and beyond it to a different path—to the path of the self-
conscious submission or trammeling of independent judgment that is
implicit in genuine obedience. We must in mature judgment decide to
become again as children. In Pascal's words, "La sagesse nous envoie à

89

l'enfance. 'Nisi efficiamini sicut parvuli' [Matt. 18:3–4]. . . . [C]'est une ignorance savante qui se connaît" (*Pensées*, #82–83 [= Brunschvicg #271 and 327]).

Yet is this move possible, or even conceivable as coherent? In the words of a thoughtful contemporary skeptic, is not "any free choice" as such "by definition, an act of non-obedience," since it "means, implicitly, reaching for and acting on our own 'knowledge' (or opinion) of good and bad, better and worse" (Kass, "Man and Woman," 16)? To this a perspective informed by the pronouncements we have previously quoted from such authorities as Luther, Milton, and Pascal, joined by Maimonides' famous pronouncement in his codification of the law,[35] would reply thus: But does not obedience in the authentic sense shine forth precisely in those cases where the inferior must surrender his independent judgment—not merely or even typically because his own judgment lacks entirely sufficient knowledge, but rather where his own judgment tells him that what is commanded is *not* evidently sensible or reasonable or intelligibly good?[36] Does not obedience come into its own as a virtue where the obedient must overcome or sacrifice, defy, his own prudential intellect in order to follow the commandment received from a superior, over and against the subordinate's better judgment? Is this not what we will see exemplified at the peak moment of the life of Abraham? But this would seem to imply that *true* obedience presupposes ignorance rather than knowledge. True obedience consists in a decision against what one knows. Is true obedience then *necessarily* a willfully blind obedience, in the telling cases?

Or must we not recognize precisely at this point that the crucial "knowledge" underlying and animating true obedience is a unique kind of cognition that, so far from being the product of autonomous reasoning or judgment, is itself an inspired gift of the revealing God? Is this not a gift received through the direct experience of the divine presence "living and breathing within" the words of commandment or of Scripture, through an experience, that is to say, that can in no way be arrived at without miraculous assistance—but that a human can somehow contumaciously and perversely reject, refuse to accept and submit to? Calvin conveys his own experience in this respect as follows:

> Enlightened by the virtue of the Spirit, we no longer believe, either on our own judgment or that of others, that the Scripture is from God, but, in a way superior to all human judgment, we know without doubt that it is

given to us from the mouth of God, by the aid of men—as if [in the last edition of 1560, Calvin omitted the word "entirely" which he had in earlier editions of 1541–57 written before "as if"] we beheld with our eye the essence of God in it. We seek not for arguments or probabilities on which to rest our judgment, but we submit our judgment and intellect to it as to a thing elevated beyond the necessity of being judged. This, however, we do, not in the manner in which some are accustomed to fasten lightly on an *unknown* object, which, as soon as known, displeases, but because we are very certain that we have in it unassailable truth. Nor are we like ignorant men who are accustomed to surrender their minds to superstition, but because we feel a divine *virtue* living and breathing in it, a *virtue* by which we are drawn and animated to obey it, willingly indeed, and knowingly, but more effectually than could be done by human will or knowledge. . . . I say nothing more than every believer experiences in himself, though my words fall far short.[37]

This does mean that the "knowledge" one has when one reaches this point is such that "one does not comprehend, what one understands; but possessing as certain, and being entirely persuaded of what one cannot comprehend, one understands better by the certainty of this persuasion than when one comprehends something by human capacity." Or in other words, "The knowledge of faith consists more of certainty than of discernment" (*apprehensione*).[38]

Yet as the italicized words in the quoted passage from Calvin indicate, the obedience here under discussion presupposes a recognizable divine "virtue." To put the point another way, true obedience entails *trust* in the judgment of the superior; the virtue of obedience to God goes with the virtue of trust in God—both are implicit in "faith." And surely this trust implies, if not the certain knowledge, then the conviction, the guiding opinion, of the wisdom and goodness and justice that are believed to be so necessarily intrinsic to the superior that they unfailingly characterize the superior as commander: "The highest proof of Scripture is uniformly taken from the character of Him whose word it is" (*Institutes* 1.7.4). The higher, obedient knowledge of good and evil would then perhaps consist in not knowledge of what ought to be done because it is best to be done in each or in any particular case, but rather a grounding knowledge of the utterly trustworthy goodness and justice of God, Whose commandments are for *this* reason always to be followed, even when they appear lacking in sufficient reason or unreasonable.[39]

So, is not obedience, precisely in this case, derivative from one's own insight into what is best in the long run—from one's own knowledgeable certainty or settled conviction that God is undoubtedly and unfailingly wise and good, even if unfathomable in the means He employs to secure the good? In other words, about this grounding "inner witness of the Holy Spirit," we may still ask, however, is there not some at least partially intelligible and hence communicable content to the divine attribute of goodness, of which the truly and fully obedient have firm inspired knowledge, as the presupposition or at any rate the necessary accompaniment of all their (nonblind) obedience?[40] Is the crucial intelligible attribute that God possesses that of being the good-in-itself, which as such makes an absolute claim upon us? But what is the articulate content to *this* notion, this notion of the good-in-itself such that the thought of it gives clarity and thus renders trust in God altogether different from blind obedience?[41] In particular, what is the relation between God's goodness-in-itself and His goodness to or for us and the rest of Creation—His loving care, His justice, and above all His mercy? Or are the latter attributes—His attributes as ruler, His political attributes—not the decisive constituents of His intelligible goodness (as both Maimonides and Calvin insist)?[42] Is it not trust in these *political* attributes that in fact underlies our quest to prove ourselves meritoriously obedient? In other words, is not knowledge of these intelligible *political* attributes, and trust in them, presupposed even or especially in the apparently most unqualified and unquestioning obedience? Let us keep these questions in mind as we ascend to the story of the binding of Isaac.

What is taught through the story of the Fall is a lesson that animates the Scripture from beginning to end. There is a manifest radical paradox at the core of what is demanded by this teaching: the just God asks man to take upon himself the responsibility for choosing *either* culpably to take responsibility for choosing for oneself, *or* to remain in (to return at once to) unqualified and more than childlike dependence on God's choosing for us. This paradox shows the severity of the test of or challenge to obedience and trust in His merciful justice that God imposes. For it is not manifestly incoherent to demand that humanity recognize that in its inability to fathom, and consequently in its unavoidable disobedience to, this fundamental command, we have no alternative except to throw ourselves, in contrite fear and hope, upon His mercy.

The Puzzle of Divine Foreknowledge

We cannot altogether avoid questions that seem raised, by the guilt of the creatures, concerning the power of the Creator. Since we are to understand the human pair as having truly violated, and thus as having destroyed forever, the original and presumably superior divine plan for Creation, does this not imply the existence of real bounds on God's knowledge and hence His power? Is there not implicit in human freedom and power a grave qualification of, or an insuperable uncertainty about, what God can guarantee for His creatures and Creation? One could further wonder whether it does not begin to appear as if God is in some degree ignorant of these limits at the outset—as if He grows in wisdom by gradually coming to know the immutable, uncreated limits to what He can expect or accomplish.

It suffices to spell out the preceding questions to recognize that if we are to preserve the meaning of the Creator's omnipotence, we must ascribe to Him foreknowledge of the disruption of His apparent original plan: "For the Most High knows every object of knowledge, and He sees from of old the things that are to come. He discloses what has been and what is to be, and He reveals the traces of hidden things" (Sir. 42:18−19). Ought we not to conclude that in and through the paradigmatic case of Adam and Eve, God means to teach us that any and every human, placed in similar circumstances, would similarly, sooner or later, choose defiance? Is this not an important sense in which we are all implicated in the story of the Fall? But if so, does not such foreknowledge suggest an absolute limit on human capacity and freedom, and hence responsibility or guilt? To such a question Milton's God replies,

> They therefore as to right belong'd,
> So were created, nor can justly accuse
> Thir maker, or thir making, or thir Fate;
> As if Predestination over-rul'd
> Thir will, dispos'd by Absolute Decree
> Or high foreknowledge; they themselves decreed
> Thir own revolt, not I: if I foreknew,
> Foreknowledge had no influence on their fault,
> Which had no less prov'd certain unforeknown.[43]

Yet (an Aristotelian logician might ask; see *On Interpretation* 18a33ff.) does not "prov'd certainty" of an outcome imply necessity, thereby foreclosing any open "possibility," and hence authentic moral choice and responsibility? But let us follow Maimonides' counsel and leave this aside, on the ground that the very meaning and implications of "knowledge" in God are inaccessible to us (*Eight Chapters,* end). Still, if God foreknew the Fall, could He have wisely planned for or intended anything that did not presuppose the Fall? In choosing to create mankind, did He not choose to create beings He knew would rebel? Or was he unable to do otherwise—unable to create morally free beings who were immune (like Himself), or who were at least not prone, to perversion? Would there not here come to light, after all, some fixed limits—in the "nature" of what is possible in a mortal creature, in the "matter" with which God has to work—before which even God must bow?[44] But this would mean that even God could not save us from the ultimate necessities inherent in nature or matter. If or since His grace was incapable of endowing us in the beginning with souls that were not inclined to rebellion, how could His grace ever subsequently acquire such a capacity? But then what would be the meaning of the promise that someday "a new heart also I will give you, and a new spirit will I put within you; and I will take away the stony heart out of your flesh, and I will give you an heart of flesh. I will put My spirit in you, and cause you to walk in My statutes, and to keep My ordinances" (Ezek. 36:26–27; cf. 11:19–20 and Deut. 30:6)? How could our souls ever be redeemed, in the sense of permanently and not merely temporarily released from sinful rebellion—and from the sentence of death that is the proclaimed condign punishment for such rebellion? Can we find recourse in the speculation that while God is unable to form a soul not prone to sin, He is nevertheless fully able to effect this goal through transformation of a sinful soul? But even or precisely if we accept such a thought, does this not mean that we are impelled down the blasphemously suspicious track of exploring the limits on God that we are presuming to think are left unstated or only hinted at in the Scripture? It is not surprising that Augustine, followed by Calvin, sternly warns us from this course. Both insist that we must never abandon the sheet anchor that is the doctrine of the Creator's omnipotence. Accordingly, both contend that God is quite capable of creating free creatures who are sinless; among the angels, we are assured, there are such.[45]

This, however, leads to the grave question, If God *could* have created a humanity or a superhumanity that was destined not to rebel, then is not our moral weakness, is not our overwhelming proneness to defiance, partly (not to say decisively) the product of *His* creative choice? Can this divine choice be made intelligible as a means to the glory of God as just judge and merciful redeemer? "It offends the ears of some," writes Calvin (*Commentary on Genesis* ad 3:3), "when it is said God *willed* this [fall]; but what else, I pray, is the *permission* of him, who has the right of preventing, and in whose hand the whole matter is placed, but his will?" A bit later Calvin adds (ad 3:7), "The eternal counsel of God that preceded the fall is not without reason, though that reason is concealed from us. We see indeed the fruit daily springing from this horrible ruin and that God instructs us in humility by our miseries, and moreover that God makes more clearly resplendent His own goodness. For He has spread through the world a more abundant grace by the Christ than He would have given in the beginning to Adam."

But perhaps we ought to recognize that we are here starting to slip into waters over our heads (Sir. 3:21–25). As regards the divine mind, and its knowledge and power and ultimate plans, we scarcely have direct evidence or experience (see Jth. 8:14). "As to why God did not sustain [Adam] by the virtue of perseverance, that is hidden away in His counsel, and it is our duty to know nothing except within the bounds of soberness" (Calvin, *Institutes,* 1.15.8 end).[46] "And as when the Lord descends to us He in a certain sense abases Himself and stammers with us, so He wishes us to stammer with Him. And this is the true wisdom, when we embrace God in the manner in which He accommodates Himself to our capacity" (Calvin, *Commentary on Genesis* ad 35:7). Ought we not to limit ourselves to those matters about which we do have direct evidence and experience? We do have direct evidence and experience in the matters pertaining to ourselves, pertaining to human action and human understanding, and pertaining to the teachings God addresses to man insofar as He makes them intelligible to man. Let us then leave behind, as "hidden in His counsel," the coexistence of God's omnipotence (and hence foreknowledge or predestination) with (fully responsible) human choice; let us consider how we are to comprehend, as a choice, the human choice of defiance.

Guilt and Punishment

Spinoza poses, in this regard, a characteristically unabashed and bracing challenge to the biblical notion of sin and the Fall. At about the same time that Milton was receiving, as he reports, divine inspiration guiding his writing of the majestic epic that was intended to "justify the ways of God to men" (*Paradise Lost,* 1.26), Spinoza wrote near the start of his (never to be completed) *Political Treatise* as follows, responding to those who "maintain, that the human mind is not produced by natural causes at all, but is the direct Creation of God, and is so independent of the rest of things that it has an absolute power to determine itself and use right reason":

> But experience teaches all too well that it is no more in our power to have a sound mind than to have a sound body. Moreover, since each thing strives as much as it can to preserve its own being, we cannot have the slightest doubt that, if it were as much in our power to live by the precept of reason as it is to be led by blind desire, all men would be guided by reason, and would order their lives wisely; which is very far from being the case. For everyone is captivated by his own pleasure. Nor do theologians dispose of this difficulty by maintaining that the cause of this impotence is the vice or sin which takes its origin from the fall of our first ancestor.[47] For if precisely in the first man there was as much power to stand as to fall, if his mind was sound and his nature whole, how, with his knowledge and prudence, could he possibly have fallen? They say that he was deceived by the Devil. Who was it, in truth, that deceived the Devil himself—who, I ask, made the very foremost of all intelligent creatures so mindless that he wished to be greater than God? For surely, if he had a sound mind, he must have been striving all he could to preserve himself and his own being? Moreover, if the first man himself was sound in mind and master of his own will, how could he possibly have allowed himself to be seduced and tricked in his mind? Now if he had the power to use right reason, he could not have been deceived; for he must necessarily have been striving as much as he could to preserve his own being and his own sound mind. But the premise is that he had this power: therefore it necessarily follows that he must have preserved his sound mind, and could not have been deceived. This, however, is shown to be false by the story told about him; and so it must be admitted that the first man did not have it in his power to use right reason, but, like ourselves, was subjected to passions.
>
> But no one can deny that man, like any other individual in nature, strives as much as he can to preserve his being. In fact, one could only

conceive man to differ from other things in this respect if one assumed that he had free will. Yet the more free we conceived man to be, the more should we be compelled to maintain that he must necessarily preserve himself, and be of sound mind; as everyone who does not confuse freedom with chance [*contingentia*] will readily grant me. For freedom is virtue or perfection: and so what betokens weakness in a man cannot be ascribed to his freedom. In consequence, it is quite impossible to call a man free because he can fail to exist, or because he can fail to use reason; he can be called free only in so far as he has the power to exist and act in accordance with the laws of human nature. So the more free we conceive a man to be, the less we can say that he can fail to use reason, and choose bad in preference to good.[48]

Now, on its own terms this objection might seem to be decisive. But the closer one looks, the more Spinoza's critique may seem to rest at bottom on assertions rather than arguments, or the more it may seem to assume what is most in need of demonstration. Spinoza's appeal to our "experience" is contradicted by the apparent experience of the divine call, a call that complements and completes the universal human experience of the sense of indignation and moral responsibility or freedom—freedom, above all, to do and to choose what is right even or especially when this involves sacrifice of one's own interests. Now, of course, Spinoza claims to demonstrate the self-contradictoriness or unintelligibility of the purported sense of responsibility and freedom. The difficulty in his demonstration is his assumption that freedom or free will means acting in order to maximize one's *own* mental and physical security. Why, we may ask Spinoza, should we assume that there is no conceivable alternative to an intelligent being's acting with a view to its own benefit or pleasure? Is not Spinoza overlooking or disregarding what is human in man ("man, *like any other individual in nature,* strives as much as he can to preserve his being")? Does not the Bible presume, more commonsensically, that an intelligent human being acts not only with a view to its own benefit and pleasure, but also with a view to what is right or noble simply; and that the simply right or noble is *not* identical with—that it is, in the crucial cases, sometimes *contrary* to—the beneficial or pleasant for oneself? Is not precisely this the significance of the divine commandment as commandment—that it calls us to obedience regardless of the (admittedly tempting) real or apparent consequences for our own benefit or pleasure?

It is true that a sanction or punishment is affixed to the commandment, but this does not necessarily imply that we are supposed to obey solely out of fear of punishment or hope of reward. Quite to the contrary, punishment and reward, blame and praise, are understood to be something we *deserve*. Now, what we mean by this deserving would make no sense if our obedience or disobedience were simply a consequence of our ignorance of the punishment. Ignorance and costly mistakes in calculation of our self-interest do not make us deserving of punishment, any more than knowledge and accurately profitable calculation of costs and benefits to ourselves make us deserving of reward. If we *deserve* punishment, it is because we failed to do what is right, because we consulted exclusively our own pleasure and benefit; the punishment in part deprives us of the profit from our ill-gotten gains. If we *deserve* reward, it is because we acted according to what was right, regardless or to the neglect of our interest and pleasure; the reward in part compensates us for our noble sacrifice.

Yet if this undercuts Spinoza's challenge to the Bible as he states it, it does not dispose of all the difficulties implicit in that challenge. In the first place, might not Spinoza point out that the biblical context of the Fall—life in Paradise, communing intimately with God—suggests that the Bible itself conceives of the obedience to divine law, away from which Eve and Adam turned, as something supremely good for them? If, in reply, we forced Spinoza to concede that despite this, the Bible as a whole plainly means, by obedience to God, in part a self-forgetting or self-sacrificing devotion to Him, might not Spinoza retort that the Bible remains on this crucial point confused or contradictory? That to make the meaning of obedience to divine law intelligible, one must decide whether that obedience is to be understood as ultimately and fundamentally good or as ultimately and fundamentally not good for the obedient (since it cannot be both at once), and that one must consider whether one can hold to the view that obedience to God's law is fundamentally bad for the obedient? In the second place, must we not concede this much to Spinoza: that there is strong plausibility in his assertion that free action presupposes some kind of rational deliberation, and that every choice by a free agent depends on, and is guided by, some opinion as to what is best—whether we conceive of the "best" as the most pleasant, or most noble or right (involving sacrifice of one's well-being), or most beneficial to oneself? (See again the words Milton ascribes to God at *Paradise Lost,* 3.108, and the similar declaration of Adam at 9.351–52.)

One might indeed resist such a concession by observing that the essence of will is not deliberation, and subsequent action in accord with what is conceived to be best, but sheer will, as the ungrounded ground: the will is spontaneous and does not depend on anything prior to the will. To borrow somewhat freely from Maimonides, "The fact that it may will one thing now and another thing tomorrow does not constitute a change in the will's essence and does not call for another cause; just as the fact that the will acts at one time and does not act at another does not constitute a change, or call for another cause" (*Guide* 2.18).

But (a Spinozist might well reply) would this not leave the will a manifestation of sheer arbitrariness (*contingentia*), disconnected from everything else that we know and that constitutes our character? In what sense would we be the owners or agents of such a will? Would its "actions" not be difficult if not impossible to distinguish from the erratic, if vigorous, tergiversations of mindlessness, or of an uncontrollable imp within us? Would not the "will" to obey God's commandment be as groundless and therefore as senseless and unsteady as the will to disobey? If Adam and Eve willed in this sense (our Spinozist might complain), it would seem that their "action," whether outwardly obedient or disobedient, was in its essence more akin to impulse, or to being possessed by impulse, than to self-possessed, perspicacious and circumspect, responsibility.[49] Now, while the Bible leaves us to speculate on the possible motives for Adam's accepting the fruit from Eve, in the case of Eve, Scripture surely indicates that she was motivated not by some sort of groundless "decision" but rather by the apparent good and beauty of the tree—as well as by the serpent's questioning of the threatened penalty and by his promise that she might become divine.

If, then, Eve was motivated by some *opinion* as to the balance of better and worse entailed in the options of obeying and disobeying respectively, must we not consider what that opinion and balance could have been? If she was responsible, then she *knew* it was wrong, and to that extent bad, to eat of the fruit. But since she decided to eat the forbidden fruit in the face of this knowledge, was her decision not based, at the moment of decision, on the supervening opinion (i.e., what appeared to her to be the knowledge) that the benefit and pleasure outweighed in goodness what was admittedly bad in doing what was wrong? But did she not then think it was on balance *better* to disobey, *worse* (or less preferable) to obey? Did she not somehow fail to grasp the fact that the right outweighed in goodness, was better than, was preferable to, the (lesser) goodness of the pleasant and apparently beneficial—for the latter appeared "impregn'd / With Reason, to her seeming, and with Truth" (*Paradise Lost*, 9.737–38)? But then is her fault not a result of some kind of confusion, ignorance, or pitiable blindness, even if only of a momentary sort?[50] (The difficulty is only removed one step and then bounces back if we suggest, with Milton's Adam, that the basic crime consists not in the deceived following of false opinion but rather in the failure of reason to remain sufficiently vigilant against becoming deceived—"Not keeping strictest watch, as she [Reason] was warn'd" [ibid., 9.363 and context]. For the question recurs, did Eve's Reason then not fail to grasp, at the crucial moment or moments, the gravity of the warning, and thus the supreme goodness or perdurability, over all other apparent goods, of the intelligible requirements of Reason's duty of maintaining vigilance? If or inasmuch as Reason exercised choice, did Reason not choose what She at that moment thought best, impressed by "reasoning words" [see ibid., 9.379, 404–5]; or else, was Reason not distracted, thus leaving Eve "mindless the while" and "unwary," and therefore, as Milton himself judges, "yet sinless" [ibid., 9.431, 614, 659]?)

But no, we may protest: if Eve was criminally responsible, she was *not* blinded by deception, confusion, or ignorance. Let us suppose, then, that on the contrary, Eve has clearly present in her mind the absolute priority, the unquestionably greater goodness, of the right over and against the pleasant and the apparently beneficial. Let us suppose that at the moment of acting she not only knew what was right but, in addition, saw unmistakably that in case of conflict the right is *better* than, *preferable* to, the pleasant and the apparently beneficial. Let us suppose that she then proceeded to act contrary to what her conscious mind clearly conceived to be best, or preferable. But was Eve not then in a condition in which she was driven or gripped or tyrannized by something other than the piloting awareness of her conscious thought and what her conscious mind prefers, of what is choice-worthy or desirable to her own mind? Is this not an even graver sort of incapacity than the blindness that issues in choice of the worse based on the mind's deceived misapprehension of it as the better? Is this not the condition of an intelligent being in the grip of a kind of nightmare in which she is no longer guided by her mind or intelligence, no longer at all the conscious author of the actions of her body and the speeches of her tongue? Is she not to an even greater degree than in our former case a pitiable victim of a kind of terrible seizure or debility?

The Bible does not explicitly raise, or even invite, these sorts of questions, which we have been compelled by Spinoza's challenge to pursue. Augustine, having begun to explore, in the passages we have quoted, the precise character of the "seduction" St. Paul ascribes to Eve, abruptly breaks off his longest commentary on Genesis with these words: "But what more is to be said? The sin [of Adam and Eve] was the result of persuasion in accordance with the way in which such persons can be tempted: the account was written, however, as it ought to be, in order to be read by all, and as it ought to be, in order to be understood by few."[51] Scripture does not critically probe moral responsibility as it comes to sight in our primary experience. As a consequence, the Bible does not need to leave moral responsibility in the very ambiguous light in which Aristotle leaves it (*Ethics* 1114b1–15a3). The Bible remains firmly within the bounds of our commonsense conviction that we and others are capable of a perversely self-conscious embrace of evil, with full awareness of the significance of our acts, and that when we act on this perverse capacity we deserve to suffer not only the intrinsic ill consequences of our embracing what we see clearly to be bad but in addition a penalty that dramatically worsens our already depraved situation.

But this last formulation brings home to us a final troubling question. However we are to understand criminal responsibility, what are the intelligible grounds for the overwhelming conviction that the guilty deserve to *suffer* for what they have done; and what are the intelligible grounds for the concomitant *hope* that they—that even we ourselves—*will* suffer the punishment that they, and we, deserve? For guilt betokens sin or vice; and sin or vice are either genuinely and severely harmful, in the most important respect, to the very soul of the criminal; or else they betoken an alienation of the criminal from *the* source of meaning for him as a being destined to devotion. Why, then, is it appropriate, why is it sensible, that such a crippled or alienated being receive, in addition to and as a consequence of its corruption or alienation, further harm or suffering? Why is it so terribly important for us that to the suffering and mutilation of the spirit that is entailed in being unjust there be added extrinsic bad consequences for the perpetrator?[52]

The Scripture may allow us a glimpse of one important part, at least, of an answer to the second of these two questions—if we reflect on the more attractive side of the Scripture's teaching on retribution. For of course the biblical God tempers retribution with *mercy*. While God expelled Adam and Eve from Paradise, and thereby from the possibility of eating the fruit of the Tree of Life and living forever, He did so not only to punish them but also to prevent their engaging in further and perhaps worse evil.[53] He did not, in the event, carry out the lawful execution that had been laid down as the retributive penalty (Gen. 2:17: "*On the day* of your eating of it, you shall surely die"). Instead, He clothed the guilty pair and then allowed them to live, in tolerable conditions, for many centuries. Most important of all, God made Adam and Eve the never-to-be-forgotten parents of the entire human race, a race to whom He subsequently offers final, eternal redemption and salvation. Now, to be sure, we must never lose sight of the fact that divine mercy, which the Bible thus exemplifies from the outset, has as its necessary premise guilt, sin, and retributive justice. Divine mercy (in contrast to divine benevolence) is bestowed only on creatures who have justly deserved—and, what is more, who contritely acknowledge that they have justly deserved—the retributive punishment that is nevertheless alleviated as the expression of a love that transcends, and might seem to contradict, even or especially while presupposing, justice. By bringing the guilt and the just deserts of the first humans to the foreground of the self-reflective reader's attention, Genesis brings to the fore the guilt and the just deserts of selfish or self-loving humanity as such. The Scripture thus guides us toward putting the concern for retributive justice in the foreground of our own existence. Inasmuch as we do so, we may understand ourselves to be putting in the background our concern for our own well-being—most obviously because justice, as retributive justice, can be said to be in a decisive sense a threat for all of us as sinners or potential sinners. We thus find ourselves apparently transcending, however belatedly and incompletely, our self-love. In this way the embrace of holy retributive justice—the confession of our guilt and of our just deserts at the hands of an angry God, even as the premise of our beseeching forgiveness and mercy—may give us the sense of a reillumination within us of the fact that we were created in the image of the holy God.[54] Through this qualified renewal of our participation in the divine holiness of justice we may recover, in an appropriately chastened manner, our self-exaltation, our sense of divinely endowed worth. Reflections such as these may give us the clue to one important meaning of the biblical teaching to the effect that it is only when, and because, we fervently acknowledge that we do not justly deserve mercy—that we instead deserve punishment—that we can begin fervently to hope for God's eternal mercy.

CHAPTER SIX

Pollution and Purgation

THE STORY OF MANKIND THAT UNFOLDS AFTER THE EXPULSION FROM
Paradise helps diminish our wonder at the Fall by showing us how deep
and intransigent is the human creature's propensity to evil. This of course
prompts in us again the question why the Creator had to create so labile a
being in His image. What prompts new wonder, however, is the reluctance God shows to curtail human evil, to exercise His policing authority.
We know of course what the Scripture eventually teaches to be the
answer to human errancy: the rule of a specific code of positive divine law,
delivered and taught through prophecy to a chosen people, who are thus
constituted "a kingdom of priests and a holy nation" (Exod. 19:6). But
the peculiarities of this answer are so great as to make it far from easy to
comprehend. Why a chosen people? Why this positive law, for just this
one people? Scripture, it would appear, intends to help us to begin to
understand the necessity, and something of the purpose, of the Mosaic law
and the chosen people by taking us through a series of divine historical
"experiments,"[1] in which we are made the vicarious witnesses of a succession of forms of social existence that do not yet know the people chosen
to receive this law, to be formed spiritually by it, and thus to exemplify its
meaning to all the world.

The first divine experiment, lasting for a millennium and a half—or in
other words for almost half of the total historical time that the Hebrew
Bible treats—shows us what humanity for the most part decays into when
left almost entirely to its own devices. Yet it is not sufficient to characterize this first and longest biblical epoch in such depressing terms. The era
from the Fall to the Flood is not merely one of divine disengagement.
God's reluctance to promulgate commandments, to make covenants, to
designate prophets or judges or kings, bespeaks His original and never-to-
be forgotten preference for a much simpler, more direct and intimate, less
"political," form of governance. The moral grandeur of the covenants,
and the law, and the lawful community that the law makes possible, is not
to be permitted to obscure the fact that covenant and law represent God's
necessarily punitive remedy for man's rebellious, sinful rejection of His

original, less "institutional" intention.[2] That original intention, and the human possibility of abiding by it, is still visible in the line descended from Seth, as opposed to the line descended from Cain.

By devoting as much space to the uneventful genealogy of the blameless Seth and his long-lived offspring as it does to the dramatic misdeeds and amazing accomplishments of Cain and his offspring, Scripture does more than indicate the purity of the genealogical line descending from Adam to Noah; it also reveals something of the character of the stock from which Noah comes, and limns that stock in sharp contrast with that of Cain. A few points stand out.

It was only after the establishment of Seth's line (i.e., after the birth of Seth's eldest son Enosh) that men began, the Bible says (or began once again), to call upon God by His name, Yahweh (יהוה). This invocation would seem to signal the recovery of some sense of intimacy with God.[3] Yet the term "intimacy," unless qualified, is too strong. After the banishment of Cain, the only appearance God makes in this whole fifteen-hundred-year era is when He is repeatedly said to have walked with, and finally to have taken away, Enoch, the descendant of Seth—in pointed contrast to the Enoch who is the firstborn son of Cain, the Enoch who achieved fame by having the first city named after him (Gen. 4:17, 5:21 and 24; see also Sir. 44:16 and 49:14). Centuries later God walked once again with a single and singular man: Noah, Enoch's great-grandson.

At the beginning of the narration of Seth's line, the Scripture pauses to remind us that "man" (אדם, "adam") is the name God gave when He created "man" in His likeness, male and female, and "blessed them" (Gen. 5:1–2). Scripture then says that after Adam had lived one hundred thirty years he begot a son in *his* likeness and image and named him Seth. We are prompted to doubt whether Cain and his descendants were begotten "in Adam's image and likeness." Do they even fully deserve the name "man/Adam"?[4] It is certainly Cain's murder of Abel, and then the deeds of Cain and his descendants, that stand in the foreground of the narrative and thereby make intelligible the second awesome parable of punitive catastrophe, the Flood.

The Descent into Sinful Anarchy

The first event we hear of in the lives of the first humans born of woman is their offering sacrifices to God. There was no suggestion of such worship in Paradise, and there is no indication that Adam and Eve were moved even after their expulsion to bring oblations—or that God in any way requested, or indicated his expectation of, such homage. Indeed, Abel and Cain have reached maturity and have toiled for some years before they are animated to make the first sacrificial offerings. It would be pedestrian to suppose that these oblations manifest a mistaken conception that God is somehow in need of food or of any material goods that men may be able to offer Him. The sacrifices are more appropriately viewed as betokening the brothers' need to express to God their overcoming of what they recognize to be their proclivity to care too little for God, to think too much of themselves and their fellow humans, to regard their possessions as merely their own, to use their goods solely for their own or merely human benefit. The votive acts presuppose, in other words, the sinking in of the experience of alienation from God. The offerings represent an effort on the part of the brothers to begin to bridge the gulf, to mend the rift, by demonstrating unselfish devotion to God (cf. Joel 2:14).

As such, the offerings are not without considerable moral ambiguity.[5] To be sure, they are most obviously a manifestation of self-deprecating generosity, humility, and even shame. But may they not also betray a hope to establish a claim on God—at the very least, on His attention? Is this presumption not what God descries underlying Cain's act of worship, as opposed to what He sees expressed in the more truly humble immolation performed by the junior brother? Does this not explain what seems otherwise or at first sight to be God's capricious preference for Abel's shepherd's offering?[6] Is this not what is betrayed by Cain's immediate reaction, of angry, wounded pride? Is this not what is suggested by God's admonition in response?

This admonition has been the source of controversy. Spinoza plausibly remarks that God's words to Cain would seem to indicate in exemplary fashion that the behavior and attitude satisfying to God are by no means beyond the reach of man, and that thus the humility God demands and expects is far from being an "impossible" virtue.[7] Calvin, on the contrary (following Luther), struggles to explain away the plain import of the text (which of course poses a sharp challenge to the Reformers' teaching that humans are incapable of good works on their own and become capable only through an infusion of divine grace). Against those who interpret the text "as if God were promising Cain that the dominion of sin should not prevail in his heart, if he were willing to labor to subdue it," Calvin argues that "the words should rather be taken as referring to Able"—that is, as promising to the elder brother, Cain, his title of rule over his junior sibling. Still (Calvin continues), even if the words be taken as referring to dominion over sin, "there is no doubt that this is an exhortation which God makes to him, declaring not what we are able, but what it is our duty to do, even if beyond our ability."[8]

Surely this much is undeniable (as Calvin stresses): Cain proves in the event unable to master his sin. Despite God's direct intervention and exhortation, Cain gives himself as prey to heinous revenge and then compounds the jealous fratricide by his notorious, remorseless answer to God's demand that he account for his brother's whereabouts: "Am I my brother's keeper?"

In a well-known and crucial passage early in the *Second Treatise of Government* (para. 11, end), Locke ironically appeals to the story of Cain's crime as purported biblical support for the Lockean doctrine that there is "writ in the hearts of all mankind" a "great law of nature," to wit that "every man, in the state of nature, has a power to kill a murderer," or that "whoso sheddeth man's blood, by man shall his blood be shed." Locke could hardly have chosen a text that illustrates more vividly how far his doctrine of a "natural law," purportedly discernible in a "state of nature," in fact stands from the plain message of the Bible. For Scripture teaches that the law Locke quotes as if it were exemplified in the Cain story is in truth laid down only many centuries later, immediately after the Flood, as a *positive* commandment of divine legislation rather than as a *natural* rule intrinsic to the human condition, written in the human heart, or knowable to unassisted reason (Gen. 9:6).[9] We note here the absence from the Scripture of the concept of *nature* in the morally normative sense, just as at the outset we noted the absence of the concept of nature in the sense of a necessitated and fixed cosmos or character of a being. The biblical substitute for the "nature" of a being, or for what is "by nature right" for a being, would seem to be "way," "customary way," and the "right way" (דרך [see, e.g., Gen. 6:12], Septuagint ὁδός; ארח [see, e.g., Gen. 18:11]).[10]

By the same token, Scripture here teaches by the example of Cain how weak in the human heart or reason is the "conscience." Only after God has inflicted punishment on Cain does Cain betray any uneasiness; and then (*pace* Martin Luther) what he expresses is a complaint that the consequence of the punishment for his admitted crime is unbearable.[11] Perhaps most amazing is what is implied as the basis for this complaint.

Cain murmurs that as a result of the banishment, which removes him from God's presence and hence His immediate protection, anyone whom Cain meets in his wanderings may kill him. Observe that Cain does *not* speak of his own feared demise as if it were an execution, a punishment; that is, he does not express trepidation that someone will kill him *because* he is guilty of the murder of Abel. His mortal anxiety seems to arise rather from his surmise that his own commission of unprovoked murder is a manifestation of the bloodthirstiness he assumes is to be found in his fellow humans, constituted like himself and prevented from acting on their vicious impulses only by the fear of God's protective providence (which Cain fears the banishment will remove from him). God, for His part, is so far from disputing Cain's gloomy assessment of the prevalent human inclination to murder strangers that He responds by putting a special protective mark on Cain and by proclaiming the deterrent threat of a very violent punishment—seven times worse than death—to be imposed on anyone who should murder Cain.

The ease with which Cain ignored God's direct warning against harming Abel and the extraordinary severity of the punishment God feels called upon to promulgate in order to protect Cain suggest that in the beginning men were not inclined to be very fearful of God, or to take His threats of punishment altogether seriously.[12] Did they not, with good reason, look upon Him as a loving and even somewhat indulgent Father, to Whom they could directly appeal for forgiveness or mitigation of punishment? Certainly the actual retributive punishment of Cain is rather mild and, we cannot help but observe, left unenforced. For although Cain was sternly condemned to wander as a "tottering vagabond" (נע ונד), in fact he brazenly "went from the face of the Lord and *settled* in the land of Nod" (i.e., "the land of the vagabond" [בארץ־נוד]; cf. Gen. 4:12 and 14 with 16). Still worse, after thus settling down, in direct contravention of the divine punitive admonition, Cain was so bold as to found the first city, or *polis* (as the Septuagint has it), and to glorify his son by naming this inaugural *polis* after him.

The urban or "political" life introduced on earth by Cain and his descendants spawns the lusty and bloodthirsty Lamech, "the first transgressor of the Law of Monogamy that was laid down in the Terrestrial Paradise" (Bayle, *Historical and Critical Dictionary,* s.v. "Lamech"). This same Lamech is also the Bible's original singer or poet. Poetry or song does not make its first scriptural appearance, after the Fall, under very favorable auspices.[13] The first song invented after the Fall is the proud ode Lamech addresses to his wives boasting of his past and future killings, killings that he conceives of as imitating—nay, surpassing—the divine punitive justice that protected his forefather Cain (Gen. 4:23–24). Scripture would appear to teach that the triumphant delight in bloody vengeance emerges in close association with a proudly hopeful belief that as a consequence or implication of successful revenge, one possesses a godlike self-protective power; and this belief gives birth to musical exultation before one's women.[14] Lamech's sons, born from the wives to whom he sings, are the beginners or inventors of the musical and metalworking arts.

The implicit animadversions on the profound linkage among life in the city or *polis,* murderous moral indignation, eros, musical inspiration, and what is nowadays called artistic "creativity" are intensified by the implicit contrast with the irenic, apolitical, unmusical or prosaic, and uninventive line of Seth.[15] It was evidently the sons of Cain (cf. Wisd. of Sol. 10:4), with their ambition, civic society, artful creativity, and excitedly perverted emulation of divine retributive justice, who over the centuries led mankind down the path to a state of sin so insidiously universal that even the other animal species were contaminated; the earth became a veritable cesspool of wickedness. In the end, the moral plague infected also the descendants of Seth, with the one great exception of Noah and his immediate family (Noah's own father, we note, had apparently been named after the bloodthirsty Lamech). God saw that "every devising of the thought in the heart of man was only evil every day"; that "the earth was filled with violent outrage"; that "the earth was corrupted because the way of all flesh was corrupted on earth" (Gen. 6:5, 11–12; see also 6:17). Is it not understandable that God, apparently in regret and sadness at His Creation, resolved to purge the earth of the animate life on it?[16] "But Noah found favor with the Lord." One man, alone in his righteousness, suffices to move a saddened and regretful God to preserve the seeds of all animate life on earth, even when all that life has become corrupt.

Before we turn to the regeneration effected through Noah, we must pause to puzzle (with Rashi) over the implications of God's "regret" at His original Creation.[17] For precisely when we find this divine regret "understandable," do we not in effect sympathize with God in his *plight,* as beleaguered just ruler—and are we not in this moment slipping into an anthropomorphization that is scandalously demeaning to God, and thereby dangerous to us? Can God's "regret" possibly betoken the same sadness and change of mind, or rueful wish that things had been done otherwise, that humans experience? This is a question prompted also by key subsequent scriptural texts: God is repeatedly said to "change His mind," to "regret," or to "repent" (נחם)—to alter His intended deeds and His plans, in response to human actions.

It is true that Scripture does twice emphatically declare, through the prophets, that "God is not human, that He would deceive, and He is not the son of man, that He would repent" (נחם). But the utter rejection of the idea of a divine change of mind may, in the first of these declarations (Num. 23:19), be taken as referring to God's unflagging fulfillment of His promises; and given that His supreme intelligible attribute is His justice—tempered, to be sure, by loving kindness or mercy—God might well be understood never to deviate from His promises, without necessarily being understood never to regret or to change His mind at all.[18] In the second case (1 Sam. 15:29), the asseveration is made in reference to God's un-wavering adherence to the word He has declared to His prophet Samuel. That word, however, is to the effect that God has "regretted" a most important action: His appointment of Saul as king (1 Sam. 15:11 and 35). What is more, the prophets Isaiah, Jeremiah, Joel, Amos, and Jonah re-peatedly teach that God is capable of "repenting" His declared plans to punish, in the face of actions on the part of the guilty signaling deep contrition.[19] In the introduction to his *Commentary on the Mishna,* Mai-monides teaches that as regards prophecies, when a true prophet predicts disasters for a people as punishment for their sins, God in His mercy may relent (Maimonides invokes esp. 1 Kings 21:29), but "when He promises a nation good tidings through a prophet, it is impossible to say that he will not keep His word . . . otherwise, there would be no way at all left to establish the authenticity of anyone's prophetic counsel" (*Maimonides' Introduction to the Talmud,* 56–57). Yet through Jeremiah, God proclaims that "if at any time I declare concerning a nation or a kingdom that I will build and plant it, and if it does evil in my sight, not listening to my voice, then I will repent of the good which I had intended to do to it" (Jer. 18:9–10).

If we take literally these scriptural texts ascribing repentance or regret and change of mind to God, can we still speak intelligibly of divine omnipotence? This question would seem to underlie the traditional or-thodox reading, expressed in Hugo Grotius's insistence that "in reality God does not change His decrees. Nevertheless He is said to change them and to be influenced by repentance (*Council of Toledo* 8.2, cited by Gratian *Decretum* 2.22.4.90) as often as He acts otherwise than His words seemed to mean; and this may happen on account of a condition tacitly understood (see Seneca *Natural Questions* 2.37), which has ceased to exist: Jer. 18:8. It is possible to find examples in Gen. 20:3, Exod. 32:14, 1 Kings. 21:29, Isa. 38:1, Jon. 3:5 and 10" (*On the Law of War and Peace,* 2.13.3.4). Grotius here follows Calvin, who argues (*Institutes,* 1.17.12) that "if no man knowingly or willingly reduces himself to the necessity of repentance, we cannot attribute repentance to God without saying either that he knows not what is to happen, or that he cannot evade it, or that he rushes his deliberation precipitately and inconsiderately." The reasoning is cogent, but is the premise certain? Can we, ought we, be sure that God's behavior in respect to regret or repentance must be intelligible in terms that we know to be true of humans? Why does Calvin *here,* in this instance, insist that what we know of human consciousness and its exhaustive possibilities must be the standard—a standard by which we dare to interpret away the plain meaning on the surface of numerous authoritative scriptural texts? Calvin goes on to stress (ibid., 1.17.13) that "because our weakness cannot reach His height, any description which we receive of Him must be brought down to our capacity in order to be intelligible." But how then do we decide which of two contradictory predications of God is the "lowered" and which is the truer to His "height"? In particular, what entitles us to be sure, in the face of numerous scriptural texts to the contrary, that God "is incapable of every feeling of perturbation"? Is the answer not that the alternative would require drawing into radical question the intelligibility of the Bible's teaching of divine wisdom and omnipotence, the omnipotence that is the ground of our awe before His inescapable judgment (and of our hopes from His limitless grace)?

So when, in this light, we understand God as having foreseen from the outset the necessity of the purifying deluge, we do not for a moment suppose that He Himself learned, or needed to learn, anything from the experience. Still, the very existence of the Scripture testifies to His concern to employ the experience as a vehicle for the teaching of mankind. In Genesis, God shows us how He begins each epoch of His rule with fatherly gentleness and loving kindness, and with the demand, if not the expectation, that His children will respond with congruent and obedient love. Their ungrateful defiance deserves condign retribution. That retribution is nonetheless long delayed, episodic, and often—not to say always—softened by undeserved mercy. God is thereby, indeed, temporarily tolerant of burgeoning criminality. But humanity finally reaps just deserts that are accordingly all the more harsh. This harshness is only apparently in contradiction to the tender love with which each stage of biblical history begins; in fact, the severity is implicit in the tenderness from the beginning. The principles of governance taught by the biblical God's example and precept are certainly the exact contrary of those principles of governance that Machiavelli claimed to have discovered to be intelligibly necessary and "humane."[20]

The Cleansing and the New Dispensation

In commencing the story of Noah,[21] the Bible for the first time mentions *justice* explicitly (Gen. 6:9). Like Enoch his forefather, Noah walked with God; but what *distinguished* Noah, what set him apart, was his being just (צדיק). The virtue of justice comes to the fore as an explicit theme in the context of a world pervaded by injustice. Among humans, at any rate, justice as a virtue presupposes injustice, or the struggle against injustice and against the temptation to injustice. The emergence of justice into the foreground of the narrative is at once a symptom of decline and a manifestation of the paradox that decline is the precondition for singular ascent.

Noah's justice is truly remarkable because of the extreme decadence of the era in which he lives or against which he is defined. Noah is "wholly"[22] just—"in his epoch," "for his generation." He is so far from being simply or unqualifiedly just that his behavior—even or precisely his act of worship after the cataclysm—provokes God to repeat, to His heart, the judgment that "the devising of the heart of man is evil from his youth."[23]

But Noah's virtue is sufficient to make him eligible not only to be saved but to be the first human hearer and sharer of God's plans (Gen. 6:13; cf. 7:1). Noah, and mankind through Noah, has now learned how desperate is the earth's need for divine rule. The time has come for a shattering intervention of omnipotence. Yet the all-powerful ruler of the universe does not simply exercise His power. He first speaks to Noah (Gen. 6:12–13). He first makes man a responsible partner in His rule. To be sure, man is, and will always remain, very much the junior partner in God's rule. And only gradually, over generations, does man grow into the capacity to assume even that junior partnership of which he is capable. In particular, the partnership represented by Noah is only the first stage. God does not tell Noah all that the narrator tells us is in God's mind. God does not speak to Noah of His sadness and regret, and He does not reveal to Noah the very severe judgment on the human character that the Scripture repeats to us before and after the Flood; indeed, God does not, in speaking to Noah, even go so far as to lay the blame for the earth's corruption on man (contrast Gen. 6:13 and 17 with 6:5–7 and 8:21). God simply informs Noah of the coming catastrophe and commands him to make an ark; He then explains the function of the ark in light of the fact that the catastrophe will take the form of a flood; in passing, He mentions the "covenant" that is to be "established" with Noah (Gen. 6:13–21). Having heard this staggering set of revelations, Noah says not a word in response and asks not a single question, not even about the wholly unexplained "covenant" or about what its terms might be: "And Noah did all that God commanded him, thus he did."[24] Noah does not think of presuming to remind God that the world ought to be saved if even a few other just men are to be found in it (see the contrast drawn with Abraham in the *Zohar* Bereshith 1.106a). Noah's justice expresses itself as unquestioning obedience. Noah thus seems to recapitulate, *mutatis mutandi,* the original childlike innocence of man.

In the repetition of the command concerning the animals to be taken onto the ark, God draws a distinction between the clean (טהרה) and the unclean. This is the first we hear of such a dichotomy in the Bible, yet Noah neither seeks nor (apparently) requires any explanation of, or any guidance in making, this crucial separation among the species. So far from being mysterious, arbitrary, or in need of special revelation, the distinction is treated as self-evident. Creation has perceptible within it, the Scripture suggests, a ranking or hierarchy that was much more obvious, at least to a "just" man like Noah, in the epochs closer to the simple beginnings, unclouded by sophistication (especially, we may add, philosophy or science). Yet when the categories of clean and unclean are later elaborated in the Mosaic dietary law (Lev. 11), principles guiding this distinction do not seem indicated in any way, and the distinction thus appears quite arbitrary. Are "clean" and "unclean," then, simple perceptible attributes of the animals, like their odors or cries—immediately and directly evident, without the need of cogitative interpretation, to a healthy or unimpaired sensibility (which has been almost entirely lost by the time of Moses)? But there may still be intelligible principles underlying the distinction between clean and unclean (even as sound waves underlie audible cries)—

principles that are also, however, no longer (or not yet) accessible to later pious people, at least at the time of the Mosaic revelation. Are we to understand that we must await a further, perhaps gradual, purgation and revelation in order to fully experience and to understand the principle of this crucial comprehensive distinction pervading animate creation? Or is the mystery of the principles underlying the distinctions in Leviticus an implicit invitation to deduction of those principles by the most astute among the pious?[25]

This prompts the further question, What is the source in Creation of the "unclean?" It is difficult to understand how certain species could have come "unclean" from God's omnipotent hands, especially since He pronounced all his Creation "very good." The "unclean" species would therefore appear to have become so in the course of the moral pollution of all animate life that preceded and made necessary the Flood. God resolved to "destroy all flesh upon the earth in which is the breath of life" because "the way of all flesh had become corrupted" (Gen. 6:17 and 12). The one sort of corruption specified is "violence" (חמס): "God said to Noah, 'I have decided to make an end of all flesh because the earth is filled with violence through them'" (Gen. 6:13). This would support Kass's suggestion ("Why the Dietary Laws?" 46–47) that underlying the distinction between clean and unclean species is divine disgust primarily at the carnivorous, as well as at those species that appear to have distorted or "done violence to" their forms or means of locomotion. At the core of the apparently arbitrary distinction between clean and unclean would, then, be a moral distinction between those species that have adhered to and those that have failed to adhere to the nonviolent "way" God intended. And once again we would see how alien is the biblical perspective to any "biology" that attempts to articulate the "natures," the "forms," of the beings as fixed or as not dependent on moral choices for which all the beings or species are to be held in some measure responsible.[26]

The fact that the fundamental distinction between clean and unclean species persists through and after the Flood would, then, be a clear signal that a perfect cleansing of life on earth is not contemplated. Still, for a brief moment the Scripture allows us to hope that the purge of the earth will allow a truly fresh start for mankind—a new beginning free, though not forgetful, of the stain of sin and the burden of punishment. But no sooner has Noah set foot again on dry land than he seizes the initiative, and we are compelled to come to terms with the crooked wood that man is. Noah offers a holocaust, the first burnt offering recorded in the Bible (for there is no indication that Abel thought to barbecue the animal he immolated). Noah's sacrificial offering cannot help but recall the sacrifices offered up by Cain and Abel, and Noah's act, like theirs, partakes of deep ambiguity. Doubtless, it is fitting and proper that Noah should feel and should express his deep gratitude for having been saved from the inundation. And he is meticulous in devoting only clean animals to God. But why slaughter so many of the very few clean animals that have been saved with him, and whose number, seven pairs, was explicitly designated by God? Might one not have hoped that Noah would gain a new appreciation of the sanctity of animal life, a new sense of kinship with the animals, especially the clean, through his many months of living together with them on the ark? That God sees a deep kinship between man and the other creatures is underlined by the indications in this context that He holds the animals morally responsible, and not only prior to the Flood; the subsequent decree of capital punishment for murder of a human being is promulgated to or for the other animals as well as to mankind.[27] Just as in the case of the offerings of Cain and Abel, so here there is no suggestion that God required the sacrifice that is performed; and indeed, given the fact that it entails the obliteration of one-seventh of all the surviving clean animals on earth, God's ambiguous reception of this dubious honorarium is not surprising.[28] God says to Himself, in effect, that He will resign Himself to the evil that manifestly pervades the human heart[29]—at least to the extent that He will never again destroy life on earth as He has just done. And as if in response to the daring if tacit request implied by Noah in the act of sacrifice that produced "the pleasing odor" of cooked meat, God not only restates the original blessing on the human race together with the commandment to multiply but for the first time makes permissible the eating of flesh while subordinating all animals to the fearsome domination of man.[30] Still, the permission to eat meat is kept within bounds by the first dietary law: "But thou shalt not eat flesh containing its life-blood" (Gen. 9:4). This lays the cornerstone for the much more elaborate dietary laws enunciated in Lev. 17:10–16 (note the emphatic extension of this dietary law to "strangers") and in Deut. 12:15–18. This foundational dietary law would appear to be intended to remind mankind forever of the limited indulgence God shows in allowing humans, after many centuries, the questionable—because necessarily violent or life-destructive—luxury of meat eating.[31]

Here again we find a vivid illustration of the gulf in outlook between the pristine Bible and the Lockean "reinterpretation." Our philosopher-physician makes the killing and consumption of flesh *the* paradigm of the natural right to property. After having previously noted with emphasis that the Scripture gave no such right to eat flesh, and hence no right of property, to Adam or to humans prior to Noah,[32] and after having remarked that the grant to Noah implies that "Mans propriety in the Creatures is nothing but that *Liberty to use them,* which God has permitted," Locke subsequently has the daring directly to contradict himself and to assert that

> God having made Man, and planted in him, as in all other Animals, a strong desire of Self-preservation, . . . spoke to him, (that is) directed him by his Senses and Reason, . . . to the use of those things, which were serviceable for his Subsistence, and given him as means of his *Preservation.* And therefore I doubt not, but before these words were pronounced, 1 *Gen.* 28, 29 (if they must be understood Literally to have been spoken) and without any such Verbal *Donation,* Man had a right to a use of the Creatures, by the Will and Grant of God. . . . This being the Reason and Foundation of *Adams Property* gave the same Title, on the same Ground, to all his Children . . . an equal Right to the use of the inferior Creatures, for the comfortable preservation of their Beings, which is all the *Property* Man hath in them. . . .
>
> Whether we consider natural *Reason,* which tells us, that Men, being once born, have a right to their Preservation, and consequently to Meat . . . : Or *Revelation,* which gives us an account of those Grants God made . . . 'tis very clear, that . . . God, who hath given the World to Men in common, hath also given them reason to make use of it to the best advantage of Life, and convenience. . . . The Fruit, or Venison, which nourishes the wild *Indian,* who knows no Inclosure, and is still a Tenant in common, must be his.[33]

The Bible, in fact, is as silent on any right to "comfortable preservation" as it is on all other Lockean human and property rights. The biblical God does not acknowledge a human "right" to meat eating but instead concedes this indulgence to his wayward and human, all-too-human creatures.

But Locke the founder of scientific anthropology goes farther in his defiance of the Bible. In his subsequent analysis of the natural foundation of the human family, he argues that only the assumption that the God of nature made the human a carnivorous beast of prey from the beginning provides a reasonable foundation for the claim that humans are by nature directed to a (more) lasting conjunction of male and female partners in procreation:

> For the end of *conjunction between Male and Female,* being not barely Procreation, but the continuation of the Species, this conjunction betwixt Male and Female ought to last, even after Procreation, so long as is necessary to the nourishment and support of the young Ones, who are to be sustained by those that got them, till they are able to shift and provide for themselves. This Rule, which the infinite wise Maker hath set to the Works of his hands, we find the inferiour Creatures steadily obey. In those viviparous Animals which feed on Grass, the *conjunction between Male and Female* lasts no longer than the very Act of Copulation: because the Teat of the Dam being sufficient to nourish the Young, till it be able to feed on the Grass, the Male only begets, but concerns not himself for the Female or Young, to Whose Sustenance he can contribute nothing. But in Beasts of Prey the *conjunction* lasts longer: because the Dam not being able well to subsist her self, and nourish her numerous Off-spring by her own Prey alone, a more laborious, as well as a more dangerous way of living, than by feeding on Grass, the Assistance of the Male is necessary to the Maintenance of their common Family, which cannot subsist till they are able to prey for themselves, but by the joynt Care of Male and Female. . . . And herein I think lies the chief, if not the only reason, *why the Male and Female in Mankind are tyed to a longer conjunction* than other Creatures. . . . Wherein one cannot but admire the Wisdom of the great Creatour. [*Two Treatises of Government,* 2.79–80]

Nothing illustrates so vividly the gulf that separates "nature's God" and "the laws of nature's God" from the biblical Creator and His law.

The biblical God's reluctant tolerance of slaughter is further qualified, and the dubiousness of meat eating still more highlighted, by the accompanying proclamation of capital punishment for the taking of human life. The permission to butcher and consume animate life requires as its complement a severely sanctioned restatement of the sacredness of human life. The biblical God does not take it for granted that humans will "naturally" refrain from cannibalism.[34] Retributive capital punishment is the lawful expression, in the context of granting permission to mankind to kill animals for food, of the fact that man alone of the beings was made in the image of God; capital punishment is the primary (though of course not the full) lawful expression of the special dignity of man as creature.

The affirmation of unique human dignity here is not, however, as complete as one first is likely to assume. For since "all" other animals, as well as humans, are here subjected to capital punishment for murdering a human, we are not justified, it seems, in attributing to the text the thought that a human who commits murder is distinguished from an irresponsible animal by being singularly graced with the capacity of being held fully accountable for his actions, and thus of receiving his just deserts—a punishment that fits the crime, a suffering that counterbalances and thus negates the willfully chosen enjoyment of domination, freedom, exploitation, and cruelty. What we can discern more unambiguously is God's honoring humankind, above the rest of the animals, with the new responsibility for faithfully and accurately executing the primary divine penal law. Foremost, moreover, is the consideration that unmutilated and innocent human life is so precious and of such dignity that the damage done and the suffering undergone in the deliberate destruction of such a life calls for compensatory suffering on the part of the perpetrator that is of the severity of a capital retributive penalty.

Yet let us not fail to note that the reason given by Scripture for the preciousness or dignity of human life is not the evident intrinsic value of that life or being in and of itself. Human life has dignity on account of the revealed truth that this being was created in the image of God (cf. Nietzsche, *Beyond Good and Evil,* aph. #60). In addition, even when this unique creaturely status of human life is clearly recognized, it does not yet *necessarily* follow, it would seem, that murder deserves capital punishment. We recall that there was no indication that in God's or the Scripture's eyes Cain deserved such punishment for the murder of Abel (Cain's sentence was rather a sort of exile); and during the many centuries prior to the Flood there was apparently no divine law of capital punishment. The Bible suggests that the specification of capital punishment as condign is due to the will of God and not simply to the "nature" of the crime. Is God's will here somewhat mysteriously arbitrary, in this specification, or is the divine will guided by additional decisive considerations, beyond retribution? We might surmise, though the Bible does not make clear, that the divine specification of capital punishment for murder at this point in history is motivated by deterrent and educative, as well as by the primarily retributive, aims. In Locke's philosophic understanding and rewriting of the Scripture, by contrast, "retribution" under natural law (or "reason, which is that law") is *wholly* limited to, or indeed defined by, deterrence and education (together with reparation)—aimed exclusively at humans. Accordingly, under "this very strange doctrine" (as Locke pointedly confesses it to be), the criminal is viewed not so much as evilly responsible and hence "deserving" to suffer but instead as having lost humanity, as having degenerated into a "savage beast," or indeed "a noxious thing," the embodiment of a human proclivity to a degenerate rabidity that must be quarantined and eliminated insofar as possible:

> And thus in the State of Nature, *one Man comes by a Power over another;* but yet no Absolute or Arbitrary Power, to use a Criminal, when he has got him in his hands, according to the passionate heats, or boundless extravagancy of his own Will; but only to retribute to him, so far as calm reason and conscience dictate, what is proportionate to his transgression; which is so much as may serve for *Reparation* and *Restraint.* For these two are the only reasons, why one Man may lawfully do harm to another, which is that we call *punishment.* In transgressing the Law of Nature, the Offender declares himself to live by another Rule than that of *reason* and common Equity, which is that measure God has set to the actions of Men, for their mutual security: and so he becomes dangerous to Mankind. . . . [E]very man upon this score, by the Right he hath to preserve Mankind in general, may restrain, or where it is necessary, destroy things noxious to them, and so may bring such evil on any one, who hath transgressed that Law, as may make him repent the doing of it, and thereby deter him, and by his Example others, from doing the like mischief. . . . I doubt not but this will seem a very strange Doctrine to some men. . . . A Murderer, . . . having renounced Reason, the common Rule and Measure, God hath given to Mankind, hath by the unjust Violence and Slaughter he hath committed upon one, declared War against all Mankind; and therefore may be destroyed as a *Lyon* or a *Tyger,* one of those wild Savage Beasts, with whom Men can have no Society nor Security: And upon this is grounded the great Law of Nature, *"Who so sheddeth Mans blood, by Man shall his Blood be shed."*[35]

The "Covenant"

The solemn promise (ברית, traditionally translated "covenant") God now announces is in this case by no means a contract or compact in which each of two or more parties voluntarily transfers his right to something in return for a congruent transfer by the other party or parties. The commitment is all on the part of God, Who makes a solemn promise without asking anything in return.[36] The "covenant" consists solely in God's promising never again to cut off all flesh by the waters of a flood, never again to allow a flood to destroy the earth. God conspicuously does not reveal to Noah the large qualification that the narrator indicates God addressed to His own heart: "for all the days of the earth."[37] Furthermore, as we have noted, the "covenant" is made with the brutes as well as with man. No speech, no acquiescence or agreement on the part of the creature, is required for the first biblical "covenant"; and, by the same token, no choice, no thought of refusal, is allowed or contemplated.[38] Accordingly, when Hobbes, the greatest originator of the modern voluntarist and consensual conception of the "social compact" as the basis of all government legitimacy, tries to propagandize the notion that the modern theory of the social compact is rooted in the biblical conception of covenant, he is compelled to avoid any mention of Noah, or of what the Bible here presents as the basic and original "covenant" (*On the Citizen,* 16.1–3; *Leviathan,* chap. 40). Hobbes's early opponent and critic, Sir Robert Filmer, cogently expostulated, "Men are persuaded that in the making of a covenant, something is to be performed on both parts by mutual stipulation, which is not always true. For we find God made a covenant with Noah and his seed, with all the fowl and the cattle, not to destroy the earth any more by a flood. This covenant was to be kept on God's part. Neither Noah, nor the fowl, nor the cattle, were to perform anything by this covenant."[39]

The Discouraging Aftermath

The Scripture confines itself to narrating a single telling vignette in the life of Noah and his sons after the momentous "covenant." Noah's drunkenness, together with his youngest son's subsequent impudicity, confirms the severe judgment God passed on Noah, and mankind in general, after as well as before the Flood—though the pious response of the elder brothers to Ham's shameless disclosure reaffirms the human capacity for right action to repair wrong. In the foreground, however, stands this deplorable sight: even Noah, even the man "fully just in that epoch," even the man who has witnessed firsthand God's terrible punishment and salvational mercy—even or especially this man—is capable of a disgusting loss of dignity, self-control, and modesty.

In a sense Noah's lapse, of course, recalls the original Fall. But the terribly burdensome consequences of that Fall, and perhaps the added terrifying experience of divine punishment through the Flood, would seem to make Noah's misdemeanor more understandable. One is tempted to conclude that, as was perhaps divined or predicted by Noah's father when he assigned his son the name Noah ("the man of the earth"; Gen. 5:29), Noah sought from the fermented fruit of the earth nepenthean relief from the toil upon the earth that was the punishment God had decreed to Adam for all mankind (Kass, "Seeing the Nakedness of His Father," 42–43).

If this was Noah's motive, the motive is rendered very questionable by the event. The Bible does not seem to hold the enjoyment of wine per se in contempt. In the words of Benno Jacob, "To possess a vineyard, to enjoy its noble fruit and to rest in the peace of its shade, was for the Israelite bliss and an ardent desire for the Messiah (for instance 1 Kgs. 5:5; 2 Kgs. 18:31; Hos. 2:17). The vine is the sign of peace and prosperity (Zech. 8:12)."[40] Still, the dark outcome of the first experience of this enjoyment paints indelibly the dangers that attend inebriating indulgence (see Nachmanides ad Gen. 9:26). The state of besotted nudity to which the intoxicant reduced Noah is a grotesque parody of the state of innocent nudity once enjoyed by mankind before it ate of the Tree of Knowledge of good and evil. The loss of shame regarding the body and especially the genitals is, from the scriptural point of view, so far from being a recovery of innocence that it is a descent into quasi bestiality; and this likely consequence of excessive drinking should be a warning against it: "Woe to him who makes his neighbors drink, you who put your venom thereto and make him drunken also, so that you may look on their nakedness" (Hab. 2:15).[41]

By disclosing to his brothers his father's disgraceful nakedness, Noah's son Ham—"the father of Canaan," as the Bible proleptically and mordantly remarks here—outdoes his father in shamelessness. Ham's is the prurience of a son who is sober, with full conscious responsibility for his lewdness—limned by the contrast with the pious modesty exhibited by his two sound brothers.[42] Each of the pair of sins here—the father's drift into drunken oblivion and the son's profanation of paternal privacy—recalls and might well appear to reenact in some measure the original sins of Adam and of Eve. But as such, the twin postdiluvian sins remind us of the profound ambiguity and hence question enshrouding the character of the original sin(s). Was the original sin a kind of irresponsible drift into oblivion, like Noah's drunkenness—as appeared the case, superficially at least, especially with Adam, in his careless acceptance of his wife's proffered gift of the fruit? Or was the original sin a deliberate and arrogant violation of a clearly understood taboo, like Ham's disclosure of his father's nakedness—as seemed more likely, superficially at least, in the case of Eve? Does the Bible intend to prod us to puzzle over this deep ambiguity concerning the nature of sin?

Equally thought provoking is a retrospective consideration of the Fall in light of the virtuous behavior of the older brothers. May not their response be taken as a kind of model of the sort of behavior God was testing to find in Adam as well as Eve? Having heard their younger brother's shameless announcement of their father's naked exposure, the elder brothers carefully contrive to cover him in such a way as deliberately to prevent their own seeing of his nudity. Is this not a suggestive manifestation of what Milton (*Paradise Lost*, 4.775) calls "knowing to know no more"? As Kass puts it ("Seeing the Nakedness of His Father," 45), "Their piety *is* a kind of (willing) blindness. They knowingly choose to live leaving some things in the dark."

Finally, we cannot avoid thinking of the punishment God the Father imposed on the future offspring of Adam and Eve when we hear the curse the furious Noah places on the head of Ham's descendants—on Canaan and thus especially the "Canaanites." Do we have here a clue to part of the motivation and meaning underlying God the Father's harsh punishments of us as descendants of our original parents?[43] But God did not, in fact, curse Adam and Eve (unlike the serpent and the ground); and does Scripture show providence ratifying so exorbitant a curse laid on the heads of unborn and thus still apparently innocent descendants? At least in the short run, the threat fails to materialize. Ham's sons do not become, in the immediately succeeding generations, the lowest slaves of the descendants of Shem and Japheth. Quite to the contrary, the Israelites, the descendants of Shem, become the lowest slaves of the Egyptians, the descendants of

Ham.[44] Yet eventually, of course, the Canaanites—as well as the Egyptians, the Amorites, and the Philistines (all numbered here among the descendants of Ham)—prove evilly degenerate[45] in their ways of life and become the unjust (and worst) enemies of the chosen people. As a consequence of this extreme sinfulness, Ham's offspring become the *justly deserving* victims of penal servitude imposed by God, on behalf of as well as through His chosen people descended from Shem. Thus Noah's curse transpires to be less a source than a foreshadowing of penal servitude, of generations yet unborn and only subsequently guilty. Or could it be that God formed the seed of Ham to be wicked from the very womb, and thus subject to just punishment and servitude, as a way of bringing about the vindication of the paternal curse? The possibility of predestination continues to haunt the narrative.[46]

The Tower of Babel

The line of Ham exhibits characteristics that recall the antediluvian line of Cain, just as the line of Shem, from which Abraham eventually springs, recalls in its apolitical simplicity and relative longevity the antediluvian line of Seth. Shem's descendants seem to be rural or even hill people (Gen. 10:30); Ham's are city builders and city dwellers. The contrast suggests to Milton the further reasonable surmise that the line of Shem, the Abramic line, should be understood as dwelling "Long time in peace by Families and Tribes / Under paternal rule" (*Paradise Lost*, 12.23–24). In other words, tribal patriarchy remains superior to political life—which, now associated with Ham's line, is to become even more closely linked to erotic deviance (among the cities, or *poleis*, associated with the descendants of Ham's son Canaan are, notably, Sodom and Gomorrah; Gen. 10:19). It would appear that even as almost the entire line of Seth eventually became corrupted by the line of Cain, so once again the pure line of Shem became eventually contaminated by the perverse lusts of the more active line of Ham; for since all mankind was punished for the building of the tower of Babel, must we not assume that all mankind participated—or at any rate consented—in its construction?

Most prominent of Ham's immediate descendants is his grandson through Cush: Nimrod, "a mighty hunter in the face of God" (i.e., in defiance of God, "as in despite of Heav'n, / Or from Heav'n claiming second Sovrantry"; Milton, *Paradise Lost,* 12.34). Nimrod's empire began with Babylon (or Babel) and other proud cities in the land of Shinar. This monstrous Babel came to be animated by a vaunting, collective ambition to build a structure that would tower up to the heavens, thereby embodying and ensuring the permanent unity of the human race, in the proud glory of its self-sufficient technical craft and godlike power and glory: "Let us make for ourselves a name." (As Kass points out, the verb here "to make" [עשה] has previously been used only by God or as applied to God and to His commanding Noah to build the ark; "What's Wrong with Babel?" 50.) It is striking that the Scripture avoids any reference to a connection of the tower-building with idolatry or what we now know to have been Babylonian religious worship (contrast ibid., 48–49). The febrile effort is presented as one of unqualified ambition, not as worship of, or even as a sign of human feelings of kinship with, the divinities or the stars. Abravanel's commentary on the story of the tower of Babel, linking that story back to the sin of Adam and then to the sinfulness of Cain and his descendants, aptly underlines the Bible's continuing deep if implicit opposition to anything like the classical political philosophers' attempts to honor and to elevate politics and civic life:

> The sins of the generation of the Tower of Babel were like the sin of Adam and Cain and his sons since, having a multiplicity of the natural things necessary for their existence, by God from heaven, freed of art and all labor, and prepared to busy themselves with the perfection of their souls, their thoughts were not set at rest by the great natural gift that their Creator had prepared for them. Rather they sought and put all their thoughts to finding the arts by which a town might be built, one comprehending all the arts and having a tower in its midst, in order to come together there and to make themselves political instead of being rustics. For they thought that the end particular to them was the political association, so that joining and company might arise among them; and that this was the highest of the human ends, together with the things that would follow from it: namely, fame, office, rulership, imaginary honors, the delight of gathering possessions, and the violence and robbery and bloodshed that follow—none of which was to be found while they were in the fields, each one by himself. [*Commentary on the Pentateuch,* trans. Sacks, in *Medieval Political Philosophy,* 257]

One may go so far as to say that "Babel is not just any city, but is *the* city, the paradigmatic or universal city, representing a certain universal human aspiration" (Kass, "What's Wrong with Babel?" 46)—so long as one adds the all-important qualification that in the Bible's view this aspiration is sinful, unnecessary, and to some extent eventually overcome, or sublimated, by the building and rebuilding and purification of Jerusalem, the "city of David," the "holy city": "Ours is a mighty city" (see esp. Isa. 26:1; 37:35; 52:1–2, 9; 60–62; 65:17ff.).

God's reaction to the building of the tower of Babel recalls His expulsion of Adam and Eve from Paradise. Just as He acted to prevent humanity's eating of the Tree of Life and thus becoming deathlessly superhuman, so now He acts to prevent humanity—as Kass notes (ibid., 51), "the children of Adam" is the Scripture's suggestive usage here—from pursuing its potentially successful, vaunting, technological and universalist ambitions (cf. Gen. 3:22 with 11:5 and Plato *Symposium* 190b–d). This means that according to the Bible (as Kass points out at ibid., 52, but retracts at 54–55), the successful construction of the tower was so far from being impossible that it was nigh-certain, absent hostile divine intervention. By fragmenting humanity into scattered nations, each with its own language, God primarily ensures not that humanity will be any purer but that it will be decisively weakened. Enormous obstacles are now placed in the way of mankind's pooling of its scientific knowledge and technical skill. The loss of a common language drastically impedes the advance of human knowledge[47]—even or especially the knowledge of the Scriptures, which necessarily will be written down in a language that has become unintelligible to the vast majority of humans no longer speaking Hebrew.[48] It is difficult not to see here a considerable spur to idolatry (contrast ibid., 55). Not least of all, God makes impossible humanity's coalescence into a cosmopolitan political community or world-state. God here initiates political life as we know it: He makes inevitable the fundamental political distinctions between friend and enemy, citizen and noncitizen, insider and outsider, not to say slave and freeborn. All such distinctions violate, no doubt, the original and persisting kinship of mankind, the kinship so vividly taught by the stories of Noah and of Adam and Eve.

Still, without all these invidious and thwarting distinctions—without the checking and balancing of competing nations divided by alien tongues—mankind, and especially its leaders, would become (the Bible teaches) intoxicated with lust for autonomy and glory and limitless in Frankenstein-like technological potential. We learn more concretely and precisely the character of this evil in the depiction of Pharaoh, the ruler whose regime comes closest to realizing the ambitions expressed in the attempt to construct the tower of Babel; and it is remarkable that Pharaoh is *not* presented as particularly idolatrous but rather as quasi-atheistic in his presumed self-sufficiency. For the Bible, one may conclude, atheism is even worse than idolatry.

Commenting on this scriptural lesson, the greatest philosophic exponent of universal peace through world government bears qualified witness to the Bible's wisdom: "Holy Writ is quite right," Kant avers,

> in regarding the fusion of peoples into one society, and their complete liberation from external dangers at a time when their culture had hardly begun, as an impediment to all further cultural progress, and a plunge into incurable corruption. . . . [For] even still now, the danger of war is the only factor which mitigates despotism; for wealth is required if a state is to be nowadays a power, but without liberty, wealth-producing business activities cannot flourish. . . . At the stage of culture where the human race now stands, then, war is an indispensable means to the still further development of human culture; and only in a state of completed culture (God knows when) would perpetual peace be of benefit to us, and only then would it be possible. ["Conjectural Beginning of Human History," in *Akademieausgabe*, 8:120–21]

Yet this means that the ambition and the hope brought to light in the story of the tower of Babel remains, for Kant and for the progressive Kantian outlook, the ultimate proper destiny of mankind.

Moreover, according to the Bible, in contrast to Kant, the fragmentation of mankind into alien and hostile nations or peoples does not only forestall great evils; it is also the precondition for a very great good. It makes possible the choosing of one people, the elevation of one people—through supreme providential demands and care—to the position of being the sole beacon of genuine enlightenment and (in the very long run) of superhuman hope, for all mankind. Indeed, the story of Noah and his progeny contributes substantially, if still largely negatively, to our understanding of why a chosen people is necessary or reasonable, given the biblical premises. The story teaches us in part by raising and then dashing our hopes. For we are momentarily allowed to hope that the human race can indeed be purged. We are tempted to hope that the solution to the human problem is to start afresh, with a few human beings who have seen (or who have been raised by parents or grandparents who have seen), with their own eyes, God's awful punishment; who have felt in the midst of that terror His sheltering wing reserved for the righteous; who have spoken directly with Him and, what is more, have been made partners in His plans and providence. But we are lured by this hope, it seems, only so that we may thus learn that even such firsthand experience of punishment and providential redemption is far from sufficient—that it is at most the first step, that it is only a bare foundation.

We are thereby better positioned to understand that what is needed is a much more protracted breeding and discipline, over many generations and through long, complex, and painful experiences. What we have next to begin to learn is that central to those experiences must be the experience of a ranking within and among the human race, a ranking—of the chosen over the unchosen—that embodies and reflects the ranking of the holy God over His Creation and the ranking of the clean over the unclean within His Creation. One must immediately add, however, that this is a ranking from which human, all-too-human pride must be expunged. Unlike Noah, God does not curse the descendants of Ham, nor bless, in contrast, the descendants of Shem and Japheth. As Strauss remarks, "Mankind will be divided, not into the cursed and the blessed (the curses and blessings were Noah's, not God's), but into a chosen nation and nations that are not chosen" ("Jerusalem and Athens," 160).

CHAPTER SEVEN

Abram from the Calling to the Covenant

THE CALLING OF ABRAM RECAPITULATES IN A SENSE THE CALLING OF Noah.[1] As with every such biblical recapitulation, the divergences are at least as instructive as the redundancies. Noah and his family were called to be the surviving remnant of the whole human race; Abram and his family are called to separate themselves, to distinguish themselves, from all the rest of the race.[2] Accordingly, Abram/Abraham and Sarai/Sarah are the first real personalities in the Bible. We gained but little sense of Noah or of his family as distinctive persons. His wife, and his sons' wives, remained anonymous. In contrast, Abraham and Sarah, their descendants and their descendants' wives, are indelibly etched in our minds as perplexing exemplars. From this point forward Genesis bristles with characters defined and to some extent ranked by unique qualities, both admirable and questionable—qualities that disclose themselves for the most part through the drama, and only to readers who do some serious thinking for themselves. "It is a characteristic of these narratives," Cassuto remarks, "not to describe the thoughts and feelings of the *dramatis personae,* but only to record their deeds, and to inform the reader through the narration of events of the ideas and sentiments that prompted their actions." Or as Alter says, "We are compelled to get at character and motive, as in Impressionist writers like Conrad and Ford Madox Ford, through a process of inference from fragmentary data, often with crucial pieces of narrative exposition strategically withheld, and this leads to multiple or sometimes even wavering perspectives on the characters. There is, in other words, an abiding mystery in character as the biblical writers conceive it, which they embody in their typical methods of presentation." Our contemporary novelist E. L. Doctorow, praising "the wisdom of the later scribes in leaving intact on the page those chronicles they felt obligated to improve upon," argues that "as a result we get more than one point of view, which has the effect, in the depiction of human character, of a given roundness or ambiguity that we recognize as realistic."[3]

Preeminent of course is Abraham, the only person in Genesis who is denominated, by God Himself (though not when speaking to Abraham), as a "prophet."[4] What kind of man is this first richly developed "hero" that the Bible sets before us? How does he come to sight as Abram, and how do his qualities unfold in dialectical interaction with the other characters about him, divine and human, in the course of the amazing drama through which we watch him live? What do we learn from this drama about God, about God's intention, and about the chosen people who embody that intention, in part by honoring and following the example of Abraham? For he is rightly designated, according to the Bible, as "the pillar of the world": "The term 'rock' was used figuratively to designate the root and principle of every thing. It is on this account that after saying: 'Look unto the rock whence you were hewn,' Scripture continues (Isa. 51:1–2): 'Look unto Abraham your father,' and so on, giving, as it were, an interpretation according to which the *rock* whence *ye were hewn* is *Abraham your father.* Tread therefore in his footsteps, adhere to his religion, and acquire his character" (Maimonides *Guide* 1.16, 3.29; see also Abravanel's *Commentary on the Pentateuch* ad Gen. 22 beg.).

Abram at the Time of the Call

Our massive initial impression of Abram is of a man characterized by singular devotion to, and trust in, the Lord. God's first words to him are a summons to personal sacrifice and risk: at the age of seventy-five, with a wife aged sixty-six, Abram is commanded (without any threat of punishment for disobedience) to leave his native land—and, what is more (cf. Gen. 20:13), his aged father and paternal home—in order to "go his own way" to a land unspecified.[5]

To be sure, it is undeniable that God in the same breath holds out the loving promise of very substantial goods that will accrue to Abram as a consequence of his obedience. So grand are these rewards, and so prominent and primary is the promise of them, that they have occasioned deep discomfort among rabbinic commentators—an unease that seems to have contributed to the amassing of legends to the effect that prior to this call, Abram had already heroically endured persecution for the sake of his belief in God, at the hands of idolaters, thereby coming to deserve this vast recompense. The noble Nachmanides thus protests that

> this portion of Scripture is not completely elucidated. What reason was there that the Holy One, blessed be He, should say to Abraham, "Leave

your country, and I will do you good in a completely unprecedented measure," without first stating that Abraham worshipped God or that he was "*a righteous man, perfect*" (Ps. 119:176)? Or, it should state as a reason for his leaving the country that the very journey to another land constituted an act of seeking "*the nearness of God*" (Ps. 73:28). The custom of Scripture is to state, "Walk before Me (Gen. 17:1) and hearken to My voice, and I will [then, therefore] do good unto you," as is the case with David and Solomon as well as throughout the Torah. . . . However, the reason is that the people of Ur of the Chaldees did him much evil on account of his belief in the Holy One.[6]

Now while Ibn Ezra cannot be gainsaid in his stubborn and skeptical stress on the fact that the Scripture itself is altogether silent on any previous sufferings of Abram, we can at least observe that the vast prospects held out to Abram are certainly not mercenary—for Abram is already a wealthy man. The divine promise is that Abram is to be the seed of a "great nation" (גוי גדול). As such, his name or glory will be brilliant; nay, his name will be not merely known as some object of historical memory or wonder or awe (like Cyrus's, for example); the name of Abraham will be, God promises, employed lovingly, as a blessing—by every family on the face of the earth. One can wonder if any man of political ambition and love of glory has ever dared to hope for, let alone has ever been promised, so total a satisfaction of his deepest longings.

But the love of glory and of being loved by multitudes to which God's promises appeal does not seem to be precisely a *political* love of glory. Abram shows no desire for, and is given no promise of, his own empire—or, for that matter, the glory of having founded an empire, or the grateful memory of having ruled a great people well. How exactly, then, are we to understand the longings of Abram to which the call, or the promise that is in the call, appeals? What if anything are we told of Abram prior to the call that would help us to understand more precisely the yearnings that surge in his heart?

Abram's people were nomadic herdsmen, and it is thus that Abram himself has prospered (Gen. 12:5, 13:5−6). His wealth in herds and slaves[7] has given him, and continues to give him, mobility and independence (he never in his life owned any land, it appears, until he bought a burial site for Sarah). He has no strong previous tie to any single country, as is indicated by the fact that both Ur and Haran can be called "the land of his kin"

(ארץ ומולדת, often translated as "native land").[8] Long before God's call,[9] Abram's father Terah had taken the whole family out of the "land of his kin" and set out for Canaan—though he had settled short of his goal (Gen. 11:31). We see that Abram comes from restless stock, already uprooted, and already directed or inclined toward what will become the divinely promised land.

The young Hegel, in his hostile analysis, descries here the clues that reveal Abraham to have been a rather unhealthy, anarchistic rebel, "alienated" from the world in general and in particular from sound, quasi-Hellenic, community: "The first act which made Abraham the progenitor of a nation is a disseverance which snaps the bonds of communal life and love. The entirety of the relationships in which he had hitherto lived with men and nature, these beautiful relationships of his youth (Josh. 24:2), he spurned."[10]

More edifying is the deuterocanonical book of Judith (5:5–9; see similarly Josephus *Antiquities* 1.7.1), which presents Achior, the leader of all the Ammonites, as sketching to the conqueror Holofernes a history of the Hebrews that characterizes Abram's family as the monotheistic victims of pagan religious persecution: "At one time they lived in Mesopotamia, because they did not wish to follow the gods of their fathers who came into being in Chaldea. They had abandoned the ways of their ancestors, and worshipped the God of heaven—the God whom they had come to know; their ancestors drove them out from the presence of their gods; and they fled to Mesopotamia, and lived there many days. And their God told them to leave the place where they were living and to make their way to the land of Canaan."

God, however, speaking through His prophet Joshua in a public oration to the chosen people, gives a less flattering version of this history (Josh. 24:2–4 and 14–15): "Beyond the Euphrates lived your fathers of old—Terah, the father of Abraham and of Nahor; and they served other gods. Then I took your father Abraham from beyond the river and led him through the whole land of Canaan. . . . [P]ut away the gods that your fathers served beyond the Euphrates and in Egypt, and serve Yahweh; and if it is displeasing in your eyes to serve Yahweh, choose for yourselves this day whom you will serve: whether the gods which your fathers served, in the region beyond the river, or the gods of the Amorites among whom you dwell. But as for me and my house, we will serve Yahweh." Calvin severely comments (*Institutes* 3.24.2), "He calls to their remembrance whence it was He took their father Abraham when He willed to receive him in His love—namely, from the midst of idolatry, in which he was, as it were, plunged with all his people."[11] Yet the Genesis text before us, describing the first call from God to Abram, is most reasonably read as presuming that Abram, along with Lot and their families, had already long ago acknowledged Yahweh as the one and only God, Creator of all. God does not here speak as if He is forming the faith of Abram, but rather as if he presupposes that faith. The two texts taken together might well seem to imply a previous complex interaction between God and Abram (as well as Lot, and their families); legends to this effect abound in the tradition and become canonical in the *Qur'an*.

Next to the strength of faith in the one God, what manifestly sets Abram apart is his childlessness—and the singularly powerful need or emptiness that therefore can be understood to gnaw at his vitals. The Scripture brings home to us the anguish of this need in an especially poignant passage. Some time after God's initial call, and after He has shown to Abram the land of Canaan and has promised the land "forever" (עד עולם) to Abram's "offspring" (זרע)—who are to be as numerous as the dust particles of the earth (Gen. 12:7, 13:14–16)—God speaks to Abram in a vision, promising him that "his reward will be very great." In response the frustrated Abram expostulates, "What can You give me, seeing that I shall die childless [ערירי]!" (Gen. 15:1–2). No divine promise seems great to Abram in the absence of children of his very own as a living presence in his life.

But why, exactly, did Abram lack children? Only by pressing this question do we uncover Abram's heart more fully, and thus explode the Hegelian reading. For the Bible makes it clear that the childlessness of the marriage of Abram and Sarai was not due to any incapacity in Abram: "Now Sarai was barren" (Gen. 16:2); after Sarah died, Abraham took a second wife, Keturah, and sired six sons (Gen. 25:1–2; see also 11:30). But so long as Sarai lived, Abram took no second wife, and at the time of his call he had not even inseminated a concubine. That he could have done so is shown by the fact that he does do so, later in the story, but that subsequent cohabitation with Hagar, his wife's slave, occurs only because his wife wishes and commands it; and after Hagar has become pregnant with his first child, a resigned Abram allows the tyrannical Sarai to drive her into despairing flight (Gen. 16:1–6). Abram's childlessness, like his first fatherhood, is a consequence and a manifestation of his wife's extraordinary hold over him. Why does she have such a hold on her husband?

The Bible stresses over and over that Sarai is astoundingly beautiful and desirable, and that she is such first and foremost to Abram, who "said to his wife Sarai, I know what a beautiful woman you are." Even at the age of sixty-six, her beauty so impresses the Pharaoh of Egypt and his princes, who are doubtless not unaccustomed to beautiful young women, that the Pharaoh eagerly selects her for his harem. When Sarah is ninety years of age, and past menstruation, she is still so attractive that she is plucked by the king of Gerar for his harem (Gen. 12:11–15, 20:2). This extraordinarily beautiful woman is, as Abraham later admits, his own half-sister.[12] Abram's passion for Sarai, and for children from her, is singular, and not only in its strength. We may venture to characterize it as a powerful erotic love of the beauty that is Abram's own kin, and that promised truly kindred offspring. In order for the young Hegel to advance his astounding interpretation of Abraham as a man who "wanted *not* to love, wanted to be free by *not* loving" (thus allowing him to characterize the Jewish impulse as the antithesis of that found in erotic Greek religion), he must maintain almost complete silence about Sarah, as if she were not present in the story (Hegel's only reference to her is to her burial place).[13]

We conclude that Abram's distinguishing passion is not so much political as it is the passion of a man overwhelmingly attracted to the unique, kindred woman whom he passionately desires to become the mother and grandmother of his offspring. He is, or could become, seriously interested in the political realm insofar as it is derivative from, and in service to, his own familial realm. Abram's inclination to identify his greatest good with the good of numerous others who see their lives as having been uplifted and fulfilled through him is the inclination not so much of a potential ruler as of a potential father, and father of fathers. In his longing for fatherhood, Abram is set apart in the Scripture. Previously, as Westermann stresses (*Genesis 12–36*, 24), "fatherhood is restricted to the genealogies" and "no one there, not even Adam, is described as the father of generations to come."

Genesis presents Abram as a man whose hungry openness to the call to become the seed of the chosen people presupposes his having experienced in the very depths of his bones the yet barren, even desperate, need and longing for offspring of his own from the one and only beautiful wife whom he loves.[14] This is not to deny, of course—it is rather to explain how it is—that once Abram, in obedience to Sarai, has begotten a son from another woman, he becomes passionately attached to that son. Abram's response to hearing the promise of the imminent birth of a son—Isaac—to his wife Sarai is the plea that his first son, Ishmael, the son born to the concubine Hagar, might find favor with God; and this is a request that God in part accepts (Gen. 17:18, 20). Abram, we may say, could never even entertain the Platonic Socrates' or the Platonic Athenian Stranger's contentions that a truly good and just society would require the abolition of the private family and fatherhood, and that "one should not look elsewhere for the model, at any rate, of a political regime, but should hold on to this and seek with all one's might the regime that comes as close as possible to such a regime" (Plato *Laws* 739c–e; cf. *Republic,* bk. 5). Abram and the people he founds stand at the opposite pole to the imagined republics of Plato.[15]

Still, Abram's deepest original yearning is not yet adequately circumscribed by his monogamous erotic and familial passion. That this is still not sufficient is indicated by the fact that the Scripture does not have God make any direct reference to Abram's own future children in the first speech He addresses to him. God, we are tempted to say, discerns within, or accompanying, Abram's passionate love for Sarai, and aching need for children from her, a more far-reaching longing—a more political longing—of which Abram himself is as yet unaware and whose importance he only gradually comes to recognize. Yet we must immediately add that Abram is brought to recognize his concern to be the originator of a great nation only because he is, to begin with, devoted above all to God. In other words, we must be wary of any attempt fully to explain Abram in terms that are limited simply to his psychological needs, erotic, parental, or political—however urgent and however sublime those needs may be. For this would surely contradict Abram's own self-understanding, that is, the self-understanding of the Scriptures: at the culmination of Abraham's story is the sacrifice of a father's most treasured mortal acquisition upon the altar of devotion to eternal omnipotence.[16] In accordance with all this is the fact that there is, of course, no hint in the story of Abram, or in the biblical patriarchal narratives altogether, of any ancestor-worship or of any potential divinization of the ancestral fathers. The strict monotheism of the Bible rules out the most common and nigh-universal human reverence for ancestors and family (Westermann, *Genesis 12–36,* 25).

Abram's Ungentlemanly Guile

It is understandable that weighty authority has characterized Abraham as "heroic" or as a "hero."[17] That he is not a hero in the classic sense, however—that he is not like the "heroes [גברים] of old, the men of renown" (Gen. 6:4); that he is not even like Nimrod, "the first [human] hero [גבר] on the earth" (Gen. 10:8)—is vividly brought home to us by the initial, and very troubling or perplexing, incident the Scripture relates about Abram after he has arrived in the promised land and has been vouchsafed the first direct appearance of God, and has begun to "invoke" or to proclaim "Yahweh [יהוה] by name."

A severe famine afflicts the promised land (which, we therefore see, from almost the very outset, is not always or necessarily a land flowing with milk and honey). Abram does not for a minute suppose that he and his folk are to be given divine dispensation or protection from the suffering and danger. He rather assumes that he must continue to live by his wits, a nomad in a risky world. He heads for Egypt, a land of plenty, relatively immune to famine, and ruled by the Pharaoh—the embodiment, in Scripture, of despotism. Just before crossing the border, Abram successfully beseeches Sarai to join him in pretending to be merely brother and sister so that he may be saved from powerful strangers who would calculate that only by murdering Sarai's husband (and perhaps in their passion being led to rape her) could they acquire her without unacceptable complications. Once in Egypt, the gambit works: Sarai is appropriated by no less than Pharaoh himself into a potentially adulterous relationship, and her "brother" gains riches as well as security—at the wrenching cost, of course, of his beloved wife's honor and companionship (Gen. 12:10–20).

This desperate dodge, Abram later discloses, is a general stratagem he conceived when God commanded him to leave his ancestral family's protection and to travel among powerful strangers who might threaten his life (Gen. 20:13). Observe the radical implication: this imposture is a policy coeval with Abram's knowing himself to be the chosen one of God; this policy of gruesome masquerade was formulated as a major part of Abram's response to the divine call. Moreover, this scheme Abraham taught to his son Isaac, by example if not by precept.[18] Abram/Abraham, as God's chosen, certainly does not appear to be what ancient Greece would call a perfect gentleman (καλὸς κἀγαθός), let alone a "hero." Abram, as God's chosen, is not a man who risks his life to keep, or to protect the "honor" of, the wife he dearly loves.[19] When self-preservation requires, he is a man fully prepared not only to lose his beloved wife, together with her honor, but also to tell grave lies, lies that may suborn others into serious sins for which they may be severely punished by God. To be sure, those potentates who arrogantly presume to take Sarai, without either her own or her "brother's" consent, or after securing that consent by implicit intimidation, are far from being altogether guiltless.

Scripture leaves us to figure out for ourselves how we are supposed to judge of Abram's premeditated and adulterous perfidy.[20] If we understand the prior account of the Fall to imply an inborn original sinfulness, or even if we bear in mind God's declaration after the Flood that "every inclination of man's heart is evil from childhood" (Gen. 8:21), it is difficult to resist Calvin's conclusion that here we see the meaning of human sinfulness even or especially in the paragon Abraham (see also Rabbi Eleazar in the Talmudic Arachin 17a). Yet Abraham himself, in the Septuagint, reports that he characterized what he was asking his wife to do as "an act of justice to me."[21] God is of course fully cognizant of Abram's scheme, and though He does not praise it, He indicates no objection whatsoever to it. That the divine silence is not disapproving seems indicated by the following observations: As we have noted, Abram employs the strategy yet a second time, and it is during that second incident that God declares him to be His prophet (and accordingly proves in deed the prophet's extraordinary powers of intercessory prayer). In addition, when Isaac is subsequently shown to have adopted the identical strategy, we again hear not a hint of divine disapproval.[22] Nay, as is underlined by Rashi and Ibn Ezra, it is precisely at the outset of the account of Isaac's imitation of his father's potentially adulterous mendacity that God tells Isaac that Abraham "obeyed My voice and kept My charge, My commandments, My statutes, and My laws"—seeming thus to make it unmistakably clear that precisely with an eye to *this* pattern of behavior there is in God's eyes no moral blemish in Abraham's entire record (Gen. 26:5).[23]

These are not the last occasions on which God will appear to tolerate or even to approve of lying as a strategy appropriate for those in desperate—or even in less than desperate but still straitened—circumstances.[24] What is more, the prophet Micaiah was vouchsafed a vision of the Lord commanding an angel to go forth and be "a lying spirit in the mouth of all [Ahab's] prophets" (1 Kings 22:19–23). We are therefore inclined to conclude that Abram, and Isaac after him, does not conceive of God as categorically prohibiting lying. Abram, of course, knows that in general it is a sin to lie, as the Bible will repeatedly teach (see, e.g., Ps. 5:7, 12:3, 28:3ff., 120:2; Prov. 3:29, 17:20, 26:24 and 28). And he knows that lying is especially sinful when the deceit regards so grave a matter as the facts that determine whether or not a contemplated act of cohabitation will entail adultery; his later response to Abimilech indicates his keen awareness of the need to excuse his gravely duplicitous conduct.[25] But he seems convinced that the justification he provides is valid (contrast Calvin, *Commentary on Genesis* ad 20:11), and God certainly does not gainsay him in this regard—though God does ensure that, at least on this second occasion, when Sarah's pregnancy looms, adultery does not occur. Now since "the Lord has not given anyone permission to sin" (Sir. 15:20), the principle underlying or implicit in Abram's exculpation would appear to be that in the absence of a positive divine commandment, what is right or wrong, sinless or sinful, is defined decisively, in pressing circumstances, by what human prudence dictates to be good—for example, conducive to one's own survival, at least or especially if one understands oneself to be chosen by God for His mission. Justice or righteousness, Abram apparently presumes, cannot be irretrievably harmful, even or especially for the just person or the one chosen by the just God.[26]

What might at first appear a deficiency in Abram's understanding of justice would seem to reveal, then, the practical if not altogether noble wisdom in his flexible understanding of justice. But this cannot help but give us pause. No one has brought out the underlying question more sharply than Pierre Bayle. Faced with the praises of and excuses for Abraham offered by Sts. Augustine and Chrysostom, and confronting Augustine's praise not only of Sarah's behavior in these incidents but also of behavior similar to hers on the part of another and much later Roman "heroine," Bayle expostulates:

> It is a strange thing, that these great lights of the Church, with all their virtue and all their zeal, did not recognize that it is not permitted to save one's life, nor that of another, by a crime.

> Who does not see that if this morality has credit, there will not be a single precept of the Decalogue from which the fear of death will not dispense us? Where are there any exceptions in favor of adultery? If a wife is not obliged to obey the commandment not to sully her body when she can

spare her husband the ultimate suffering, then she won't be obliged to
obey, when it is a question of saving her own life. . . . It follows that, in
order to avoid death, one can with impunity violate the law of chastity. So
why will not a similar reason permit murder, robbery, bearing false witness, abjuring one's religion, etc.?[27]

To be sure, Bayle thus ignores Calvin's insistence (*Commentary on Genesis*
ad 12:11 and 20:2) that these stories in no way suggest that Abram acted
out of concern for mere personal self-preservation ("as certain impious
dogs yelp"). Rather, "when he reflected that the hope of salvation was
centered in *himself,* that *he* was the fountain and the source of the Church
of God, that unless *he* lived, the benediction promised to him, and to his
wife, was vain, he did not estimate his own life according to the private
affection of the flesh but, inasmuch as he did not wish the effect of the
divine vocation to perish through his death, he was so affected with
concern for the preservation of his own life, that he overlooked every
other thing. So far, then, he deserves praise, that having a just end for
living he was ready to save his life at any cost." It is only (Calvin concedes)
"in devising this indirect method, by which he subjected his wife to the
peril of adultery," that Abraham "seems to be by no means excusable."
"He ought," Calvin judges, "to have cast his care upon God." Calvin thus
argues that it is the teaching of the Bible that even the highest and clearest
vocation from God is never meant to dispense with the categorical character of the imperatives of morality as articulated in the Decalogue.[28]

To this condemnation one might reply, in admittedly abashed defense
or mitigation of Abraham, that the legislation of the Ten Commandments
introduces a more sublime and true categorical absoluteness into "morality" that was unknown to Abraham, because such absoluteness is not
sufficiently evident prior to positive (revealed) divine legislation. This
would seem to imply, however, that the Bible does not endorse the notion
of a strict or categorical "natural" law.[29]

Besides, this points to a further question. Does not the problem of
Abram's apparent injustice to his fellow men pale in comparison to his
apparent injustice to God—his seeming lack of trust in God's providential
protection?[30] Or could it be that there is a clue to a defense even of this last
and gravest charge, a clue perhaps to be found in what at first may strike us
as one of the least attractive features of these incidents: the apparent lack of
manliness or dignity that they exhibit? Could it be that what one is

initially tempted to call Abram's (and later, Isaac's) lack of manliness is, according to the Bible, a manifestation of the much higher virtue of humility? Augustine observes (*City of God* 16.19) that "if Abram hadn't taken every precaution against danger that he could have taken, he would have tempted rather than hoped in God." The touchstone of medieval Jewish mysticism, the *Zohar* (Bereshith 1.82a), remarks on the episode involving the Pharaoh: "This is one of the trials which Abram endured without complaining against God." The *Zohar* follows *The Avot of Rabbi Nathan* (chap. 33, p. 132). Abram can be said to demonstrate here that even though God has promised him a great future, he does not presume to think that he can therefore take for granted divine protection. As the *Midrash Rabbah* comments (on Gen. 40.3), "Famine assailed Abram, yet he did not protest nor murmur against the Lord" (contrast von Rad, *Genesis,* 234). On the second occasion, involving Abimilech, Abraham demonstrates his belief that even after God has declared that He will be a shield, even after God has confirmed the covenant, even after Sarah has become pregnant, God's providence nonetheless presupposes that Abraham has first done all that he can do on his own to save the lives of himself and his wife.[31] In considering Abraham's motivation in this repeat episode, where the king in question (Abimilech) turns out to be manifestly more moral than was the Pharaoh, Luther plausibly suggests (LG, *Werke,* 43:91–92, 105, 107, 112) that we bear in mind the fact that the incident occurs soon after Abraham has witnessed the destruction of Sodom and Gomorrah, horrible indications of how vicious the people are who dwell in the cities located about him: " 'So why,' you will ask, 'did Abraham fear so pious a man?' I judge the fact to be so on account of the horrible example of those five cities. He experienced there such human malice, that God Himself testified to the effect that in the entire region there were not five just men to be found" (ibid., 107). Luther aptly compares the behavior of the prophet Elijah: "Since Abraham has no certain word from heaven that his wife is to be protected, he does what reason persuades of, and hopes that by such a lie he and his wife will be protected. . . . When Elijah killed the prophets of Baal, he was impelled by the spirit of God [1 Kings 18:40]; yet the same later on, when Jezebel's wrath has been announced, fears for himself, and withdraws into the desert, looking out in this way for his own life [1 Kings 19:1–4]. This he does of his own will, for he is not commanded by God to withdraw. Reason kept telling him that he would be safe, if he hid in the desert" (ibid., 104–5). Nevertheless,

Luther eventually concedes, "this does not entirely excuse Abraham" (ibid., 114).

Assisted by St. Chrysostom, we may, however, go further. Implicit in Abraham's deportment would appear to be an insight made more explicit by David in Ps. 34:19 (see also 51:18–19): "The Lord is close to the brokenhearted; those crushed in spirit He delivers." When one seriously contemplates the fear and the humiliation that must have animated Abram's desperate strategy (and Sarai's acceptance of it)—when one tries to imagine the horror, abasement, and despair that both must have experienced when she was taken away, apparently forever, by the Pharaoh's minions—one wonders whether anything could have sustained them except the hope that God, precisely in allowing them to be so crushed, was following His characteristic bent, displaying what the ingenuous St. Chrysostom characterizes, in his discussion of this gruesome story, as "the extent of the Lord's inventiveness: when He allows terrible things to reach a climax, then it is that in turn He scatters the storm and brings peace and quiet and a complete change of fortunes so as to teach us the greatness of His power."[32] As Montesquieu repeatedly proves, the principle that men call "honor" is indeed at the opposite pole to the principle of biblical religion.[33]

A much less agonizing humility is manifested in Abram's comportment toward his nephew in the next major incident of his scriptural story. A quarrel between his herdsmen and those of his nephew Lot is resolved by Abram's granting to the nephew the choice of whichever part of the land he may wish for grazing (Gen. 13:5–10). Abram exhibits here more than avuncular complaisance. As Cassuto observes, "This, too, is a test and trial for Abram: he was hoping to become a great nation (Gen. 12:2), yet now, even though he was still childless, he was compelled, out of his love of peace, to separate himself from his brother's son, who was to him as a son."[34]

Abram's Manliness

In foolish but typically human fashion, Lot chooses to settle in the rich land ("land like Egypt") next to the city of Sodom. As a result, he is swept up with the Sodomites when they are captured after their defeat as rebels by their lord Chedorlaomer, king of Elam. Abram—who is here for the first time called "Abram the Hebrew," that is, Abram the beginner of a great nation (Gen. 14:13; cf. 11:14)—meets this family emergency by organizing and executing a shrewd nighttime military action that proves beyond any doubt both his courage and his competence as a commander.[35] We are not to suppose, then, that extraordinary humility and wily peaceableness preclude the possession and exercise of warrior virtues, when they are needed and when it is prudent that they be displayed and employed. Ibn Ezra comments on the phrase את־חניכיו (trained men): "Abraham had trained them many times for battle. This is the meaning of the term, even though Scripture does not previously note that Abraham trained young men for war." It is true that Abram's one military victory is a nocturnal operation rather than a pitched battle. Josephus (*Antiquities* 1.10) goes further, and beyond the Scriptures, in supposing that the enemy was caught in bed, drunk. Josephus nevertheless concludes that by this victory Abram "demonstrated, that victory does not depend on multitude, and the number of hands, but the alacrity and courage of soldiers overcome the most numerous bodies of men."[36]

Nor, we next see, does Abram's humility obviate a proud sense of independence from other humans, a sense grounded in his keen awareness of his dependence on God. When the king of Sodom expresses his gratitude for the rescue, by offering Abram all the possessions the latter has recovered, Abram—"being not only of a pious, but of a lofty mind"[37]—refuses, swearing an oath in the name of "God most high, the Maker of heaven and earth": "You shall not say, 'It is I who made Abram rich'" (Gen. 14). Abram here exemplifies, one may say, that dignified humility that the Bible regards as the mean between the extremes of haughty arrogance (or *hubris*) and vileness or abasement.[38]

Trust in God as Justice

Yet Abram still has no children. And as time passes, it becomes more and more inconceivable that, or how, he might ever have children. If we are attuned to the mysterious suspense of this wonderful drama, we are impelled (with Abram—cf. Ginzberg, *Legends of the Jews*, 1.228) to wonder: Could the rescue of Lot signify that God meant that Abram's "offspring" were to be his descendants through his nephew Lot?[39] But Lot and Abram have now separated, and immediately "after Lot had parted from him," Abram was told by God that he and his offspring would be given *all* the promised land forever—and that his offspring would be as numerous as the dust particles on the earth (Gen. 13:14–16). Besides, the rescue of Lot does not reunite the families; Abram's steward is in line to be his heir (Gen. 15:3). God's promise has thus become progressively more and more inscrutable, bewildering, straining credibility.

In this situation, and in the aftermath and apparently as a consequence of the splendid military victory and the proud refusal of gifts (Josephus *Antiquities* 1.10; Nachmanides ad Gen. 15:1), God appears to Abram for the second time, and this time the account of the direct revelation is unprecedented. To begin with, the narration is introduced by a formula— "the word of the Lord came to" (היה דבר־יהוה אל־)—that is unique in the Hexateuch but is found frequently in the prophetic books.[40] What is more, God manifests Himself to Abram as a voice in an ecstatic night vision (במחזה)—"also a prophetic mode of experience" (Alter, *Genesis* ad loc.). When the divine voice speaks, it assures Abram that he need not fear and then makes the pronouncement—for the first time to Abram or to anyone in the Bible—"for you *your reward* [שכרך] is very big." These features of the event may signal that the moment has arrived when Abram clearly achieves the rank of prophet.

In response, apparently sensing and taking advantage of the rank to which he has been elevated, Abram is so bold as to remonstrate with the visionary voice, addressing God by His name, Yahweh. But as Alter perceptively remarks, since "God remains impassively silent in the face of Abram's brief initial complaint," Abram has to summon the will to "continue and spell out the reason for his skepticism about the divine promise."[41] Abram, as we have already observed, is a man who is desperate in his longing for a son from his beloved wife. But it is by no means necessary to reduce his desire to merely the longing for such a son and heir. The Scripture "indeed ascribes to Abram a disposition which is naturally inherent in all men, but this does not mean that Abram did not look higher, when he so strongly desired to be the progenitor of an heir"; the earlier promise—"in thy seed shall all nations be blessed"—"contains in itself the whole gratuitous pledge of salvation" (Calvin, *Commentary on Genesis* ad 15:2).

Abram's persistence evokes a penetrating and unambiguous divine response. He is assured by God that "the issue of your loins shall be your heir" and is taken out to view the starry sky and told that "so many will be your offspring." Calvin acutely remarks (ad loc.), "The sight of the stars was not at all superfluous, but was intended to strike the heart of

Abram with this thought, 'God who by His word alone suddenly produced a host so numerous, by which He might adorn the previously vast
and desolate heaven; shall not *He* be able to replenish my desolate house
with offspring?' "

Nevertheless, Abram is not given a clue as to how this nigh–incredible
promise might be fulfilled. His trust in the promise is accordingly of the
utmost merit; it is a manifestation, Scripture says, of his justice (צדקה). By
"justice," in this context, Scripture would seem to mean, most simply, the
willingness to give God His due, and what is due to God is *trust,* even or
especially in the absence of earthly plausibility or evidence (Gen. 15:4–6).
The Bible certainly implies, through this paramount case, that an exemplary faith such as Abram's is inseparable from, and perhaps tantamount
to, justice. Such faith is moral, in that it expresses a sense of obligation;
such faith is faith in God as a judge. Martin Luther's comment takes us still
further: "Our Lord God thus asks nothing more from us humans than that
we give to Him alone the honor that is His due, and that we hold Him to
be our God, that is, that we do not hold Him to be some vain and
whimsical deity, but rather a just and truthful God. . . . To thus give to
God such honor from the heart is certainly a wisdom above all wisdom, a
justice above all justice, a service to God above all service to God, a
sacrifice above all sacrifices. . . . Whoever thus believes and trusts in God's
word, as has Abraham, he is just before God; for he has such a faith as gives
to God the honor that is due to Him—that is, he gives to God what is
owed to Him and what it is a duty to give."[42] Luther suggests that Abram
does not act out of self-interest, that he rather acts out of duty or obligation, that he even makes a "sacrifice" inasmuch as he lays aside his prudential calculation as to what is best for him to aim at and to work for in
the future. He entrusts his future concerns to God not out of prudence
but rather out of honor or devotion to God—to God as one Who is not
whimsical but just and truthful. To such a degree does Abram's faith
bespeak a transcendence of self-concern.

The First Stage of the Covenant

Still, the Bible cannot, or at any rate it does not, leave matters here.
Sacrificial trust is not the sole or apparently the sufficient basis for Abram's
adherence to God and to God's word. When, after an indefinite interval,[43]
God speaks yet a third time to Abram, revealing that it is He who brought

Abram not only out of Haran but, even earlier, out of Ur, and then renews the promise of the land, Abram dares to ask how he can *know* (ירע)—not just believe or trust (אמן)—that he will own the land. Ibn Ezra observes in his comment on this passage that "Abraham had complete faith in God's word that he would beget a son who would be his heir. It was only with regard to the possession of the land that he asked for a sign." Ibn Ezra then rather cryptically adds, by way of a clue to the explanation, "He acted like Gideon." Ibn Ezra would appear to refer to Judg. 6:34–40, which he apparently interprets as follows: Since the land of Israel could be legitimately or justly taken away from its Canaanite owners only if they remained unrepentant sinners, it was uncertain whether the promise or prophecy of the land grant would necessarily be fulfilled. Gideon, like Abram before him, knew that, given the contingent possibility of human repentance, and God's strict adherence to justice, "all prophecies are conditional." In particular, all grants of land belonging to other peoples are conditional. "God's oaths, on the other hand, are unconditional." Ibn Ezra interprets Abram as in effect asking that the prophecy or grant be made certain by an oath—such as was indeed immediately afterward given in the covenant. Such a request, Ibn Ezra means to say, was reasonable, being based on a proper conception of divine adherence to justice. He thus refutes the Midrashic suggestion (Mas. Nedarim 32a) that Abram sinned in asking for a confirmatory sign.[44]

Yet it is not perfectly clear that it *was* simply a covenant, and *not* some further sign, that Abram was in fact requesting. Certainly in reply to Abram's insistent question God orders him to participate in a complex sacrificial ritual,[45] after which, just before sunset, Abram is overtaken by a "dreadful" sleep of "darkness" and terror, framing the first dream vision, or prophetic revelation during sleep, in the Bible. In this dreadful dream God reveals the crucial outlines of His very trying plan for the chosen people in the coming centuries, while assuring Abram himself of a ripe old age and a peaceful death. When the sun sets, there appears—apparently not in the dream, but after Abram has awoken—the uncanny sight of a smoking oven-pot and a torch passing between the sacrificial meats that Abram had prepared and tended prior to the dream vision.

Against Ibn Ezra, whose commentary he gives evidence of knowing well, Spinoza takes this passage as a proof text for his thesis that according to Holy Writ, "prophecy by itself cannot involve certainty, since, as this now shows, it depends solely on the imagination; and thus the Prophets were not certain of God's revelation by that revelation itself, but by some sign, as is patent from Abraham (see Gen. 15:8), who, having heard God's promise, demanded some sort of sign [*aliquod signum*]; he, who believed in God, and did *not* ask for a sign, in order to have faith in God, but rather in order to know that it was indeed by God that the promise had been made" (*Theologico-Political Treatise,* chap. 2, p. 16 [or para. 3]). Yet (Spinoza goes on to observe) even evidently miraculous signs convey in themselves no certainty, according to the Scripture itself: "For in Deuteronomy, chap. 13, Moses warns" that "God makes even signs, and miracles, to test the people. And Christ gave this same warning even to his disciples, as is declared in Matthew, chap. 24, verse 24." "And although," Spinoza slyly adds, "this seems to show prophecy and revelation to be a very doubtful thing, it nevertheless has, as we said, much certainty." To be sure, Spinoza adds, "as I have said, the Prophet's own certainty was as such merely moral, since no one can justify himself to God, nor boast, that he is the instrument of God's piety, as Scripture itself teaches."

Spinoza thus claims that our text shows that the paradigmatic prophet Abraham himself was always uncertain as to whether it was God or merely his own imagination that was speaking to him. In the present instance he received such confirmation as he ever got by the "sign," that is, by the passage of the smoking oven-pot and torch. But of course, the train of skeptical thought started by Spinoza leads one to wonder whether this sign was not just another part of the dream—or a product, once again, of a vivid and impassioned imagination.

But does this line of thought start from a plausible reading of the text before us? Is Abraham in fact being presented as doubting whether the voice he hears is really that of God, as opposed to being merely imaginary? Would this degree of doubt not be such as might arise only in someone (like Spinoza) who has not himself had that personal experience that the faithful report as divine revelation? It may well be true, as Kant insists, in the context of a discussion of Abraham's experience, that "it is absolutely impossible for a human through his senses to grasp the infinite, distinguish it from sensory existents, and *recognize* it as such." But from this does it necessarily follow, as Kant claims and seems to think, that "if God should really speak to a man, the latter could still never *know* that it was God who spoke to him"?[46] May there not be a kind of certainty granted to a human by revelatory grace, experienced not "through his senses"? On Spinoza's and Kant's side, it must be noted that we know of philosophers who seem to have had some such experiences and who nevertheless sometimes doubted their divine provenance, subsequently if not at the moment.[47] What is more, Spinoza goes on to show that Scripture itself testifies to such doubts arising even in those who have such experience: "The same is made even clearer," he notes, "from the story of Gideon; for thus indeed he says to God, 'and make for me a sign (that I may know) that it is you who are speaking with me'; see Judges, chap. 6, verse 17; and" (Spinoza adds rather more tendentiously) "God also says to Moses [Exod. 3:12] 'and this may be for you a sign, that it is I who send you.'"

Spinoza here draws our attention to an earlier part of the Gideon story that does not so easily fit into what we have gathered is Ibn Ezra's explanation. The doubt Spinoza raises is not so easy to dispose of, even on the basis of the Scriptures—not to speak of the fact that many faithful believers have testified to the uncertainty of the experience of God's presence.[48] Yet, to repeat, the Scripture does not seem to suggest that Abram, at least (or for that matter virtually any of the other prophets), ever had much doubt that it was in fact God's voice that was being heard, in dream and in vision.[49] A notable exception is the young Samuel (1 Sam. 3), but this story hardly supports Spinoza (as he is compelled to admit).[50] For although Samuel at first repeatedly failed to recognize that the voice addressed to him was the voice of God, he never considered the voice to be in his imagination and never asked for or needed a further miraculous sign in order to confirm that it was not in his imagination; once the high priest Eli had informed him that the voice was not his own and must be that of God, Samuel recognized the voice as such without any hesitation or doubt (see also John 20:15–17).

Maimonides, we may observe, offers an interpretation of the biblical presentation of the prophetic experience that takes an uneasy—and not transparently coherent—stand somewhere between the subversive doubts of Spinoza and the *surface* message of the scriptural text (which never mentions the imagination, but which therefore, Maimonides points out, slips toward corporealism inasmuch as it attributes a human voice to God Himself, rather than to an image of Him in the human imagination). According to Maimonides, God communicates with His prophets (except in the unique case of Moses)[51] by way of an "overflow" to the bodily faculty that is the imagination, and hence always "in a dream and in a vision" (Num. 12:6–8). In his thematic treatment of prophecy, Maimonides asserts that the difference between a true prophet of the Lord and a

mere imaginative visionary is this: "If this overflow reaches both faculties—I mean both the rational and the imaginative—as we and others
among the philosophers have explained, and if the imaginative faculty is
in a state of ultimate perfection owing to its natural disposition, this is
characteristic of the class of prophets. If again the overflow only reaches
the imaginative faculty, the defect of the rational faculty deriving either
from its original natural disposition or from insufficiency of training, this
is characteristic of those who govern cities, while being the legislators, the
augurs, and the dreamers of truthful dreams" (*Guide* 2.37). But it is to the
example of Abraham, in obeying the command to bind and to prepare to
slaughter his son Isaac, that Maimonides later appeals to show that

> it should not be thought that what the prophets hear or what appears to
> them in a parable is not certain or is commingled with illusion just because
> it comes about *in a dream and in a vision,* as we have made clear, and
> through the intermediary of the imaginative faculty. Accordingly [Scrip-
> ture] wished to make it known to us that all that is seen by a prophet in *a
> vision of prophecy* is, in the opinion of the prophet, a certain truth, that the
> prophet has no doubts in any way concerning anything in it, and that in his
> opinion its status is the same as that of all existent things that are ap-
> prehended through the senses or through the intellect. A proof for this is
> the fact that [Abraham] hastened to slaughter, as he had been commanded,
> *his son, his only son, whom he loved,* even though this command came to him
> *in a dream or in a vision.* For if a dream of prophecy had been obscure for the
> prophets, or if they had doubts or incertitude concerning what they ap-
> prehended *in a vision of prophecy,* they would not have hastened to do that
> which is repugnant to nature, and Abraham's soul would not have con-
> sented to accomplish an act of so great importance if there had been a
> *doubt* about it.[52]

However this may be, the scriptural text with which we are now
wrestling clearly shows that God found it appropriate or understandable
that Abram seek to undergo some *experience* that would give vivid confirmation to his faith—not, it would seem, as Spinoza claims, Abram's faith
that the voice came from God, but rather his faith that God would, or that
He could, perform what He had promised. Now, this does indeed force us
to ask precisely what it was of which God understood Abram to be not yet
sufficiently convinced.[53]

The "sign," as Spinoza calls it—the miraculous passage of the smoking oven-pot and the torch—might well have helped to indicate, or to remind of, or to underline, God's power, if not His omnipotence. And thus there would be some merit to Spinoza's stress on the importance of that sign. But the text would appear to suggest that it was above all the *dream* experience itself that gave Abram the reassurance that he sought. The plunge into the "terror" (אימה), the "great darkness" (חשכה גדלה), of the dream experience, followed immediately by the vivid prophetic reassurance of a secure future life culminating in a comfortable and even hopeful death (a death in the prospect of living on through one's infinite descendants), would then be what gave Abram the more secure confidence, or sense of knowing, that he sought. To speak more precisely, the text would appear to suggest that it was the vivid emotional experience of initial black terror, followed by immediately consequent hopeful reassurance of salvation, that made Abram cease seeking firmer knowledge than he had already been vouchsafed. For Abram asks no further questions, even in the face of a truly puzzling prognostication. In particular, he does not ask why it is necessary or right that his offspring be enslaved and oppressed for four hundred long years. When God next appears to him, Abram immediately falls on his face before God and then listens—without any questions—to the astounding divine instructions to circumcise himself and his household (Gen. 17:3).

This dramatic account of Abram's demand for, and reception of, a "sign" confirming God's promise would seem to illuminate what the Bible means when it teaches that "the fear of the Lord is the beginning of wisdom" (or, perhaps more literally, "the first principle of knowledge" [יראת יהוה ראשית דעת]; Prov. 1:7).[54] The "fear" referred to is a fear of the loving and just God, Who inspires not sheer terror but awe, Whose presence can or ought to remind us of our lowliness and exposedness, but only in the all-embracing context of His providential and redeeming capacities.[55]

The Completion of the Covenant with Abraham

Apparently within the great darkness of the dreadful dream, God explicitly formalizes the grant of the land in a solemn covenant. As a matter of fact, He does more than formalize the previous grant; He vastly enlarges it. He now gives to Abram's posterity all the land between the Nile and the Euphrates—a veritable empire (cf. Sir. 44:21). The "covenant" at first appears to be as unconditional and uncontractual a promise as was the covenant God made with all mankind through Noah: "Certainly," as Wevers remarks, Abram "was only a silent partner."[56] Yet it transpires that this is not the last word of God's covenant with Abram. Many years pass before God once again appears to him to elaborate, and finally to clarify the character of, this most fundamental covenant.

In the meantime, Abram's domestic situation becomes immensely complicated (Gen. 16). At the age of eighty-six, he at last begets a son of his own, through Hagar, in somewhat uxorious obedience to the (understandably) impatient—and short-sighted—insistence of Sarai (contrast Luther, LG, *Werke,* 42:579ff.). The advent of Ishmael is the (rather predictable) occasion of lasting enmity between Abram's beloved wife and her proud—and hence persecuted—slave girl Hagar, the mother of Abram's cherished son Ishmael. For thirteen years Abram apparently bears this unhappy family tension with bewildered patience, sustained in all likelihood by the natural belief that this one and only son is to be the vehicle for the fulfillment of ·God's promises (Luther, LG, *Werke,* 42:602; cf. Augustine *City of God* 16.26). But all of this turns out to be a trial Abram must undergo in order (we may surmise) to learn to transfer his most passionate paternal hopes from his thirteen-year-old firstborn, the object of so much love[57] and the source of so much grief, to a son who is wholly and unmistakably—because miraculously—a blessing from God. Abram must learn that the paternity that counts most is the paternity utterly dependent upon God. The chosen people are emphatically not the same as the offspring of Abraham. Family, paternal love, descendants, are not by themselves the most important things. They can become truly important only when they are distinguished by singular or miraculous divine blessing.

When Abram is ninety-nine years old, the truly astonishing provisions of the covenant are revealed to him at last. Before we consider those provisions let us first note again how different the divine covenant, even in this case, is from the sort of covenant, and the interpretation of the biblical covenant, that has been made the ground of obligation by the modern political theorists of the social contract. At no point is Abram asked to give his *consent* to anything, and least of all to God's rule over him; nor is he ever asked to swear any oath; nothing really resembling a contract between two parties is made. As God later indicates, the only oath sworn was His own; Abram's part was obedience (Gen. 26:3 and 5), along with the vocation of teaching justice, understood to be the way of the Lord (Gen. 18:19). The Scripture paints a vivid contrast between the kind of covenant God makes with Abram (and Noah) and the very different kind of contractual covenants, forged by mutual promises and oaths, that are made between Abraham and Abimilech, and then later between Isaac and Abimilech, at Beer-sheba (Gen. 21:27–32, 26:28–31), or the mutual covenant sworn between Laban and Jacob in Gilead (Gen. 31:44–54).[58]

Hobbes nevertheless dares to claim that in this text (Gen. 17:7–8), *"Abraham promiseth for himselfe and his posterity to obey as God, the Lord that spake to him: and God on his part promiseth to Abraham the land of Canaan for an everlasting possession. . . .* [B]y which Abraham obligeth himself, and his posterity, in a peculiar manner to be subject to Gods positive Law."[59] In *De Cive* (16.4) Hobbes goes so far as to say that our text shows that "God wished to acquire obedience to himself by paying for it and through contract [*pretio & per contractum*]." Hobbes's imposition on the text, outrageous as it may be, is nonetheless illuminating. This "reading" helps us to see, by way of contrast, just how alien the authentic biblical notion is to the voluntarism, individualism, and utilitarianism of Hobbes's theory of contract. This is not to deny, of course, that at the foundation of this covenant there is, as we have seen, pervading Abraham's faith a deep sense of obligation, or of what is owed to God.[60]

When we focus on the specific provisions of God's promise or covenant, we are taken aback to find, to begin with (Gen. 17:4–8), that Abram is now informed for the first time that he is to be the progenitor not just of a single people, however great, but of very many different peoples—of a "multitude" (המון, *hamon*) of nations, ruled by many different kings. That, indeed, is the reason why his name is henceforth forever changed: to "father of a *multitude*" (אברהם, *Avra-ham;* not "father of a people" or even "father of the chosen people"). How are we to understand this momentous disclosure, made unforgettable by its becoming the basis for Abraham's new name? How can Abraham be *both* the father of a chosen, singular people and, simultaneously or by virtue of the same ascription, father of a "multitude of nations" or of different kingdoms? Are we not meant to see from the very outset that the mission or destiny of the chosen people is transcending of national particularity? Yet it is so in such a way as not to obliterate or to blur—nay, in such a way as, paradoxically, to heighten or to intensify—the chosen people's distinguished particularity. Let us also observe that God does not say that Abraham is to be the father of *all* nations; God does not articulate what could be called, strictly speaking, a cosmopolitan vision. The fact that all families will bless themselves by Abraham (Gen. 12:3) does not imply that they, still less their kings, will look upon him as their father (but contrast Rom. 4:11–12). The political shape of the future of Creation as a whole remains hazy, but there would appear to be foretold here at least three ranks of nations: the singular chosen people, the many peoples who will trace their lineage to Abraham, and other peoples who will not do so, even though as families they bless themselves by Abraham. And let us not forget that in His initial promise to bless those who blessed Abram, God also said that He would curse those who cursed Abram; Abram and his peoples will (always?) have enemies (see Calvin's *Commentary on Genesis* ad 12:3).

In the second place, God renews—that is, once again changes—the grant of land to Abraham and his posterity. The land that is promised to Abraham and his offspring is now limited again to Canaan. What is the meaning of this return from the expansive to the narrow land donation, immediately following the vast expansion of Abraham's promised progeny? Did the earlier, expansive promise, of all the land between the Nile and the Euphrates, refer to the land that was to be given to Ishmael's descendants as well as to Isaac's (cf. Gen. 13:14 and 17:8 with 15:18–21)? Or did it refer to some distant future, in which the Hebrews would spread their rule out from Canaan? But God does not suggest that the chosen people will establish a single empire with a single emperor or monarch. On the contrary, He speaks of kings, in the plural. Much later, at Gen. 35:11, God promises Jacob, when naming him Israel, that an "organized assembly" (or perhaps "league"; קהל) of nations shall spring from him (this answers the blessing or prayer of Isaac at Gen. 28:3). What is to be the precise political relationship between these Hebrew nations or kingdoms and the Ishmaelite nations or kingdoms? Between these and all the other nations of the earth? It is noteworthy that God does not say a word about future *republican,* let alone *democratic,* forms of rule. As father of many nations, Abraham is to be the father of many *kings.*[61]

Here the text seems to mark a pause in the amazing divine revelations (Gen. 17:9). But—to repeat our earlier observation—the Abram (now Abraham) who fell on his face does not raise his head to utter a word, much less pose any questions. This silent, submissive posture is apparently altogether gratifying to God, Who proceeds to a yet more staggering new provision of the covenant: the ritual mutilation of the genitals of all males in Abraham's household and all the males belonging to the peoples descended from Abraham.[62]

Not for a moment does the Scripture suggest or hint that circumcision was a practice adopted from or in imitation of any neighboring peoples—least of all the Egyptians, among whom Abraham had previously sojourned.[63] It is certainly not the case, as Westermann claims, that "according to Josh. 5:2–9 the Israelites took over the rite of circumcision when they came into the land of Canaan" (*Genesis 12–36*, 265; this is higher criticism run riot). As Maimonides—the greatest legal scholar, and also the preeminent medical authority, in traditional Judaism—teaches, the most obvious purpose of circumcision is the weakening of the male sexual capacity and pleasure: "The fact that circumcision weakens the faculty of sexual excitement and sometimes perhaps diminishes the pleasure is indubitable." Closely related would appear to be the aim of setting before any potential adult male convert the trial of submitting to a mark that incurs shame among most if not all other peoples, as well as being frighteningly painful: "Now a man does not perform this act upon himself or upon a son of his unless it be in consequence of a genuine belief. For it is not like an incision in the leg or a burn in the arm, but is a very, very hard thing."[64] Finally, this mark, and the gulf it establishes, not only distinguishes but unifies the chosen people. The peculiar nature of the pain, of the debility, and of the shame serves to underline the fact that dedication to God calls for a severe mastery over and ruthless subordination of sexual appetite and pleasure. It is surely no accident, Maimonides observes in the same passage just quoted, that it was the chaste Abraham who was the first to be called upon to enact ritual circumcision. But of course we must add that since the commandment applies to Ishmael as well as to Isaac, circumcision is the mark uniting those singular peoples, descended from Abraham, who recall not only his chastity but above all his dread in the presence of God; who share in that dread, and who understand the dread and the circumcision to be in part their response as mortal, hence reproductive, hence sexual, creatures—created in the image of God—to the presence of the holy or pure God Who as Creator utterly transcends His mortal, reproductive creatures, and especially their sexuality.[65]

The rebarbative severity of the circumcision commandment—which had brought Abraham to his feet, though he had dared utter no word—is closely linked to, and finds a glorious compensation in, the last wonderful piece of news. Only when Abraham painfully mutilates, and thus in a sense offers as sacrifice, his reproductive organ will God give, through it, His miraculous reproductive blessing. Sarah, past the age of menstruation (Gen. 18:11), is to bear Abraham a son, from whom, God emphatically adds, the promised multitude of nations and the kings of peoples will spring. In speaking previously of a multitude of nations and of kings, God did *not,* then, have in mind the descendants of Ishmael, He now makes clear. And we have noted before the evident pain or anxiety this causes Abraham in this scene. Nevertheless, Abraham's immediate response is to fall again on his face before the Lord and, this time—for the first time in his life in our hearing—to burst out in laughter.[66]

The promised son is to be called Isaac, "Laughter" (יצחק), evidently in memory of Abraham's laughter, the first laughter we have heard in the Bible, the exultant laughter of a pious man whose fondest hope has been fulfilled, against all hope, by the grace of God—a man for whom nothing is too difficult, for whom every pious hope is a potential reality.[67] But Isaac's name also immortalizes the later laughter of Sarah—the blame-worthy, dangerous laughter of a doubter, whose laughter came to be transfigured, through initial terror of the Lord, into a pious and grateful joy akin to that of her husband (cf. Gen. 17:17 with 18:12–15 and 21:6). Sarah, inspired to prophecy on that occasion, foretells that her unexpected and undeserved felicity at the birth of her own son is to inspire joyful exultation in all who hear of her motherhood; and we see again the intermingling of particular and universal promise that is characteristic of God's covenant with Abraham. Sarai, as the mother of royalty, is henceforth to be called Sarah, "Princess" (שרה). Her new name, no less than that of her husband, is a memorable reminder of the transnational future destiny of the chosen people. It would also appear to be, we may add, a reaffirmation of the monarchic or nonrepublican character of that future. The mark of circumcision, and the intense, chaste devotion to family that it partly signifies, defines the exclusivity of the chosen people. Yet those people are to be recognized as the model and the beacon for others. Besides, some of the "others"—the offspring of Ishmael (ישמע־אל, meaning "And God hears"; see Gen. 17:20)—belong within the group of the circumcised kin. We meet others, beyond the pale of kinship, who nonetheless know of and worship the one true God, without having had to learn of Him from Abram; the most prominent in the immediate context is Melchizidek (מלכי־צדק, "Righteous King"), the king of Salem and a priest of God, who called upon God as "maker of heaven and earth" and whose priesthood Abram recognized by donating to him a tithe from the spoils of war (Gen. 14:18–20). There are still others whom God visits in dreams—notably Abimilech (Gen. 20:3ff., 21:22–23). Others, in particular the Hittites, recognize Abraham as "one elevated by God among us" (Gen. 23:6). In short, the choosing and the elevation of Abraham and his seed by no means leaves the rest of mankind in spiritual darkness; Scripture suggests that there is no reason why those who encounter Abraham, directly or secondhand, should not recognize him as the "elevated one of God among us," and thus take to heart, or even imitate or join, the way of life of the Hebrews.[68]

Conversely, there is nothing in the covenant to suggest that the elevation of the chosen people justifies their turning their backs on the rest of the human race. All to the contrary, the Bible highlights and clarifies Abraham's special sense of responsibility for his fellow man by the incidents it narrates immediately after the report of the circumcision covenant that sets him and his household apart from the rest of humanity.

The Lord and two accompanying angels appear, in the form of three human travelers,[69] while Abraham rests at the entrance to his tent in the heat of the day—perhaps still recuperating from the circumcision (*Talmud, Baba Metzia 86b*). Abraham greets the strangers with a hospitality that is at once fervent, lavish, and delicately self-effacing. In his invitation, he offers, as his visitors' "servant," simply to provide them some water to wash their feet, a shady place to rest, and "a morsel of bread" (פת־לחם) before they continue their journey. When the unknown travelers accept, Abraham springs into action to provide a magnificent repast (Gen. 18:2–8). His hospitality is limned by the contrast with the utterly corrupt Sodomites' attempted homosexual rape of the two angels, still disguised as human travelers, the very same evening.

Yet there is one inhabitant of Sodom who is not depraved. Lot, who inhabits Sodom as a resident alien, exhibits an astonishingly sacrificial sense of the duty of hospitality, outstripping even that of his uncle. Only the angels' use of their special powers prevents the worst from happening to both Lot and to his daughters as a consequence of his heroic defense of the strangers.

CHAPTER EIGHT

Abraham at the Peak

THE BEHAVIOR OF THE SODOMITES WOULD SEEM FULLY TO JUSTIFY
God's decision to extirpate the city and everyone in it, with the exception
of Lot and his family; the Scripture stresses that the rapacious mob included "all of the people, in its entirety, from the young to the old" (Gen.
19:4).[1] But prior to the visit, God makes the portentous decision to allow
Abraham the opportunity to share in, or indeed to contribute to, the ver-
dict. More precisely, the Lord determines to inform Abraham of an investigation[2] that He, through His two angels, intends to carry out into the reports that have reached Him concerning the outrageous sinfulness of the
cities of Sodom and Gomorrah. And the narrator takes the remarkable
step of letting us listen to the conversation God had with Himself in determining so to inform Abraham, and thus to open up the possibility that
Abraham will respond by seeking to influence the divine deliberation.
This inner divine conversation lets us see directly the reason God takes
Abraham into His confidence; and that reason sheds clearer light on Abraham's mission, and on the meaning and purpose of the chosen people.[3]

For the reason is that Abraham is to "become a great and mighty
nation, and all the nations of the earth are to bless themselves by him,
because," God now explains, enlightening all of us as to His providential
design, "I have singled him out [literally, "I have known him"; ידעתיו] *so
that* he may command his children and his household after him to heed
the way of the Lord by doing what is just and in accordance with right
judgment [צדקה ומשפט; perhaps hendiadys], *so that,*" God does not fail to
add, "the Lord may bring to Abraham what He promised to him" (Gen.
18:18–19). Abraham is, in the words of Philo (*On Abraham* 4–6), "a living
rational law, the model for the later, particular written laws." The teaching
of justice, by precept and example, is the truest blessing Abraham represents for mankind.[4] The teaching of justice is the heart of Abraham's, and
the chosen people's, mission. Now, if Abraham is to teach his people—and
through his people, the world—what justice means in word and deed, he
must show that he knows what justice is; and for this it is not enough
merely to act justly and to obey God. God's soliciting Abraham's reaction

to the impending investigation is a necessary step in Abraham's testing and his education, but it is above all a showing forth, to us and for our meditation, of Abraham as an embodiment and thus as a teacher of the *knowledge* of justice. In reacting to God's disclosure of His intended judicial investigation, Abraham discloses—first for himself, and then, by his example, for all others—a new depth to his concern for justice.

Abraham's Insistence on Divine Justice

Abraham responds by venturing to remind God, fearfully and in all humility, but with relentless moral insistence, of the requirement that even God—that God above all—must adhere to *intelligible* justice.[5] Abraham here proves that his pious obedience is not a slavish submission, his terror not an abject terror. His compliance is not simply with God as the Almighty Ruler of all the earth; it is, most fundamentally, an obedience to God as "the Judge [השפט] of all the earth," and God as Judge sanctions a justice (משפט) that is not simply whatever He declares to be justice (Gen. 18:25). The Bible here teaches that God vindicates a concept of justice known to man, apart from—though of course indurated and clarified by—the fiat of God.[6] This justice that man knows independently of revelation, this justice that is presupposed by revelation, man can humbly call upon God to uphold.[7] Abraham brings to full explicitness here a crucial ingredient of his experience of God that was hitherto always implicit. He experiences the presence of God, and the call of God, conjoined with the experience and demand of an intelligible justice. Without this latter co-present experience and demand, it is impossible to imagine what the experience and call of God would be for Abraham. This is not to say for one moment, however, that the experience of God is ever, for Abraham, merely some kind of Kantian postulate evidently presupposed by or necessary to the experience of justice. As will be made vivid in the binding of Isaac, Abraham experiences God as the living God, as the shattering Presence, as the most important and unmistakable voice in his life. (From the biblical point of view, the adherent of philosophy indulges in the idlest of speculations if or when he wonders how this experience, and the apparent evidence it provides for the existence of the God experienced, would alter, for Abraham or for the countless others of us who have experienced some degree of something akin, if the intelligibility of the attribute of justice were to alter.)

We are certainly now given a deeper insight into what the Scripture means when it says that fear of the Lord is the beginning of wisdom; we now understand better one of the most important ingredients of that dread that descended upon Abram in the dream. Sheer terror, at God's overwhelming and mysteriously alien power to harm one, is doubtless present, at the core.[8] But counterbalancing and mitigating, and thereby defining, that terror, is awe—the conviction that one is in the presence of a Being superior not just in might but in right.[9] The fear of the Lord includes the trust that God will use His overwhelming power to uphold what is right and to chastise what is wrong. The fear of the Lord is the fear of one's Judge, and of His judgment. The fear presupposes one's awareness of one's own proclivity to do wrong, since "the devising of the heart of man is evil from his youth" (recall Gen. 8:21). The fearfulness before God is, then, simultaneously also a hopefulness and even a confidence before God; the fear of the Lord includes the belief that His power to inflict infinite suffering is inseparable from His power to do infinite good—each in proportion to merit, softened by mercy. In the words of Mary's Magnificat (Luke 1:50), "And his compassion, from generation to generation, is for those who fear him."[10]

But does not the fact that Abraham here repeatedly reminds or challenges God imply that he has some worry that God will not act justly, or will not do so unless prompted by Abraham to do so? It is certainly the case that Abraham feels the need to take an active role in pointing out to God and urging upon Him the just course of action. But there is no need to conclude that Abraham thinks it conceivable that God could act tyrannically, or in a deliberately or at any rate grossly unjust fashion. He may well suppose that the danger is that God would act without having taken full cognizance of the relevant but unobtrusive facts (i.e., of the presence in the city of an obscure scattering of righteous men). This does indeed imply that Abraham does not, at this moment, suppose God to be simply omniscient, or even meticulous in His investigations—and therefore in His judicial judgments. After all, in saying that He intended to carry out an investigation, God left Abraham with the impression that He was not, to begin with, in full possession of the relevant facts. Ibn Ezra takes this to mean that Abraham was aware that "God who is All knows the individual in a general rather than in a detailed manner." But then if the biblical, like the Aristotelian, God exercises only a general providence—since He does not cognize individuals because his pure and incorporeal intelligence is not immersed in the sense perceptions that depend on the organs of the body—how could God ever come to exercise the particular providence required by just judgment? How could He have saved Lot and his family in particular? Ibn Ezra laconically adds, "This interpretation is correct, although it is a great mystery." For our part, we must observe that at Gen. 19:13 the angels tell Lot that God sent them not to investigate but simply to destroy Sodom; in other words, God was in fact fully apprised of the moral character of the populace. In saying that He needed to investigate, it would appear that God told Abraham a benevolent and noble lie, in order to further the latter's education. And against Ibn Ezra, it would seem truer to the text to suggest that Abraham may have feared that God would be so revolted by the massive sinfulness of the vast majority in Sodom that He would overlook or not seek out the small and (comparatively) eclipsed just minority in the city. After all, this is by no means the sole occasion upon which Scripture shows how doubt concerning the evident justice in the workings of God's providence can afflict men who are exemplars of pro-found piety; it suffices to refer to David's Psalms.[11]

Let us now try to clarify more exactly the intelligible principle of justice to which Abraham calls the Lord's attention. Abraham implicitly agrees that the Sodomites, if wholly unjust, ought not to be left to wallow in their iniquity but ought to suffer in addition severe hurt, even capital punishment, even mass capital punishment. But, "will You sweep away the just along with the wicked" (Gen. 18:23)? To begin with, if a consid-erable number—fifty—of the Sodomites are exceptions, if they are just, then those fifty and their families ought to be immune to the punishment rightly visited on the unjust. Nay, Abraham goes further: the whole city ought to be forgiven (נשא) for their sake.

We are compelled to ask, How does the existence of a big enough number, or a large enough percentage, of righteous men somehow im-munize the rest of the population against otherwise deserved punish-ment? Abraham would seem to proceed on the premise of a certain degree of collective guilt or responsibility. Does he not conceive of the civic community as being to some extent a kind of whole, of which each of its members is a part? Does he not suppose that in a city—as in a family, though to a lesser degree—the life and deeds and spirit of each individual, living among and in daily intercourse with the rest, must shape and be shaped by the life and deeds and spirit of the rest? After all, the virtue of justice is an emphatically social virtue, which the righteous can practice only in and through their habitual interactions with their fellows. To find fifty men living a just way of life within a city would be to find a city that allows, even if it does not actively support, just social existence.[12]

But if this is so, then Abraham would be fearing that God might be quite careless in His inspection of the merits of the city. Perhaps, then, Abraham only means that though the city in its wickedness may be actively hostile to the just men and their attempt to lead lives reflecting justice, still, since the city at least tolerates so many just men in its midst, it should be spared at any rate the ultimate punishment.

Abraham may also have in mind the simple fact that the city in question is the righteous men's home, to which they are inevitably attached and whose protection and support, however exiguous, they need (consider here how even the heroic Lot lingers with regret when he is commanded to depart the totally devilish Sodom; Gen. 19:16–22).

In the event, God agrees, without explaining His principle, that if He finds fifty just men in Sodom, He will "*forgive* the whole place for their sake."[13] With the most humble pertinacity, Abraham takes another step. Suppose there are five less than fifty; will God destroy the whole city for want of the five? God replies that He will not destroy the city if He finds there forty-five just men. Neither Abraham nor God speak any longer of "forgiving" (נשׂא) the whole city. Does this mean that the city as a whole may suffer more or less serious punishment, but without being eradicated? If so, no explanation is offered of why the city that is the home of forty-five righteous men loses the immunity granted to, if not deserved by, the city that is the home of fifty. And what of a city in which there were fewer than ten just men? Would so few indicate a city in which there was no redeeming social significance to their presence?

Abraham did not begin by asking, What if only *one* just man is found in the city? And he does not continue to press God any further after He has agreed that if ten just men are found, the city will not be annihilated. Yet this need not mean that God is depicted here as not being equally provident for every last just individual.[14] There are good reasons of delicacy dictating Abraham's ceasing his questions at the point where he does. He indicates that he fears he may already have gone too far in pressing God. Does he not mean that he recognizes that he has received more than enough assurance that God will attend to the deserts of the just, no matter how few they be?

Moreover, it is reasonable to suppose that Abraham wishes to avoid any suspicion of special pleading for his nephew Lot and the latter's immediate family. To plead with God for a hypothetical single just man living in Sodom might suggest, if not necessarily deception, then perhaps self-deception, in Abraham's purportedly just concern for the fate of the anonymous righteous men of Sodom. For Abraham knows that Lot settled among the Sodomites. Throughout his dialogue with God, Abraham meticulously avoids any intercession for his kinsman. His expressed—and, I think we must understand, his genuine—concern is not for his nephew and the latter's family but rather for the fate of the nameless and unknown just among the alien Sodomites.[15]

In the event, of course, Lot proves himself to be a man of heroic justice and hospitality—the sole just man dwelling in Sodom—and God accordingly "remembered Abraham and removed Lot from the midst of the upheaval" (Gen. 19:29). In the light of what has preceded, God's "remembering Abraham" is most righteously understood, not in the sense of God's doing Abraham, through his family, a favor, but rather in the sense of God's bearing in mind Abraham as the evoker of the principle of justice to which Abraham had appealed. God does not, indeed, for the sake of the one just man refrain from destroying the city; instead, He simply saves the just man and offers his innocent family salvation as well. God, we may say, completes or spells out fully what was implied in and from the beginning of Abraham's abashed appeal to the idea of justice. God exemplifies the principle of just desert as He states it in His word delivered through the prophet Ezekiel.[16] No doubt God does also simultaneously gratify Abraham's family feeling. Abraham would be inhuman if he were not also concerned about the fate of his kin, and God would be inhumane were He not to appreciate that concern. But both show here that concern for kin is absolutely secondary to concern for justice, or, more precisely, to concern for the just deserts of those who are just. To be sure, since Abraham is himself dedicated to justice, and since he can reasonably hope that his nephew Lot remained just, resisting corruption, while living among the Sodomites, Abraham cannot simply divorce his concern for the fate and desert of the just or of those dedicated to justice from his concern for his own and his nephew's fate and desert. But he can implicitly insist that he makes the deserved welfare of his nephew and of himself strictly secondary, or subordinate, to his concern for the deserved welfare of the just as such. Indeed, his strict subordination of his concern for his own desert is a precondition of his and his family's becoming deserving.

This last thought might well lead one to ask, however, whether Abraham's passionate focus on the deserts of the just and unjust does not betray a concern for justice in which what is paramount is concern for the rewards—for the benefits one reaps, the immunities one wins, as a consequence of having been just. But if Abraham's, if the righteous man's, justice (and piety), if his apparent subordination or sacrifice of his own good, if his apparent devotion to the good of others, are all in fact pursued with a view to receiving the reward that enhances his own good or avoiding the penalty that detracts from it, then the just man would seem no longer to differ radically in motivation and goal from the unjust; the two sorts would seem to differ chiefly in the clarity and the accuracy of their insight into how to acquire what is best for themselves. Moreover, the just man would seem no longer so clearly to merit the recompense or reward for which he hopes, since he did not truly subordinate his own good to something beyond himself. The core of the just man's self-understanding would appear to become incoherent and self-canceling; for he aims at or devotes himself to attaining a good that will accrue to him only if he does not aim at or devote himself to attaining that good. It would appear necessary, then, to insist that Abraham, and the righteous man as such, while of course concerned for the benefit and happiness of the just, in some sense including himself, aims only secondarily at this goal (his own, or even their, deserved reward); the just person as such devotes himself primarily to justice (and piety) itself, and to God and God's law as the supreme instantiation of righteousness, which the Abrahamic man treasures apart from or even in the absence of reward. And such a person, in his loving concern for other humans (e.g., for his own son, such as Isaac), seeks and longs above all for their similar devotion and ordering of priorities. To be sure, this has the paradoxical implication that the just man's chief concern for those whom he loves is not for their good. Rather, his chief and overriding concern is for his loved ones' pious justice, which entails their subordination or even sacrifice of their good.

Yet even God, in the conversation with Himself that we were privileged to be given access to, spoke as follows: "I have singled him out *so that* he may command his children and his household after him to heed the way of the Lord by doing what is just and in accordance with right judgment, *so that* the Lord may bring to Abraham what He has promised to him" (Gen. 18:19; see also Deut. 6:24).[17] Nehama Leibowitz (*Studies in the Book of Genesis,* 168), responding to a deep unease expressed over

160

this passage by the rabbinic commentators, appeals to a comment by Nachmanides (ad Deut. 29:18) explaining that the meaning of the Hebrew term for "so that" here (*lemaʿan,* or לְמַעַן) does not necessarily suggest *purpose* but may mean simply *result,* even unintended; this, she claims, allows the conclusion that "the first *lemaʿan* in our text expresses result deliberately purposed by the subject, and the second, a situation where the man is the unconscious instrument, the result brought about without the deliberate intention of the doer. Abraham did not command his sons because he wished to receive reward but the reward came automatically."

The difficulty Leibowitz fails to note is that her suggested reading would mean that God too does not purpose the reward he promises, which would render His pronouncement incoherent; the second "so that" must refer to at least God's intended purpose. One is tempted to try to overcome the grave difficulty by distinguishing between two levels of the divine just purpose—between God's *chief* purpose (to promote justice, and thus to promote deliberate sacrifice or subordination of self-concern in Abraham and other just persons) and His *secondary* purpose (to distribute the fitting and justly deserved reward for such selflessness, and punishment for selfishness). Part of what makes Abraham meritorious would be that he—as a just person or in order to be just—maintains a similar set of priorities. Doing so would be following or "keeping" what God in this same crucial pronouncement (Gen. 18:19) declares to be "the way of the Lord" (דֶּרֶךְ יהוה). In order for a human "to understand and to know" God, he must understand and know Him as the Exerciser of justice; nay, he must understand and know that this is God's *pleasure,* that God "*takes delight*" in exercising justice (Jer. 9:22–23; see also Isa. 65:12, 66:4; Hos. 6.6). To follow this model would be to attain the good life, to be in the best human condition or to be blessed (Jer. 22:15–16; Isa. 26:7–8 and 56:1–2).

Yet then it is necessary to take another step, and thereby to confront a deeper perplexity. For does this last not imply that in devoting himself to justice and piety, the just man is necessarily thereby seeking his own greatest good and highest pleasure? Is he not aspiring to become sublime, is his soul not reaching for purification and exaltation and (as much as possible) assimilation to the divine, by his becoming or being just, by his enactment of what is right?[18] To the extent that he succeeds, does not the just man even thereby enjoy the most pleasant life, mirroring the "delight" God Himself takes in exercising justice? Does not knowing God as the Being Who delights in justice mean knowing that on the highest level justice is supremely good—good for, the joy and flourishing of, the one who is just—and that in being or pursuing justice knowingly, the just being knowingly pursues its own good? Is not aspiring to or seeking the "godlike" transfiguration of one's own soul, in and through the stern but invigorating exercise of justice and (merely apparent) "sacrificial" devotion, equivalent to the pursuit of the greatest of all conceivable goods for the very core of one's own being? Is not the deserved extrinsic reward *therefore* merely supplementary, and a matter of secondary concern? But why, then, would desert—punishment as well as reward—be a matter of any great concern? And more fundamentally, would this understanding of justice as the supreme benefit for the just person not take away the ground for a coherent notion of desert? For if in devoting himself to justice, if in becoming just, a man like Abraham fulfills and completes himself and is thus successfully devoted to his own greatest good and self-interest, how is it that he comes to merit great additional reward (compensatory benefit) beyond his justice? And how is it that the man devoted to injustice, who as such utterly abandons and harms to the utmost his own interest, comes to merit great additional (compensatory) harm? Abraham's passionate plea, a plea welcomed by God, for the deserving claim of the just to salvation, in the midst of the deserved destruction that must be visited upon the unjust, would seem to indicate the response that justice, taken together with piety, is *not* understood to be good for the just man; justice entails—not always, but in the decisively revealing cases—*sacrifice* of the just man's good, for the sake of something beyond himself, out of a concern that leaves behind self-concern. Justice, taken together with piety, is noble or sublime; and *as such*—that is, not as good, but rather as bad, for the just—justice is the all-important thing.[19] Whether this can in fact be maintained would seem to be a crux question we are prompted to address to the Bible's narration of Abraham's greatest trial.

The Binding of Isaac

"And it was after these things," the Scripture says, "that God tested Abraham" (Gen. 22:1). Of course Abraham has already been tested, in many major ways, yet the test that we must now contemplate eclipses all others. "*It was after these things*": in order to understand the precise nature of the test, and of the grandeur exhibited in Abraham's response, we must view this drama in the light of what has preceded.

The immediate antecedent is the "covenant" (Gen. 21:32) sworn between Abraham and Abimilech—an incident that, while not in itself of enormous import, nevertheless brings home again the sanctity of covenants from the biblical point of view, and thus recalls to our minds the supremely sacred covenant that God Himself has made with Abraham.

Previously, and of course far more passionately significant for Abraham, was the birth and then the weaning of Isaac, and the consequent expulsion of Ishmael from the household, leaving Isaac as Abraham's sole filial comfort.

Prior to this, the Scripture told of Abraham's attempted deceit of Abimilech, a narration that underlined (again) the length to which Abraham is ready and feels himself entitled to go in order to care for his own security, when he discerns no conflict with explicit divine injunction. (This story, as we have noted, would appear to suggest that there is no absolute biblical prohibition on lying or even on adultery.)

But most important and revealing of all was the amazing colloquy between God and Abraham on *justice* that preceded the destruction of Sodom and Gomorrah. Only if we bear that dialogue in mind will we reflect properly on, and appreciate correctly, the import of the fact that in this case, despite the horror of what is commanded, Abraham raises no objections. Seen as the sequel to Abraham's interrogation of God regarding the justice of his intended punishment of Sodom and Gomorrah, Abraham's unquestioning obedience in binding Isaac for slaughter cannot be viewed as a manifestation of an unwillingness or incapacity to challenge God as to His adherence to the standard of intelligible justice. The Bible, we may say, sets before us the task of trying to understand how or in what sense Abraham continues to recognize the justice of God even or especially in this most terrible demand.

The great philosophic moralist Kant, confident that this task is impossible, states in a nutshell his rejection and supposed refutation of the Bible by proclaiming this peak event as the paradigm of a falsifiable revelation:

> That it is not God whose voice he believes he hears man can in some cases
> be sure; for if that, which through it is commanded him, is contrary to the
> moral law, then no matter how majestic the apparition may be, and seem-

ing to surpass the whole of nature, he must consider it an illusion. We can use, as an example, the myth of the sacrifice that Abraham was going to make by butchering and burning his only son at God's command (the poor child, without knowing it, even brought the wood for the fire). Abraham should have replied to this supposedly divine voice: "That I ought not to kill my good son is quite certain; but that thou, who appearest to me, be God—of that I am not certain, and never can be," not even if this voice rings down from (visible) heaven.[20]

Looking back to the Scripture to discover a response to Kant's searing challenge, we may observe to begin with that this supreme call to Abraham confirms what we have already seen evidenced (most recently in the account of Abraham's deception of Abimilech): the biblical conception of justice is not confined by absolutely unexceptionable moral laws—including even the (almost total) prohibition on taking innocent human life. A fuller or higher dimension of justice than lawfulness in itself is the dimension of justice as the common good, which in its widest sense means the common good of all Creation, constituted by God's sagacious but inscrutable plan for the happiness of the whole, in accordance with desert. Yet we must never forget that the desert that trumps all other is the desert accorded to God Himself, and not merely because of or in accordance with what He has done for the rest. In sharp contrast to Kant, the Bible teaches that it is not law, it is not even divine law, it is only the divine Lawgiver, that is simply good, in and of itself—with a goodness that transcends even His activity of lawgiving or ruling. God as the perfect being, as the Holy One, simply because of His perfection or holiness, rightly claims the devoted subordination and even occasional sacrifice of each creature, including created law itself. Or in other words, justice demands that Creation pay tribute to a perfection in the Creator that transcends even His justice or creating. Moreover, while the Bible would seem to agree with Kant that God's justice—and, we may add, His perfection altogether—must as a whole be intelligibly recognizable to humans, it is precisely on the basis of that recognition that the Bible shows God permitting and commanding particular actions whose justice and goodness are not always entirely intelligible, and that therefore demand some crucial degree of faithful or trusting obedience. Yet we must immediately add that this means that God's serious demands cannot appear simply capricious or arbitrary from the human moral perspective. Let us then try to see how these general and still somewhat abstract principles become concretized and thus more real by trying to articulate what are the considerations of *justice,* recognizable by Abraham and by us, that forestall his questions on this gruesome occasion.

To begin with, it may be argued that the same facts that properly make Isaac uniquely precious to Abraham give God the *right* to ask for the sacrifice of him. Isaac was the wholly unexpected and undeserved gift of divine grace, a gift given not unqualifiedly but having as its unambiguously explicit purpose the fulfillment of the divine plan for the common good of the universe—a good culminating in devotion to the Godhead as the supreme and supremely demanding Good that is good-in-itself, and not only or chiefly a source of overflowing good for devoted humans. Only as such was the son to be supremely treasured by his human father Abraham. God now reveals that He has a plan far more complex or mysterious than the plan as it appeared to be communicated previously to Abraham. Part of God's plan, it now transpires, was the tempting and testing of Abraham to ensure that he would in fact utterly devote himself to God—following God's will even or especially when the son who was brought into being as the instrument of that plan proved to be recallable. The blessing that Isaac represents, it would appear, turns out to be even more ambiguous, even more of a temptation, than the blessing represented by the firstborn son, Ishmael. Just as Abraham had to learn to relinquish Ishmael, he must now learn not only to relinquish but personally to sacrifice (in the most literal sense) the even more beloved Isaac.

Yet Isaac is an innocent individual. Even if nothing is demanded from Abraham that he has a right to insist on keeping, is he not being asked to commit murder? Feeling this moral difficulty acutely, the Jewish tradition is full of commentary and Targumic translations that in various ways make Isaac a willing partner in the sacrifice.[21] But as Ibn Ezra stubbornly remarks in his commentary on these verses, "Scripture says nothing concerning Isaac's great self-sacrifice." And this accords with Isaac's being still a minor, wholly in the charge of his father. "If Isaac was an adult at this time," Ibn Ezra continues, "then his piety should have been revealed in the Scripture and his reward should be double that of his father for willingly having submitted himself to the sacrifice." But Isaac was not an adult; he was incapable of mature consent, and so the Scripture indicates no such consent (in striking contrast to Jephthah's daughter; Judg. 11:34–40). Nevertheless, and to repeat, the Abraham who has shortly before reaffirmed God's justice through daring questioning raises here no objection. Must we not understand Abraham to conceive of God as imbued with the right, as Creator and Ruler of the universe, but also on account of His perfection, to demand the sacrifice of any one of his innocent creatures for the greater good of His whole, crowned by Himself and the worship of Him—a good whose future and somehow all-encompassing fullness is known only to the just God?

Yet God promised, in a solemn covenant, that "Sarah your wife shall bear you a son, and you shall name him Isaac; and I will maintain My covenant with *him* as an everlasting covenant for *his* offspring after him" (Gen. 17:19). In asking for the immolation of Isaac, God breaks, or cancels, or retracts, the unambiguous words of His sworn covenant. How is this consonant with intelligible justice?

The principle of justice implicitly underlying God's commandment and Abraham's unquestioning obedience would seem to be this: in the case of a divine promise accruing to one's own benefit, one must be prepared to accept the apparent drastic modification of that promise and thereby to manifest one's greater devotion to God and to God's will than to any benefit, or any avoidance of harm, to oneself. Every covenant with God, it would seem, must be understood with this proviso—which would be, to say the least, a considerable qualification of divine covenant, but one that even the philosophic moralist at least entertains: "It is represented that when God bestows a promise on us, we are justified in demanding what he has promised us and expecting from his justice that it will be fulfilled. But promises of this kind, where someone pledges a wholly undeserved benefit to another, do not appear actually to bind the promisor to grant this benefit to the other. Or at least they do not give him the right to demand it" (Kant, *Lectures on Philosophical Theology*, 125).

But in the event, of course, God's promise holds. Through His angel, God prevents the sacrifice of Isaac. Through His angel, God reaffirms His covenantal promise and even slightly but significantly enlarges it. Not only are Abraham's descendants to be as numerous as the stars and the sands, they "shall take the gates of their enemies" (there will, then, indeed be need for war, but not, it would seem, forever; cf. Gen. 24:60). Not only will all the nations of the earth bless themselves by Abraham, they will bless themselves by his descendants as well (Gen. 22:17–18). Now, however, it is revealed to Abraham that all this has been contingent on, all this is the reward for, his willingness to sacrifice Isaac: "*because* you have

done this, and have not withheld your son, your one and only [יחידך]."
God, it would seem, always knew that this test was a provision of the
covenant, and doubtless also knew that Abraham would pass the test; God
was at no time in uncertainty as to whether He could keep the covenant
He swore.

After all, if God had actually allowed the sacrifice, then the God of the
Bible, His covenants, His word, His justice, His very holiness and perfection, would have utterly altered in their meaning. If God had broken or
retracted His solemn covenant, then it would follow that for His ad-
dressees there would be no telling when He would do so again. What is
more, if God breaks His explicit and unambiguous word, or if His promise must be understood with the proviso that it is retractable, then God
knows, in His wisdom, at the moment when He utters the word that it
does not mean what it says. His covenant or promise would then in the
decisive respect cease to be a covenant or promise, either for those to
whom it is addressed or for God Himself. But God is the Rock (Gen.
49:24): "The Rock! Whole is his action, for all His ways are of righteous
judgment [משפט]: a God of faithfulness [אמונה] and without injustice
[עול]; just [צדיק] and upright is He" (Deut. 32:4). God's covenant is more
solid than granite. Therefore, insofar as God lays, on those to whom He
has promised precious goods, the commandment that they sacrifice precisely those goods out of obedience to His will, this commandment is
seen from the divine perspective as a hurdle that the chosen must and will
vault in order to become deserving of those promised goods.

But this takes us to the deepest and most momentous puzzle in divine justice—concerning the human virtue that God tests and confirms
through His extraordinary demands. For if God knew that His righteousness necessarily implied that His covenantal commitment was unwavering, did not Abraham also know this—if or since Abraham knew God as a
just God? Yet if Abraham knew this, then in what sense could he ever
truly have believed he was being asked—nay, in what sense could he ever
truly have been asked—to sacrifice the goods promised to him by the
covenant? Let us note that the angel of God does not precisely say that as a
result of Abraham's evident readiness to slay his beloved son on the pyre,
God now knows that Abraham *loves,* or is devoted to, God; what the angel
precisely says is that now God knows that Abraham *fears* God (כי־רא אלהים
ידעתי; Gen. 22:12). What exactly is the new dimension of this "fear" that
is revealed in this all-important passage? Does the fear include a serious

doubt as to whether God keeps His word and solemn covenants? But would such a fear not be impious? Does not the pious fear of God include the awed certainty, the trust, that the just God abides by His covenants (though often in ways utterly unforeknowable to mankind)? That He sustains or saves, through often astonishing events, precisely those who, out of their God–given sense of justice and piety, show themselves ready to sacrifice everything they have to Him and to His just will? Is this not why Abraham tells his servants, on the third day of the horrible journey, that he *and Isaac* will return to them after worshipping? Is this not why, in answer to Isaac's bewildered question, Abraham assures his beloved son that the Lord will provide a sheep? To this sort of question Calvin responds that "the Apostle answers, that Abraham's confidence in God's word remained unshaken, because he could hope that God would be able to cause the promised benediction to spring up, even out of the ashes of Isaac (Heb. 11:19)."[22]

But if Abraham was confident that on account of a resurrection he would not in fact have to lose Isaac, does not the whole drama become rather histrionic? Would we not then have to suppose that while Abraham did believe that he had to bring about the momentary extinction of his son Isaac, he remained sure that in an utterly unforeseen and unforeseeable way, Isaac would spring again to life, and thus the apparent "sacrifice" would in fact lead to the fulfillment of the covenant, and thus of Abraham's hopes? But in that case Abraham never abandoned his deepest hopes; while momentarily "sacrificing" Isaac, he never sacrificed his long-range prospects; he never laid aside the guiding concern with his own good—as dependent, to be sure, on divine favor.[23] But for precisely what, then, was he subsequently rewarded? For having run the risks and made the temporary sacrifices reason can calculate to have been necessary in order best to secure his own interests? (See Heb. 11:19: Abraham "was rationally calculating [λογισάμενος] that God was able to raise from the dead.") Yet Abraham's desert depends on his having truly subordinated or abandoned his own good. The narrative risks losing not only its coherence but its bleak and moving grandeur when we attribute a long-range prudential motivation or understanding to Abraham. In the words of Martin Luther, "If he had known that this was only a trial, he would not have been tried. Such is the nature of our trials that while they last we cannot see to the end." "Abraham could not have believed," Luther continues, "that he was thus being tested, because then he would have remained certain of the promise, thinking, 'God is doing as parents are accustomed to do from time to time, when they test children and take away a treat or some such thing, that they soon thereafter restore'; but when God commands that the son be taken away, he leaves no hope, but simply leads Abraham into a contradiction—and God, who previously seemed the highest friend, now seems made an enemy and a Tyrant."[24]

We seem, then, compelled to recognize that during the period in which Abraham was responding to God's ghastly call—when he split and packed the wood, while he wended his way on the long three days' journey with his beloved son, when he (disingenuously) told his servants that he would return with Isaac, when he loaded the wood on the boy's back, when he (untruthfully) answered his son's touching question, when he bound the boy, and finally at the gruesome moment when he raised the knife—that during all this, the prophet was devastated by the thought that he was indeed sacrificing everything conceivably good for himself. But as Benno Jacob contends, was Abraham not precisely thereby, at some level, sustained and even exalted by the austere thought that he was achieving and exemplifying the highest virtue of character—that he was himself becoming a better being in the deepest sense, achieving the peak of human existence, through what he was choosing to do?[25] Or must we not carefully insist that in Abraham, during the decisive three days, there was no thought whatsoever of his own supreme good, of his own elevation in his devotion? Surely his sacrifice was to and for the God to Whom he was showing himself utterly devoted. Every hope was abandoned, and for the sake not of nothing but of God.

But what did Abraham conceive God to be, this Being to Whom Abraham was proving his utter dedication by total sacrifice? What did Abraham think gave God the undeniable claim to unqualified devotion?[26] Was He, is He, not the awesome God of the covenant,[27] the just Judge of all the earth? Is He not the guarantor of the universal common good, of the goodness of justice and devotion—above all for the just? "Abraham had a single consolation in this incredible temptation: that he knew he had a commandment from God" (Luther, LG, *Werke* 43:211). When the angel quotes God's very own words of resolution to reward Abraham mightily for his willingness to sacrifice his son, the angel reports (Gen. 22:16) God's swearing, for the sole time in the Hexateuch, the rare oath, "by Myself."[28] According to Isa. 45:23, God explains this singular oath as His invoking His attribute of justice (צדקה; see similarly Jer. 22:3–5, 44:22–26, 49:12–

13, 51:11–14; Amos 6:8). God here seems thus to indicate with passion and with awesome weight that in this resolution we see as clearly as we can ever see what God IS, in His own eyes, in His resolution to enact righteousness.

> Thus says Yahweh:
> Let not the wise man glory in his wisdom;
> And let not the mighty man glory in his might;
> Let not the rich man glory in his riches;
> But in this let him who glories glory:
> That he has insight [שכל] into and knows Me,
> That I am Yahweh, Who practice kindness,
> Justice and righteousness, on the earth. [Jer. 9:22–23]

Starting on the page following that from which the previous long quotation from Luther is taken, Luther proceeds to say, "I have stated what the trial of Abraham was, namely, the contradiction of the promise. Therefore his faith especially shines forth here, because he obeyed the commandment of God with such a prompt spirit, and because, although Isaac was to be sacrificed, nevertheless he in no way doubted the fulfillment of the promise, even though he was ignorant of the manner of fulfillment, while he trembled and feared—what else could a father do? Nonetheless, he clings to the promise, that in the future Isaac will have another descendant . . . even after a thousand years."[29]

Abraham's unequaled deed is infinitely clearer to us than the coherence of the thought that was in his heart. But no one asked him what he was thinking in his heart. Perhaps the Scripture means to leave this dialogue for us to articulate on our own; but perhaps it implicitly commands us not to press such questions too far (contrast Rembrandt's remarkable drawing depicting a deeply troubled young Isaac listening to his father's explanation).[30] The story of Abraham culminates in what is perhaps the deepest mystery of the Torah. We conclude that the pious righteousness that Abraham exemplifies is a virtue of action rather than of speech.[31]

Scripture records no further speech of God or His angels with Abraham. The remainder of Abraham's life story makes vivid the rewards God bestowed on him as the just deserts of his virtue—rewards whose premise must be that their anticipation could not have been motivating Abraham's mind throughout his radically sacrificial ordeal. It is notable that not only did he live to see his heir, Isaac, wealthy and well married (and the father of two sons), but in addition Abraham was granted a second large family. He was afforded not only the distant prospect of a kind of immortality to be achieved through a great nation of numerous generations of descendants and their vivid memories of him and his beloved Sarah; he also was granted the simpler and more direct gratification of living in the bosom of a prosperous home blessed with many fine sons. In short, we are inclined to say, Abraham died having been granted everything for which a father could reasonably wish. Furthermore, when we consider the fact, implicit in Genesis and made explicit by Isaiah (41:8; see also 2 Chron. 20:7), that God cared for Abraham as "My friend" (אהבי), it seems reasonable to conclude, as do the sages,[32] that God "loved" Abraham; and the love overflowing from eternal omnipotence is infinite in its potential blessing.[33]

CHAPTER NINE

Kierkegaard's Challenge

Søren Kierkegaard lays a deeply troubling challenge to any and every attempt such as ours, inspired by Socrates, to shed some light on what is at stake in the crux text recounting Abraham's binding of Isaac for sacrifice—and thus on the core teaching of Scripture altogether. If Kierkegaard is right, then the entire enterprise of this book is misguided; and therefore we cannot avoid a sustained confrontation with Kierkegaard. For Kierkegaard claims that the philosophic rationalism rooted in Socrates can never grasp the moral and human meaning of faith as it is paradigmatically exhibited in the story of Abraham on Mount Moriah: "If faith is nothing but what philosophy makes it out to be, then Socrates already went further, much further, whereas the contrary is true, that he never reached it."[1] The faith that authentically experiences God's commandments or their moral meaning remains "a paradox, inaccessible to thought" (66), "which no thought can master, because faith begins precisely there where thinking leaves off" (64). "Abraham is the representative of faith, and that faith is normally expressed in him whose life is not merely the most paradoxical that can be thought but so paradoxical that it cannot be thought at all" (67). Kierkegaard does not mean, however, that the moral meaning of the experience of faith is ineffable. He proceeds to demarcate that meaning by indicating the precise sense in which philosophic rationalism fails and errs in its attempt to comprehend it.[2]

Kierkegaard's argument may be characterized as having two moments, one more negative and one more positive, the first of which proves to be less disconcerting for philosophic rationalism than does the second. To begin with the negative and less perturbing moment, Kierkegaard asserts that the philosophers in their attempt to understand faith have ignored or avoided what he calls the "teleological suspension of the ethical," in which he finds the source of the "*angst*"—the profound moral dread, and concomitant "strife with God"—that is intrinsic to the crescendo moments of genuine faith. Kierkegaard takes it for granted that the ethical rationalism originated by the Greeks and above all Socrates reaches full maturity in the thought of Hegel (he refers in particular to Hegel's

Philosophy of Right, pt. 2, subsec. 3), who teaches that the ethical is the universal, to which the individual must subordinate himself; every moral imperative or commandment must be understood as a principle applicable to and obliging all moral beings. From this it follows, Kierkegaard observes, that every duty toward God is in fact such only incidentally, as a particular expression of a universal duty. Nay, the truly divine or highest becomes the universal ethical principle itself. " 'God' is used in an entirely abstract sense as the divine, i.e. the universal"; and the individuality of God "becomes an invisible vanishing point, a powerless thought" (78).[3]

Kierkegaard retorts that the living God experienced in faith is an Individual, or the supreme Individual, revealing Himself to chosen human individuals and surpassing in rank and priority any principle or set of principles. As is nowhere made more vivid than in the story of Abraham on Mount Moriah, the living God issues singular commandments to specific human individuals requiring and testing the capacity for "personal" worship of precisely this transmoral, supreme status of the Divine Individuality as "absolute." The purest manifestation of divine revelation comes in a call that tests a specific human individual's *angst*-ridden capacity to make a sacrifice that requires apparent violation of moral principle or law. Yet Kierkegaard adds that in the final analysis the violation is only apparent—Abraham is no murderer, though he would have to be on Hegelian or philosophic terms—for every moral principle and law must be understood to receive its true dignity from its subordination to the individual Creator. The call to Abraham presupposes and transcends dialectically, it does not set aside, the otherwise inviolate prohibition against a father's taking the life of his innocent and otherwise untroubled son, at least where the common good does not evidently require such killing. "The paradox can also be stated by saying that there is an absolute duty toward God. . . . [I]f this duty is absolute, the ethical is reduced to a position of relativity. From this, however, it does not follow that the ethical is to be abolished, but it acquires an entirely different expression, the paradoxical expression—that, for example, love to God may cause the knight of faith to give his love to his neighbor the opposite expression to that which, ethically speaking, is required by duty" (80). Kierkegaard denies that the binding of Isaac can be understood as analogous to "tragic" instances of human sacrifice, in which, on good Hegelian-rationalist grounds, the wrenching sacrifice of innocent life is justified by appeal from the lawful prohibition on murder to the higher, translegal but still moral, principle of the common good (it is thus that Kierkegaard understands not only Euripides' *Iphigenia at Aulis* but also Jephthah's slaying of his daughter): "For I should very much like to know how one would bring Abraham's act into relation with the universal, and whether it is possible to discover any connection whatever between what Abraham did and the universal—except the fact that he transgressed it. It was not for the sake of saving a people, not to maintain the idea of the state, that Abraham did this" (69–70).

As is clear from the thoughts presented earlier, we are inclined to respond that Kierkegaard exaggerates when he contends that the admitted paradox exhibited in the binding of Isaac is one that "suspends the ethical," at least as the ethical is articulated by classical rationalism. On the one hand, as we have tried to show, once one takes into account—as Kierkegaard does not adequately do—the overall scriptural context, or the story of Abraham taken as a whole, it is by no means implausible to ascribe to Abraham on Mount Moriah a conception of God as embodying that "universal" which is loving concern for the common good of the whole, governed by unvarying principles of distributive justice. And on the other hand, it turns out that Kierkegaard himself does not for one moment actually conceive of God as ever leaving behind His recognizably "universal" moral attributes as a just governor. As we have seen, Kierkegaard characterizes faithful obedience as an "absolute *duty*" that does "not abolish" but only gives "different, paradoxical expression" to the ethical. Accordingly, Kierkegaard allows himself to entertain only a mitigated version of the thought that God, leaving behind recognizable universal principles, "was only making sport of Abraham"; for Kierkegaard conceives of the "sport" as issuing in a future great and just recompense. What is more, Kierkegaard then almost immediately insists that, in any case, this thought—that God was whimsically playing with him on Mount Moriah—was not in Abraham's mind: "Abraham's faith was not of this sort, if there be such faith; for really this is not faith but . . . is separated from it by a yawning abyss within which despair carries on its game" (33–35). "Faith is convinced that God is concerned about the least things" (45). Above all, Kierkegaard explicitly grounds his discussion in a conception of God as ruling the universe in unwavering fidelity to the universal principle of distributive justice, which is realized in the "world of the spirit" though not in the "outward world" (38).[4]

This is by no means to deny Kierkegaard's point that the living God of

Scripture is an Individual Who is far more than abstract principle, far more even than His political attributes; and that the pious human individual's personal relationship to this richly mysterious and lovable but also fearful Individuality is not done justice by the Hegelian categories. But a moment's recollection of Homer suffices to make it clear that Kierkegaard has fallen too much under the Hegelian historicist spell when he writes that "such a relationship to the deity paganism did not know. The tragic hero does not enter into any private relationship with the deity, but for him the ethical is the divine" (70). By the same token, one can doubt on the basis of Aristotle's *Ethics* "the necessity of a new category if one would understand Abraham" in his recognition of a duty to sacrifice to the divine individuality strictly for the latter's own sake. Aristotle's account of the moral life drawn from general opinion supplements the peak of justice, understood as lawfulness, with another, prior peak of "magnanimity" or "greatness of soul," which exists not so much in "the universal" as in the individual who realizes this supreme virtue (*Ethics* 1123a34ff.). The individual Aristotle has primarily in view is a human, but the only specific individual example to which he refers in this context is Zeus, god of gods. The individual with greatness of soul possesses perfection and, what is more, crowns his excellence with a self-consciousness that demands from those who witness him the greatest of external goods: "that which we assign to the gods." Such a being is "pleased in a measured way by the greatest honors given by serious men, as thereby happening upon what belongs to him, or even less—for of completely perfect virtue there is no honor equal to what is deserved; not that he won't accept honor, since they are not able to distribute to him anything greater." Now, without diminishing the enormous distance between Aristotle and the Bible, and without denying that Aristotle would judge the commandment to sacrifice Isaac as so extreme as to be prima facie incredible, we submit that the demand is not one that so "suspends the ethical" as to exist in "other categories besides those which the Greeks possessed or which by consistent thinking can be derived from them" (65). Kierkegaard concedes that his case collapses "if in any way it is possible to explain how Abraham can be justified in sacrificing Isaac when thereby no profit accrues to the universal" (89).

Only now, after having cleared away Kierkegaard's misleading stress on the "suspension of the ethical," are we in a position to see clearly the more daunting aspect of his argument—which may well produce consternation in the Socratic rationalist. Kierkegaard insists that the philosophers remain stuck at attempting to comprehend pious sacrifice as a species of the tragic, or what he calls the "infinite resignation." This is, he grants, the first great moment in the unfolding or "dialectic" of faith—but only the first. This first devotional moment may well express "love of God," but this tragic-heroic love of God is not yet that joyfully anguished experience of the intimate presence of God in one's existence that truly deserves the name "faith." The tragic-heroic love of God is at most "the surrogate for faith," which is still missing. The tragic hero sacrifices to God—or to whatever he conceives to be highest—that finite being which he most loves in earthly existence, having abandoned every falsely comforting expectation of saving the finite sacrificial beloved or receiving it back. But in enacting this virtue, "the knight of infinite resignation" is at some level confident of winning—though not out of belief in his own merit, if he is a Christian knight—the infinite: "What I gain is myself in my eternal consciousness." "A purely human courage is required to renounce the whole of the temporal to gain the eternal; but this I gain, and to all eternity I cannot renounce it" (59). Now, in this tragic experience Kierkegaard for his part sees no inconsistency: "There is no absurdity in this for the understanding" (57). Yet the author of *Fear and Trembling* stresses that if or insofar as he can imagine himself taking Abraham's place and acting only in this tragic spirit and not going beyond this, then he "would not have loved Isaac as Abraham loved": "That I loved him with all my soul is the presumption apart from which the whole thing becomes a crime, but yet I did not love like Abraham," since "if I had got Isaac back again, I would have been in embarrassment." For "he who with all the infinity of his soul has performed the infinite movement and cannot do more, only retains Isaac with pain"—and this shows that at bottom I made the infinite movement "in order to find myself and again repose in myself": "For he who loves God without faith reflects upon himself, he who loves God believingly reflects upon God" (46–47).

So what sort of reflection upon God is this, that distinguishes the truly believing Abrahamic love of God? What is this belief or faith that dialectically incorporates but transcends the moment of infinite resignation? Kierkegaard answers, "Abraham believed":

All that time he believed—he believed that God would not require Isaac of him, whereas he was willing nonetheless to sacrifice him if it was required. He believed by virtue of the absurd; for there could be no question of human calculation, and it was indeed absurd that God who required it of him should the next instant recall the requirement. . . . Let us go further. We let Isaac be really sacrificed. Abraham believed. He did not believe that some day he would be blessed in the beyond, but that he would be happy here in the world. God would give him a new Isaac, could recall to life him who had been sacrificed. He believed by virtue of the absurd; for all human reckoning had long since ceased to function. [46–47]

At first one might think that Kierkegaard means to say that the two moments—of resignation, and of confidence in recovery—are successive, or separated by, at the very least, a moment of time; but this proves a misleading impression. It is only the unbelievers, the tragic heroes, who "vacillate an instant, and this vacillation shows that after all they are strangers in the world" (52). The man of true faith "every instant is making the movements of infinity," "but he does this with such correctness and assurance that he constantly gets the finite out of it, and there is not a second when one has a notion of anything else" (51). On the one hand to make a committed "movement" to sacrifice what one most treasures, and on the other hand to believe *simultaneously*, with serene confidence, that one has *thereby* already won the secure possession or immediate reposses-sion of what one "sacrifices"—this is utterly "absurd," because patently self-contradictory (affirming what is denied in the same breath). But according to Kierkegaard, the fully self-conscious realization of this in-coherence is so far from having the effect of making faith tied to such absurdity evaporate that it turns out to be the "divine madness" in which alone genuine faith thrives and finds its "elevation." The paradox of faith

on the one side has the expression for the extremest egoism (doing the dreadful thing it does for one's own sake); on the other side the expression for the most absolute self-sacrifice (doing it for God's sake); . . . faith is this paradox, and the individual absolutely cannot make himself intelligible to anybody. [81] . . . To be able to lose one's reason, and therefore the whole of finiteness of which reason is the broker, and then by virtue of the absurd to gain precisely the same finiteness—that appalls my soul, but I do not for this reason say that it is something lowly, since on the contrary it is the only prodigy. [86]

"Humanly speaking," the fully self-conscious believer "is crazy and can-not make himself intelligible to anyone. And yet it is the mildest expression, to say that he is crazy" (86).[5] This "dialectic of faith is the finest and most remarkable of all; it possesses an elevation, of which indeed I can form a conception, but nothing more" (47). According to Kierkegaard, it is in this absurd dialectic and only in this state that the human conscious-ness genuinely experiences God's call, hears the angel, and is vouchsafed the otherwise inarticulable vision of the ultimate divine reality that totally dethrones human reason. This state of quasi insanity is not one that a human can induce in himself by himself; it is a "miracle."[6]

Kierkegaard's testimony to the meaning of faith as exemplified in Abra-ham can hardly be dismissed as that of someone lacking intelligence or moral seriousness, who is pontificating about an experience that he can safely be presumed never himself to have had.[7] And the fact that Kierke-gaard shows a deep misunderstanding of what Socrates was about—he characterizes Socrates' life (the "most interesting life ever recorded") as centered on an awareness of ignorance that makes him an "intellectual tragic hero" (79, 92, 110n, 126)—suggests that the challenge cannot be dismissed as constructed artificially by a debater who saw clearly what his refuter was aiming at and proceeded cleverly to figure out what response might eristically confound his opponent. But precisely because we take Kierkegaard's testimony and claim with the utmost seriousness, we have every right and duty to ask what evidence supports it. Do any believers report unambiguously and clearly that their religious experience is cen-tered on the specific absurdity that Kierkegaard describes? The experi-ence may be at its core "unthinkable," but it, *and certain criteria for it,* are by no means incommunicable: "Whether the individual is in temptation or is a knight of faith only the individual can decide. Nevertheless it is possible to construct from the paradox several criteria which he too can understand who is not within the paradox" (89). Through deploying these criteria "one may have an opportunity to see whether the move-ment on the part of a particular person is true or fictitious" (55). And on one thing we agree absolutely with Kierkegaard: his emphatic declaration that "a free-born soul" would "above all not permit his soul to be de-ceived by itself" (61). Now, Kierkegaard readily admits that his interpreta-tion of Abraham is controversial or hardly self-evident and hence does not constitute decisive evidence in itself.[8] He further concedes that "perhaps it is not possible to do what the believer proposes, since it is indeed unthinkable." "Or if it could be done, but the individual had misunder-stood the deity—what can save him?" (71). Kierkegaard himself stresses that what is decisive in determining the truth of his claim—namely, the claim that a specific, self-conscious, absurdity that is tantamount to a kind of insanity defines the existence of Abraham and of every believer who truly experiences God's call—is empirical evidence of the existence, "the relation to reality," of such believers: "Upon this everything turns," since, Kierkegaard concedes, "the prodigy is so likely to be delusive" (52).

Kierkegaard is insistent that belief is not belief—it is merely Philistinism masquerading as belief—unless it begins in the moment of infinite resignation, of anguished sacrifice that seeks eternity beyond. Without that, one "sucks worldly wisdom out of the paradox" and seeks to "swindle God out of the first movement of faith." Kierkegaard is still more insistent on what it is that elevates faith beyond tragic heroism: the confidence in having won guaranteed immediate possession or repossession of that which was committed to "sacrifice" (he never provides a comment on Matt. 27:46, Mark 15:34). Now, as Kierkegaard points out, this has the discomfiting evidentiary consequence that while the "knights of the infinite resignation are easily recognized," those "who carry the jewel of faith are *likely to be delusive,* because their outward appearance bears a striking resemblance to that which both the infinite resignation and faith profoundly despise—to Philistinism" (49; my italics).[9] The author of *Fear and Trembling* goes further: he candidly confesses that "in my practice I have not found any reliable example of the knight of faith, though I would not therefore deny that every second man may be such an example." Of still greater moment, he repeatedly declares that he himself has no personal experience whatsoever of such faith. While he admires Abraham in a "crazy way," he cannot really "comprehend" him; while he can *think* himself into the tragic hero, "into Abraham I cannot think myself" (44–45, 48; see also 51). But here we must not overlook the fact that Kierkegaard ascribes this book to a pseudonymous author by the name of Johannes de Silentio; and this appears to mean that for didactic purposes Kierkegaard has ironically hidden or only pointed off toward what may be his own decisive personal (and postphilosophic) experience of revelation.[10]

But is Kierkegaard's implicit testimony to the character of that experience unwavering? In fact, his disturbing claim becomes more problematic on its own terms (and therefore less disturbing) as the "dialectical lyric" of *Fear and Trembling* unfolds. For as the work proceeds, the author is drawn into describing the experience of faith in categories that bring it, willy-nilly, into closer and closer congruence with the supposedly superseded

Socratic interpretation of faith as an extreme form of tragic heroism or resignation looking to eternity.

At first we hear, as we expect, that the man of faith lives "joyfully and happily every instant by virtue of the absurd"—"every instant" seeing "the sword hanging over the head of the beloved," finding not "repose in the pain of resignation, but joy by virtue of the absurd" (61). We are assured that despite faith's *angst*-ridden moment, the man of faith lives in "the most beautiful and assured harmony with existence" (60). The "simple" man of faith outdoes the impressively tragic "dancer" in his unique ability "to transform the leap of life into a walk, absolutely to express the sublime in the pedestrian" (51–52). The man of faith manifests such everyday satisfaction that he is easily mistaken for the Philistine: "He belongs entirely to the world, no Philistine more so" (50). He does not fundamentally regard his life as a heroic resignation or sacrifice from which he looks and hopes for a distant reward in a future eternity (for then what would at bottom distinguish the "knight of faith" from the tragic hero?). Abraham "did not believe that some day he would be blessed in the beyond, but that he would be happy here in the world" (46–47). When the apparently terrible call came, Abraham answered "joyfully, buoyantly, confidently, with a loud voice—'Here Am I.' We read further: 'And Abraham rose early in the morning'—as though it were to a festival" (36).

But even or precisely in the midst of this initial celebration of the temporal joy suffusing Abraham's experience of the acme of faith, Kierkegaard betrays the fact that, contrary to his claim that this experience is continuous and continuously satisfying, what Abraham won above all by his single moment of "faith" was emphatically *not* a continuation of the paradigmatic experience of faith but rather liberation forever from that terrible moment, and projection toward a future happiness in the fulfilled promise of personal immortality: "In marching home from Mount Moriah thou hadst no need of a panegyric which might console thee for thy loss; for thou didst gain all and didst retain Isaac. Was it not so? *Never again* did the Lord take him from thee, but thou didst sit at table joyfully with him in thy tent, *as thou dost in the beyond to all eternity*" (37; my italics).

In the latter part of the essay, this hint of a predominant "infinite resignation" in Abraham burgeons until the portrait of Abraham (or of the man of faith) as sufferer living in hope of joy beyond this life replaces the portrait of him as reveler surmounting *angst*. We hear that "martyrdom," and the consequent deserved hope for immortality, is greater, not less, in the man of faith than in the tragic hero; we hear that faith is distinguished from tragic heroism not by its winning immediate temporal joy but by its existing in a more austere resignation: "Even the most tried of tragic heroes walks with a dancing step compared with the knight of faith, who comes slowly creeping forward." One who perceives the "terrible" suffering of faith

> will at least have a presentiment of the marvelous glory this knight attains in the fact that he becomes God's intimate acquaintance, the Lord's friend, and (to speak quite humanly) that he says "Thou" to God in heaven, whereas even the tragic hero only addresses Him in the third person.
>
> The tragic hero is soon ready and has soon finished the fight, he makes the infinite movement and then is secure in the universal. The knight of faith, on the other hand, is kept sleepless, for he is constantly tried. . . . The hero's concentration Abraham also has, even though in his case it is far more difficult. [88–89]

The "knight of faith" undergoes "the martyrdom of being uncomprehended" (90), while "the tragic hero does not know the terrible responsibility of solitude"; for the man of faith, his "unutterable sighs are torture" (123). But as a consequence of this tortured martyrdom, "think what he attained! . . . [Y]ea, so completely has he forgotten it that afterwards there would not even be the least inkling of his pain if God Himself did not recall it, for God sees in secret and knows the distress and counts the tears and forgets nothing" (129).

Thus (as Socrates would have predicted) Kierkegaard would appear to be incapable of steadfastly sticking with his attempt to attribute to the faith of Abraham, or of anyone, the absurd or indeed insane specific contradiction originally claimed.[11] He is drawn back to a recognizably traditional or "pre-Kierkegaardian," Socratic, understanding of faith in terms of "infinite resignation" or tragic heroism—in which, Kierkegaard has stressed, he at any rate discerns no fundamental contradiction. We are left doubting whether Kierkegaard ever fully grasped in his bones, or found it possible to live believing in, what was meant when he characterized faith as self-consciously and unabashedly "absurd" in his original, precise, anti-Socratic sense; and so we find even Kierkegaard's own testimony to, or interpretation of, religious experience indecisive in supporting his deeply disquieting claim.

Conclusion

PATRIARCHY, THE SCRIPTURE TEACHES, IS THE CORNERSTONE OF THE right way of life for mankind. The chosen people are a people of patriarchal families. Genesis presents, for all the future generations, models that are meant to guide the Hebrew fathers (and, through them, all fathers everywhere) in their understanding of their sublime responsibilities—and of the grave dangers and temptations that attend those responsibilities. Through the story of Abraham the Bible shows forth the exemplary patriarch, in all his pious glory. But patriarchy in and of itself, even patriarchy inspired by the model of Abraham, is far from sufficient. In Abraham's successors, Isaac and Jacob, we witness the decisive limitations of patriarchy, the problems that necessarily attend patriarchy, even when sprung from an Abraham:[1] we learn the crucial reasons why a society of patriarchs requires broadening to a fraternal society (consider Gen. 50:18—end) regulated and guided by a detailed legal code, by the rule of law, finally enforced by a lawful King of Kings.

What Scripture will mean by the rule of law is the absolute rule of positive divine law: a code of law made for, but not by, men; a code of law recognizable as wise by human reason (Deut. 4:6–8; cf. 26:18–19) but not deducible from human nature by human reason. In order to understand the character and the need for such a rule of divine positive law, Israel (and we, vicariously) must first experience the unqualified rule of man over man, unlimited by any such higher positive law; and in order to grasp fully what such rule implies, in order to see the ultimate direction toward which it tends, we must watch as the seed of Jacob experience life under a purely human regime in its full development.[2] We must witness the great drama of Egyptian enslavement and Mosaic liberation—the drama whose culmination is the promulgation and reception of the divine law. This legislation lies at the heart of the magnificent structure of the Torah, and its exploration would be, and has been—in the hands of Maimonides above all—the peak of the encounter between political philosophy and the Bible.

The present book has confined itself to a preliminary task: that of probing and clarifying the divine law's foundations, laid down in Genesis. At the beginning of Genesis we were confronted with the challenge of the biblical conception of omnipotence, with its correlate, Creation. Then the account of the eating of the fruit of the Tree of Knowledge put squarely before us the Bible's root understanding of sin and of human responsibility for evil. Through following the subsequent unfolding of mankind's story from the murder of Abel to the destruction of Babel, we began to grasp the scriptural justification for a, or rather the, chosen people—and thereby the basic premises of the political science or royal art implicitly ascribed by the Scripture to Divinity. In the figure and the drama of the exemplary Abraham we learned the decisive lesson about the Bible's understanding of what is humanly most admirable or meritorious.

I hope to have demonstrated how these foundational teachings of the Bible are illuminated when they are interrogated from the perspective of political philosophy. At the same time, I have tried to indicate how political philosophy can contribute to clarifying and legitimating its own doings through such an interrogation. This dialogue requires an approach to the Scripture that treats it as a text to be heeded, and questioned in all seriousness, because one takes seriously the possibility that it may provide the answer to the most important question—the question, How ought I to live? If the Bible is true, then what is called for above all is obedience to the biblical God as simply authoritative. Philosophy as such—so long as it remains true to itself—cannot wholly surrender to such obedience, but philosophy can strive to understand what it might mean to do so; philosophy can thereby bring the legitimacy of its own independence into question, and can thereby seriously entertain the possibility of such surrender. But since this very questioning, since this very interrogation of philosophy by philosophy, remains a philosophic self-questioning, there is entailed a simultaneous questioning of what it is we ought to be and to do, if we are or were to accept the Bible's authority. And given what we have seen to be the anchoring role of justice in the Bible's teaching about itself and about God, there is absolutely required, sooner or later, the raising and the answering of the question, What is justice (righteousness)? What is contained in this OUGHT, how is it intelligible, and to what extent must it be intelligible? Most profoundly, one is required to live with, and to observe what one undergoes when and as one lives with, the full answer that emerges. The danger for us today is that we remain at too great a skeptical distance ever to enter into such a dialogue and such an excogitation; and therefore we risk wallowing in longing for God instead of grappling with God—as Jacob and Socrates, each in his radically different way, teach us to do.[3]

Notes

Introduction

1. In the century that saw the most intense theological and philosophic commentary on the Bible, the overwhelming emphasis was on this portion of the book of Genesis. See Williams, *The Common Expositor,* chap. 1. See also the remarks of Westermann, *Genesis 1–11,* ix and 1.

2. "Ut homines humanis sensibus et humanis rationcinationibus" (St. Augustine *The City of God against the Pagans* [henceforth cited as *City of God*] 18.41 beg.; cf. 18.37 beg.). See also Calvin, *Institutes of the Christian Religion* (henceforth cited as *Institutes*), 2.2.3, commenting on Cicero's *On the Nature of the Gods* 3.88: "There you have in sum the conviction of the philosophers, namely, that the reason which is in the human understanding suffices to conduct us well and to show us what is good to do." For Calvin's explicit criticism of Socrates on account of this, see 1.5.13; for the grave existential implications of this criticism, see esp. 1.10.3 and 1.14.10. The great political theologian John Milton—chief theorist and state paper writer of Cromwell's regime—presents in his *Paradise Lost* Socratic dialectic as the preoccupation of the most rational of Satan's fallen angels as they confront their own eternal damnation: "Of good and evil much they argu'd then, / Of happiness and final misery, / Passion and Apathy, and glory and shame, / Vain wisdom all, and false Philosophy: / Yet with a pleasing sorcery could charm / Pain for a while or anguish, and excite / Fallacious hope, or arm th' obdured breast / With stubborn patience as with triple steel" (2.555–69; see also 10.830). According to Milton's *Paradise Regained,* Satan's temptation of Christ culminated in an attempt to impress the latter with the wisdom of Socrates and the wise proponents of the virtuous contemplative life exemplified by Socrates. See the dialogue between Satan and Christ at 4.235ff. and esp. 309–11, where Christ exclaims, of Socrates and all those who follow in his wake, "Alas! What can they teach, and not mislead, / Ignorant of themselves, of God much more, / And how the World began, and how Man fell, / Degraded by himself, on grace depending?" See also Milton's *Christian Doctrine,* 1.13 beg.: "I assume that no one thinks you should look for truth among philosophers and schoolmen rather than the Bible!" And see Martin Luther's *Lectures on Genesis* (henceforth cited as LG, with references to volume and page of the Weimar Kritische Gesamtausgabe as *Werke*), 43:94 and 240, 241.

3. See, e.g., Locke, *Essay Concerning Human Understanding,* 4.18.7–10.

4. Xenophon *Apology of Socrates to the Jury* 4–9. See, in a similar vein, Cicero's interpretation of his own personal religious experience as reported in *On Divination* 1.58–59.

5. Aristotle *On Prophecy in Sleep* 462b21–22, 463b15, and 464a21–22. Contrast Maimonides *Guide of the Perplexed* (henceforth cited as *Guide*) 2.36. See also Aristotle *Nicomachean Ethics* (henceforth cited as *Ethics*) 1179a22–32 and the pronouncement of Apollonius of Tyana (the greatest pagan saint or prophet of whom we have extensive hagiographic records, born ca. A.D. 172) to the king of India: "The gods' first providential care is for those who philosophize with virtue; and secondly for those who are sinless and are reputed never to have committed any injustice. They grant to those who philosophize the sound understanding of the difference between the divine and the human things; but to those who are otherwise decent in their lives they grant a sufficiency, so that these latter will not become unjust through at some time being in want of the necessities" (in the account of Flavius Philostratus *Things Pertaining to Apollonius of Tyana* 2.39; see also 3.18 end).

6. *The Incoherence of the Incoherence,* as quoted and translated in Kogan, *Averroës and the Metaphysics of Causation,* 222. Cf. Aristotle *Metaphysics* 1047b31–48a24 and esp. 1048a13–14.

7. A comment such as that of Gerhard May (*Creatio ex Nihilo,* 4 n. 10: "For Plutarch," the true being or "ὄντως ὄν is God—for Plato it is the Ideas: *Phaedr.* 247e; *Repub.* 10 597d; *Tim.* 27d–28a") drastically oversimplifies. In the context of the very passage May cites here from the *Republic* (597bff.), Plato has Socrates suggesting that the Ideas are made by God. But above all, such a characterization ignores the theology of Plato's *Laws,* with its conspicuous silence on the Ideas. As has been judiciously remarked, Plato's *Laws* provide us with our "most differentiated and most intensive image of polis religion. At the same time the essential lines of the situation which was to hold for the next 600 years becomes visible: the conflict between philosophical and traditional religion is denied" (Burkert, *Greek Religion,* 337; see also 325: "Plato himself feels free to speak about god and gods only at the playful level of myth"; and 327: "Plato kept it his secret").

8. *Stromata* 5.4.24; 5.9.56; 5.10.65 and 66; see also 5.14.89–90. See similarly Augustine *City of God* 6.1, 6.4, 7.5.

9. Locke, *The Reasonableness of Christianity as Delivered in the Scriptures* (henceforth cited as *Reasonableness of Christianity*), 144.

10. Ibid., 155 and 158. There is a gulf between this assessment of the status of revelation and that taught by Maimonides. The latter does not tire of repeating the pronouncement of the Talmudic sages that "the Torah speaketh in the language of the sons of man"—meaning, according to Maimonides, that the

Bible speaks in accordance with "the imagination of the multitude," thereby bespeaking the "wily graciousness" of God (*Babylonian Talmud* [henceforth, unless otherwise indicated, the source of our Talmudic citations], Yevamoth 71a and Baba Metzia 31b; Maimonides *Guide* 1.14, 26, 29, 33, 46, 53, 57, 59; 3.13, 32, 54; see also 2.47). But Maimonides insists that especially the highest, Mosaic, revelation discloses a truth or truths that crosses and thus humbles philosophic reason (see esp. *Guide* 2.17, 20, and 25). Compare Pascal, who invokes the Talmud and Maimonides in insisting that "proof" of the truth of the Bible depends on uncovering the "double" or "hidden" or "secret" sense of the prophecies in it, but who insists that the clue to the hidden meanings must be found within the New Testament (*Pensées*, #274–76, 501–3 [= Brunschvicg #642–43, 691, 659, 571, 675]; and see #272 [= B. #687]: "It is not permitted to attribute to Scripture meanings that it has not revealed to us that it has. . . . Still less to say that this is the manner of the philosopher's stone"). See also Calvin, *Institutes,* 1.13.1. Milton, it is to be noted, resists all esoteric interpretation of the Bible: "Let there be no question about it: they understand best what God is like who adjust their understanding to the word of God, for he has adjusted his word to our understanding, and has shown what kind of an idea of him he wishes us to have" (*Christian Doctrine,* 1.2, p. 136).

11. *Ethics* 1178b8–12. See also *Politics* 1325b29–30. There is no need to quote here Hobbes's blasphemous remarks (*On the Citizen* 15.14) on this Aristotelian conception of God.

12. *Leviathan, with Selected Variants from the Latin Edition of 1688,* ed. Curley, chaps. 12, paras. 6–8 (in the light of appendix to Latin ed., chap. 3, paras. 6–8) and chap. 31, paras. 2–5. All subsequent references to *Leviathan* will be to the useful paragraph numbers in this excellent edition.

13. See Pangle, "A Critique of Hobbes's Critique of Biblical and Natural Religion" and *The Spirit of Modern Republicanism,* part 3.

14. *Pensées*, #131 ("Humiliez-vous, raison impuissante!") and the section of his thoughts that Pascal himself labeled "Soumission et Usage de la Raison," esp. #167, 170, 173, 174, as well as 235 (= Brunschvicg #434, 269, 268, 273, 270, 771). Compare, however, #200 and 505, as well as 821 (= B. 347, 260, 252).

15. *Confessions* 10.6. See similarly Calvin, *Institutes,* 1.5.13 (1.5.14 in Latin version) and 3.2.14–15. Augustine, imagining a personal meeting with Moses in which he could ask and get answers in Latin as to what was intended by the words of Genesis, turns to ask of God rhetorically, "But if I could understand him, how would I *know* he was speaking the truth? If I learned this, would it be from him?—Within me, within the very home of my thinking, without Hebrew or Greek or Latin or barbarian tongue, Truth, without the organs of ear or tongue, nor the sound of syllables, would say: 'he speaks the truth!'; and I would immediately with *certainty* say to that human, Your servant: 'You speak the

truth!' " (*Confessions* 11.3). See also 2 Pet. 1:16–21, together with Matt. 17:1–
9; 1 Cor. 2:12 ("But we have not received the spirit of the cosmos, rather the
spirit that is from God, so that we might have *knowledge* of the things granted to
us through grace by God") and 13:9 ("for we *know* in part"); 2 Tim. 1:11–12
("but I am not ashamed: for I have *knowledge* of what I believe in"); 1 John 2:20
("And you have an anointment from the Holy One, and you *know* all things. I
have not written to you because you do not have *knowledge* of the truth, but
because you do have *knowledge* of it"); and Heb. 11:1 ("faith is proof-rooted-in-
the-test-of-cross-examination [ἔλεγχος] of matters that are invisible"). "It follows," Milton comments, "that implicit faith, which blindly accepts and so
believes, is not real faith at all. Unless, that is, it is only a temporary state, as in
novices and new converts . . . or in those who are dull of understanding and
practically unteachable" (*Christian Doctrine*, 1.20, p. 472). Contrast the amazingly weak, late-modern characterization of "faith," and of the meaning of Heb.
11:1, found in Voegelin, *The New Science of Politics*, 122: "Uncertainty is the very
essence of Christianity. The feeling of security in a 'world full of gods' is lost
with the gods themselves; when the world is de-divinized, communication
with the world-transcendent God is reduced to the tenuous bond of faith, in the
sense of Heb. 11:1." Voegelin claims as his authority, for this very weak conception of faith and interpretation of Heb. 11:1, St. Thomas Aquinas's *Summa
Theologica*, 2nd part of the 2nd part, question 4, article 1 [henceforth cited as ST
2a–2ae qu. 4 a. 1]. But what we find in that text of Thomas is in fact the
following: faith as defined in Heb. 11:1 means "the *firm* adhesion of the *intellect*
to the non-apparent *truth*. . . . For when we describe faith thus, we distinguish it
from opinion, suspicion, and doubt, which do not make the intellect adhere to
anything *firmly;* when we go on to say, 'of things that appear not,' we distinguish
it from science and understanding, the object of which is something apparent. . . . Faith is that *certainty* of the mind about absent things which surpasses
opinion but falls short of science." To be sure, Thomas, schooled by Maimonides (see *Eight Chapters,* chap. 7) and Aristotelian science, recognizes more clearly
than do Augustine, Milton, and Barth the difference between even the most
"certain" faith and knowledge in the strict sense (see also Calvin, *Institutes,*
3.2.14).

    16. Barth, *Church Dogmatics,* 3:1, pp. 6–10, 22; cf. also pp. 32–33, on "the
knowledge of the secret of creation." Milton admonishes, "In religion, we should
beware above all of exposing ourselves to the charge which Christ brought
against the Samaritans in John 4:22—'you worship something you do not know.'
Assume, too, that in matters of faith, that saying of Christ, 'we, however,
worship something that we do know,' should be regarded as axiomatic" (*Christian Doctrine*, 1.6, p. 288; see the full elaboration at 1.17–21). See Milton's
testimony to his own experience of very extensive direct revelation (*Paradise*

Lost, 1.1–32, 3.1ff., 9.21ff.). On the experience of revelation promised to "each individual believer" (*Christian Doctrine*, 1.30, pp. 580ff., referring esp. to 2 Cor. 4:2–3), see *Paradise Lost*, 12.511–13 and *Paradise Regained*, 4.288–90 (Milton's unorthodox doctrine of the "Holy Spirit" must be kept in mind; see *Christian Doctrine*, 1.6 as a whole). See also Pascal, who describes the "certainty" of "faith" in the "hidden God" as a "sentiment of the heart" put into the heart by divine grace (*Pensées*, #7, 90, 110, 149 end, 172, 242, 380, 394, 424, 427, 432, 444, 446, 781, 793, 921 [= Brunschvicg #248, 337, 282, 430, 185, 585, 284, 288, 278, 194, 557, 586, 242, 737, 518]). Pascal's remarkably rationalist "psychology" of faith, as induced and sustained by "custom," in #821 (= B. #252), must be supplemented by his more comprehensive if briefer statement in #808 (= B. 245): "There are three ways to believe: by reason, by custom, by inspiration. The Christian religion, which alone is correct, does not admit at all among its true children those who believe without inspiration." Pascal's famous reflections on the "wager" with which every unbeliever in his "uncertainty" is confronted obviously do not apply to those whose hearts have been already "inclined" by grace (#418, 429, 577 [= B. #233, 234, 229]). For the darker side of the life that rotates about this experience, see (in addition of course to the Psalms of David), Calvin, *Institutes*, 3.2.17–20, 3.2.24 end; and Martin Luther's accounts of his *Anfectungen*, which he reports took him so far as sometimes to cry out, "Our Father Who art in Heaven . . . Who knows whether it is true?!" (see Bainton, *Here I Stand*, chap. 21, "The Struggle for Faith").

17. Scholem, "Revelation and Tradition as Religious Categories in Rabbinic Judaism," in *The Messianic Idea in Judaism*, 292, 298, 301–2, translating from Isaiah Horovitz, *The Two Tables of the Covenant* (Amsterdam, 1689), which is commenting on the Talmudic Chagigah 15b.

18. See also Pascal, *Pensées*, #835 (= Brunschvicg #564): "The prophecies, the miracles even, and the proofs of our religion . . . are such that one cannot say that there is no reason to believe in them. Therefore, . . . it is not reason that can determine the refusal to follow this evidence, and thus it can be only lust and malice of the heart. And thus there is sufficient evidence for condemnation, even if there is not sufficient evidence to make one believe."

19. See Strauss, *Philosophy and Law*, chap. 1, n. 2: "If 'religion' and 'politics' are *the* facts that transcend 'culture,' or, to speak more precisely, the *original* facts, then the radical critique of the concept of 'culture' is possible only in the form of a 'theologico-political treatise,'—which of course, if it is not to lead back again to the foundation of 'culture,' must take exactly the opposite direction from the theologico-political treatises of the seventeenth century, especially those of Hobbes and Spinoza." Heinrich Meier comments, "Er spricht von einem *theologisch-politischen* Traktat, d.h., von einer philosophischen Schrift, die sich der theologischen und der politischen Alternative stellt und in der Ausei-

nandersetzung mit den Forderungen der Politik und der Religion zur Philosophie hinführt. Der theologisch-politische Traktat hat, mit anderen Worten, einen sowohl elenktischen als auch protreptischen Charakter. Wo aber kann die Prüfung ansetzen, wenn die anspruchsvolle Alternative nicht länger präsent ist oder wenn ihre Konturen im Vielerlei der bloßen Privatsachen, in dem alles mit allem kompatibel erscheint, bis zur Unkenntlichkeit verschwimmen? . . . Wenn eine Gründung geschichtlich ausgeschlossen erschien, so konnte doch eine geschichtliche Gründung 'wiederholt,' nämlich in ihren fundamentalen Prinzipien gedacht werden. Ebendas war es, was Strauss in *Philosophie und Gesetz* unternahm" (*Carl Schmitt, Leo Strauss und "Der Begriff des Politischen,"* 184–85).

20. O'Donovan and O'Donovan, eds., *From Ireneus to Grotius,* xv–xvi.

21. See Pangle, *The Ennobling of Democracy,* part 1; Derrida, "How to Avoid Speaking," 76–77; Caputo, *The Prayers and Tears of Jacques Derrida;* and Owen, *Religion and the Demise of Liberal Rationalism.*

22. Though it is to be noted that so weighty an authority as Augustine finds the theological speculation in the Platonic dialogues to be sufficiently "congruent" with the biblical that he is of the opinion that no one can rule out the possibility that Plato acquired at least secondhand knowledge of much of the content of the Hebrew Scriptures. See *City of God* 8.11 (which qualifies somewhat *On Christian Doctrine* 2.28). Augustine follows several earlier Christian authorities (not to mention Philo Judaeus, whose writings are full of this sentiment). See Justin Martyr *First Apology* 59–60 and *Second Apology* 10.8; Clement of Alexandria *Stromata* 1.22, 5.14 (Clement cites the great Hellenizing Aristotelian Jew Aristobulus of Alexandria [ca. 145 B.C.; for Aristobulus see Eusebius *Preparation for the Gospel* 13.12ff.] and also Numenius, the leading Platonist of the third century), as well as *The Teacher* 1.8 and *Protreptic Speech to the Greeks* 6 (suggesting that Xenophon also shows familiarity with the Hebrew Scriptures in his Socratic writings); and Origen *Against Celsus* 6.19. So also Luther, in the opening of LG, *Werke,* 42:4; Luther follows his cicerone, Nicholas of Lyra. Among modern scholars, see Robbins, "The Influence of Greek Philosophy on the Early Commentaries," 229–30. Also Bickerman, "The Historical Foundations of Postbiblical Judaism," 77 and 84: "As cuneiform business documents of the Persian period show, the Jews in the Babylonian Diaspora rubbed shoulders with . . . Lydians and Ionians"; so "when a later Jewish author thought that the Greek sages had learned loftier conceptions of God from Moses, they were probably wrong, but the surmise does not any longer appear absurd in the light of recent discoveries." And on the other hand, recent scholarship has proposed that the Bible, even or especially early sections of Genesis, shows dependence on the Hesiodic *Catalogue of Women* (Van Seters, "The Primeval Histories of Greece and Israel Compared," 1–22; Hess, "The Genealogies of Genesis 1–11 and Comparative Literature," 251–53).

23. See Strauss, *Philosophy and Law,* 76: "The interpretation of Platonic philosophy . . . has to begin not from the *Republic,* but from the *Laws:* from the *Laws,* in which Plato undoubtedly stands closest to the world of revealed law, since it is there that, in accordance with a kind of interpretation anticipating the philosophic interpretation of the revealed law among the medieval thinkers, Plato transforms the 'divine laws' of Greek antiquity into truly divine laws, or recognizes them as truly divine laws. In this approximation to revelation without the guidance of the revelation we grasp at its origin the unbelieving, philosophic foundation of the belief in revelation [*die ungläubige, philosophische Grundlegung des Offenbarungsglaubens;* see also 61, 69, 81]. Plato's approximation to revelation furnishes the medieval thinkers with the *starting-point* from which they could understand revelation philosophically. But if they were not to lose faith in revelation because of Plato, then it had to be the case that Platonic philosophy had suffered from an *aporia* in principle that had been removed only by revelation." (The translation has been altered slightly to make it more literal; cf. the original, now available in Strauss, *Gesammelte Schriften,* 2.64; see also 49, 56, 68.) See also Strauss's last published work, *The Argument and the Action of Plato's Laws,* 6–7 and 172.

24. Even the greatest and most influential critique of classical rationalist philosophy ever undertaken, while it specifically targets certain "followers of" Socrates, Hippocrates, Plato, and Aristotle (in particular, al-Farabi and Avicenna) and raises grave doubts about the adequacy of classical metaphysics, nonetheless insists that "all significant thinkers, past and present, agree in believing in God and the last day; that their differences reduce to matters of detail extraneous to those two pivotal points (for the sake of which the prophets, supported by miracles, have been sent)"; "those prominent and leading philosophers are innocent of the imputation that they deny the religious laws"; "they believe in God and His messengers," but "they have fallen into confusion in certain details beyond these principles, erring in this, straying from the correct path, and leading others astray" (Al-Ghazali *The Incoherence of the Philosophers,* intro., sec. 7, p. 3).

25. Plato *Laws* 899b. Cf. Virgil *Eclogues* 3.60 ("All things are full of Jove") and Aristotle *Parts of Animals* 645a19–24 ("And even as it is reported that Heraclitus said to some strangers who wanted to meet him, and had paused after entering, because they saw him warming himself at a stove—he bid them come on in boldly, since the gods were there too—so as regards the inquiry into each of the animals one ought to proceed without bashful hesitation, since in all of them there is being, that is by nature, and is beautiful").

26. *Der Römerbrief,* xi–xii. For further discussion of the precise limitations of scientific-historical criticism, and a defense against the charge of being "an enemy of historical criticism," see the preface to the second edition, xvi–xx.

There Barth stresses (xiv–xv) that the book was written as a "part of the conversation of a theologian with theologians," but that "if, despite this warning, non-theologians also grasp the book—and I know of some, who will understand what is in it better than will many theologians—that is for me a great joy; for I am convinced that its content is important for everyone, because its questions are the questions of everyone." Barth further noted that the deepening in his understanding of the Scripture that had occurred between the first and the second, revised edition was due in major part to his "becoming better schooled in the authentic orientation of the thought of Plato" (xiv). To forestall misunderstanding I should add, however, that I cannot follow Barth when he rejects Augustine's allowance of the possibility of an historically unfolding divine intentionality in Genesis that gives a richness of meaning that might even have transcended the understanding of the human writer. Cf. Barth's *Church Dogmatics,* 3:1, p. 64, with Augustine *Confessions* 12.18 and 12.31.

CHAPTER 1. *The Twofold Account of Creation: and the Hermeneutical Problem*

1. See Fradkin, "God's Politics." The political attributes of God and His heavenly realm, even prior to Creation, are in the foreground of the inspired political theologian Milton's epic, *Paradise Lost,* esp. 1.40ff.; 5.600ff., 772ff., 840; 10.86–87.

2. Philo of Alexandria *Creation of the Cosmos* 2 (the Platonic notion of legal "preludes" [προοίμια] is developed in *Laws* 719b–723d). Philo goes on to contend that the account of creation teaches that "one who is obedient to the [Mosaic] law becomes, by so doing, a citizen of the world." In what sense this may be true will become clearer as we proceed.

3. Strauss, "On the Interpretation of Genesis," 8. Cf. Jacob, *The First Book of the Bible,* 5: the Bible "describes things according to appearances and these never change. It will always appear as if there is a heaven just as, in spite of Copernicus, the sun still rises and sets."

4. The attempts of Cassuto (*A Commentary on the Book of Genesis,* 1:84–96, 101–2, 108, 127–29) to resolve the contradictions do not seem to do justice to the massive and primary impression the two accounts give of being contrasting accounts. See similarly Cassuto's *Documentary Hypothesis and the Composition of the Pentateuch,* 70–78. Augustine usefully catalogues the difficulties in his *On the Literal Interpretation of Genesis, in Twelve Books* (henceforth cited as *Genesis XII*), 7.28. For a discussion of the old Latin text of Genesis that Augustine used, and a translation of the same, see appendix 2 to his *The Literal Meaning of Genesis,* trans. Taylor.

5. Pascal, *Pensées*, #236 (= Brunschvicg #578): "Fundamental premise: Moses [as presumed human author of Scripture] was a clever man. If, then, he governed himself by his wits he should not have put in anything that was directly contrary to a clever wit. Therefore all the very obvious weaknesses are in fact strengths. . . . What is more obvious than that [these] could not have been concerted?"

6. Strauss, "Jerusalem and Athens," 152; "On the Interpretation of Genesis," 8.

7. "It must even be said that the first without the second, like the second without the first, would not express what ought to be said here" (Bonhoeffer, *Creation and Fall,* 41; see similarly Rosenzweig, "The Unity of the Bible," 23). In order to endorse this judgment, we do not have to reject observations such as Gunkel's (*Genesis,* 28–29), agreeing with Wellhausen (*Prolegomena to the History of Israel,* 304–5) that in contrast to the more sophisticated account in Gen. 1, "natural science has not made any connection with Gen. 2 and 3"; that "Gen. 2–3 offers a much more immature concept according to which Yahweh 'forms' his creatures with his own hand. Consequently, this narrative is full of naïve anthropomorphizations of God." We need only insist that in its present context—as the sequel to the first account—the naiveté appears no longer unselfconscious; and that even strictly on its own terms, the second account expresses and invites profound subtlety of moral and theological speculation— rendering dubious Gunkel's further and unnecessarily patronizing claim that "the horizon of the myth reaches no farther than the farmer." It is to be noted that Gunkel concluded the introduction to his famous commentary by conceding the possibility of discerning a "unity in the variety of Israel's religion" expressing "the providence of God who spoke childishly to children and then maturely to adults" (lxxxvi).

8. This does not mean that we simply close our minds to the possibility that Moses was in some miraculous way the author of the Pentateuch. And we are receptive to the view articulated by Brevard Childs: that "when correctly interpreted, the Mosaic authorship of the Pentateuch is an important theological affirmation," i.e., of "the continuity of the faith of successive generations with that which had once been delivered to Moses at Sinai" (*Introduction to the Old Testament as Scripture,* 134–35; see also 62–64). The scriptural indications of Moses' own writing activities are at Exod. 24:3, 34:27, and, above all, Deut. 31, as well as Ezra 6:18, Neh. 13:1, 2 Chron. 25:4. A sophisticated scholarly attempt to defend Mosaic authorship is Leiman's *The Canonization of Hebrew Scripture.* See the critical discussion in Childs, *Introduction to the Old Testament as Scripture,* 55–56, 58.

9. Wellhausen, "Die Composition des Hexateuchs." For Wellhausen's own

development of the full implications, see his *Prolegomena to the History of Israel* (for his account of his indebtedness and relation to previous scholarship, see his introduction).

10. The most informative brief critical account of the history of higher criticism that I have found is Houtman, "The Pentateuch." Also very helpful are Blenkinsopp, *The Pentateuch,* chap. 1, and, most recently (1995), though more sketchy and popular, Whybray, *Introduction to the Pentateuch,* chap. 2 ("Who Wrote It? Problems of Composition")—which is rooted in the author's compendious *The Making of the Pentateuch.* All these correct the rather breezy, complacent, and misleading remarks found in Speiser's introduction to *The Anchor Bible: Genesis,* xx–xxiii. For a good critical review of the early- and mid-twentieth-century literature on the Pentateuch, see Knight, "The Pentateuch," in *The Hebrew Bible and Its Modern Interpreters,* ed. Knight and Tucker. Von Rad's famous *Genesis: A Commentary* arranges the text and commentary so as to identify and separate out, in accordance with the mid-twentieth-century scholarly consensus, the various hypothesized documentary strands. See also the running identification and discussion of sources postulated for each biblical section in Speiser's *Anchor Bible: Genesis.*

11. Included in "P" are Gen. 1:1–2:4; 5:1–27, 30–32; 9:1–17, 28–29; 11:10–27, 31–32; 12:4–5; 17; 23; 25:7–10, etc. Blenkinsopp (*The Pentateuch,* 132 n. 17) gives a list of lexical terms exclusive to or highly characteristic of "P." The conventional scholarly dating has been disputed with increasing vigor, on substantive and linguistic grounds. Arguing for a later date is Vink, "The Date and Origin of the Priestly Code"; arguing for a much earlier date are Kaufmann, *The Religion of Israel,* 174–211, and Avi Hurvitz, "The Evidence of Language in Dating the Priestly Code." Contending that "P" is properly understood not really as a "source" but rather as a late redactional revising and supplementing of the basic stratum that is the "JE" narrative are, e.g., Cross, *Canaanite Myth and Hebrew Epic,* 293–325; Childs, *Introduction to the Old Testament as Scripture,* 146–47; Rendtorff, *Das überlieferungsgeschichtliche Problem des Pentateuch,* 112–42; and the same author's "The 'Yahwist' as Theologian?" (indeed, Rendtorff largely breaks with the documentary hypothesis and simply denies the existence of "J" or the "Yahwist"; see similarly Blum, *Die Komposition der Vätergeschichte*). Blenkinsopp (*The Pentateuch,* 118–20) has rejoined with strong arguments for "P" as a source rather than as a late editorial stratum.

12. For a good brief account, by a leading authority of the documentary thesis, of the differences between the hypothesized sources "J" and "P," see Noth, *A History of Pentateuchal Traditions,* 8–37.

13. Gunkel himself went very far in deconstructing the "J" source. See esp. *Genesis,* lxxiii: "J is neither a unified work itself nor does it trace back to older, self-contained, unified works. Rather it was constituted by the combination of

several, indeed of many hands. . . . 'J' and 'E' are, thus, not individual authors but narrative schools."

14. Von Rad, *Das erste Buch Mose: Genesis,* 17 (I have corrected the Marks translation, p. 24). See also von Rad, *Genesis,* 95 ("Genesis, chs. 2f.," exhibits "the highest command of every artistic means"), and Westermann, *Genesis 12–36,* 571.

15. Von Rad, *Genesis,* 36. See also 159–61, 167–68, 209–10, 217, and von Rad, "The Form-Critical Problem of the Hexateuch."

16. Von Rad, *Genesis,* 26. For a survey of debates over "E," see Craghan, "The Elohist in Recent Literature." The principles invoked to separate "E" from "J" are described in the first chapter of Noth's *History of Pentateuchal Traditions,* 38–41—which, however, stresses the common traits of "J" and "E," tracing them to a common source, yet another hypothesized document "G" ("Grundlage"). Scholars subsequent to von Rad and Noth have increasingly argued for a much later dating of "J." See Winnett, "Re-examining the Foundations"; Van Seters, *Abraham in History and Tradition* (which is dedicated to his teacher Winnett); Schmid, *Der sogenannte Jahwist;* and Blenkinsopp, *The Pentateuch,* 64–65 (with a list of words used in the "J" sections that are otherwise attested only or primarily in postexilic texts), 73, 78, 91. The sections of Genesis that have usually been ascribed to "J" include 2:4–4:26; 6:1–8; 9:18–27; 10:8–19, 21, 25–30; 11:1–9, 28–30; 12:1–4, 6–20, etc.; those ascribed to "E" include 20:1–8, as the first chunk, then 21:8–34, 22:1–19, and so forth.

17. Von Rad, *Genesis,* 40–41; see also 94, 115, and esp. 73 (deferring to Humbert's *Etudes sur le récit du Paradis et de la chute dans la Genèse*). See also Westermann, *Genesis 12–36,* 573. Contrast the subsection "Redaction" in Knierim's contribution to *The Hebrew Bible and Its Modern Interpreters,* 150–53, and the classic statement by Eissfeldt, *The Old Testament,* 240: "Pentateuchal criticism has become accustomed to denote as redactors those who brought the material together, in distinction to the compilers or authors of the individual 'documents' . . . ; there is a distinction, for the most part clearly recognizable, between the author, organically shaping the material, and the redactor working *mechanically.*" But near the end of Knierim's essay, very considerable concessions are made to the possible fruitfulness of the new and as yet somewhat unorthodox respect for the Redactor: "Our exegetical tradition suggests that redaction criticism continues to be an appendix to literary criticism and that its proper role in the methodological system has not yet received the attention it deserves. *This deficit affects our concept of the system in its entirety*" (156; my italics).

18. Childs (*Introduction to the Old Testament as Scripture,* 148–50), disputing the "misleading" typesetting in the *Biblia Hebraica Stuttgartensia,* insists that the "priestly genealogical formula" that first appears in Gen. 2:4 ("these are the generations of the heavens and the earth") must be syntactically understood to

serve as an introduction to the second account which *follows,* and not as a conclusion to the *first* account (the formula is always followed by the genitive of the progenitor and never of the progeny; Skinner, *A Critical and Exegetical Commentary on Genesis,* 41). This shows that here "P" has been written or rewritten in such a way as presupposes and subordinates "J." So (Childs concludes), "the two originally different accounts have not been simply juxtaposed," and "to read them in this fashion as has usually been done" is to "disregard the essential effect of the canonical shaping which has assigned the chapters different roles within the new context of the book of Genesis."

19. Houtman, "The Pentateuch," 194 and 198. See similarly Thompson, *The Origin Tradition of Ancient Israel I,* 116.

20. *The Origin Tradition of Ancient Israel I,* 49; see also 155–56. The crumbling of the consensus is evident in Westermann's somewhat sprawling and disjointed commentary, which, while it continues to orient itself by a qualified version of the documentary hypothesis, does have the merit of admitting how serious were the criticisms raised by Cassuto above all. See *Genesis 1–11,* 569ff., esp. 572, 574, 578–79; and *Genesis 12–36,* 30–58, 126, 406, and esp. Westermann's words at 571–73: "The interpretation given here, over against the view of the classical source theory, shows that the patriarchal story as transmitted is considerably more unified than previously thought." See Childs's severe judgment on Westermann's work as a whole: "In Westermann's huge commentary all the problems inherent in the traditio–critical method reached their zenith, but in a complexity which threatened to devour exegesis. . . . [I]t seems already clear that his contribution will not lie primarily in the area of Old Testament theology. The concluding theological section, which rises as a vestige from a former generation, has been lost in the innumerable levels of literary and cultural development" (*Introduction to the Old Testament as Scripture,* 142). Let us here remark that Wellhausen himself, in contrast to some of his epigones, had to acknowledge that the book of Genesis as we have it manifests an artistic unity, created out of originally "detached narratives": "To weave them together in a connected whole is the work of the poetical or literary artist" (*Prolegomena to the History of Israel,* 296; see also 295).

21. Blenkinsopp, *The Pentateuch,* 25–27. See also 120–26 and 130; Childs, *Introduction to the Old Testament as Scripture,* 119–27; Anbar, "Genesis 15"; Van Seters, *Abraham in History and Tradition,* 249–78; and Schmid, *Die Sogenannte Jahwist,* 35–36. Rendtorff (*The Problem of the Process of Transmission in the Pentateuch,* 99; see also esp. 200) has argued that the Pentateuch as a whole "in its ideas and language is closely related to Deuteronomy." The tendency to dissolve E as a distinct source is very marked in Westermann (see *Genesis 12–36,* 401–2, 412, 453, 464, 472, 554, and esp. 571–72). Late-twentieth-century scholarly con-

sensus is thus far from what is suggested in Harold Bloom's rather fabulous preface and introduction to his and David Rosenberg's *Book of J* (1990).

22. Childs, *Introduction to the Old Testament as Scripture*, 15, 41, 52–54, 58–59, 62–64, 67, 73, 75–76, 78; see also 16, 40, 157–58; and for specific application to Genesis, see esp. 148–50. As internal evidence for the process of law-governed canonization signaled in what are acknowledged to be some of the earliest strands of the Scripture, Childs refers to Exod. 24:1–11, Deut. 31:24ff., Josh. 1:8 and 4:10 (62–63). For an updated restatement, see Childs, *Biblical Theology of the Old and New Testaments*. See also Strauss, "Jerusalem and Athens," 151: "Memories of memories are not necessarily distorting or pale reflections of the original; they may be re-collections of re-collections, deepenings through meditation of the primary experiences."

23. Alter, *The Art of Biblical Narrative*, 13–15, 20, 24, 34–35, 100 n, 103–4, 138, 141–42. See the review article by Fradkin, "Biblical Interpretation and the Art of Writing." Northrop Frye went so far as to complain that for historical criticism, "disintegrating the text became an end in itself" (*The Great Code*, xvii). The scholarship Alter and Frye criticize is usefully surveyed in Knight and Tucker's *Hebrew Bible and Its Modern Interpreters*. See esp. Knierim's contribution ("Criticism of Literary Features, Form, Tradition, and Redaction"), which concedes that "the atomization of methods and results in historical exegesis has become a major concern for everybody. Some have called it a scandal" (126; see also 128). Yet Knierim opens his survey of biblical exegesis by defensively reissuing, in the face of what he calls "the upsurge of additional methods of interpretation," the self-imposed, ruling imperative of mainstream "historical interpretation": to keep itself free of the contamination of "hermeneutical methods which concentrate on the principles of relevance, validity, or accessibility of the ancient texts for us," whether such hermeneutics be "based on theological or philosophical preconceptions"; and in a footnote, no fewer than fourteen leading scholarly works are introduced as expert witnesses that "affirm" this self-denying ordinance (123–24). As Thompson acidly observes, "Biblical and historical scholarship in the past generation seems to have had on the whole no feeling for a bible text as literature, with a meaning in itself" (*The Origin Tradition of Ancient Israel I*, 41). In the last few years David M. Carr (*Reading the Fractures of Genesis*) has reconsidered and reformulated traditional historical scholarship in a spirit much more open to and respectful of the interpretative approach that focuses on the (qualified) integrity of the final form of the text. But despite his deep bow to what is referred to as "synchronic" in contrast to traditional "diachronic" or historical scholarly analysis (the jargon comes from the linguistic theorizing of Saussure; see Barr, "The Synchronic, the Diachronic, and the Historical"), his conclusions from rearticulation of the

latter have disappointingly little to contribute to the former (see part 4, "Moving Forward").

24. See Rosenberg, "Meanings, Morals, and Mysteries." See similarly Fokkelman, *Narrative Art in Genesis,* 5–6.

25. *Art of Biblical Narrative,* 19; see also 32 n (taking to task Licht's *Storytelling in the Bible*), but contrast 46. Childs has become somewhat disillusioned with the theological shallowness of much holistic literary interpretation of the Scripture (see *Biblical Theology of the Old and New Testaments,* 722–23). See Barr's aculeate observation on the "religious vacuity of some literary readings" recently ("The Synchronic, the Diachronic, and the Historical," 11).

26. *Art of Biblical Narrative,* 19. See also 132–33; Alter, *Genesis,* "To the Reader," xl–xlii; and Houtman, "The Pentateuch," 186.

27. Van Seters, *In Search of History* and *Prologue to History;* Whybray, *The Making of the Pentateuch.* In his more popular 1995 *Introduction to the Pentateuch,* while continuing to suggest that "the Pentateuch may be regarded as to all intents and purposes the work of a single author" (26), Whybray prudently declares that "the important question is not one of the sources available to the compiler but what the Pentateuch was intended to mean in its present form" (13; see also 134–36).

28. *Commentary on the Book of Genesis,* 2.34 and 2.307; *Documentary Hypothesis and the Composition of the Pentateuch,* 82, 103–4. See similarly Martin, *Stylistic Criteria and the Analysis of the Pentateuch.* For further vigorous discussion and application of Cassuto's interpretative "hypothesis," see his *Commentary on the Book of Genesis,* 1.12, 56, 71–76, 93–94, 185, 189, 190, 193, 266–67, 2.38, 142–43, 184–85, 234–36, 269–70, 273, 293–94, 299, 336–38, and *Documentary Hypothesis,* esp. 72–73, 102–3. In the latter work, however, Cassuto concedes that "there were current among the Israelites in regard to the names of Esau's wives, and likewise with reference to other topics that similarly recur in contradictory versions, two divergent traditions; but the Torah did not wish to reject one in favour of the other, and therefore found room for both in its text, leaving it to the reader to choose one of the versions or to find a way of reconciling them as he deemed fit" (68).

29. Strauss, "Jerusalem and Athens," 163 (my italics). See also his "On the Interpretation of Genesis," end. From this statement, and even more so from his detailed exegesis of Genesis, it is obvious that Strauss does not take the hermeneutic path explicitly indicated by Maimonides throughout the *Guide*—that is, a reading that ascribes to the Bible an esoteric or hidden, quasi-philosophic, teaching that differs radically from the surface or exoteric teaching. Strauss's divergence from Maimonides' esoteric interpretation follows from the fact that Strauss writes his exegesis as a philosopher: "The finding that the *Guide* is devoted to the explanation of the secret teaching of the Bible" is for Strauss

"pregnant with the consequence that the *Guide* is not a philosophic book" ("On the Literary Character of the *Guide for the Perplexed*," in *Persecution and the Art of Writing*, 42; see the context).

CHAPTER 2. *Creation and the Meaning of Divine Omnipotence*

1. See also ad 17:1: "It is not in nature that the rains should come in their due season when we worship God"; such things "are all miracles by which the disposition of natural law is overpowered, except that no change from the natural order is noticeable." See similarly Luther, LG, *Werke*, 43:233–34.

2. See Guitton, *Le temps et l'éternité chez Plotin et Saint Augustin*, 207.

3. *The Incoherence of the Incoherence*, trans. Van den Bergh, 1:97 and 273. See also Kogan, *Averroës and the Metaphysics of Causation*, 107 and 218. We find Cicero in the dialogue *On Divination* (2.37) attacking his brother's version of Stoic "philosophy" with the following words: "The city of philosophy, I believe, you surrender, while defending its outworks; for, by wishing divination to be true, you overthrow reasoning on the basis of nature. . . . [You say, of the entrails of the sacrificial victims,] 'god snatches away,' or 'some force destroys or consumes.' So then the genesis and the end of all things is *not* due to nature, and there will be something which either comes into being out of nothing [*ex nihilo*] or suddenly disappears into nothing! What natural philosopher ever said this?" See also ibid., 2.86, and *On the Nature of the Gods* 3.92; Lucretius *On the Nature of Things* 1.149–264; Parmenides, in Diels-Kranz (henceforth D-K) B 8.7–8 and 8.12–13; Empedocles, in D-K B 12; Diogenes of Apollonia, in Diogenes Laertius 9.57; and Aristotle *Metaphysics* 1062b24–26.

4. *Critical and Historical Dictionary*, s.v. "Luther," n. KK. Compare Calvin, *Commentary on Genesis* ad 19:26: "Since God created men out of nothing, why is it not licit for Him, if He sees fit, to reduce them again to nothing? If this be granted, as it must be, why, if He should please, may He not turn them into stones?" Biblical support for Calvin's remark may be discovered in the words of John the Baptist: "And do not start saying to yourselves, 'we have Abraham as our father'; for I say unto you that God has the power from these stones to raise up children for Abraham" (Luke 3:8). Karl Barth properly stresses that "presupposing the certain knowledge of God in His word, it is actually the case that the existence and being of the world are rendered far more problematical by the existence and being of God than vice versa. For how far do we know about the world and nature and history and above all ourselves with a certainty which makes quite indisputable the knowledge and statement that they and we really are, and really are what we are?" (*Church Dogmatics*, 3:1, p. 6).

5. *City of God* 21.8. On the precise meaning of divine omnipotence, expressed in providence and rooted in Creation, see Calvin's *Institutes*, 1.16.3. As

Calvin later remarks (2.2.17), the core of the biblical notion is to be found "even in Homer," where "it is said that men possess reason and prudence, not only according as Jupiter has distributed to each, but according as he leads them day by day, οἶον ἐπ' ἦμαρ ἄγῃσι." We may add to Calvin's observation that comparable in the decisive respect (though of course by no means identical) to the biblical outlook is the view easily accessible to the Greco-Roman philosophers by way of Hesiod's purported revelation from the Muses in *Theogony* 116–17 ("Now at the very first, Gaping Emptiness [Chaos] came into being; and after that / Broad-bosomed Earth, a safe seat forever for all / The immortals who possess the peak of snowy Olympus") as well as by way of utterances such as these of Pindar: "The power of the gods makes a light achievement out of even what surpasses what one would swear or hope possible" (*Olympian Odes* 13, l. 83); "For from the gods spring [ἔφυν] all the devisings of mortal virtues, and the wise, and the mighty with their hands, and the eloquent" (*Pythian Odes* 1, ll. 41–42); "To me nothing ever appears to be incredible among the wonders of the accomplishing gods" (*Pythian Odes* 10, ll. 48–50); and "By the power of god, unsullied light can spring forth from dark night, and the pure light of day be hidden by dark cloud" (frag. quoted in Clement of Alexandria *Stromata* 5.14). Voltaire (*Philosophical Dictionary*, s.v. "Genesis" and "Matter") is thus plainly in error when he asserts (in support of his claim that Creation out of nothing was a notion that could not have been known to the Bible) that "not a single author in antiquity has ever said that something was drawn out of nothingness." In order to sustain this assertion, Voltaire finds himself compelled to rewrite, in effect, the crucial lines of Hesiod's *Theogony*. It is amazing to find Westermann (*Genesis 1–11,* 44) repeating Voltaire's grave error. According to William Foxwell Albright, evidence suggests that the solar monotheism introduced into Egypt for about fifteen years around 1375 B.C. (roughly two generations before Moses), a cult with which Mosaic religion "probably has some indirect connection," placed "constant stress on the one God as creator of everything" ("The Biblical Period," 11, and *From the Stone Age to Christianity,* 165ff. and 205ff.).

6. Augustine *Genesis XII* 6.16.27; see also 6.14. Calvin remarks that "it seems but little consonant with reason, that Moses declares birds to have come out from the waters: that is why there are mockers who have seized upon this as an occasion of calumny"—to which Calvin responds, "Why should it not be lawful for Him, Who created the world out of nothing, to bring forth the birds out of water? And what greater absurdity, I pray, has the origin of birds from water, than that of the light from darkness?" In discussing the condition of Creation after the Flood, Calvin notes that the irregularity of weather patterns testifies to the fact that "the order of nature" or "the order of the world" is indeed "disturbed by our vices," introduced with the Fall. And he later argues

that without the "miraculous" intervention of divine providence, the "wild beasts without number" would "rend, tear, and devour everything human." Yet on the other hand, Calvin concedes that the evidence of the science of nature adduced by "the philosophers" requires us to understand that the rainbow occurred as a natural phenomenon even prior to its being designated as the sign of God's covenant with Creation through Noah (*Commentary on Genesis* ad 1:20, 8:22, 9:2, 9:13; see similarly Nachmanides *Commentary on Genesis* ad 9:12).

7. *City of God* 21.7. See also 21.8 and Milton's *Paradise Lost,* 2.577ff., describing "A Universe of death, which God by curse / Created evil, for evil only good," where "Nature breeds Perverse, all monstrous."

8. *Spirit of the Laws,* 1.1 (my italics). See also Montesquieu's defiant but somewhat disingenuous response, at the beginning of *The Defense of the Spirit of the Laws,* to his orthodox religious critics' severe censure of this opening.

9. *Discourse on Method,* part 5, in *Oeuvres,* 6:43 and 45. See also Descartes, *Principles of Philosophy,* 2.22.

10. *Historical and Critical Dictionary,* s.v. "Epicurus," n. S. See similarly Maimonides *Guide* 2.1; Rousseau, *Letter to Beaumont,* in *Oeuvres complètes,* 4.956–57; and Lucretius *On the Nature of Things,* Bailey's commentary, 2.624, 628. But contrast Aristotle *Metaphysics* 1062b24–26: "For that nothing comes into being from not being, but all from being, is a settled opinion [*dogma*] of *almost* (σχεδόν) all those concerned with nature."

11. *The Refutation of All Heresies* 8.17.1–2; see also 10.28. The word "plagiarize" (κλεψιλογεῖν) was invented by Hippolytus to characterize the heretics, and especially the Gnostics, in their "theft" of the ideas of Plato and other Greek philosophers. See also Tertullian *Against Hermogenes* 1 ("Turning away from the Christians to the philosophers, from the Church to the Academy and the Porch, he learned there from the Stoics how to place matter on the same level with the Lord") and Robbins, "The Influence of Greek Philosophy on the Early Commentaries," 228.

12. *Long Commentary on Metaphysics XII,* as quoted and translated in Kogan, *Averroës and the Metaphysics of Causation,* 209.

13. Plato *Timaeus* 41–43; Maimonides *Guide* 1.28, 2.12; Philo *On the Eternity of the World* 28–31, 125–26. See also Aristotle *On Respiration,* esp. 478b23ff., and Lucretius *On the Nature of Things* 3.425ff.

14. Gen. 18:14. See also Job 42:2, Matt. 19:26, Mark 10:27, Luke 1:37; Augustine *City of God* 16.26, referring to the miracle of Isaac's conception ("When, however, God's work is evident at the point where nature is vitiated and ceasing, *there* is grace more evidently made intelligible"); and Soroush, "The Sense and Essense of Secularism," 65–66 (quoting and commenting on *Mathnavi,* bk. 3, vv. 3576–77). Montesquieu's attempt to give a law-governed interpretation to Creation and hence to divine providence flies in the face of

Bayle's marshaling of seven moral, physical, and metaphysical arguments to demonstrate the "paradox" that "once this impiety [of limits, rooted in the nature or laws of "matter," to divine power] is laid down," it is "less absurd to contend, as did the Epicureans, that God was *not* the Author of the World, and that he does *not* involve himself in conducting it, than it is to contend, as did several other philosophers, that he formed it, that he preserves it, and that he was its director. The conclusion of these latter was true, but that does not prevent their having spoken self-contradictorily." Bayle follows up his sevenfold refutation of the Platonists with an even bolder imaginary dialogue between Epicurus and a priest—with whom, Bayle argues, Epicurus "would have his greatest advantage." Epicurus would confront the priest with the question, " 'Are the gods contented, or discontented, with their administration? Beware of my Dilemma: if they are happy with what happens under their Providence, they are pleased with evil; if they are discontented, then they are unhappy. . . .' The Priest would respond that they do not like evil, that they regard it as an offense which they punish severely, which is the cause of plagues, wars, famines, shipwrecks, floods, etc. To which Epicurus would reply: 'I conclude from your answer that they are unhappy; for there is no life more unhappy than that of being continually exposed to offenses, and continually obliged to avenge oneself. Sin does not cease among men; it follows that there is not one moment in the day when the gods are not receiving affronts; . . . the gods have no sooner finished avenging themselves on one nation, when they must commence the punishment of another. And that is always recommencing; what sort of a life is that? What more atrocious existence could one imagine for one's worst enemy? I much prefer to attribute to them a tranquil state, without any cares' " (*Historical and Critical Dictionary,* s.v. "Epicurus," nn. S and T). Ernst Cassirer characterizes Bayle's monumental work as "the real arsenal of all Enlightenment philosophers" (*Philosophy of the Enlightenment,* 167); Emile Faguet terms it "the Bible of the eighteenth century" (*Dix-huitième siècle,* 1 and 6). For the best introduction to Bayle's theologico-political thought, see Bartlett, *The Idea of Enlightenment.* Bayle's argument quoted here, we may note, recalls that of Tertullian in *Against Hermogenes* 10ff.

15. *Genesis XII* 4.3.7 and 4.4.10; see also 4.2 and 4.7.14: "Six is the first perfect number because it is the sum of its parts. . . . We cannot, therefore, say that the number six is perfect precisely because God perfected all His works in six days, but rather we must say that God perfected His works in six days because six is a perfect number."

16. *Special Laws* IV 186; *On Abraham* 268; *Creation of the Cosmos* 46.

17. It is here, consequently, that Islam takes its stand, rejecting the beliefs in the Trinity and in the divinity of the Messiah Jesus as blasphemously incoherent denials of intelligibly omnipotent monotheism: "Verily, they are unbelievers

who say, 'The Messiah, son of Mary, is God.' You ask them: 'Who could prevail against God if He had chosen to destroy the Messiah, son of Mary, and his mother, and the rest of mankind?' . . . He creates what He pleases, for God has the power over all things. . . . He can punish whom he please and pardon whom He will." "They are surely infidels who say, 'God is the Christ, son of Mary.' But the Christ only said, 'Oh children of Israel, worship God who is my Lord and your Lord.' Whoever associates a compeer with God, will have Paradise denied him by God, and his abode shall be Hell." "And when God will ask: 'Oh Jesus, son of Mary, did you say to mankind: *Worship me and my mother as two deities apart from God?*' Jesus will answer: 'Halleluja. Could I say what I had no right to?' " "Jesus was only a creature whom We favored and made an example for the children of Israel. If We pleased We could have put angels in place of you as trustees on the earth. . . . Let not Satan misdirect you" (*Al-Qur'an* 5.17–18, 72, 116; see also 3.77–84 [though the Christian version of the Gospel "sounds like the Scripture, in fact it is not"], 4.171, 9.30–32).

18. Barth, *Church Dogmatics*, 3:2, pp. 153–54. Barth assembles a list of orthodox patristic authorities who embraced this version of Platonic eternity.

19. The same question is more acutely raised by Leon Kass's recent radical version of a Platonizing interpretation of biblical "Creation" (an interpretation inspired by an understandable wish to reconcile evolution with Creation). Kass suggests that we are to understand the species of the biblical creatures as being "present *potentially* in the world, even before they were called forth into being (that is, created)" ("Evolution and the Bible," 37).

20. Thomas Aquinas *Writing on the Book of "Sentences" of Peter Lombard* (henceforward cited as *On Sentences*), bk. 2, dis. 1, qu. 1, a. 1 and 2, "Solutions"; a. 5, reply objs. 7, 9, 12, 13, 14, reply to args. 2; *On the Eternity of the World; Commentary on Aristotle's Physics*, secs. 989–90; *On Separated Substances* 9; ST 1a qu. 46, a. 1 reply obj. 6; Luther, LG, *Werke*, 42:11.

21. Philo's *Creation of the Cosmos* 13–28 teaches that God first *created* even the ideas, or an incorporeal archetype of the cosmos; still, this was done in conformity to certain preexisting forms of "perfection." Seemingly more radical is Tertullian *Against Praxeas* 5–8 and *Against Hermogenes* 18, stressing Prov. 8:22–25, which teaches of God's "creating" or at any rate "originating" [קנה] even or precisely "Wisdom"; yet this wisdom Tertullian equates with the Son and with Reason: "For God is rational and reason was first in Him" (*Against Praxeas* 5).

22. At the other extreme we have the radically antiphilosophic *Zohar's* doctrine on Creation, as summarized by Gershom Scholem, according to which matter not only did not preexist but was not even brought into being by God's initial Creation: "Only the Fall has caused God to become 'transcendent.' . . . All creation was originally of a spiritual nature and but for the intervention of

evil would not have assumed material form" (*Major Trends in Jewish Mysticism,*
224; see also 90–91 [the medieval Hasidic doctrine], and 231: "It is to sin" that
man "owes his corporeal existence, born from the pollution of matter by the
poison of sin" [referring to Ezra ben Solomon and Moses de Leon, probably the
author of the *Zohar,* as well as to *Zohar* sec. 3, p. 83b]; also 275, 280 [Moses
Cordovero and Isaac Luria], 305). For the *Zohar's* radical interpretation (in sec.
1, p. 15) of the opening line, or three words, of Genesis, see Scholem, ibid., 221.
The danger here is a drift toward pantheism or even myth, gnosticism, and
polytheism (ibid., 12–13, 28–29, 34–35, 265ff; see also Scholem's "Kabbalah
and Myth," in *On the Kabbalah and Its Symbolism,* esp. pp. 100–109).

23. In support of Ibn Ezra's pronouncement, it would seem that there is
some likelihood that at least the original basic meaning of ברא is "divide," "cut
off," or "separate" (see Josh. 17:15, 18; Ezek. 23:47; and Dantinne, "Création et
séparation"). On the other hand, consider Strauss's exploration of the implications of the fact that at the beginning of Genesis "this term, *bara,* is used
synonymously, at least apparently, with the Hebrew word for doing or making,
asah," which twice in this special context is applied to the peculiar "making" of
"the fruit tree making fruit" ("On the Interpretation of Genesis," 9).

There is no word in ancient Greek for "creation." As Westermann notes
(*Genesis 1–11,* 100), "Of the 46 times that the Septuagint encounters the Hebrew ברא = create, it renders it by κτίζω only 17 times; κτίζω is not found in
Genesis; only ποιεῖν is used. κτίζω and ברא seem to have the same meaning only
after the Greek translation. The Septuagint translators had no Greek equivalent
of the Hebrew ברא." See also W. Förster's article "κτίζειν" in the *Theologisches
Wörterbuch zum Neuen Testament,* ed. Kittel et al.: "Since the days of Alexander
the Great, κτίζειν in the Hellenistic sense has had particular reference to the
autocratic ruler with aspiration to divinity, who irrespective of what was there
before, causes a *polis* to arise by his word or command or will (backed by his
power), thus acquiring divine honor in this city, since it owes its very existence
wholly to him as its κτίστης" (see in this regard Philo *Creation of the Cosmos* 17ff.
and *On Dreams* 1.76). The use of κτίζειν thus does not rule out an eternal
material, and this fits the Septuagint's rendering into Greek of the opening
verses, as was noted already by Clement of Alexandria (*Stromata* 5.14.90). As for
the Hebrew word (יצר) that is employed for the "creation" of man in the second
account (Gen. 2:7, translated by πλάσσω in the Septuagint), see Humbert,
"Emploi et portée bibliques du verbe *yasar* et de ses dérivés substantifs," and
Westermann's critical discussion, *Genesis 1–11,* 203–5. Barth observes (*Church
Dogmatics,* 3:1, p. 17) that "it is significant that without a single exception the
Septuagint carefully avoided the familiar Greek verb δημιουργεῖν as a render-
ing of the Hebrew words used to denote the creative activity of God to the
Greeks. . . . When δημιουργός is used of God in Greek literature it is to describe

Him as the One who has transformed the world from ἀταξία into κόσμος. . . . In evident awareness of this, the Septuagint does not wish to equate Him with the demiurge of Greek philosophy and mythology." (The same cannot be said of Philo, of course, who insouciantly uses δημιουργός as a term for the Creator.)

24. Westermann, *Genesis 1–11,* 109. The ambiguity is reproduced rather than resolved in von Rad's commentary, which thus fails to recognize, let alone confront, the depths of the difficulty (*Genesis,* 46–49). Justin Martyr, the celebrated early Christian apologist, complacently and incoherently takes it as a matter of course (in striking contrast to his disciple Tatian) that Genesis agrees with the doctrine of Plato's *Timaeus* (indeed, that the latter was taken from Genesis). Creation took place through God working as a craftsman upon a preexisting and uncreated raw material, yet "God alone is ungenerated and on account of this is God, and all the rest is generated and destructible." Cf. *Apology I* 10.2, 20.4, 59.1–5 (quoting the Septuagint of Gen. beg.), and 67.7 with *Dialogue with Tryphon* 5.4–6. Clement of Alexandria continues to speak similarly (cf. *Stromata* 5.14.89–90 with 5.14.92). Barth recognizes the difficulty, but his attempt at a solution is of dubious coherence (*Church Dogmatics* 3:1, sec. 41, esp. pp. 106–7). Robert Alter's recent new translation goes very far in construing the opening of Genesis in such a way as to deny Creation *ex nihilo,* though his commentary does not draw attention to the radical moral and theological implications. Alter's characterization of Creation in his and Kermode's earlier *Literary Guide to the Bible* (34) similarly leaves things at reproducing the problematic ambiguity of the scriptural text. Westermann (*Genesis 1–11,* 95–98) usefully collects and compares the major diverse arguments for how the syntax of the first lines is to be construed and what the theological implications are of the alternatives. In the second account of Creation, Adam and Eve are of course not created *ex nihilo*—and Augustine (*Genesis XII* 7.5ff.) alertly struggles with the relevant and very far-reaching question of whether or not the text can be construed as indicating that at least their *souls* were so created (the alternative being that God may face limits in the spiritual or immaterial as well as in the material realms of being).

25. Around 124 B.C. See Momigliano, "The Second Book of Maccabees."

26. ὅτι οὐκ ἐξ ὄντων ἐποίησεν αὐτὰ ὁ θεός. Some later and less reliable or perhaps manipulated manuscripts switch the key words and read ἐξ οὐκ ὄντων. But as May observes (*Creatio ex Nihilo,* 7 n. 27), the fundamental issue is not affected. The phrase "*ex nihilo*" comes into the theological tradition from the Vulgate translation of this line.

27. For prefigurations of corporeal resurrection, see Job 19:25–26, Isa. 26:19, Ezek. 37:1–14. For strong affirmation, see Dan. 12 (also John 5:28–29, Acts 24:15, 1 Cor. 6:14–15 and above all 15:12ff.).

28. 2 Macc. 7:9, 11, 14, 23, 28–29 (see the editorial note ad loc. in the *New*

Oxford Annotated Apocrypha). On resurrection see also 12:44–45, 14:46, and Dan. 12:2–3. The closest thing to a reference to Creation out of nothing in the pre-Hellenistic Scripture is probably Job 26:7, but see 28:25–27 and 38 entire. Ambiguity similar to that of the mother's formulation in 2 Maccabees is expressed in a more sophisticated form in Philo's *Creation of the Cosmos* 81; *Allegories of the Sacred Laws* III 10; *On the Change of Names* 46; *On the Decalogue* 58 and 111; *On the Indestructability of the Cosmos* 19; and *Life of Moses* II 99–100 and 267. However, in *Creation of the Cosmos* 8–10 and 171 and *Questions and Answers on Genesis* I 64, Philo seems to assume the existence of an uncreated matter (see similarly *Allegories of the Sacred Laws* II 19; *On Plantation* II 3; *On Dreams* 1.241; *On the Special Laws* I 47ff. and 266, III 180, IV 187; *Who Is the Heir of Divine Things* 134 and 160; and *On Flight and Discovery* 8–12). What is more, Philo stresses that this matter in its wildness and death is radically alien to God, prior to His working upon it (*Creation of the Cosmos* 21–23, 33; *On Flight and Discovery* 198). Indeed, in *Allegories of the Sacred Laws* II 329 Philo even declares that it was not "lawful" (θέμις) for God to touch the matter, and therefore He could not Himself have worked upon it directly. Insofar as Philo attempts to put together divine omnipotence and the eternity of matter, he follows the line of those Stoics Cicero declared most "superstitious" (*On Divination* 2.86 and *On the Nature of the Gods* 3.92). For a full discussion of the Jewish sources, see Schmuttermayr, " 'Schöpfung aus dem Nichts' in 2 Makk 7,28?" and May, *Creatio ex Nihilo*, 6–26, both of which draw on Weiss, *Untersuchungen zur Kosmologie des hellenistischen und palästinischen Judentums*. Sorabji (*Space, Time, and the Continuum*, 203–9) argues with some hesitation (and not altogether convincingly) for Philo's articulation of Creation *ex nihilo* on the basis of somewhat obscure passages from the two treatises *On Providence* known almost entirely in Armenian translations.

29. ἐξ ἀμόρφου ὕλης. See Augustine's uneasy comment on this testimony, which he concedes is of canonical Scripture (*On the Literal Interpretation of Genesis: An Unfinished Book*, chap. 3 end).

30. Even so sophisticated a thinker as Tertullian fails to remain intransigent in his grasp of the basic issue. At one point he is willing to argue that resurrection, and even Creation *ex nihilo,* may be understood as not ruling out uncreated matter (*On the Resurrection of the Flesh* 11).

31. See esp. Irenaeus *Against the Heresies* 2.14. As Scholem pointed out ("Schöpfung aus Nichts und Selbstverschränkung Gottes"), the first unqualified statement of Creation *ex nihilo* (in some respects uncannily foreshadowing the Lurianic Kabbalah, as well as the later doctrine of "negative attributes") is found in the idiosyncratic Gnostic Christian heresy of the philosophically learned Basilides of Syria (writing ca. A.D. 125), whose views are available to us in the polemic against him in Hippolytus *Refutation of All Heresies* 7.20ff. For an

intelligent analysis of Basilides' views (which included an explicit interpretation of the opening of Genesis), insofar as they can be deduced from Hippolytus's polemic against them, see May, *Creatio ex Nihilo,* 67–84. For the "Platonism" of the Gnostics in general, see Jonas, *The Gnostic Religion,* 33–34, 191 n. 24, 193–94, 286.

32. For the deep connection between the doctrines of Creation, resurrection, immortality of the soul, and the response to Platonic philosophy, see Pelikan, *The Christian Tradition,* 1.50–55.

33. *Refutation of All Heresies* 10.32.1. See also Irenaeus *Against All Heresies* 2.1.1, 2.30.9, as well as 2.10.2–4 and 4.20.1, identifying "substantium" with God's will—in opposition to "Anaxagoras and Empedocles and Plato" (2.14.4; for the confrontation with Plato, see also 3.25.5). Irenaeus becomes the foundation of "the Church Doctrine of *Creatio ex nihilo,*" but it is to be noted that "the biblical creation story moved somewhat into the background; nowhere did Irenaeus expound it consecutively" (May, *Creatio ex Nihilo,* 174–75).

34. According to Williams (*The Common Expositor,* 45–46), the explosion of thirty-five or more Renaissance and Reformation commentaries on Genesis all argue for Creation *ex nihilo* not on the basis of positive scriptural interpretation but instead negatively, in a dialogue with and against the philosophers, beginning with Aristotle. But contrast Luther (LG, *Werke,* 42:5): "As to Lyra's belief that a knowledge of the philosophers' opinion concerning matter is essential because on it depends the understanding of the six days of activity—I don't know whether Lyra understood what it was that Aristotle called 'Matter.' Unlike Ovid, Aristotle does not designate the shapeless and crude chaos as matter. Therefore, disregarding these needless opinions, let us turn to Moses as so much the better teacher, because we can follow him with greater safety than the philosophers, who, without benefit of the Word, debate about unknown matters." Yet Luther is compelled to proceed (ibid., 42:6–8) to an exegesis of the first two verses as describing the creation of heaven and earth as "not such as they now are, but rather rude and formless bodies [*rudia et informia corpora*]."

35. *Guide* 1, intro., 1.50, 2.29. As Joseph Albo observes (*Ikkarim* 1.3, p. 51), "Maimonides also, the author of the *Guide of the Perplexed,* in chapter twenty-five of the second part, says that his belief in creation *ex nihilo* was not due to the authority of scriptural texts—texts can be interpreted—but to the fact that it is a true doctrine, and therefore the texts must be interpreted to harmonize with this doctrine. . . . For the Torah does not oblige us to believe absurdities, which are opposed to first principles, or any imaginary notions which the reason cannot conceive. But a thing which can be conceived by the mind, we are obliged to believe, though it is opposed to nature, for example, resurrection of the dead and the miracles of the Torah. An absurd idea, however, which can not be conceived by the mind need not be believed even if it is plainly expressed in

the Torah." According to Al-Ghazali (*Incoherence of the Philosophers,* Seventeenth Discussion, On Causality and Miracles, 179), when the philosophers say to the believers, "We help you by maintaining that every possible thing is within the power of God, while you help us by maintaining that whatever is impossible is not within [divine] power. . . . Now then what, according to you, is the definition of the impossible?"—"[We believers] answer: the impossible is not within the power [of being enacted by God]. The impossible consists in affirming a thing conjointly with denying it, affirming the more specific while denying the more general, or affirming two things while negating one of them. What does not reduce to this is not impossible, and what is not impossible is within [divine] power" (see Maimonides *Guide* 3.20 end). In struggling to understand the opening sentences of the Bible, Augustine addresses God as "my God, in whose breast there is no contradiction [*deus meus, in cuius sinu non est contradictio*]" (*Confessions* 12.25). As a consequence, see, e.g., Augustine's striking thesis in *Genesis XII* 8.22 and context: "Motion in space and time is impossible for God"; and 10.25: "I do not judge that Tertullian was so foolish, as to believe that even the nature of God was capable of suffering, so that Christ not in body only, or in body and soul, but in the Word Itself through whom all things were made, would be believed to be capable of suffering and subject to change"; as well as Augustine's fundamental hermeneutic principle, which he states as follows: "If in the words of God, or in the words of someone called to play the role of a prophet, something is said which cannot be understood literally without absurdity, there is no doubt that it must be taken as spoken figuratively in order to point to something else" (11.2). See also Augustine's words of complaint against a common misunderstanding of the meaning of omnipotence (*Against Faustus the Manichean* 26.5): "This means that if God is omnipotent, He could make those things which are true, by the very fact that they are true, to be false." Thomas Aquinas is more cautious (*On the Eternity of the World*): "It is said that it cannot be the case that an affirmation and a negation be simultaneously true, although some say that God could make this so. Others, however, say that not even God can make this so because in fact it is nothing. It is, finally, clear that God cannot make it to be the case, because the very affirmation by which this is held to be so implies its own denial. Still, if it should be held that God is able to make it that things of this sort come to be, the position is not heretical, although I do believe that it is false, just as that the past has not been includes within itself a contradiction." See similarly Milton's words, in *Paradise Lost,* 10.799–801: "contradiction, which to God himself / Impossible is held, as Argument of weakness, not of Power." Contrast the more dogmatic teaching of the same author's *Christian Doctrine* on the meaning of "omnipotence": "It is to be noted, however, that the power of God is not exerted in those things which imply a contradiction—2 Tim. 2:13, Tit. 1:2;

Heb. 6:18" (1.2, pp. 145–46, 148; 1.3, p. 156; 1.7, p. 311). But Milton's insistence on the impossibility of contradiction leads him into the iconoclastic position of denying the Trinity as absurd (1.5, esp. p. 212). In contrast, see Pascal, *Pensées,* #177 (= Brunschvicg #384): "Contradiction is a bad mark of truth. Several things certain are contradicted." Consider, finally, Luther, LG, *Werke,* 43:27–28: "So it is not sufficient to be a rhetorician. The rhetorician must be a dialectician, so that he may judge between worthy arguments and axioms (thus indeed are named solid, certain, and true statements) and mere 'likelihoods.' . . . Even in moral business axioms are to be sought. . . . But it is in matters of Theology that we ought to use to the greatest extent such firm and certain reasonings."

36. *Confessions* 12.8. See the preceding appeal to philosophic doctrines of matter in 12.6; also 7.5 as well as *On the Literal Interpretation of Genesis: An Unfinished Book,* chaps. 3–4; *Genesis XII* 1.14–15 and 8:20; and *Two Books on Genesis against the Manicheans* 1.6. See also Thomas Aquinas ST 1a qu. 66 a. 1 and 2. Compare Luther (LG, *Werke,* 42:5–9, 13–14, 19, 25–26), who understands the word "water" in the opening verses of Genesis to be the designation of "that rude mass of heaven and earth," appealing to 2 Pet. 3:5 ("By God's Word long ago the heavens were, and the earth was formed out of water and by water"). Yet Luther adds (42:7), "With Augustine's statement in his book *Confessions*—that matter is almost nothing, so close to nothing that there is no intermediate reality—I disagree entirely. How can you apply the term 'mere nothing' to something that is the sort of thing and substance which Moses calls heaven and earth?" One could do so, Luther submits, only if one means "matter" in the sense of "something like wood which is not yet a box or bench. But the philosophers call this 'secondary matter.' "

37. *Confessions* 12.24. Augustine here very much qualifies his much more assertive and unhesitating interpretation of the opening of Genesis in his early polemical work *Two Books on Genesis against the Manicheans* 1.3.

38. This line is reminiscent of Lucretius *On the Nature of Things* 5.259 ("The parent of all things herself the tomb of all"), with the addition of the "perhaps." Lucretius is speaking of the earth, in the course of one of his arguments proving that the earth is *not* immortal.

39. See also 1.10, 3.1–21 and 708ff., 4.665–6, 5.179 and 577–78, 7.90–93 and 211ff. See also Milton's remarkably dramatic youthful (written 1628) Latin poem on *"Pater omnipotens,"* entitled *"Naturam Non Pati Senium."* Contrast two major "sources" for Milton, Guillaume du Bartas's *La sepmaine, ou Création,* Day One or "The Chaos," and Day Two or "The Elements"; and Milton's personal friend Hugo Grotius's *Exile of Adam,* act 2 (pp. 123–25 and 130–31 of Kirkconnell's *Celestial Cycle*).

40. It goes without saying that in Milton's dogmatic work *Christian Doctrine,*

these doubts at the foundation of the errors underlying the angelic rebellion are largely laid to rest. See bk. 1, chap. 7, and also chap. 32, p. 627.

41. See *Theologico-Political Treatise,* in *Opera,* chap. 2, p. 38, l. 32–p. 39, l. 13; chap. 6 (beg.), p. 81, ll. 16–23 and p. 81, l. 31–p. 82, l. 7; and Strauss's discussion of these passages and their import, "How to Study Spinoza's *Theologico-Political Treatise,*" in *Persecution and the Art of Writing,* 198–200.

42. In his understanding of the rabbinic sages' attitude toward Greek philosophy, Spinoza has in mind such Talmudic pronouncements as the repeated remark, "Cursed be the man who would breed swine and cursed be the man who would teach his son Grecian Wisdom" (Baba Kama 82b–83a; Menachoth 64b; Sotah 49b); or the less pungent but equally mordant reply of Rabbi Ishmael to the question of Ben Damah (Menachoth 99b; see also Sotah 49b): "May one such as I who have studied the whole of the Torah learn Greek wisdom?—He thereupon read to him the following verse, 'This book of the law shall not depart out of thy mouth, but thou shalt meditate therein day and night.' [Josh. 1:8] Go then and find a time that is neither day nor night and learn then Greek wisdom." See also *Mishnah,* Pirke Avoth 3.23; the story of Aher in the Talmudic Chagigah 15b; and the deuterocanonical book of Sirach (3:21–24).

43. Hegel reveals his full Montesquieuian "agenda," so to speak, by interjecting the following passionate remark: "The true 'miracle' or wonder is the appearance of spirit in nature, and the true appearance of spirit is, in its fundamental aspect, the spirit of humanity and its consciousness of the world. (For knowledge of the world means, that the world in all this confusion and contingent manifoldness still contains lawfulness and reason everywhere—relatively speaking, *this* is wondrous.)" The very grave question is, How does Hegel understand himself to have *knowledge,* knowledge that satisfies his intransigent criteria for knowledge (as opposed to mere conviction, tantamount to "belief" or "faith"), that this apparent "wonder" is true—in the face of the contrary original biblical claim, purportedly grounded in the direct experience of miraculous divine intervention by direct revelation?

44. See Al-Ghazali's *Incoherence of the Philosophers,* Seventeenth Discussion. The appeal to the fixity of nature makes its appearance in Christian apologetics directed against philosophically informed pagans. See notably chap. 6 of Eusebius *Against the Writings by Philostratus about Apollonius of Tyana, Occasioned by the Parallel Drawn by Hierocles between the Latter and Christ.*

45. In the New Testament, which has come under a certain influence of Greek philosophy, φύσις (and derivatives) is found sixteen times, while in the Septuagint it is found only in the Hellenistic books Wisdom of Solomon (7:20, 8:19, 12:10, 13:1, 19:20), 3 Maccabees (3:29), and 4 Maccabees (1:20; 5:7, 8, 25; 13:27; 15:13, 25; 16:3).

46. See the *O.E.D.*, s.v. "miracle," #1; Augustine *Against Faustus the Manichean* 26.3; Thomas Aquinas ST 1a qu. 105 a. 7 and 8; Spinoza, *Theologico-Political Treatise,* chap. 6; Strauss, *Natural Right and History,* 81–84, as well as the same author's "Jerusalem and Athens," 151. The Revised Standard Version translates פלא as "miracle" at Ps. 78:12. Consider the lengths to which Philo must go in order to force upon the text of Genesis a version of a Platonic conception of nature (*Creation of the Cosmos,* 8–9, 24–29).

47. The term (מקרה) is translated in the Septuagint as σύμπτωμα. For the philosophic-theological significance of this latter Greek term, see Aristotle *On Prophecy in Sleep* 462b27–463a3 and 463b1ff. See also *Physics* 199a3–6 and context.

48. Eccles. 2:14 and 15; 3:19; 9:2 and 3. See also the use of the verbal root (קרה) at Num. 11:23, Isa. 41:22, Eccles. 9:11, Dan. 10:14. See similarly the connotation of the other word for accident (פגע) at 1 Kings 5:18 and Eccles. 9:11 (at both points, the Septuagint uses ἀπάντημα). Calvin, discussing Ps. 107, teaches that all apparently fortuitous occurrences are in truth providential (*Institutes,* 1.5.8). See similarly Thomas Aquinas ST 1a qu. 103 a. 7 and qu. 116.

49. *Institutes,* 1.16.2, 8, 9. See the unfolding meaning of "Chance" in Milton's *Paradise Lost,* beginning from the fallen angels' self-delusion and culminating in God's pronouncement (1.133; 2.233, 550ff., 965; 7.172). See also Milton's *Christian Doctrine,* 1.2 beg. and 2.5, p. 690: "The casting of lots is in effect an appeal to the divine power for explanation or arbitration in uncertain or controversial matters." See similarly Plato *Laws* 690c.

50. Translated from ben Gabbai's "עבודת הקודש" (written 1531), in Scholem, *The Messianic Idea in Judaism,* 300. See similarly Nachmanides' comment ad loc. on the word "said" in Gen. 1:3 and Maimonides *Guide* 3.20 end.

CHAPTER 3. *The Ontological Implications of the Unfolding of Creation, for Creatures and Creator*

1. Cf. Ps. 115:16 with Cassuto, *Commentary on the Book of Genesis,* 1:20, and Barth, *Church Dogmatics,* 3:1, p. 18.

2. God's total power over, even His capacity to nullify, the sidereal splendors is stressed in Neh. 9:6, Job 9:7, Ps. 8:4, Isa. 13:10, Jer. 51:15, Ezek. 32:7–8, Joel 3:15, Amos 8:9, Hab. 3:11. See also 1 Kings 8:27; 2 Chron. 2:5, 6:18; and Jehudah Halevi's Song #1, ll. 30–33, in *Three Jewish Philosophers,* 3rd part, pp. 132–33: "Who shall say he hath not seen Thee?— / Lo, the heavens and their hosts / Declare the fear of Thee / Though their voice be not heard." See also Jacob, *The First Book of the Bible,* 7; Barth, *Church Dogmatics,* 3:1, pp. 166–67; and Westermann, *Genesis 1–11,* 119: "Heaven in the Old Testament is simply

something created; it has no divine character at all. . . . [I]t is part of 'not God.' . . . There is no indication at all in the Old Testament that God created heaven for himself to live in as happens, for example, in Egypt."

3. Thomas wrestles unsuccessfully with this manifest incongruity (ST 1a qu. 67 a. 4). See Calvin's *Institutes*, 1.16.2: "The Lord, that He reserve to Himself the entire glory of these things as His own, willed that light should exist, and that the earth should be replenished with all kinds of herbs and fruits, before He made the sun. No faithful man, therefore, will make the sun either the principal or necessary cause of those things which existed before the creation of the sun, but only the instrument that God employs, because He so pleases; though He can without it act equally well by Himself." See similarly Calvin's *Commentary on Genesis* ad 1:3 and Theophilus of Antioch *To Autolycus* 2.15 beg. Barth comments (*Church Dogmatics,* 3:1, p. 153), "As Basil has rightly perceived (*On the Hexateuch* 5.1), . . . the author is maintaining this against every solar cult, and especially the Egyptian" (see also 120–21 and esp. 158–60). Cassuto observes (*Commentary on the Book of Genesis* 2:101–2) that in the account of the Flood, "the Torah does not refer to the heat of the sun as one of the factors contributing to the evaporation of the waters, although it would have been but logical to mention this detail." In contrast, in the Sumerian myths of the Flood, from which the biblical account may be derived, "stress is laid on the action of the God Samas at the end of the Flood, when he shed his light in the heavens and on the earth." See also von Rad, *Genesis,* 49.

4. *Church Dogmatics,* 3:1, p. 135. See also Strauss, "On the Interpretation of Genesis," 15. The Septuagint, unlike the Hebrew text, *does* have God declaring the work of the second day to be good—or, more precisely, "beautiful, noble" (καλόν, the term used throughout chapter 1 by the Septuagint for the Hebrew טוב). On the appropriateness and the moral and aesthetic significance of the Greek term in this context, see Wevers, *Notes on the Greek Text of Genesis* ad loc., and consider the meaning of טוב at Gen. 6:2.

5. "The expression 'lamps' is meant to be prosaic and degrading" (von Rad, *Genesis,* 53).

6. Barth, *Church Dogmatics,* 3:1, p. 159. See also Strauss, "On the Interpretation of Genesis," 15.

7. Repeatedly we hear in the Scripture reports of the incursion, even into the very bosom of Israel, of star- or sun-worship (2 Kings 17:16, 21:3ff., 23:5; Jer. 8:2, 10:2; Ezek. 8:16; Amos 5:26; cf. Job 31:26–28). See also Maimonides *Mishneh Torah: The Book of Knowledge* 66a–67a; Gunkel, *Genesis,* 110; and Barth, *Church Dogmatics,* 3:1, sec. 41, pp. 165–66. The Talmud generally combats astrology (e.g., in suggesting that Abraham learned from God of the falseness of the science; Genesis Rabbah 44.12, Shabbath 156a) but as a continuing presence, and

sometimes as accepted by the Sages (Shabbath 119a, 156b, Palestinian Shabbath 8d, Berachoth 64a). Openness to astrological superstition creeps back into even so thoughtful an authority as Nachmanides (see his comment on Gen. 1:15–18) and remains a problem in the Christian tradition, epitomized most notably by Pope Leo X and Melanchthon—whose influence on the original editors of Luther's *Lectures on Genesis* seems to have introduced the surprisingly qualified toleration of astrology there (see LG, *Werke*, 42:33–34, and Pelikan's introduction to vol. 1 of the American translation, p. xi). See Calvin's *Warning Against Astrology*. And consider Barth's very defensive comment on the failure to condemn astrologers in the New Testament account of the three Magi (*Church Dogmatics*, 3:1, sec. 41, pp. 165–66). For the continuing struggles throughout the Hellenistic period over the status of the heavenly bodies, see Jonas, *The Gnostic Religion*, chaps. 1 and 10.

8. For the implications of the philosophers' astral piety, see esp. Plato *Laws* 885e7–886a8, 886d4–e2, 888e4–890a2, 898d3–899b9, taken together with 966e2–968a1; *Apology of Socrates* 18a7–19d7, 23d2–7, 26d1–e2; Cicero *Tusculan Disputations*, bk. 5 sec. 10; Aristotle *Physics* 196b1–4 and context; and *Metaphysics* 1074b1–11. For a high expression of the opposing, still vigorous, pre- or antiphilosophic Greek understanding of the divinely mysterious heavens, or more precisely of the unpredictable "meaning" of a solar eclipse, see the fragment of Pindar's (Ninth) Paean to the Thebans, preserved in Dionysius of Halicarnassus "On Demosthenes" 7.

9. Cf. Deut. 4:19–20 with 17:3 and also Wisd. of Sol. 13:1–9. Lucretius, who does not deign to count Aristotle and Plato among the philosophers who have made "divine discoveries" (*On the Nature of Things* 1.734–39 and context), argues that ignorance of the genesis and hence the nature of the visible heavenly bodies is the chief reason why human beings began (ibid., 5.1205ff.)—and continue, even the sophisticated (ibid., 5.82ff., 6.58ff.)—to grovel in the "misery" of fearful belief in ruling providential divinity.

10. Aristotle *On Respiration*, esp. 472b27; *On Youth and Old Age, on Life and Death*, beg. (modern science modifies this only by substituting "oxygen" for air; see Nuland, *How We Die*, 118ff., which begins with the famous aphorism of Hippocrates, "The human is an obligate aerobe"). See the paraphrase of Anaximenes, D-K A7 ("Limitless air he said to be the first cause, from which comes into being the things that come into being and have come into being and will be, both the gods and the goddesses"; see also D-K B3); Diogenes of Apollonia, D-K A4–5, B2–5; Aristophanes *Clouds* 264 (see also 230, 393, 627, 763); *Birds* 692–97; and Philemo 91.4, in *Comicorum Atticorum Fragmenta*, ed. Kock. In *Creation of the Cosmos* 29, Philo fills in the "gap" in Genesis by identifying "darkness" as "air"; and in *On Plantation* 3 he identifies "the heavens" as "aether."

11. Thomas was misled by the Vulgate translation rooted in the Septuagint to suppose that the words for "and all the host of them" (זכל־עבאם) actually read "and all their array/adornment" (Sept.: πᾶς ὁ κόσμος αὐτῶν).

12. Strauss, "On the Interpretation of Genesis," 10–12. See also his "Jerusalem and Athens," 152–53. Cf. Barth, *Church Dogmatics,* 3:1, pp. 168, 170, 174. Westermann, in ignorance of Strauss's crucial interpretive discoveries, hopelessly declares, "All attempts to bring the works of creation into a systematic order must be given up" (*Genesis 1–11,* 89; see also 123). I demur from Strauss only inasmuch as he seems certain that the sun and moon, despite their mobility, are presented as lifeless. Strauss rightly stresses that the adjective "living" or "alive" (חי) appears only when the creation of the animals is narrated, at Gen. 1:20 (so far as I am aware, this adjective is never applied to plants in the Hebrew Scripture). But the two "lamps" are assigned the activity of "ruling" (ממשלה) the day and the night (though not, Strauss stresses, ruling the earth, let alone humanity). This at the least would seem to raise a question: Can the unalive be rulers? (See Ginzberg, *Legends of the Jews,* 1.23–24, 80.) Herder, referring also to Ps. 19:5–7, comments, "Kings of the world are they; but only under God; his Vicars, his creatures and messengers. . . Sun, Moon, Stars also become living: they are given their homes and pavilions in heaven" (*On the Spirit of Hebrew Poetry,* dialogue 3, in *Schriften zum alten Testament,* 726–27). See also Westermann, *Genesis 1–11,* 127: "P is speaking polemically: he must establish in every way possible his thesis that the sun and the moon are creatures and nothing more. How difficult this was is demonstrated by one of the functions assigned to the sun and the moon; they are to rule, vv. 16 and 18. . . . Ruling is a personal function; even in Gen 1 there persists an echo, however faint, of the divinity of the sun and the moon, so deeply ingrained in the Ancient Near East." But contrast Maimonides *Mishneh Torah: The Book of Knowledge,* Laws Concerning Idolatry, chap. 1 and 2 (beg.); and Calvin, *Institutes,* 1.11.1.

13. See Bonhoeffer, *Creation and Fall* ad loc. ("Uncreated freedom is worshipped by created freedom"); Kass, "Evolution and the Bible," 36 ("Genesis stresses more [man's] freedom of motion and action, less his theoretic intellect"). We may note in this connection that the biblical account thus ignores the fact stressed by the philosophic biologist: the existence of the class made up of "many" immobile animals (dwelling in water). Accordingly and significantly, the philosopher defines the nature of animals by capacity for awareness, or perception (at a minimum, as in the case of the sponge, touch), and not by capacity for local motion (Aristotle *History of Animals* 487b8–15, 489a15–19; *Parts of Animals* 651b4–5, 653b23–24, 666a35, 681a10ff.). For the philosopher, in contrast to the Scriptures, we may conclude, the human is the supreme animal on earth by virtue of supreme awareness rather than by virtue of supreme mutability.

14. *Ideas for a Philosophy of the History of Mankind* 10.6. See similarly Strauss, "Jerusalem and Athens," 154, and Cassuto, *Commentary on the Book of Genesis* 1:49–50. On the sea monster as "the one exception," see the apt comments by Robert Sacks in "The Lion and the Ass," 43, and Barth, *Church Dogmatics*, 3:1, p. 173: that the "sea monsters" (תנינם) are the first to be mentioned among the sea-dwellers, and that the verb for "create" is specifically applied to them, "denotes in the context of Old Testament thinking an act of demythologisation the importance of which we cannot overlook." Contrast, however, Ginzberg, *Legends of the Jews*, 1.30–34.

15. See notably Hesiod *Theogony* 120ff.; Parmenides, D-K B 13; *Gilgamesh*, trans. by Gardner and Maier, tablet 1, column 2, ll. 16–17, 27–28, 35; column 4, ll. 8ff.; column 3, ll. 8–19; and Vriezen, *The Religion of Ancient Israel*, esp. 73. Cf. Frankfurt et al., *Before Philosophy*, esp. chap. 8. Strauss comments ("On the Interpretation of Genesis," 13), "The fundamental dualism, male and female, is replaced by the fundamental dualism, distinctness, or otherness, and local motion." This latter dualism "does not lend itself to the assumption of two gods, a distinguishing god and a moving god, as it were."

16. Barth observes (*Church Dogmatics*, 3:1, p. 170) that in the prior creations, including vegetation, "there was no question of any such blessing, nor was it demanded." But, "in addition to the special capacity for movement, it appears that the need of divine blessing belongs necessarily to the animal creation, especially if it is to continue and multiply in new individuals. A thing is blessed when it is authorized and empowered, with a definite promise of success, for one particular action [here, reproduction] as distinct from another which is also a possibility [sexual indulgence]." In other words, procreation "requires divine permission." We add that this may help explain why the text (Gen. 1:11–12) dwells so on the relatively pure mode in which the plants reproduce: through "seed" without coupling, without "the spontaneous association of two mutually adapted beings" (Jacob, *The First Book of the Bible* ad loc.)—and hence without need for a "permissive" blessing or restrictive commandment. The verb used to express the act of plant reproduction (עשה) is also used here as one of the words for God's act of creation. To be sure, this leaves unexplained the lack of an express mention of a blessing of the land animals other than man; and I am unconvinced by the labored explanations offered by Jacob and others.

17. The difficulty is indicated in the teaching of *The Avot of Rabbi Nathan* (chap. 2, p. 23): "Adam, too, was born circumcised, for it is said, 'And God created man in His own image.' Seth, too, was born circumcised, for it is said, 'And (Adam) begot a son in his own likeness, after his image.'" Cf. Plato's *Symposium* 190a8–b6 and 191b5–d3. Gunkel errs, however, when (*Genesis*, 13) he assimilates Aristophanes' teaching on the love of the couple to that of the Bible.

18. See also Gen. 30:2 and Calvin's comment ad loc.: "Jacob is angry, because his wife ascribes nothing to the providence of God, and, by imagining that children are the offspring of chance, would deprive God of the care and government of mankind." Also Gen. 33:5 and Calvin's comment ad loc. Cf. *Midrash Rabbah* on Gen. 8:9.

19. The maculate character of procreation is a second reason, closely linked to or an entailment of omipotence, why the *Qur'an* condemns the Christian divinization of Jesus as God's "son": "It does not behove God to have a son. Too immaculate is He! When He decrees a thing he has only to say: 'Be,' and it is. Jesus only said: 'Surely God is my Lord and your Lord, so worship Him. This is the straight path.' But the sectarians differed among themselves. Alas for the unbelievers when they see the Terrible Day!" (19.35–37).

20. See esp. Lev. 12; 15; 18, above all 18:24–25; 20:10–23; 23:3, 10–15. See also Bonhoeffer, *Creation and Fall,* 78–81 (commenting on Gen. 3:7), culminating in: "If the dogmatics of the Church saw the essence of original sin in sexuality, this is not such nonsense as Protestants have often said from a point of view of moralistic naturalism. The knowledge of good and evil is originally not an abstract knowledge of ethical principles, but sexuality; i.e. a perversion of the relationship between persons. And since the essential nature of sexuality consists in destruction, the dark secret of the originally sinful being of man is in fact preserved from generation to generation in continuing procreation. The objection, which refers to the natural character of sexuality, is not conscious of the highly ambivalent character of all so-called 'natural' things in our world."

21. Gunkel, *Genesis,* 113; Exod. 3:6, 24:10–11, 33:18–23; Num. 12:8; 1 Kings 22:19. See also Maimonides *Guide* 1.3–5.

22. Westermann, *Genesis 1–11,* 114: "P does not understand light as the sphere of God as in Ps. 104:2, or in 1 Tim. 6:16 or in Jas. 1:17; nor could P say: . . . 'God is light and in him is no darkness at all,' 1 John. 1:5. These passages do not preserve the boundary between creator and creature which for P was absolute." See also Aalen, *Die Begriffe "Licht" und "Finsternis" im Alten Testament, im Spätjudentum und im Rabbinisimus.*

23. Contrast, however, Cassuto, *Commentary on the Book of Genesis,* 1:26, and Augustine *Confessions* 12.3 as well as *Two Books on Genesis against the Manicheans* 1.3–4.

24. ST 1a qu. 73 a. 2. The reference is to Augustine's *Genesis XII* 4.8–19, which exhibits considerably more puzzlement over what could be the intelligible meaning of God's "resting" than Thomas suggests (but see 4.15 beg. for the view Thomas endorses). See also Thomas's *On the Sentences* 2.15.3.3. Barth even declares (*Church Dogmatics,* 3:1, p. 98), "The goal of creation, and at the same time the beginning of all that follows, is the event of God's Sabbath freedom, Sabbath rest and Sabbath joy, in which man, too, has been summoned

to participate." This is "a rest which takes precedence over all man's eagerness and zeal to enter upon his task. *Man is created to participate in this rest*" (my italics; see also 181–82 and 213ff.).

25. *Creation and Fall*, 13 and 40. Augustine, in sharp contrast (endorsed by Barth), rebukes those who would thus "bring ridicule upon one who asks about the things above and bring praise upon one who answers falsely" (for "*aliud est videre, aliud ridere*"). "I would rather reply," Augustine continues, "that what I don't know, I don't know" (*Confessions* 11.12 and Barth's *Church Dogmatics*, 3:1, pp. 69–70).

26. *On the Sentences* 2.1.1, art. 2, reply obj. 5. For a helpful introduction to and exploration of the tradition of discussion of the intelligibility of divine immutability and atemporality, see Sorabji's *Time, Creation, and the Continuum*, chaps. 8–9 and 13–19.

27. Scholem, *Major Trends in Jewish Mysticism*, 11–12, 22, 38–39, 65–66, 225, 322–24; *On the Kabbalah and Its Symbolism*, chap. 3, "Kabbalah and Myth."

28. See Cassuto, *Commentary on the Books of Genesis*, 1:59, which invokes Isa. 11:7 and 65:25 as evidence that in the Messianic era the original vegetarianism of all animate creation will be reestablished. The Aristotelian Thomas Aquinas (ST 1a qu. 96 a. 1 reply obj. 2), following Augustine (*Genesis XII* 3.16), characteristically demurs from such a reading, on the grounds that "the nature of animals was not changed by man's sin, as if those whose nature now it is to devour the flesh of others, would then have lived on herbs, as the lion and falcon." Contrast Milton, *Paradise Lost*, 11.182ff.

CHAPTER 4. *Creation and Divine Solicitude for Mankind*

1. Sacks attempts to show ("The Lion and the Ass," 37–45)—followed by Kass, in his attempt to reconcile evolution and Creation ("Evolution and the Bible," 38–39)—that "under the surface" of the first account of Creation there is a "deeper sense," which teaches that "the most fundamental difficulties lie not in the heart of man, but in the heart of being." As Sacks stresses, his specific interpretations of the verses stand or fall by the peculiar—and, it seems to me, unwarranted—construction he puts on the repeated and (for his interpretation) crucial phrase "And it was so" (ויהי־כן) at Gen. 1:7, 9, 11, 15, 24, and 30. Most massively, this reading would reduce the biblical Creator to the Platonic demiurge and thus remove the Bible's cornerstone (and the radicalism of its challenge to philosophy).

2. Strauss, "Jerusalem and Athens," 155. See also his "On the Interpretation of Genesis," 17.

3. See Wevers, *Notes on the Greek Text of Genesis* ad 2:24, for the universalistic significance of the Septuagint's switch from ἀνήρ to ἄνθρωπος in this verse.

We cannot, however, go so far as von Rad (*Genesis,* 82): "One must say, in fact, that in this statement the entire narrative so far arrives at the primary purpose toward which it was oriented from the beginning."

4. *Politics* 1253a2–3 and context (see Thomas Aquinas *Commentary on the Politics of Aristotle* ad loc., esp. secs. 35 and 39); 1278b18–30; see also the slightly more qualified formulation of Aristotle at *Ethics* 1097b11. See also Plato *Republic* 369b–370b, *Laws* 678–682; Cicero *Republic* 1.38–41, 3.1–7, 4.3. Note the contrast between Richard Hooker's discussion of the character of human sociability as revealed by the beginning of the Bible (*Of the Laws of Ecclesiastical Polity,* 1.10.3–4, esp. 4 end) and the text of the beginning of Aristotle's *Politics* that Hooker adduces. Hooker is following Thomas (ST 1a qu. 96 a. 4), who attempts with rather conspicuous lack of success to force Aristotle's teaching onto the text of Genesis and onto Augustine's interpretation of that text (in *City of God* 19.14–15).

5. E.g., 1 Kings 19:19–21. And of course the status of the teacher becomes very high in the *Mishnah*. See, e.g., *Mishnah,* Pirke Avoth 4.12 ("Let the reverence for thy teacher be as the fear of Heaven"), and the Talmudic Metzia 33a. The importance of finding a "companion" to study together with is stressed in *The Avot of Rabbi Nathan,* chap. 8.

6. One of the very few times when friendship is briefly lauded in Scripture is in the deuterocanonical book of Sirach 6:14–17, 9:10; see also 22:21–22 and Prov. 17:17 and 18:24 as well as 27:9–10. Contrast Deut. 13:6, Ps. 55:12–14, Prov. 19:4–7. In Milton's *Paradise Lost,* intimate friendship other than that of the married couple makes its appearance only in the subversive connivance of Satan and "his next subordinate" (5.671ff.; contrast 8.445–51). In *Christian Doctrine,* 2.11, however, Milton lauds friendship as a Christian virtue (while failing to adduce a single New Testament text in support of this claim). In Grotius's *Exile of Adam,* Satan's first gambit (which proves unsuccessful) is to conceive a plot to seduce Adam through an appeal to friendship. See "Argument" and act 1 beg. as well as act 3, esp. l. 953, where Satan says, "My way is to please my friends," to which Adam replies, "Indeed, which is the same as ruination!" (pp. 96–97, 110–11, 148–55 of Kirkconnell's *Celestial Cycle*). A possible "source" for Grotius's rendition of the story is *Al-Qur'an* 7.21.

7. See Pangle, "The Hebrew Bible's Challenge to Political Philosophy." In Milton's *Paradise Lost,* classical republican principles and practice are manifested in the assembly and the policy of the fallen angels under Satan's leadership and example. See not only bk. 2 but also 9.665ff. and 10.427ff., as well as *Paradise Regained,* 4.251–71. Consider also what was revealed to Adam concerning the original "cities" of men at *Paradise Lost,* 11.638ff.

8. Gen. 2:16–18 and 3:17. See Rabbi Tahlifa's remark in the *Mishnah Rabbah* on Exod. 28:2; and Luther LG, *Werke,* 42:79–80. In the Septuagint, as

Wevers remarks ad loc. (*Notes on the Greek Text of Genesis*), "though woman has not yet been created and the text has only Adam addressed by the Lord God, nonetheless the second person verbs of this verse are all in the plural, contrary to the Hebrew text. . . . [T]he plural is proleptically introduced."

9. Westermann (*Genesis 1–11*, 235–78) endorses a consensus originating with Wellhausen that makes the rather preposterous attempt to understand the "good and evil" in question here as purely utilitarian, or as having nothing to do with "moral knowledge." The incoherences and unclarity that result are remarkable.

10. Cf. Bonhoeffer, *Creation and Fall*, 66–69. I cannot follow Bonhoeffer in interpreting the serpent as "only suggesting the possibility that man has perhaps misunderstood," and as thus introducing the idea of a God Who appears morally superior to the true God.

11. In the influential poetic retelling of Creation by Alcimus Ecdicius Avitus, *Poematum de Mosaicae historiae gestis libri quinque* (A.D. 507), Eve is presented as asking the serpent to explain to her what God meant by the word "death."

12. Contrast, however, Augustine's interpretation, according to which Adam and Eve were eating regularly of the Tree of Life, and thus securing themselves against death, prior to their expulsion (*Genesis XII* 11.32; *City of God* 13.20). In the second-century pseudepigraphical *Revelation (or Apocalypse) of Moses,* as Adam is being expelled from the garden he pleads with God for a taste of the Tree of Life, which God refuses, declaring that this would render Adam immortal—and promising that after the resurrection Adam will be given the taste that frees him from mortality (Alexander and Donaldson, eds., *The Ante-Nicene Fathers,* 8.568).

13. Gunkel goes so far as to adduce, as a parallel to Eve's fall, "the Wolf's seduction of Little Red Riding Hood or the disguised Queen's seduction of Snow White" (*Genesis,* 17; cf. 11 and 31–32).

14. Maimonides *Eight Chapters,* chap. 5, pp. 76–77, and chap. 8, p. 88.

15. *The Questions Concerning Liberty, Necessity, and Chance, Clearly Stated and Debated between Dr. Bramhall, Bishop of Derby, and Thomas Hobbes of Malmesbury,* Animadversions upon the Bishop's Reply no. 10.

16. *Schriften zum alten Testament,* 797–98. For an anticipation, see Grotius, *On the Law of War and Peace,* 2.2.2. Consider the deliberate awkwardness of the introduction of "wickedness" and "punishment" into Kant's tongue-in-cheek Rousseauian reconstruction of the account of the Fall as the "transition from the crudeness of a merely animal creature to the state of humanity" ("Conjectural Beginning of Human History," in *Akademieausgabe,* 8:115–116, 123; contrast *Religion within the Limits of Reason Alone,* 1.4). Hegel's reading (*Lectures on the Philosophy of Religion,* 2.419–28 and 3.224–33) essentially follows that of Kant. For a contemporary version, explicitly reading into the Scripture Rousseau's

account of the evolution of mankind from the "state of nature"—and appealing also to Kant (but without Kant's delicious or malicious irony)—see Kass, "Man and Woman." See similarly Kass's "What's Wrong with Babel?" 44 and 51 (on the "so-called" Fall, and the "so-called" punishment, as a "rise into civilization"); "Why the Dietary Laws?" 44; and "A Genealogy of Justice," 46. Rousseau himself, it is to be noted, stressed prominently the absolute incompatibility between his account of the original state of nature and the biblical account of the origins: "Il est évident, par la lecture des Livres Sacrés, que le premier Homme ayant reçu immediatement de Dieu des lumières et des Preceptes, n'étoit point lui-même dans cet état [de Nature]" (*Discours sur l'origine et les fondemens de l'inégalité parmi les hommes*, in *Diskurs über die Ungleichheit / Discours sur l'inégalité*, 70).

CHAPTER 5. *Creation and the Meaning of Good and Evil*

1. Even the conservative Benno Jacob, in order to maintain the strictly "educative" interpretation, must contend that there was no punishment involved in the transformation of the existence of man and woman and the expulsion from Eden (*The First Book of the Bible*, 27–33). Contrast Ginzberg, *Legends of the Jews*, 1.74ff.

2. Wisd. of Sol. 12: 3–4, 8, 10, 15–16, 25–26. See also the subsequent explanation of Num. 21:6–9 (the punishment of the Hebrews through the serpents' bites), in contrast to the destruction of the Egyptians through plagues of locusts and flies: "For when the terrible anger of wild animals came upon your people . . . , your wrath did not continue to the end; they were troubled for a little while as a warning . . . our enemies were killed by the bites of locusts and flies, and no healing was found for their soul, because they deserved to be punished by such things. But your sons were not conquered even by the fangs of venomous serpents. . . . To remind them of your oracles they were bitten, and then were quickly saved, so that they would not fall into deep forgetfulness and become unresponsive to your kindness" (Wisd. of Sol. 16:5–6, 8–11).

3. Speaking of the difference between the way God punished the truly wicked Pharaoh and his fellow oppressors and the way He "disciplined" the oppressed Hebrews, the Wisdom of Solomon says (11:10), "For you tested them as a parent does in warning, but you examined the ungodly as a stern king does in condemnation." Clearly, Adam and Eve and humanity in them were treated more like the Pharaoh than like the Hebrews. Milton disposes of, and thus highlights, the difficulty by introducing the angel Raphael to instruct Adam: "God to render Man inexcusable sends Raphael to admonish him of his obedience, of his free estate, of his enemy near at hand; who he is, and why his enemy and whatever else may avail Adam to know" (*Paradise Lost*, bk. 5, "The

Argument"; see further 5.229ff.: "this let him know, / Lest wilfully transgressing he pretend / Surprisal, unadmonisht, unforewarn'd. / So spake the Eternal Father, and fulfill'd / All Justice"; at 7.71ff. we learn that the warning has been grasped and appreciated by Adam; at 9.252ff., that Adam has fully explained the warning to Eve; see also 8.635–43). Gunkel (*Genesis*, 32–33) states the central problem succinctly: "The sin the man committed is indeed portrayed, when its psychological origin is described, as a child's sin. But in the context of the curse, it is maintained with great gravity that it was a transgression." But then, exemplifying the interpretative shallowness into which the giants of the higher criticism often fall, Gunkel disposes of further reflection in the following patronizing words: "One may clarify the myth by remembering the relationship of the Israelite farmer to his servants, a relationship very often compared to the religious relationship in ancient Israel. . . . These ideas and attitudes of the myth are admittedly deficient and inferior when compared to those available to us Christians. No historically educated individual will take offense at this claim: the many prophets and thinkers and poets who have lived since this ancient narrative have not lived in vain. Nevertheless, it is fitting 'not to disdain small beginnings.' "

4. Accordingly, comments such as von Rad's (*Genesis*, 257), suggesting that "in ancient Israel one accepted life not with a defiant claim to endlessness but from the start with resignation, as something limited, something assigned to man, in which then the state of satiation was to be reached" (see similarly Gunkel, *Genesis*, 22, 31–32), fail to reckon fully with the abyss in human existence opened up by the Fall (this is not to deny that there are to be found in Scripture attempts to reconcile humans with their mortality; see, e.g., Sir. 30:17, 41:3–4; but contrast 25:24). Westermann's comparison (*Genesis 1–11*, 213–14, 272) with the import of the Tree of Life in the Near Eastern parallels, especially the Gilgamesh epic, would seem to have an implication exactly the opposite of the one he draws; what is striking is the dissimilarity or radical disagreement (in the Gilgamesh, the tree provides a magical antidote to the otherwise inexorably fated mortality of humans). On the appalling significance of mortality and the depth of the human concern to surmount it, the Bible agrees from the outset with Plato's Socrates and with Lucretius—against Aristophanes (cf., Plato *Phaedo* 67e, *Symposium* 192e–193a, 206a, and Lucretius *On the Nature of Things* 3.1053–94 with Aristophanes *Birds* 586–610) as well as against the moderns: Bacon, *Essays*, "On Death"; Spinoza, *Ethics*, bk. 4, props. 67–68; Locke, *Essay Concerning Human Understanding*, 2.21.37–38, 45, 46, 55, 60 beg., 64, 65, 68, 69–70, and also 2.20.6 end and 2.28.12; Hume, "On the Immortality of the Soul," sec. 2. But contrast Locke's (early and never published) *Questions Concerning the Law of Nature*, no. 5, pp. 160–63: "If man were his own author, able to give himself being and producing himself in the nature

of things, he would endow himself with (not to mention perfect knowledge of all things, and greater power in natural things) a sempiternal duration of existence; since it is not possible to conceive of anything so hostile and inimical to itself that it could give itself existence without at the same time preserving itself, or that would willingly abandon existence after the conclusion of a brief course of time." Let us also note that the central horror as the Bible presents it is *not*, contrary to what Hobbes tries to teach, the thought of "violent" or painful death, i.e., of the remediable ills that may attend death; the horror is the thought of death itself. Compare Pascal, *Pensées*, #138 (= Brunschvicg #166): "Divertissement. La mort est plus aisée à supporter sans y penser que la pensée de mort sans péril."

5. See Milton's vivid allegory of Death and its meaning in *Paradise Lost*, esp. 10.610ff. (Death as extinction had no place in Creation as it came from God's hand and will eventually again be totally eradicated.) See also Barth, *Church Dogmatics*, 3:2, pp. 598–99 and 616–20. The Council of Carthage (A.D. 417) proclaimed, "If anyone says that Adam, the first man, was created mortal, so that, whether he sinned or not, he would have died from natural causes, and not as the wages of sin, let him be anathema" (Bettenson, ed., *Documents of the Christian Church*, 83).

6. Contrast the much less provocative formulation of a superficially similar denial of original sin in Locke's "source" and friend, Philip van Limborch, *A Compleat System, or Body of Divinity, both speculative and practical: founded on Scripture and Reason*, in *John Locke and Christianity*, ed. Nuovo, 47–48.

7. *Summa contra Gentiles* (henceforth cited as SCG) 4.52. See also Augustine *On Free Choice of the Will* 3.18, sec. 175; the Talmudic Shabbath 55a ("R. Ammi said: There is no death without sin, and there is no suffering without iniquity"); Luther, LG, *Werke*, 42:244; and Milton, *Christian Doctrine*, 1.11, p. 385.

8. SCG 4.51. See similarly *On Evil* qu. 4 a. 1, obj. 19; qu. 4 a. 8, obj. 8. See also the Talmudic Makkoth 24a ("Moses had said, The Lord is . . . visiting the iniquity of the fathers upon the children and upon the children's children, unto the third and unto the fourth generation [referring to Exod. 20:5–6 and 34:7; Deut. 5:9]; Ezekiel came and declared, the soul that sinneth, it shall die"), as well as Berachoth 7a and Taanith 11a. In the first great martyrology, recounted in 2 Macc. 7, we hear the martyrs testifying that their sufferings are punishments for their *own* sins (2 Macc. 7:18 and 32; but consider the reference to the innocence of the baby martyrs at 8:4). Contrast, however, the very different, quasi-Stoic account of the same martyrdom in 4 Macc. 8ff., where, esp. in 17:21–22 (along with 1:11 and 6:29), the sufferings are interpreted as an atonement or ransom, by the virtuous, for the sins and the punishment deserved by the rest of the errant Jewish people (see similarly Lev. 26:39–40, Tob. 3:3–4; for

the key source of the idea of the sufferings of the innocent as atonement for the guilty, see Isa. 53). Sir. 23:24–25 teaches that an adulterous wife's "punishment will extend to her children," but it is unclear whether this means more than that her punishment will necessarily bring indirect suffering, especially through disgrace, on her children, who will be therefore almost irresistibly prone to bad conduct; the same ambiguity appears in 41:5–9.

9. ST 1a–2ae qu. 81 a. 1. See similarly *On Evil* qu. 4 a. 1, 2, and 6; *Compendium of Theology* 1.196; and Milton, *Christian Doctrine,* 1.11, pp. 384–85. There seems to be a resemblance here to the doctrine of the predominant theologian of the Eastern Orthodox tradition, Maximus Confessor (d. 662), especially as developed in *Questions to Thalassius on the Scripture* 5.21. See Pelikan, *The Christian Tradition,* 2.182.

10. Exod. 20:5, 34:7. See also Num. 14:18, Deut. 5:9, Jer. 32:18, Lam. 5:7. Milton notes (*Christian Doctrine,* 1.11, pp. 386–87) that "accordingly penitents are ordered to confess both their own sins and the sins of their fathers: Lev. 26:40 and Neh. 9:12." And he insists that "it is not only a constant principle of divine justice but also a very ancient law among all races and all religions, that when a man has committed sacrilege (and this tree we are discussing was sacred), not only he but also the whole of his posterity becomes an anathema and a sin-offering." "This feature of divine justice," Milton continues, "was well known among other nations, and never thought to be unfair. So we find in Thucydides 1.126.11; and Virgil Aeneid 1.39–41."

11. Ezek. 18 as a whole. See also Deut. 24:16, echoed in 2 Chron. 25:4. In 2 Chron. 33:11, King Manasseh is presented as having suffered condign punishment and then as having shown contrition that reunited him with God. But in 1 Kings 24:3–4 and Jer. 15:4, the Babylonian destruction of Judah is explained as punishment of Judah for the sins of Manasseh, dead for two generations. Contrast also the similarly differing retributive explanations for the destruction of Jerusalem in 2 Kings 24:19–20 and in 2 Chron. 36:11–17. The latter contrasts are plausibly accounted for by historical criticism in terms of the difference in the conception of retributive justice held by the Chronicler in contrast with the earlier scriptural authors (see, e.g., Bickerman, "The Historical Foundations of Postbiblical Judaism," 81–82). But this does not, of course, dispose of the fundamental difficulty in the account of the Fall, i.e., in the very foundation of the Bible.

12. ST 1a–2ae qu. 81 a. 2. See similarly *On Evil* qu. 4 a. 8 and *Compendium of Theology* 1.197. Compare the doctrine of the Lurianic Kabbalah (based on *Midrash Rabbah* on Exod. 40:3): "Every soul" is "outraged and degraded by the fall of Adam, whose soul contained all souls" (Scholem, *Major Trends in Jewish Mysticism,* 278–82).

13. *Institutes,* 2.8.19–20 and 2.1.8. See similarly Adam's reasoning in Milton's *Paradise Lost,* 10.822–34 (and Fish's acute comment on ll. 822–24 in *Surprised by Sin,* 283–84).

14. *Institutes,* 2.3.5. See also 2.5.1 and 2.5.11, as well as *Commentary on Genesis* ad 9:25 and Milton, *Paradise Lost,* 10.822–28. In the light of what we find in Augustine's commentaries on Genesis, however, it is reasonable to question whether Calvin has not overstated, if not misrepresented, the Augustinian position. Cf. the somewhat cryptic *On the Literal Interpretation of Genesis: An Unfinished Book* 1.3 end with the more mature and lucid discussion in *Genesis XII* 6.9 and esp. 10.14ff. (on infant baptism), where we are referred to these words of Wisd. of Sol. 8:19–20: "As a child I was well-endowed, and a good soul fell to my lot; and being good above the common, I came to a body undefiled."

15. *Commentary on the Pentateuch: Genesis,* intro., 10. See similarly Rashi's commentary, explaining the term מצות, ad Gen. 26:5. And see Luther, LG, *Werke,* 42:109, together with Bainton, *Here I Stand,* 170.

16. *Pensées,* #60, 61, 66, 81, 85, 86, 103, 131, 149, 205, 269 end, 418 beg., 520, 729, 793, 840 (= Brunschvicg #294, 309, 326, 299, 878, 297, 298, 434, 430, 489, 692, 233, 375, 931, 737, 843).

17. *Institutes,* 1.2; 1.7.4 ("The sovereign proof of Scripture is commonly taken from the character of God Who speaks in it"); 1.9.2; 1.10.3 [1.10.2 in Latin ed.] (on the "face of God" as centered upon His justice); 1.17.1.

18. See the Talmudic Shabbath 55a–56b; Ginzberg, *Legends of the Jews,* 1.102 and n. 142; and the view of the early Kabbalah as reported in Scholem's *On the Kabbalah and Its Symbolism,* 108 (see also 115): "Adam's sin is perpetually repeated in every other sin." See also Luther, LG, *Werke,* 42:131, and Adam's cogitation in Milton's *Paradise Lost,* 10.826–27 (but contrast the angel Michael's revelation at 11.427).

19. Augustine *On Free Choice of the Will* 3.24. See also *City of God* 14.13 and 14.17 and Calvin's *Commentary on Genesis* ad 2:9: Adam's "sin proceeded from an evil conscience; whence it follows, that a judgment had been given him, by which he might discriminate between vices and virtues."

20. See the response of Abraham ("I go in mine integrity," Ps. 26:1) to Satan's attempt to involve him in a dialogue on the way to the binding of Isaac, in the legend or Aggadah found in Mann, *The Bible as Read and Preached in the Old Synagogue,* 1.63.

21. See 1 Tim. 2:13–14 and Augustine's interpretation of this New Testament passage in *City of God* 14.11 (see also *Genesis XII* 11.5 and 11.30). Thomas Aquinas (ST 1a qu. 94 a. 4 reply obj. 1) follows Augustine: "Though the woman was deceived before she sinned in deed, still it was not till she had already sinned by interior pride. For Augustine says (*Genesis XII* 11.30) that 'the woman could

not have believed the words of the serpent, had she not already acquiesced in the love of her own power, and in a presumption of self-conceit.'" Elsewhere (ST 2a–2ae qu. 163 a. 1 reply obj. 4) Thomas adds, "This does not mean that pride preceded the promptings of the serpent, but that as soon as the serpent had spoken his words of persuasion, her mind was puffed up, the result being that she believed the demon to have spoken truly." The sin that preceded the eating of the forbidden fruit must have been a mortal and not merely a venial sin, according to Thomas (ST 1a–2ae qu. 89 a. 3; *On Evil* qu. 2 a.8 reply 1; see also ST 2a–2ae qu. 163 a. 1 and 2, "On the Contrary"). Yet compare the gloss that Thomas reports on 1 Tim. 2:14: "Having had no experience of God's severity, it was possible for him to be so mistaken as to think that what he had done was a venial sin" (ST 1a–2ae Q89 a. 3 obj. 1); and see Thomas's curious "Reply." For some clarification, see Thomas's *Disputed Questions on Truth,* qu. 18 a. 6 obj. 11 and reply.

22. See Thomas Aquinas ST 2a–2ae qu. 163 a. 2 obj. 2 and reply. The link between the philosophic or scientific quest for "nature" and the desire for the fruit of the Tree of Knowledge of good and evil is brought out in the words of C. S. Lewis's Queen of Perelandra (his fictional analogue to the biblical Eve, who differs from Eve in that she resists the Devil—with the help, to be sure, of a fallen human): "And why should I desire the Fixed except to be sure—to be able on one day to command where I should be the next and what should happen to me?" (*Perelandra,* chap. 17, p. 208). See also Augustine *Confessions* 2.6 end.

23. Cassuto, *Commentary on the Book of Genesis,* 1:143, commenting on Gen. 3:1: "In order to make the word-play more apparent, Scripture uses in the previous verse the form ערום and not עירום which occurs subsequently in verses 7, 10, 11, and it prefers the full to the defective mode of spelling." I have not, however, been able to follow Cassuto's interpretation of this wordplay, when he takes it to support his contention that the serpent is not meant to have here an independent existence but is "an allegorical allusion to the craftiness to be found in *man himself.*"

24. Fradkin, "God's Politics," 92. Compare Milton, *Paradise Lost,* 5.358–60. But Milton claims that prior to the Fall there was a guiltless sense of shame that the pair (especially the female) would have exhibited, even through blushing (8.501–11, 619; 9.312–13; cf. 9.1058, 1079).

25. Compare Augustine *Genesis XII* 11.4: "It seems to me that man would have had no future prospect of any special praise, if he were able to lead a good life simply because there was none to persuade him to lead an evil life; since both by nature he had the power, and in his power he had the will, not to consent to the persuader." Yet must we not then add that since God punished the serpent as well, and the serpent's progeny for all time, it would seem that the serpent cannot have been *merely* an instrument in God's plan; the serpent too, it

would seem, was being tested; and if he had not chosen to succumb to the temptations of his own cunning, then some other means of testing Adam and Eve would presumably have had to have been awaited or devised?

26. *Paradise Lost,* 4.637, 775. Stanley Fish (*Surprised by Sin,* 265–67) has plausibly suggested that Milton's *Samson Agonistes* culminates in a "truly heroic moment" (l. 1384) when Samson exhibits the kind of faithfully resigned or surrendering wisdom that "could have been" also exhibited in Adam's case.

27. *Genesis XII* 8.14.32, 8.16.34. See similarly Adam's words in reaction to Eve's dream in *Paradise Lost,* 5.116ff.

28. LG, *Werke,* 42:49–50, 55, 86–87, 105–6; see also 83–84. See similarly Thomas Aquinas ST 1a qu. 94 a. 1 and 3; qu. 95 a. 3 (Adam before the Fall had all the virtues); qu. 100 (Thomas repeatedly lays stress on Eccles. 7:30: "God made man right/just—יָשָׁר"); and Milton, *Paradise Lost,* 3.98; 4.293 and 443; 5.205–9, 524ff., 548–49; 6.327, 396–97, 401–3, 431–32; 7.61, 296, 493; 8.217ff., 352–55, 364–68 (Adam as well as God knew that it was not good for Adam to be alone), 496–500 (Milton assigns the narrator's interposition to Adam); also 5.130–35 and 9.312–13 (Adam and Eve could feel remorse as well as shame prior to the Fall), 9.343ff.; 11.87–89; 12.560 (the fallen Adam recognizes the kind of limited knowledge with which he ought to have been satisfied). See also Barth, *Church Dogmatics,* 3:1, 260–66 (though contrast the rather unclear 286–87) and 3:2 (sec. 44), 129–31, 197–98. Compare the words of C. S. Lewis's King of Perelandra: "We have learned of evil, though not as the Evil One wished us to learn. We have learned better than that, and know it more, for it is waking that understands sleep and not sleep that understands waking. There is an ignorance of evil that comes from being young: there is a darker ignorance that comes from doing it, as men by sleeping lose the knowledge of sleep. You are more ignorant of evil [on Earth] now than in the days before your Lord and Lady began to do it" (*Perelandra,* chap. 17, p. 209). For a further intriguing intimation as to the character of the knowledge mankind might have had if the temptation to eat of the fruit of the tree of knowledge had been resisted, see the Queen of Perelandra's words: "I thought that I was carried in the will of Him I love, but now I see that I walk with it. I thought that the good things He sent me drew me into them as the waves lift the islands; but now I see that it is I who plunge into them with my own arms and legs, as when we go swimming" (ibid., chap. 5, p. 69; contrast, however, Augustine *City of God* 14.17). The Judaic Kabbalistic tradition similarly lays stress on the idea of a superior Messianic knowledge of the good, rooted in the Tree of Life and prior and superior to the knowledge contained in the original sin by which man came to eat of the fruit of the Tree of Knowledge (a crucial text here is Prov. 3:18). See Scholem, *The Messianic Idea in Judaism,* 22–24, 40–41, 68–74, 148–49; *Major Trends in Jewish Mysticism,* 232, 236–37, 275 ("the true purpose of the Torah"); and *On*

the Kabbalah and Its Symbolism, 71–75, 108. See also Abravanel *Commentary on the Pentateuch* ad Gen. 11:1–9.

29. *Genesis XII* 11.31 beg. See similarly Milton, *Paradise Lost,* 9.1053–54 and context. Yet in this very passage of his commentary, apparently without noticing the difficulty, Augustine refers us, as to a "parallel usage," to another revealing biblical employment of the phrase "their eyes were opened," where Luke (24:31) means the change from ignoring to recognizing Christic.

30. *Compendium of Theology* 1.188 ("The Tree of Knowledge of Good and Evil"); Augustine *Genesis XII* 8.6, 8.13–15. See similarly St. Chrysostom *Homilies on Genesis* 16.14 and 16.16–17; Calvin's *Commentary on Genesis* ad 2:9 and 3:22 (the tree is only a "symbol": "There never was any intrinsic efficacy in the tree"); Milton's *Christian Doctrine,* 1.10, p. 352; and the rendition of the fall of Adam and Eve in *Al-Qur'an* 2.30–39, 7.19–27, 20.116–29.

31. LG, *Werke,* 42:71–73, 80, 84, 169; Augustine *Genesis XII* 8.13.29.

32. For "Tree of Knowledge," the book of Enoch (32:3) has "Tree of *Phronesis*" and says that after eating its "holy fruit" Adam and Eve "knew a great practical wisdom [ἐπίστανται φρόνησιν μεγάλην]."

33. Hegel, *Lectures on the Philosophy of Religion,* 2.425–27, 3.226. See again Kass, "Man and Woman."

34. *Commentary on the Pentateuch* ad Gen. 11:1–9, quoted in part in Leibowitz, *Studies in the Book of Genesis,* 17–22, and in part in *Medieval Political Philosophy,* ed. Lerner and Mahdi, 256–59. Abravanel's interpretation represents a rejoinder to and a decisive tempering of the more radical interpretation of Maimonides (*Guide* 1.2). Spinoza, outdoing or challenging the Platonism of Maimonides on its own ground, suggests that the Tree of Knowledge is in fact the Tree of Ignorance, above all because eating its fruit produces an obsessive fear of death together with eroticism, thus obscuring the pursuit of one's true advantage (*Ethics,* bk. 4, scholium to prop. 68).

35. Maimonides *Laws of Kings* 8.11, as translated and discussed in Spinoza, *Theologico-Political Treatise,* chap. 5 end. See the discussions in Cohen, *Jüdische Schriften,* 3.346ff., and Strauss, *Spinoza's Critique of Religion,* "Autobiographical Preface," 23–24.

36. In Grotius's *Exile of Adam,* act 4, ll. 1112–13 (pp. 162–63 of Kirkconnell's *Celestial Cycle*), Eve replies to the serpent, "The cause of the command is uncertain: but certain it is that we must obey. Whatever it means, God forbids." See Westermann, *Genesis 1–11,* 223–24: "The meaning of the commandment becomes clearer when it is compared with the duty imposed on man in v. 15. The duty of tilling and keeping the garden is something comprehensible; the command need not be comprehensible, and such is the case here."

37. *Institutes,* 1.7.5 (my italics); see also 1.8.1, 1.8.13. For the perverse rejection of what this knowledge conveys, see 1.9; for the periods of doubt that in-

evitably overshadow this "certain knowledge," however, see 3.2.17–20, 3.2.24 end; and compare Spinoza, *Theologico-Political Treatise,* chap. 15.

38. Calvin, *Institutes,* 3.2.14. See also Pascal, *Pensées,* #7 (= Brunschvicg #248): "La foi est différente de la preuve. L'une est humaine et l'autre est un don de Dieu. *Justus ex fide vivit. . .* cette foi est dans le coeur et fait dire non *scio* mais *Credo.*"

39. See Calvin's *Commentary on Genesis* ad 3:1 near the end: "Very dangerous is the temptation, when it is suggested to us, that God need not be obeyed, except insofar as the reason of His command is apparent. The true rule of obedience is, that we being content with a bare command, should persuade ourselves that whatever He enjoins is just and right."

40. Pascal, *Pensées,* #174 (= Brunschvicg #270): "Saint Augustine. Reason would never submit itself if it did not judge that there are occasions when it ought to submit itself. It is therefore just that it submit itself when it judges that it ought to submit." See also #182 (= B. #272).

41. A key philosophic discussion of the concept "good-in-itself" is found in Aristotle's *Ethics* 1096b8–21; cf. 1113a23–30, 1155b21–26, 1156b19–20, 1157b26, 1158a25.

42. Maimonides *Guide* 1.54; Calvin, *Institutes,* 1.2 and 2.2.15–18. See also Luther, LG, *Werke,* 42:672: "It is enough to say, 'thus it pleases Him, thus it is beneficial, thus it is salutary; otherwise he would have done differently.' " "Abraham does not think, as we do, 'Why does God command this? What utility is there in this ugly and obscene thing [circumcision]?' . . . He cuts the throat of this pestilence, 'Why?' . . . He makes reason a prisoner, and acquiesces in that one thing—which is, that He, Who commands, is just, good, and wise; therefore He cannot command what is not just, good, and wise, no matter what reason judges, no matter if reason cannot understand."

43. *Paradise Lost* 3.111–19. Cf. the words of the *Mishnah,* Pirke Avoth 3.15: "Everything is foreseen, but the right [of choice] is granted, and the world is judged with goodness, and everything is in accordance with the preponderance of [man's] deed[s]." See also Augustine *City of God* 15.25, 17.7, and esp. 22.2.

44. See the questions Pierre Bayle has "Zoroaster" raise in the imaginary dialogue in n. D to the article "Manicheans," as well as the Manichean rebuttals of Origen's arguments presented in n. D to the article "Origen," in the *Historical and Critical Dictionary.* Commenting, in nn. F and G to the article "Marcionites," on the weakness of the early Church Fathers' arguments purporting to refute the dualistic heresy of Marcion (who opposed the just "hidden God" to the tyrannically moralistic God of the Old Testament, the God of creation and of justice), Bayle acerbically remarks that if, for the Marcionites, "a man with as much spirit as Descartes had had the management of this affair, one would not so easily have refuted the system of the two principles" (see the Cartesian

arguments Bayle proceeds to develop in the context). Bayle characterizes as follows the position that a self-conscious believer like himself, schooled in modern rationalist theological debates, must assume as regards the opponents of the faith: "Revelation is the sole magazine of arguments which one must oppose to those people; it is only by that avenue that we are able to refute the pretended eternity of an evil principle. But when we wish to determine in what manner the Creator conducted Himself, in regard to the first sin of the creature, we find ourselves very embarrassed. All the hypotheses, which Christians have established, parry poorly the blows which are struck: they all triumph when they act offensively; but they lose all their advantage when they have to endure an attack. Our ideas on this subject are not clear, except to the extent that enables the war to be continued eternally, like those princes who lack the force to prevent the ravaging of their frontiers, and who are powerful enough to carry out raids against the enemy." See also nn. E, G, H, L, and M to the article "Paulitians"—where, among other things, Bayle states, "The hypothesis of the Platonists is at bottom only a branch of Manicheanism."

45. Augustine *On Free Choice of the Will* 3.5; Calvin, *Institutes*, 1.15.8 end, citing Augustine's *Genesis XII* 11.7–9 (q.v.), as well as Augustine's *On Rebuke and Grace* 11.

46. See also Augustine *Genesis XII* 11.3–4, where in wrestling with the question "why God allowed man to be tempted," or why God allowed the Devil to use the serpent as he did, Augustine concedes that while "the will to do harm can come from any perverse spirit," the "power to do it can come only from God"—"and this," Augustine concludes, "must be because of some hidden and sublime justice, because there is no iniquity in God." Explicitly following the lead of St. Paul and Augustine, Calvin goes further to confront the question of the justice of the implied divine predestination of the many whose fall is permanent or who do not ever find redemption. Calvin insists that while we can be certain that this most fundamental dimension of God's Creation and providence is just, we must resign ourselves to the fact that we cannot fully grasp its justice (*Institutes*, 3.24, esp. subsecs. 12, 14, and 17 end). Augustine suggests as a partial explanation the need to instruct by example other fallible men, and the goodness of creating not only perfect but also imperfect but perfectible beings: "looking not to His own interests from the works of the good" (*Genesis XII* 11.9–11). C. S. Lewis allows his angels to suggest that "in the Fallen World He prepared for Himself a body and was united with the Dust and made it glorious for ever. This is the end and final cause of all creating, and the sin whereby it came is called Fortunate" (*Perelandra*, chap. 17, p. 215).

47. Spinoza probably has in mind Calvin above all, who speaks (*Institutes*, 1.15.8) of "the great darkness of the philosophers," who have "looked for a beautiful and complete building in a ruin, and fit arrangement in disorder"—

"the Fall of Adam being hidden to them." At first, "every part of the soul was formed to rectitude. There was soundness and integrity of mind, and the will was free to choose the good. If any one objects that it was placed, as it were, in a slippery position, because its faculty and power were weak, I answer, that the degree conferred was sufficient to take away every excuse." For the corruption of the Vulgate text attributable to the insidious influence of the "philosophers," see Calvin's *Commentary on Genesis* ad 8:21.

48. *Political Treatise,* chap. 2, secs. 6–7, in *The Political Works,* 268–73. I have altered the translation to make it more literal.

49. Augustine verges dangerously close to such a position in his account of "the many wills" he found within his "one nature" during his struggle prior to conversion (*Confessions* 8.8–10). Al-Ghazali (*The Incoherence of the Philosophers,* 179) concludes from the nature of the impossible that "we understand by the will the seeking after something known. If, then, a quest is supposed without knowledge, there would be no will. This entails the denial of what we have understood by will."

50. "The bewitchment of the base obscures the noble things" (Wisd. of Sol. 4:12). Augustine, commenting on Paul's 1 Tim. 2:13–14 ("Adam was not seduced, but the woman was seduced and fell into sin"), writes, "In fact, Adam under interrogation did not say, 'The woman whom Thou gavest to be my companion seduced me and I ate'; but, 'she gave me fruit of the tree and I ate.' On the other hand, the woman said, 'the serpent seduced me.' . . . It was, therefore, in some other way that he was deceived. . . . According to the Apostle, a seduction in the proper sense occurs when one is persuaded to accept as true what in reality is false; i.e., that God forbade Adam and Eve to touch the tree because He knew that if they touched it they would be like gods, as if He who made humans grudged them divinity" (*Genesis XII* 11.42.58 and 60). Commenting a bit earlier (ibid., 11.5) on the condition within Adam that induced the Fall, Augustine writes, "On the one hand, those who rejoice in the pleasures that bring death cannot be free of the fear of suffering; on the other hand, those who do not feel the whole evil of their desertion on account of the stupor induced by their great pride, are seen to be *much more miserable* by others who *have been able to recognize* this" (my italics). Two chapters later (11.7) we read, however (again in reference to the Fall), of "those however who have by themselves chosen evil, and have willingly and culpably corrupted a praiseworthy nature." See also *Confessions* 2.4–6. Calvin shows that he fundamentally misunderstands what is at issue in Plato's teaching that vice is due to ignorance when he misinterprets Plato's Socrates, in the *Protagoras,* as meaning to say that the ignorance in question is ignorance that sin is sin, or that injustice is injustice (*Institutes,* 2.2.22). The ignorance is in regard to the good, as to whether injustice is not better than justice in any given case. As Calvin must concede (in what is truly a remarkable

concession), "Never would Adam have dared to show any repugnance to the command of God if he had not been incredulous as to His word; for an effective curb to moderate and to restrain all his bad appetites, would have been the *knowledge* that he had nothing *better* than to cultivate justice by obeying the commands of God, and that the ultimate *happiness* of life was to be loved by Him" (ibid., 2.1.4 end, my italics; see similarly *Commentary on Genesis* ad 3:6). Differing with Augustine, Calvin like Luther traces Adam's disobedience down beyond pride to the foundation, in infidelity or disbelief. But Calvin never even addresses the question of how, or on the basis of what, a rational being can responsibly choose what is to be its foundational belief as to what is good, the opinion that guides all its other choices (ibid. and *Institutes*, 2.1.4). Must not all conscious choice rest ultimately on unchosen insight or conviction? A few pages later Calvin declares, "I do not ask, however, that man should voluntarily yield without being convinced, or that, if he has any virtue, he should turn his thought away from it, that he may thus be subdued to true humility; I only ask that he dispense with *foolish* self-love [*folle amour de soy-mesme*]" (ibid., 2.2.11 end). See also Grotius, *Exile of Adam,* act 4 (pp. 172–75 of Kirkconnell's *Celestial Cycle*).

51. *Genesis XII* 11 end. The twelfth book leaves behind the text of Genesis to speculate on a vision of the "Third Heaven" that was afforded St. Paul.

52. The uneasiness that even Calvin feels at this question is evident in the truly amazing comment inserted into his discussion of Gen. 3:19 (*Commentary on Genesis* ad loc.): "They who have thought that punishments are effected as a kind of compensation have been preposterous interpreters of the judgments of God. For God does not consider, in punishing the faithful, what they deserve; but what will be profitable to them in future; and thus fulfills the office of a physician rather than of a judge." A few pages later (ad 4:10–11) we read, "This is a wonderfully sweet consolation to good men, who are unjustly tormented, to hear that their own sufferings, which they silently endure, go into the presence of God of their own accord to demand vengeance. . . . [W]hat is more, God will be the more prompt to avenge us if we modestly endure everything. . . . This doctrine concerns not only the condition of the present life . . . but also puts us in hope of a better life; we must accordingly hold that those for whom God has such great care could not fail to survive after death. That should also very much terrify people given to audacity and violence . . . that God declares that He takes in hand the causes which are bereft and abandoned of every human defense; that He does not do so on account of the request of another but by his own nature, and that he will certainly take vengeance on misdeeds. . . . God constitutes the earth the minister of his vengeance." See similar comments ad 9:20, 9:22, 9:25, 11:7.

53. Compare Gen. 3:22 with Fradkin, "God's Politics," 88 and 90. See also 2 Macc. 6:13–16 and St. Chrysostom *Homilies on Genesis* 17.

54. "And exalted is the Lord of Hosts by just judgment; the Holy God is proved holy by retributive justice" (Isa. 5:16). See Milton, *Paradise Lost,* 3.210 (without retributive expiation, Justice itself dies) and the words of Satan at 4.108–9 ("So farewell Hope, and with Hope farewell Fear, / Farewell Remorse") as well as the words of the fallen Adam at 10.1041–46.

CHAPTER 6. *Pollution and Purgation*

1. See Strauss, "Jerusalem and Athens," 159—which is followed by Kass, "What's Wrong with Babel," 44, and "Educating Father Abraham: The Meaning of Wife," 16.

2. See Fradkin, "God's Politics," 89: "Man's original simplicity is not merely the Bible's starting point but its original standard. In its light it is still less surprising that during this period God undertook no political activities. In fact God's avoidance of such activities down to the flood testifies to the endurance of the standard during this period."

3. Gen. 4:26. On the reiterative meaning of the verb היחל in this verse, see Cassuto, *Commentary on the Book of Genesis,* 1:246–48. On the "personal character" of God that is expressed by the name יהוה in contrast to the "transcendental" connotation of the designation Elohim, see ibid., 87, and, more extensively, Cassuto's *The Documentary Hypothesis,* 31–32.

4. Maimonides' answer is an unambiguous no (*Guide* 1.7). So interpreted, Gen. 5:1–2 does not then support, as Gunkel claims (*Genesis,* 113), the thesis that to be created "in the image and likeness" means, in the Scripture, to "resemble in form and appearance."

5. The ambiguity is hinted at by the fact that, as Sacks ("The Lion and the Ass," 69) observes, "in Hebrew the words *he also* [גם־הוא, applied to Abel] make it clear that Cain was the initiator of sacrificing."

6. God's preference seems otherwise perplexing, since what Cain offered was the fruit of an edaphic vocation very close to the gardening that God had assigned Adam before the Fall (Gen. 3:23); and in God's curse upon Adam after his fall, He "equates man and farmer" (Gunkel, *Genesis,* 22). Cain, as eldest son, can be understood to have quite properly carried on his father's farming vocation (Calvin, *Commentary on Genesis* ad 4:2; cf. Sacks, "The Lion and the Ass," 68; according to Williams, *The Common Expositor,* 219–20, the Renaissance and Reformation commentaries are pretty much agreed on the nobility of the farming vocation followed by Cain as a continuation of Adam's gardening). Some, however (and most prominently Rousseau, "Essay on the Origin of Languages," chap. 9), have suggested that the principal (though not the sole) reason for God's acceptance of Abel's offering and His rejection of Cain's is that "the pastoral life is closer to original simplicity than the life of the tillers of the

soil" (Strauss, "Jerusalem and Athens," 157; see the fuller elaboration in Fradkin, "God's Politics," 93); and this is closely akin to the reflection that "God was more delighted with Abel's oblation, when he was honored with what grew naturally of its own accord, than he was with the invention of a covetous man, and gotten by forcing the ground" (Josephus *Antiquities* 1.2.1; see similarly Abravanel *Commentary on the Pentateuch* ad Gen. 11:1–9; that God indeed prefers the earth as it is, prior to human work upon it, is suggested by Exod. 20:22). It is certainly the case that Abraham and the patriarchs were emphatically herdsmen and not farmers (cf. Gen. 46:34). Yet the life of tilling the soil would appear to be the life led by Seth and his line, culminating in "Noah, the man of the earth," while it was Jabal, the descendent of Cain, who was "the ancestor of those who dwell in tents and amidst herds" (Gen. 4:20 and 9:20). But as regards this last, Abravanel replies that "Jabal, too, in making an effort to purchase sheep, mixed art with the work of God, something that had not previously been done. Thus it is said of him that he was 'the father of all such as dwell in tents and have cattle.' All the sons of Cain pursued the superfluous things" (ibid. ad Gen 11:1–9, trans. Sacks, in *Medieval Political Philosophy*, ed. Lerner and Mahdi, 256–57).

7. *Theologico-Political Treatise,* in *Opera,* chap. 2, p. 28 (para. 9). See similarly Ibn Ezra ad Gen. 4:7 and Nachmanides commenting on Gen. 4:7 ("Thus He taught him concerning repentance, that it lies within his power to return any time he desires and He will forgive him"), as well as St. Jerome, who paraphrases: "Because you have free will, I advise that sin should not have dominion over you, but that you should have dominion over sin" (*St. Jerome's Hebrew Questions on Genesis,* trans. Hayward, p. 34).

8. *Institutes,* 2.5.16. See also *Commentary on Genesis* ad 4:7 and the similar uneasy discussion of 6:8 and 7:1. Calvin is well aware (see *Institutes,* 2.2.4 and 9, 3.24.13) that his doctrine contradicts the authority of St. Chrysostom, whose view of the relation between grace and human effort is stated most lucidly and simply in *Homilies on Genesis* 58 end.

9. Contrast John Fortescue's more earnest, though not entirely successful, attempt to reconcile Thomistic natural law with the scriptural story of Cain: *The Nature of the Law of Nature and Its Judgment upon the Succession to Sovereign Kingdoms* 2.28.

10. See Strauss, *Natural Right and History,* 81–84; Maimonides *Guide* 2.29 (which refers us to *Babylonian Talmud,* Abodah Zarah, 54b); and Sacks, "The Lion and the Ass," 85, which also discusses the etymology of the medieval Hebrew term that was pressed into service to translate the Greek philosophic word "nature." Contrast Thomas Aquinas ST, supplement to the 3rd part, qu. 6 a. 2 obj. 1 and reply; and St. Jerome *Commentary on Ezechial* ad 1:7.

11. Luther, following Jerome, translates: "Meine Sünde ist größer, denn daß

sie mir vergeben werden möge." His rather labored defense of this translation is found in his *Lectures on Genesis* ad loc. This seems an over- or mistranslation (it is conspicuously corrected in our contemporary popular editions of his translation), although as Westermann points out (*Genesis 1–11*, 309), Luther is correct in saying that the word עָוֹן connotes "sin" as well as "punishment," or "punishment for sin."

12. The text thus gives some color of plausibility to Hobbes's nonetheless irreverent reading, according to which the story of Cain and Abel is a major scriptural proof of the Hobbesian teaching on the state of nature as mankind's original condition: "But someone may say: there has never been a war of all against all. What! Did not Cain out of envy kill his brother Abel, a crime so great he would not have dared it if there had at that time been a common power which could have punished him?" (Latin *Leviathan*, as translated in the Curley edition, chap. 13, para. 11, n. 7). According to Hobbesian theology, prior to a contractual appointment of God as the sovereign ruler of consenting humans, God rules only by natural right and inflicts as punishments for violations of natural law nothing except the natural consequences of misbehavior (*Leviathan*, chap. 31, esp. para. 40).

13. That poetry can be redeemed, however, is indicated by the fact that versifying made its initial appearance in the first words quoted from Adam, prior to his fall (Gen. 2:23); and this is not to mention the fact that God, of course, speaks in verse prior to the Fall (Gen. 3:14ff.).

14. It is noteworthy that the second song or poem of a human being after the Fall is Noah's angry curse on the descendants of his erring son Ham (Gen. 9:25–27); music and excessive indignation seem to go all too easily together, in the biblical view.

15. All the more if we take into account how far the Bible departs from the Babylonian traditions that it apparently makes use of here. See Cassuto, *Commentary on the Book of Genesis* 1:252–67, 283–85. Westermann's most self-consciously original contribution to the interpretation of Gen. 1–11 is his employment of the purported Sumerian background to attempt to read into this portion of Scripture a record of "human achievement" in the "progressive" laying down of the "foundations of present-day civilization" and "culture" (*Genesis 1–11*, 56–62, 328, 342–44; see similarly 555, on the tower of Babel). The remarkable homiletic interjection at 344 seems to indicate that this preposterous reading is animated by Westermann's profound concern to reconcile an explicitly Cartesian outlook with the Bible, in order to secure the status and meaning of late-twentieth-century technology. See the more sensible statement of Blenkinsopp, *The Pentateuch*, 70: "It is difficult to avoid the conclusion that technological progress is being linked with moral degeneration, as in Hesiod's *Works and Days.*"

16. As for the puzzling and allusive reference in Gen. 6:1–4 to the story of the "sons of God" who took the "daughters of men" as their wives and sired the "giants," the "men of renown," see Cassuto, *Commentary on the Book of Genesis*, 1:291–301 for a sensible and plausible interpretation. Cassuto fails to observe, however, that Scripture here makes the important point that God had intelligent creatures who were potential alternatives to the human creatures. God was free to terminate His experiment with humans, to turn the earth over to "the sons of God," but He freely chose, in His grace, to continue our race on earth, despite our grave failings.

17. The Septuagint avoids introducing the idea of divine regret into the text and at 6:6 has God merely "pondering" (διενοήθη) and then at 6:7 "becoming angry" (ἐθυμώθην).

18. Yet at Exod. 32:14 it is only after Moses has implored God to remember the promise He made to Abraham that God "repents" of His intention to destroy the chosen people on account of their sins and thereby, it would seem, to render nugatory the covenant with Abraham (see similarly Ps. 106:45). For a recent serious and honest, if not altogether successful, struggle to make sense of this instance from Exodus, see Wildavsky, *The Nursing Father*, 99–106. For the important difference between Jewish and Christian perspectives on the difficulty whose crux text is 1 Sam. 15, see Pelikan, *The Christian Tradition*, 1.22.

19. Isa. 38:1–6 (= 2 Kings 20:1–7); Jer. 18:7–10, 26:3, 42: 10; Joel 2:13–14; Amos 7:3, 6; Jon. 3:9–10 and 4:2. See similarly 2 Sam. 24:16 together with 1 Chron. 21:15, and consider Gen. 19:17–22 and Luther's discussion, LG, *Werke*, 43:79ff. See also *Midrash Rabbah* on Gen. 27:4. In the deuterocanonical book of Judith (8:16–17), when the heroine upbraids the elders for seeking to test God and insists that "God is not, like a human, subject to threats; nor like a son of man, to be turned by entreaty," she nonetheless immediately draws the paradoxical conclusion, "Therefore while we await salvation from Him, let us call upon Him to help us; and He will hear our voices, if such is His pleasure." See also Jth. 9:12; the Targum attributed to Jonathan ben Uzziel ad Gen. 25:21; and the Talmudic Yevamoth 64a as well as the *Midrash Rabbah* on Gen. 63:5, on the "reversal of destiny" effected by the prayers of the righteous.

20. See esp. *The Prince*, chaps. 6, 17; *Discourses on the First Ten Book of Titus Livy*, 1.26.

21. This section is one that provides some of the clearest evidence of the editorial splicing together of distinct versions or traditions that have not in their details been rendered consistent. We hear, for example, that there was *only one* pair, male and female, of each species (6:19–20; 7:14–16), but then again that there were *seven* pairs of clean and one pair of unclean animals (7:2–3, 8–9); and that the Flood lasted forty days (7:4, 12, 17; 8:6; or sixty-one, if we count every day until the ground dried out [8:6–12]), though we also hear of a duration of

one hundred and fifty days (7:24; 8:3), which goes with the five months that is said to have elapsed from the beginning of the deluge until the grounding of the ark on Ararat (8:4); and so forth. But Westermann judiciously warns that "when commentators exegete the flood narratives of J and P separately, as they generally do, there is danger that justice will not be done to the individual narrative form as it has come down to us. One cannot avoid the fact that R's composite narrative has something important of its own to say, and that the scope of its effect belongs neither to J nor to P but to R" (*Genesis 1–11*, 431).

22. I follow Cassuto (*Commentary on the Book of Genesis*, 2:48–49) in taking תמים adverbially. Cf. the parallel constructions at Job 12:4 and Num. 19:2.

23. Gen. 8:21, which slightly softens the judgment passed at 6:5. Compare *Midrash Rabbah* on Gen. 28:8–29.2 and 30:9: "In the street of the totally blind, the one-eyed man is called clear-sighted"; Rashi ad Gen. 6:9; and St. Jerome's *Hebrew Questions on Genesis* ad 6:9. But Ezek. 14:14 and 14:20 invoke Noah along with Daniel and Job as exemplars of justice (see also Sir. 44:17–18).

24. Gen. 6:22; cf. 7:5. See Cassuto's apt comments (*Commentary on the Book of Genesis*, 2:59, 71). Wevers (*Notes on the Greek Text of Genesis* ad 6:9) draws attention to the fact that the Septuagint speaks of Noah as a just "human being" (ἄνθρωπος), not a just "man" (ἀνήρ), though the Hebrew term is איש; the translators evidently sensed that manliness is not an attribute of Noah. Calvin (*Commentary on Genesis* ad loc.) presents a vivid and evocative catalogue of the extraordinary character of the demands God here places on Noah and on his credulity, thus bringing out how deep and amazing is his obedience, or how grave and pressing were the temptations not to believe and to obey. "The most grievous temptation of all was," Calvin concludes, "that Noah was commanded to descend, as into the grave, for the sake of preserving his life, and voluntarily to deprive himself of air and vital spirit; for the stench of the dung alone, pent up, as it was, in a closely filled place, might in three days have stifled all the animals inside! Let us reflect on the heavy struggles of the holy man—so various, and long-continued—in order that we may know that he had a heroic virtue, in following to the end what God had commanded him."

25. For a suggestive attempt at such a deduction, see Kass's "Why the Dietary Laws?" Contrast Montesquieu's ridicule in *Persian Letters*, #17–18.

26. For the articulation by Plato of a theological outlook that shares something with the Bible in this regard, see *Laws* 896–97—a theological/cosmological account that is conspicuously silent on the Ideas or Forms. This Platonic theology moves almost insensibly, however, from a spiritual dualism to a reaffirmation of ignorance or irrationality as the source of evil.

27. Gen. 6:12 and 9:5. See Alter, *Genesis* ad loc.; and Cassuto, *Commentary on the Book of Genesis*, 2:54, 127, which refers us to Exod. 21:28–32, where it is

made evident that under the Mosaic law animals continue to be held criminally responsible to some extent.

28. Kass, "Seeing the Nakedness of His Father," 43 n. 1; Alter, *Genesis* ad loc.: "The thanksgiving sacrifice is evidently a requisite narrative motif taken from the Mesopotamian traditions, but the Hebrew writer's attitude toward it may be more complicated than meets the eye."

29. Calvin (*Commentary on Genesis* ad 8:21) cogently protests the softening mistranslation found in the Vulgate, which has God saying that the thoughts of the human heart are merely "inclined" to sin (*in malum prona sunt*)—probably the result, Calvin says, of the text being "corrupted, by those who dispute too philosophically concerning the corruption of human nature." On the other hand, it is not as clear as Calvin claims that this text proclaims original sin, or the fact that humans are "born evil."

30. God conspicuously does not repeat to Noah the permission he gave Adam to "subdue" the earth. As Leibowitz sensibly comments (*Studies in the Book of Genesis*, 76), "It was not necessary to repeat this blessing in the case of Noah and his sons since mankind had more than fulfilled the mission entrusted to them in this sphere and even abused their trust."

31. Later rabbinic theologians read into this passage the seven so-called Noahdic commandments, binding on non-Israelite and Israelite alike: prohibition on eating the flesh of living animals, on murder, on idolatry, on blasphemy, on incest, and on theft, and the requirement of the acknowledgment of (especially judicial) authority.

32. Here as is so often the case, Locke implicitly rejects without discussion Calvin's understanding. Contrast the latter's *Commentary on Genesis* ad 9:3.

33. *Two Treatises of Government*, 1:39, 86–87; 2:25–26. See also Rousseau's wicked observation ("Essay on the Origin of Languages," in *Oeuvres complètes*, 5.397–98): "When one reads that Abraham served a calf to three people," one can "judge what terrible gluttons of meat were the men of those days. To conceive of the meals of the ancients, one has only to watch those of savages nowadays (I almost slipped and said, 'of Englishmen')."

34. See Edwards, *Notes on Scripture*, #347 (p. 329), and Kass, "A Genealogy of Justice," 46.

35. *Two Treatises of Government*, 2.8–9 and 2.11. See also Plato *Laws* 857bff.

36. Cassuto (*Commentary on the Book of Genesis*, 2:68) notes the parallel to what "was given to Phineas when God declared (Num. 25:12): 'Behold, I give to him My *covenant* of peace.'" According to Westermann, "The studies of A. Jepsen and E. Kutsch have shown that the basic meaning of the word is not 'covenant.' A. Jepsen describes it as a solemn assurance" (*Genesis 12–36*, 113). Wevers suggests that the Septuagint preserves something like this distinction by

using διαθήκη rather than συνθήκη to translate ברית in every case except one (*Notes on the Greek Text of Genesis* ad 6:18): "A *sun*-compound implies partners setting up an agreement together. But the ברית is something that God sets up; only he determines both the responsibilities and the benefits of the divine-human relationship. For this the Septuagint chose the δια-compound which meant 'testament, will,' thus a word in which only the testator determines the terms, and the relationship flows basically in one direction." Unfortunately, the matter of terminology in Greek is not quite as neat or unambiguous as this comment by Wevers suggests, since, on the one hand, the Septuagint also uses the δια-compounds to render the words for covenants that are unquestionably made between two equal (human) partners (see Wevers on διέθεντο διαθήκην at Gen. 21:27 and 21:32) and, on the other hand, in colloquial Attic Greek the word διαθήκη can mean "contract" (e.g., Aristophanes *Birds* 440–43) as well as "last will" (e.g., Aristophanes *Wasps* 589). We may add the observation that the Latin word *testamentum,* which means not "covenant" but rather the formal declaration of a person's wishes as to the disposition of property after death, was chosen in early Church Latin (though not in Jerome, who used *foedus* and *pactum* in translating ברית) to translate the Greek διαθήκη, and thus the Hebrew ברית—and this is why *testamentum* came to have the meaning of "covenant between God and man" (from which is derived the English "New Testament," "Old Testament") as well as its proper original Latin meaning of "last will." The *O.E.D.* under "testament" explains this "misuse of the word" as probably "largely due to the use of διαθήκη (in the sense of 'covenant') in the account of the Last Supper," and a consequent "association with the notion of a last will or testament."

37. Cf. Gen. 8:22 with 9:11 and *Midrash Rabbah* on Gen. 34:11. In Isa. 24–27 we hear a prediction of a future apocalyptic scourging and purification of the entire earth.

38. See Wevers, *Notes on the Greek Text of Genesis* ad 9:16–17: "Note that Noah is not mentioned anymore and it would appear that the eternal covenant is between God and 'all sentient life in all flesh'. . . . The divine covenant turns out to have been made between God and his animate creation without the intervention of Noah."

39. *Observations Concerning the Originall of Government, Upon Mr. Hobs Leviathan, Mr Milton against Salmatius, H. Grotius De Jure Belli,* "Observations on Mr Milton," sec. 10 beg.

40. *Das erste Buch der Tora, Genesis* ad loc. See similar passages at Gen. 49:11ff., Judg. 9:13, 1 Kings 4:25, Ps. 104:15, Hos. 2:15, Mic. 4:4, Amos 9:13.

41. Von Rad's and Cassuto's appraisals of the moral implications of Noah's discovery of wine and subsequent drunkenness seem too lenient on Noah and on the intoxicant (von Rad, *Genesis,* 132–33; Cassuto, *Commentary on the Book*

of Genesis 2:159–61; but contrast the citation of Hab. 2:15 on p. 152). It is true that there are passages, such as the two that Cassuto adduces (Ps. 104:15, Judg. 9:13), that indicate God's approval of wine, but there are as many indicating the qualification on that approval, especially insofar as wine conduces to drunkenness. See, e.g., Gen. 19:32–33; Lev. 10:9; Deut. 21:20, 29:5, and 32:32–35; I Sam. 1:14–16 and 25:36; 2 Sam. 11:13; Prov. 20:1 as well as 23:20–21 and 29–32; Eccles. 2:3; Isa. 5:11–12 and 22 as well as 28:1–3 and 7–8; Jer. 13:13; Luke 21:34; Rom. 13:13; I Cor. 6:10; Gal. 5:21; Eph. 5:18; I Pet. 4:3–4 and 5:8. See also *Midrash Rabbah* on Num. 10:4 and 10:8; the Talmudic Sanhedrin 70a–b; Berachoth 29b; Pesachim 113b; and Ginzberg, *Legends of the Jews,* 1.168 (the grape as the forbidden fruit of the Tree of Knowledge). The asceticism that sets apart the Nazirite includes qualified abstention from wine (Num. 6:3–4 and 20; Judg. 13:4; Amos 2:12). It is noteworthy that in the lavish meal Abraham prepares for the three angelic visitors (Gen. 18:6), he serves no wine but only milk and curds, "although the region of Hebron is, indeed, the classic locale for viticulture in Palestine (cf. the legend of the spies in Num. 13)" (Gunkel, *Genesis,* 195).

42. As Cassuto remarks (*Commentary on the Book of Genesis,* 2:150), one may well surmise that in the "source," Ham's deed "had a coarser and uglier character than the Biblical tale." Indeed, this is the way "the Talmudic sages understood the story (see Sanhedrin 70a: 'Rab and Samuel [differ], one maintaining that he castrated him, and the other that he abused him sexually') and in like vein Ibn Ezra" (and, we may add, Rashi). But Cassuto goes on to argue persuasively that it is inappropriate to read such sordid overtones into the present biblical account: "Even conduct like that portrayed in the present narrative was something that the sensitive Israelite conscience found shocking and regarded as an unforgivable sin. . . . [I]t is the seeing itself, the looking, that is accounted by the refined sensitivity of the Israelite as something disgusting."

43. Kass ("Seeing the Nakedness of His Father," 45) explains the cruel aptness of Noah's curse: "Measure for measure, Noah 'unfathers' Ham by driving a wedge between him and his (youngest) son Canaan. Should the curse be effective, Canaan (whose name is from a root meaning 'to be low') will blame his own misfortunes on his father's misdeed, precisely in the matter of filial piety."

44. Cassuto's attempt (*Commentary on the Book of Genesis,* 2:168–69) to vindicate Noah's curse by explaining what is meant by the Canaanite enslavement to the children of Shem (that the Scripture refers to the subjection mentioned in Gen. 14:4), while ingenious, strikes me as too contrived. The subjection to which Cassuto refers us does not consist in the *enslavement* of the Canaanites, let alone in their being the *lowest* of slaves to the descendants of Shem.

45. See ibid., 2:149–50: "The *sons of Ham*—especially those of them who came in direct contact with the children of Israel, namely, the Egyptians and

Canaanites—acted in sexual matters in accordance with customs that the Israelite conscience regarded as utterly abominable. Not without reason does the section on Forbidden Relations begin with these words (Lev. 18:3): 'You shall not do as they do in the land of Egypt, where you dwelt, and you shall not do as they do in the land of Canaan, to which I am bringing you.'"

46. Pascal, *Pensées*, #232 and 236 (= Brunschvicg #566 and 578): "On n'entend rien aux ouvrages de Dieu, si on ne prend pour principe qu'il a voulu aveugler les uns et éclaircir les autres. . . . Il y a assez d'obscurité pour aveugler les réprouvés et assez de clarté pour les condamner et les rendre inexcusables." See also #237 (= B. 795), where Pascal refers to the authority of Isa. 8:13–14.

47. Of course, this is not the case if one accepts Rousseau's impious contention concerning the nature of "the first language." See "Essay on the Origin of Language," chap. 3, whose thesis—that the original language was imaginative or figurative without any awareness of the difference between illusion and reality—is summarized as follows (*Oeuvres complètes*, 5.381–82): "In the beginning speech was solely poetry; learning to reason came only long afterward. . . . Since the illusory image presented by passion manifested itself first, the corresponding language was the first to be invented; it later became metaphoric when a clarified spirit recognized the error of the beginning." Consider the striking example Rousseau provides by way of illustration. The editor notes, "[Rousseau] n'évoque pas l'hébreu; mais voir les nombreuses allusions à la Bible."

48. Since Adam spoke Hebrew (Gen. 2:23: אשה, from איש; cf. Gunkel, *Genesis*, 13), we may conclude that this was the language that God originally created for humans, or created humans to speak, up until the punitive fragmentation.

CHAPTER 7. *Abram from the Calling to the Covenant*

1. See Cassuto, *Commentary on the Book of Genesis*, 2:250–51, for parallels in the details of the genealogies of Noah and of Abram.

2. "Just as, in the flood of waters, the one household of Noah survived to restore the human race, so in the flood of the many superstitions throughout the whole world, the one household of Terah survived, in whose custody is the planting of the city of God" (Augustine *City of God* 16.12).

3. Cassuto, *Commentary on the Book of Genesis*, 2:303; Alter, *Art of Biblical Narrative*, 126; Doctorow, intro. to *The First Book of Moses, Called Genesis*, p. x. See similarly Fokkelman, *Narrative Art in Genesis*, 115–16. The great but somewhat obtuse Gunkel, writing of course in ignorance of twentieth-century artists and exercising his surprisingly limited aesthetics, characteristically stresses the primitive character of the scriptural writers' understanding. Though the narrator (Gunkel concedes) "had insight into the psychic life of his hero [Abraham],"

he "was unable to make these inner processes so clear that he could articulate them." "These simple artists did not know how to reflect, but they were master observers" (*Genesis,* xxxv–xxxvi).

4. Gen. 20:7. Cf. *Midrash Rabbah* on Gen. 30:10. Westermann (*Genesis 12–36,* 27) refers us also to "the importance of Abraham for Islam, where he is the most frequently mentioned biblical figure in the Koran" (actually, Moses rivals him in this regard); Islam "can be described as the religion of Abraham." More authoritative is Baidawi *The Secrets of Revelation and the Secrets of Interpretation* 3.89: "Islam is essentially the sect of Abraham" (quoted and translated in Katsh, *Judaism in Islam,* 105 n. 8 (see also 172, referring to *Al-Qur'an* 3.61). See esp. *Al-Qur'an* 2.124ff. (God constituted Abraham the *Imam* to mankind) and 4.125 ("And God chose Abraham as friend," *Khalil Allah*); also 6.74ff. and 21.51ff.

5. I follow Cassuto (*Commentary on the Book of Genesis,* 2:309–11) in my interpretation of לְךָ ־לֶךְ in Gen. 12:1. The full magnitude of the challenge laid before Abram by the initial call has been most fully appreciated by St. Chrysostom. See the elaboration in his richly humane thirty-first homily on Genesis.

6. *Commentary on Genesis* ad 12:2, pp. 167–68. The mortal trial and miraculous salvation of Abraham are related by Nachmanides previously, following Rashi, in commenting on Gen. 11:28 (pp. 156–61). Nachmanides and Rashi depend on traditional commentary such as *Midrash Rabbah* on Gen. 38:13, 39:3 and 8, 49:11; on Lev. 27:5, 36:4; on Eccles. 3:18; and the Talmudic Eiruvin 53a. See also Ginzberg, *Legends of the Jews.* 1.175, 193ff. The legendary persecution and the miracles by which God saved the life of Abraham play a major role in the Qur'an's account of the story of Abraham. See esp. *Al-Qur'an* 21.69–70 as well as 29.24 and 37.97–98. Nachmanides also depends heavily here on Maimonides, who mentions the threat to Abram's life and God's miraculous salvation of Abram in *Mishneh Torah: The Book of Knowledge* 66b, and elaborates in the *Guide* (3.29) on the basis of what he has purportedly read in a certain idolatrous "source" concerning this drama. But in the *Guide* Maimonides reports all this as hearsay and states as certain only that Abram suffered damage to his reputation among the ignorant idolaters: it was because he endured this rather insignificant slight, Maimonides declares, that God made Abram the great initial promises in Gen. 12:3 (for Maimonides now—at 3.29, in striking contradiction to his asseverations a few pages earlier, at 3.24—avers that "to come near to this true deity and to obtain His good will, nothing is required that is fraught with any hardship whatever"). See also Ibn Ezra ad loc. Calvin (*Commentary on Genesis* ad loc.) is far less exigent than the Rabbis: "The Lord would command in vain, unless he added confidence in his grace and benediction, in order to give us courage. I have before touched on this in the history of Noah, but I do not repeat it without reason, for this passage requires something to be said of it; and

the repetition of a doctrine of such great moment ought not to seem at all superfluous. For it is certain that faith cannot exist, unless it be founded on the promises of God."

7. It is to be noted that Genesis treats slavery as an unremarkable and customary institution. There is nothing in the text that corresponds to such comments as that of Calvin, who pauses to insist that slavery represents a "violent infringement of the order of nature, because men were created to have and to continue a mutual society among themselves; and although it be useful that some have superintendence over others, still it was necessary to preserve a condition of equality, as among brothers" (*Commentary on Genesis* ad 12:5). Contrast Milton's *Christian Doctrine*, 2.15, which on the basis of numerous scriptural passages treats without pejorative comment the duties of masters and slaves as a major part of the Christian virtues.

8. Gen. 11:28, 31; 12:1. See Cassuto's helpful discussion (*Commentary on the Book of Genesis*, 2:273–75)—which is indeed contradicted, however, in its understanding of the precise meaning of the expression ארץ ומולדת as grammatically hendiadys, by the unfinished posthumous appendix (ibid., 2:309, 311–12).

9. Calvin's attempt to place the call of Abram at the time of the transplantation by Terah seems unconvincing. It is part of his more general and unconvincing attempt to depict Abram as a sinner not distinguished from those around him by anything except God's grace (*Commentary on Genesis* ad 11:31 and ff.). See similarly Kass's characterization of Abram as a "godless" man prior to the call ("Educating Father Abraham: The Meaning of Fatherhood," 33).

10. *Hegels theologische Jugendschriften*, 245–46 (= *Early Theological Writings*, 185).

11. See similarly Calvin's *Commentary on Genesis* ad 11:28 and 112:1; and Milton's *Paradise Lost*, 12.122.

12. Gen. 20:12; cf. 20:16. Such a union with one's half-sister is repeatedly and emphatically forbidden by later law, on penalty of excommunication (Lev. 18:9 and 11; 20:17), but it was apparently possible through royal dispensation at the time of David (2 Sam. 13:11–13).

13. *Hegels theologische Jugendschriften*, 246–47 (= *Early Theological Writings*, 185–87).

14. I am indebted to the penetrating discussion of the meaning and place of erotic love in the Hebrew Bible by Fradkin, "With All Your Heart and with All Your Soul and with All Your Might."

15. "'To honor father and mother and to follow their will to the root of one's soul'—this was the tablet of overcoming that another people hung up over themselves and became powerful and eternal thereby" (Nietzsche, *Thus Spake Zarathustra*, "On the Thousand Goals and a Goal"; see the context).

16. Maimonides *Guide* 3.24. See also such Talmudic passages as Berachoth 17a and b; Avodah Zarah 19a; *Mishnah, Pirke Avoth* 1.3 and 4.2. Contrast Kass, "Educating Father Abraham: The Meaning of Wife," 19.

17. Barth, *Der Römerbrief,* 104–5 (ad Rom. 4:3–5), speaks of Abraham's "heroisches Erleben und Handeln" and characterizes him as "der geistig-sittliche Heros." "O virum viriliter!" proclaims Augustine (*City of God* 16.25 end). For a rich discussion of the specific meaning and place of "heroism" in the Hebrew Bible, see Fradkin, "Poet-Kings."

18. Gen. 26:7–11. See Calvin, *Commentary on Genesis* ad loc.: "Without doubt Isaac was so led by the example of his father, so that being instructed by the similarity of the circumstances, he might become associated with him in his faith." But Calvin understands the intended "instruction" to be the rejection of Abraham as a moral model in this important case. This particular lesson, Calvin is compelled to concede, Abraham himself obviously failed to learn, as is shown by his repetition or continuation of his prevaricating policy in the subsequent story of his and his wife's comportment toward King Abimilech. "Therefore we perceive," Calvin concludes, "in the example of the holy patriarch, how easily we forget both the punishments and the indulgence of God." In the repetition with Abimilech, Abraham's "deplorable indifference is even less excusable," since, according to Calvin, Abram himself on the earlier occasion probably recognized the evil of his own action in regard to Pharaoh, as is indicated by the fact that "no answer on the part of Abram is recorded here" (i.e., at Gen. 12:18, in response to Pharaoh's "just expostulation"): "Perhaps he assented to the just and true reprehension" (ibid. ad 12:18 and 20:2).

19. Herder, *Spirit of Hebrew Poetry,* in *Schriften zum Alten Testament,* 881: "Müssen wir einen Hirtenrater nicht als einen galanten Schäfer oder als einen Ritter von Profession betrachten, der zehntausendmal für seine Geliebte zu sterben weiß." Compare also the rabbinic saying from *Tanchuma Vayeira* 12, quoted by Nachmanides (ad Gen. 19:8—in severe criticism of Lot's "evil heart" in offering his daughters to the Sodomites): "It is the custom of the world that a man fights to the death for the honor of his daughters and his wife, to slay or be slain."

20. I am not convinced by Wildavsky's heroic and ingenious attempt to overcome what he recognizes to be the grave moral difficulties (luridly high-lighted in Voltaire's nasty article "Abraham" in his *Philosophical Dictionary*) by interpreting all three stories as symbolic prefigurations of the drama of the chosen people in Egypt. This is the latest in a long line of attempts to interpret away the story's problematic implications through highly allegoric readings. See *Assimilation versus Separation,* chap. 1, "No Foreigner Can Control Israel: The Wife-Sister Motif Prefigures the Joseph Stories." See also Wildavsky's *Nursing Father,* 245 n. 41.

21. At Gen. 20:13 the Septuagint renders חסד as δικαιοσύνη. On the other hand, at 20:16 the Septuagint puts into Abimilech's mouth the morally chastising expostulation "ἀλήθευσον" (tell the truth!)—thus rendering the obscure נכחת (usually taken to mean "you are vindicated, upright").

22. Gen. 26:7–11. As Pierre Bayle observes (in direct contradiction to Calvin, *Commentary on Genesis* ad loc.), the second employment of this ruse might seem to be excused by the enormous and unlooked-for success that the first employment of it had brought about—very much through God's (apparently uncensorious) direct intervention (*Historical and Critical Dictionary*, s.v. "Abimilech," n. A). Rashi (ad 19:29) goes so far as to say that Lot's *chief* merit in God's eyes consisted in his not having said anything in protest or condemnation of Abraham's deceit concerning Sarah in Egypt.

23. See also the Prayer of Manasseh 8 and the Talmudic Baba Bathra 17a. Rashi (ad loc.) interprets מצות (commandment) as an act that ought to be forbidden, even if the Bible did not forbid it, as for example robbery with violence or murder; with this Rashi contrasts חקות (statutes), which he interprets to mean an injunction, such as the prohibition on eating swine's flesh, for which there is no other reason than God's decree (see similarly Maimonides *Eight Chapters*, chap. 6 end). Rashi further interprets תורה (law) as meaning, even in this passage, the written and oral law delivered to Moses on Sinai (which Abraham must then somehow have anticipated and obeyed in its entirety!—this is not an unusual traditional view, despite the fact that Abraham later serves meat with milk to his three visitors: Ginzberg, *Legends of the Jews*, 1.292 and 5.187 n. 51, 235 n. 40, 259 n. 275). Ibn Ezra (ad loc.) more plausibly identifies תורה (law) in this passage with Abraham's circumcision of himself, his children, and his servants; and it is noteworthy that Ibn Ezra also departs from Rashi inasmuch as he identifies חקות (statutes) with moral rules based on *reason*—yet as the context indicates, this would mean that precisely insofar as these rules are based on reason, they cannot be strict laws. See similarly Maimonides *Eight Chapters*, chap. 6.

24. See Joseph at Gen. 42:7 etc.; the midwives in Exod. 1:15–21 (see also the homiletic comment on this passage by Savonarola, *Sermons on Exodus* 4); the deceitful scheme God Himself proposes to Moses at Exod. 3:18; the lies told by the blessed harlot Rahab in Josh. 2 and 6; Ehud in Judg. 3:15ff. and Jael in Judg. 4:18ff.; Michal in 1 Sam. 19:13ff. and Jonathan in 1 Sam. 20: 6ff.; the lies of Joab (2 Sam. 14) and of Jeremiah (Jer. 38:24–27); the entire drama of Judith in the deuterocanonical book of that name and Judith's remarkable prayer, linking God's favoring deadly deceit to His being the "God of the humble" (esp. Jth. 9:9–11: "Put in the hand of me, a widow, the strength to do what I have devised. By the deceit of my lips strike down the slave with the ruler and the ruler with his servant; crush their arrogance by the hand of a woman! For your

strength lies not in numbers, nor does your mastery depend on the powerful. But you are the God of the humble, helper of the inferior ones, upholder of the weak, protector of the forsaken, savior of those without hope—yes! Yes! The God of my father and the God of the inheritance of Israel, the Despot of the heavens and of the earth, Creator of the waters, King of Your whole creation! You will hear my prayer and make my deceitful speech produce wounds and hurt"). Ibn Ezra (ad Gen. 27:19) presents a list of prevarications committed by admirable figures—David (1 Sam. 23:2), Elisha (2 Kings 8:10), Micaiah (1 Kings 22:15), Daniel (Dan. 4:16)—and adds the significant lie Abram told his servants on Mount Moriah (Gen. 22:5). One could add other significant lies of David (e.g., at 1 Sam. 21:3–10, 14, 27:10). Compare Torquato Tasso's praise of the bold public prevarication that was the heroic deed of the Christian martyr Sophronia: "Noble lie! now when is the truth / So beautiful that it can be preferred to you? [*Magnanima menzògna! or quando e il vero / Si bello che si possa a te preporre?*]" (*Jerusalem Delivered*, 2.22–23).

25. Contrast Augustine *Questions on the Heptateuch* 1.26: "Abraham wished the truth to be concealed, but not to utter a lie." See similarly *City of God* 16.19 and *Against Faustus the Manichean* 22.36. Augustine is followed by Gratian (*Decretum* 2.22.2.14) and by Grotius (*On the Law of War and Peace*, 3.1.7 end), who assimilates the action of Abraham to the politic and self-preservative deception practiced by Jeremiah (Jer. 38). But Jeremiah, we cannot help noting, felt no need to excuse his deception. (In a subsequent discussion, we may add, Grotius criticizes what he regards as the insufficiently forthright teaching of Augustine on the moral status of lying: ibid., 3.1.16.) For a sympathetic discussion of the strengths and weaknesses of Augustine's attempt, especially in his treatises *On Lying* (*De Mendacio*) and *Against Lying* (*Contra Mendacium*), to establish the principle that "the testimony of Scripture warns against nothing so much as lying, by anyone, in any circumstances" (*On Lying* 21.42), see Fortin, "Augustine and the Problem of Human Goodness," 32–33. Augustine's position may not, however, be quite as "unique" as Fortin suggests. See the Talmudic Sanhedrin 92a (see also 89b): "R. Eleazar also said: Whoever dissembles in his speech is as though he had engaged in idolatry." See similarly, among many such typical passages in the Talmudic literature, Chullin 94b and Pesachim 113b. But consider, in apparent contradiction, the words approvingly attributed to Jacob in Megilah 13b as well as Baba Bathra 123a: "Rachel said to Jacob, 'Is it permitted to the righteous to indulge in trickery?' He replied. 'Yes: with the pure thou dost show thyself pure and with the crooked thou dost show thyself subtle.'" At Gen. 33:13 Jacob deceives Esau without any apparent divine disapproval (*pace* Calvin's comment ad loc.)

26. Cf. Wildavsky, *The Nursing Father*, 245 n. 41. One may note that Abram would appear to accept or agree with the principle on the basis of which

Socrates refutes Cephalus's inadequate understanding of justice at the beginning of Plato's *Republic* (331c1–d3, 332a11–b2)—though it is true that Socrates' example does not go so far as Abram's; but this may betoken the fact that Abram, or the authors of his story, do not yet grasp the full implications or ambit of the Socratic principle.

27. *Historical and Critical Dictionary*, s.v. "Abimilech," n. A end, together with "Acindynus (Septimius)," n. C (observe Bayle's cross-references). Bayle is responding to St. Chrysostom's *Homilies on Genesis* 32 and 45 (q.v.) and Augustine's *On the Lord's Sermon on the Mount* 1.16 and *Against Faustus the Manichean* 22.37.

28. See also Calvin's comment ad 19:8, on the moral error of Lot in offering his daughters to the mob of Sodomites; and the similar position assumed by Milton, despite his apparently latitudinarian approach (*Christian Doctrine*, 2.13, pp. 760ff.).

29. The categorical character of the imperatives of natural law is highlighted by Franciscus Vitoria, *Reflection on Dietary Laws*, qu. 1, a. 3: "Even if everyone agreed that it was necessary to fornicate to save one's life, it would not be lawful to do so . . . no fear, even of death, can excuse an act forbidden in natural law." See similarly Franciscus Suarez, *On Laws and God the Lawgiver*, 2.15–16: "Simply and absolutely, none of the Commandments of the Decalogue admits of dispensation, even by the absolute power of God. So holds St. Thomas (ST 1a–2ae Q100 a. 8)." For the categorical character of the imperatives of natural law according to Thomas, see ST 1a qu. 79 a. 12; 1a–2ae qu. 94 a. 4–6; qu. 95 a. 2–3; qu. 96 a. 4; qu. 97 a. 1 and 4; qu. 99 a. 2 reply obj. 2; qu. 100 a. 1 and 3 as well as (above all) a. 8; 2a–2ae qu. 66 a. 5, 7, 8; but compare 1a–2ae qu. 95 a. 1.

30. It is this latter and graver sin for which Abram is chiefly accused not only by Calvin but by Nachmanides in their commentaries on this passage (see similarly Cassuto and his discussion in *Commentary on the Book of Genesis*, 2.353). Von Rad (*Genesis*, 37) goes so far as to interpret Abram as acting "as though God's promise could not be relied upon at all, that is, in complete unbelief," and thus as "betraying" God's "plan of salvation."

31. See St. Thomas More's interpretation of this "tribulation" of Abraham, in *A Dialogue of Comfort against Tribulation*, 1.16.

32. *Homilies on Genesis* 32.24. See also 45.21 and Luther LG, *Werke*, 42:572, on "what God is by nature. He is the savior and the liberator from death; but before He saves, He destroys; before He brings to life, He plunges into death—that is His way, so that He may make everything *ex nihilo* (Heb. 11:3)."

33. *Spirit of the Laws*, 2.5, 3.8 in conjunction with 3.10 (an interpretation of the book of Esther), 4.2–4., 5.14, 8.21, 12.29. See the more restrained but weighty comment by Churchill, *The Gathering Storm*, bk. 1, chap. 17 ("The

Tragedy of Munich") end: "It is baffling to reflect that what men call honour does not correspond always to Christian ethics."

34. *Commentary on the Book of Genesis*, 2:366. See similarly St. Chrysostom *Homilies on Genesis* 31.16. Josephus (*Antiquities* 1.7) goes so far as to assert that Abram had adopted Lot as his son.

35. Calvin (*Commentary on Genesis* ad 14:13) alertly points to the grave moral question concerning Abram's behavior in this instance raised by the Christian tradition of natural law: How was it "lawful for Abram, a private person, to arm his family against kings, and to undertake a public war?" For under all versions of natural law, it is absolutely forbidden for those who are not legitimate rulers to undertake war against rulers, no matter what their crimes. Calvin responds that Abram is on solid ground because "he had already been created king of that land. And although the possession of it was deferred to a future time, yet God willed to give a singular example of the power which He had granted him, and which was hitherto unknown to men."

36. Rashi (ad Gen. 14:15 and 15:1) follows a Midrash that insists that the victory was effected through a divine miracle; no mention is made of any military courage or skill on Abram's part. Ibn Ezra subsequently indicates (ad Gen. 15:1) that there was indeed decisive divine assistance. Calvin says that Abram here exhibited "heroical virtues"—which must, however, he insists, be attributed entirely to divine grace (*Commentary on Genesis* ad 14:13).

37. Grotius, *On the Law of War and Peace*, 3.16.3.2. Milton (*Christian Doctrine*, 2.9, p. 735) links this incident with the previous, as the leading exemplification of the Christian virtue of high-mindedness, defined as "in seeking or not seeking riches, advantages, or honors, in avoiding or accepting them, a man behaves as befits his own dignity, rightly understood. Abraham, for example, did not reject the gifts of the king of Egypt, Gen. 12:13 and 20:14, though he did those of the king of Sodom, Gen. 14:22–23; and he refused to accept Ephron's field when it was offered to him, except at its correct market price, 23:13." (Years later, when Sarah dies, Abraham refuses to accept a burial plot as a gift from Ephron the Hittite but insists on paying, in the presence of the Hittite public, the full market price for title to the land.)

38. Cf. Maimonides *Eight Chapters,* chap. 4 beg. (but contrast *Mishneh Torah: The Book of Knowledge* p. 48b).

39. This of course does turn out to be the case, in a dark and fantastically complex manner that merely human foresight could hardly guess: the House of David, culminating in the Messiah or Christ, descends from the son born of Lot's incestuous relation with his eldest daughter, the descent being by way of Ruth the Moabite—a tribal name after the Founder, whose mother named him Moab, meaning "from my own father" (see Sept.), thus reminding for all time

of the incestuous origins. See the narrator's abrupt, pregnant reference to the "Moabites *of this day*" in Gen. 19:37 together with Ruth 1:4 and 4:13ff.

40. Wevers, *Notes on the Greek Text of Genesis* ad 15:1; von Rad, *Genesis,* 178.

41. Alter, *Genesis* ad loc. See Alter's earlier explanation (ad Gen. 9:12) of what is conveyed by the "common convention of biblical narrative," "when a speaker addresses someone and the formula for introducing speech is repeated with no intervening response from the interlocuter": "It generally indicates some sort of significant silence." Calvin (*Commentary on Genesis* ad loc.) remarks that Abram here "seems to conduct himself with little modesty."

42. Quoted by Barth, *Der Römerbrief,* 130 (ad Rom. 4:20). To this quotation Barth adds his own words: "Wer's fassen mag, der fasse es: *Das* ist das Ende und der Anfang der Geschichte." This passage must be kept in mind if one is to understand Barth's later commentary on Rom. 9:15–16 (see esp. p. 366: "Eben der Gott, für den *menschliche* Begrifflichkeit schliesslich nur noch die Bezeichnung 'Despot' übrig haben dürfte, gegen dessen Herrschaft sich der *Mensch* nur empören kann, den der *Mensch* um keinen Preis Gott nennen möchte, *ist* eben Gott"). See also the Talmudic Makkoth 24a and also Rashi on the beginning of Genesis, quoted in *Midrash Rabbah* on Gen. 1:2: "Elohim (God) is His attribute as a God of justice, and the opening verse of the Bible, IN THE BEGINNING ELOHIM CREATED, is an assertion that He created the world on the basis of justice and truth." See also the summary in James, *The Varieties of Religious Experience,* lecture 1, pp. 32–35, of evidence from the history of Christian criteria for distinguishing true from false mystical experience—with special reference to Jonathan Edwards and St. Teresa.

43. As Alter comments (*Genesis* ad loc.), "Since this covenant is sealed at sunset, it can scarcely be a direct continuation of the nocturnal scene just narrated."

44. Ibn Ezra's suggestion of the difficulty or doubt that was troubling Abram gains support if we follow Kass, "A Genealogy of Justice," 47, in interpreting God's cryptic subsequent remark about the Amorites as meaning, "The Amorites, who now inhabit Canaan, are not yet sufficiently wicked to warrant expelling them from the land."

45. As Alter observes (ibid.), "Covenants in which the two parties step between cloven animal parts are attested in various places in the ancient Near East as well as in Greece" (the Scripture itself indicates the custom at Jer. 34:17–20; see also von Rad, *Genesis,* 181–82). Alter further provocatively insists that "existing translations fudge the vivid anthropomorphism here: *'ish,* literally, 'man,' means 'each' but is a word applied to animate beings, not to things, so it must refer to the two parties to the covenant facing each other, not to the animal parts"; and so Alter translates Gen. 15:10, "And he took all of these and clove

them through the middle, and *each set his part opposite the other,* but the birds he did not cleave."

46. *Conflict of the Faculties,* in *Akademieausgabe,* 7.63.

47. See Cicero *On Divination* 1.58–59 and 2.139–42; Xenophon *Apology of Socrates to the Jury* 4; and Aristotle's *On Prophecy in Sleep* as a whole. Compare also Rousseau's *Letter to Malesherbes,* 12 January 1762, and *La nouvelle Héloïse,* part 3, letter 18, in *Oeuvres complètes,* 1.1135–36 and 2.353–54. See above all Nietzsche, *Ecce Homo,* "Thus Spoke Zarathustra," sec. 3.

48. Augustine's commentary (*City of God* 16.24) on this vexing passage, with its attempt to introduce Luke 1.34 as a parallel, sidesteps rather than confronts the massive difficulty.

49. Calvin repeatedly insists (*Commentary on Genesis* ad 15:2 and 26:24 and 28:16; *Institutes,* 1.6.2 beg.) that "since Satan is a wonderful worker of lies and deceits, and has many illusions with which to delude in the name of God, it was necessary that some sure and notable distinction should appear in true and heavenly oracles, which would not suffer the faith of the holy fathers to waver." But Calvin does not or cannot explain what that distinction or "clear and unambiguous mark engraven on the visions of God" could be—and why Satan, or the human imagination, or both together, cannot also ape this manifestation.

50. *Theologico-Political Treatise,* in *Opera,* chap. 1, para. 8, p. 17: "The voice, with which God called Samuel, may be suspected to be real, since it is said at the end of 1 Samuel 3 that 'and again God appeared to Samuel in Shiloh because God revealed Himself to Samuel in Shiloh by the word of God'; which is to say, God's manifestation to Samuel was nothing other than God's showing himself by that word, or nothing other than that Samuel heard God speaking. Nevertheless, since we are forced to distinguish between the prophecy of Moses and that of the other prophets, it is necessary to say that this voice which Samuel heard was imaginary—which indeed can be gathered from the fact that it resembled the voice of Eli, which Samuel was much accustomed to hear, and hence was prone to imagine."

51. On which see also Maimonides *Eight Chapters,* chap. 7 end.

52. *Guide* 3.24 (see also 2.44–45, on Samuel; Maimonides does not, however, discuss either the specific text over which we are now puzzling, Gen. 15:8, or for that matter Judg. 6:17). Precisely in what sense Abraham's rational intellect could have had no doubt about the wisdom of his action in the case of the binding of Isaac we must consider when we arrive at our detailed discussion.

53. As Wildavsky remarks (*The Nursing Father,* 87), Hirsch underestimates the difficulties in this passage when he claims that it is "impossible" that Abram "lacked confidence in God's guidance" (*The Pentateuch,* 276).

54. See also Prov. 9:10; Ps. 111.10; Job 28:28; Jth. 16:16; Sir. 1:14–28, 4:17,

19:20, 21:11; *Mishnah,* Pirke Avoth 3.9 and 3.17; *The Avot of Rabbi Nathan,* chap. 22; the repeated Talmudic quotations of the verse from Proverbs in places such as Berachoth 17a; and Otto, *The Idea of the Holy,* chap. 14.

55. See James's rich and illuminating summary of "religion's secret" (*The Varieties of Religious Experience,* lecture 2 end): how man, in the grip of what appears from the empirical evidence of firsthand reports to be the most distinctive religious experience, "falls on the thorns and faces death, and in the very act annuls annihilation"—an experience which, fully to understand, "you must yourself have been a religious man of the extremer type."

56. *Notes on the Greek Text of Genesis* ad loc. Accordingly, Hobbes ignores this scriptural text in his account of God's covenant with "Abraham" (*Leviathan,* chaps. 35 beg. and 40 beg.; *On the Citizen,* 16.3).

57. That Abram and Ishmael never ceased to cherish one another is signaled by Abraham's distress in Gen. 21:11 and by the fact that Ishmael returned to help bury his father, as well as by the fact that the story of Abraham concludes with the genealogy of the line of Ishmael (Gen. 25:9, 12–18). See also Ginzberg, *Legends of the Jews,* 1.264.

58. See Filmer, *Observations Concerning the Originall of Government,* "Observations on Mr Milton," sec. 10: "[In] Genesis 17:9–10, God covenants with Abraham, saying 'Thou shalt keep my covenant . . . every male child among you shall be circumcised.' Here it is called God's covenant, though it be to be performed only by Abraham." Filmer's overstatement brings out the one-sidedness that is insufficiently indicated in discussions such as that by von Rad, *Genesis,* 181–82 and 195–96.

59. *Leviathan,* chap. 35 beg. Cf. chap. 40 beg.; Hobbes's italics purport to indicate direct quotation (see Curley's editorial note ad loc., p. 273 n. 6).

60. Though their discussion applies not only to the covenants in Genesis but also to the later covenants, especially that between God and the whole Israelite nation at Sinai, the characterization provided by Daniel J. Elazar and Stuart A. Cohen is still illuminating for our purposes: "A covenant is much more than a contract—though our modern system of contracts is related to the covenant idea—because it involves a pledge of loyalty beyond that demanded for mutual advantage, often involving the development of a certain kind of community among the partners to the covenant, and ultimately based upon a moral commitment" (*The Jewish Polity,* 9).

61. See Filmer, *Observations Upon Aristotles Politiques, Touching Forms of Government, Together with Directions for Obedience to Governours in dangerous and doubtfull times,* near the end, in *Patriarcha and Other Writings,* 284: "As God hath exalted the dignity of earthly kings, by communicating to them his own title by saying they 'are gods' [Ps. 82:6]; so on the other side he hath been pleased as it were to humble himself by assuming the title of a king to express his power, and

not the title of any popular government. We find it is a punishment to have 'no king,' Hosea 3:4, and promised as a blessing to Abraham, Genesis 17:6, 'that kings shall come out of thee.' " Consider the Scripture's wondering praise of the Roman republic in 1 Macc. 8:12–16: "They have subdued kings far and near, and as many as have heard of their fame have feared them. Those whom they wish to help and to make kings, they make kings, and those whom they wish they depose; and they have been greatly exalted. Yet for all this not one of them has put on a crown or worn purple as a mark of pride, but they have built for themselves a senate chamber, and every day three hundred twenty senators constantly deliberate concerning the people, to govern them well. They trust one man each year to rule over them and to control all their land; they all heed the one man, and there is no envy or jealousy among them."

For a good introduction to the subsequent development, within the Jewish political tradition, of the more republican notion of government through the *edah,* see Elazar and Cohen, *The Jewish Polity* (esp. "An Introduction to the Jewish Political Tradition," 11–20, and "Epoch I, Ha-Avot: The Forefathers," 47), as well as Elazar, ed., *Kinship and Consent.*

62. Calvin stresses (*Commentary on Genesis* ad 17:11 and 17:23) how "absurd and ridiculous this command would at first sight appear": "Who will say that it is a suitable thing that the token of so elevated a mystery should be placed and located in the shameful parts of man?" It "was necessary for Abraham to become a fool, in order to prove himself obedient to God." Abraham must have wondered, "What does this mean, that I cannot be saved unless I, with one foot almost in the grave, thus mutilate myself?" "We know that he had a great multitude in his household, nearly equal to a people. It was scarcely credible that so many men would have suffered themselves to be wounded, apparently to be made a laughing-stock."

63. See esp. Jer. 9:24–25. Contrast the rather Machiavellian or proto-Voltairian observation of Shaftesbury, in the context of his argument for the Egyptian derivation of much of the priestly Hebrew religion (*Characteristics of Men, Manners, Opinions, Times,* 6.2.1): " 'Tis certain that if this holy patriarch, who first instituted the sacred rite of circumcision, within his own family or tribe, had no regard to any policy or religion of the Egyptians, yet he had formerly been a guest and inhabitant in Egypt (where historians mention this to have been a national rite: Herodot. 2.36, 'The Egyptians practice circumcision: other peoples leave the genitals as they are, save for those who have learned from them.') long ere he had received any divine notice or revelation concerning this affair." Shaftesbury links this observation up with his ingeniously subversive explanation (partly on the basis of Tacitus *Histories* 5.3 and Justinus Junianus 36.2, as well as Acts 7:22) of the very strange passages on circumcision in Exod. 4:25–26 and Josh. 5:4ff., esp. 5:9. See similarly the article "Circumcision" in

Voltaire's *Philosophic Dictionary.* Contrast Spinoza, *Theologico-Political Treatise,* chap. 3 end. Spinoza stands closer to the Scripture inasmuch as he stresses the unique or distinguishing character of the Jewish practice of circumcision (though he also links the rite with a general "emasculation of the spirit" brought about by the Jewish law).

64. *Guide* 3.49. See similarly Philo *Questions and Answers on Genesis* 3.47. Consider, however, Gen. 34:13–24.

65. On the other hand, since the mark of circumcision sets off the peoples of Abraham in a most dramatic way, it is a misunderstanding to say, as does Westermann (*Genesis 12–36,* 270), that "the promise concerning Ishmael means that the effect of God's blessing extends beyond Israel to *other nations as well.* That *universal* trait which appeared in Gen. 1 and 10 continues here."

66. Some commentators adopt the interpretation embodied in the Revised Standard Version, which (departing from the King James version) has God reply to Abraham's question with an emphatic no—as if Abraham had asked something, for Ishmael, which God is refusing; as if, in other words, Abraham had asked that not Isaac but instead Ishmael be made the heir. In this case the laughter would perhaps have to be interpreted as a laughter of incredulity or doubt. I am inclined to say that such a reading and translation exaggerate the very mildly adversative sense of the Hebrew word אבל (yes, but . . .).

67. See Augustine *City of God* 16.26 ("Abraham's is a laughter of joy, not the scoffing laughter of doubt") and Rom. 4:20, as well as Philo *Questions and Answers on Genesis* 3.55 and Calvin, *Commentary on Genesis* ad 17:17 and 18:12. But Richard Hooker (sermon 1, in *Works,* 3.472) interprets this comment by St. Paul as follows: "I answer, that this negation [of doubt] doth not exclude all fear, all doubting; but only that which cannot stand with true faith. . . . [T]hat Abraham was not void of all doubtings, what need we any other proof than the plain evidence of his own words (Gen. 17:17)." Similarly, Barth reads this laughter of Abraham as expressing "höhnenden Skepsis" (*Der Römerbrief,* 129; but see also 359: " 'Isaak' means 'one laughs.' Why? And how? Doubtful about the *impossible* possibility, or enthusiastic about the *possible* impossibility? The step from one to the other is not so big, as those suppose, who do not know actual doubt or actual enthusiasm").

68. 1 Macc. 12:19–23 reproduces the text of a letter sent by King Arius (309–265 B.C.) of the Spartans to Onias I (320–290 B.C.), the high priest of Israel, saying, "It has been found in writing concerning the Spartans and the Jews that they are brothers and are from the race of Abraham [ἐκ γένους Αβρααμ]."

69. Von Rad (*Genesis,* 199–200) underlines the "strangeness and singularity" of "this way of [God's] appearing," but Gunkel (*Genesis,* 192–93) refers us to Judg. 6:14 ff. and 13:2ff, esp. 13:8, as well as Tob. 5:4ff. Von Rad follows Gunkel in remarking the striking parallelism to Greek accounts of divine visita-

tions, particularly *Odyssey* 18.485–87—commenting that "such similarity requires that one think of some connection, no longer distinguishable, with our narrative, or better, with one of its previous stages." But von Rad fails to note that precisely this Homeric passage, and the conception of divine mutability that it conveys, was singled out by the Platonic Socrates as illustrative of a theologically unacceptable denigration of divinity as "willingly making itself worse" through self-alteration from a perfect to an imperfect beauty and goodness of form (*Republic* 381; but see also *Sophist* 216). Von Rad's failure to grasp the difficulty is indicated in his illogical comment, "It is quite understandable that Yahweh visits Sodom in disguise, for it would have been unthinkable for Israel to allow even the possibility of Yahweh's coming into contact with the sin of Sodom" (*Genesis,* 212). The Hellenizing Josephus, better trained by Plato and perhaps with an eye to Judg. 13:16 and Tob. 12:19, insists that no food was actually ingested by the threesome but that they only *appeared* to consume the meal Abram served to them (*Antiquities* 1.11.2). The issue of course becomes moot on the basis of the New Testament (see, e.g., Acts 10:41).

CHAPTER 8. *Abraham at the Peak*

1. To be sure, one cannot help but wonder about the infants. Are they to be understood as necessarily corrupt from birth, given who their parents are, and thus what their upbringing must inevitably be? See Maimonides *Guide* 1.54 end, referring to Deut. 20:14ff. Luther opines that "about the children we are saying nothing; they are preserved, though the manner is unknown to us—as is proved by the place in Jonah [4:11] about those who are ignorant of the difference between the right and the left" (LG, *Werke,* 43:41). Contrast, however, Luther's closing remark on Sodom: "God is not moved even by the innocent by virtue of age; He snatches away everything, so that His anger against sin may be made manifest" (ibid., 45). Luther draws our attention to the fact that at Matt. 10:15 Christ unflinchingly "pronounces that the punishment of the Sodomites will be seen to be more tolerable than that visited on cities which hear and do not accept the Gospel" (ibid., 85). See also Christ's approving invocation of the punishment visited on Lot's wife (Luke 17:32).

2. The idea that God has to carry out an investigation in order to discover the truth of reports of wrongdoing is obviously perplexing and perhaps best understood as a figure of speech (see also Gen. 11:7). Nachmanides (ad Gen. 18:20) is severely critical of Ibn Ezra's assertion, commenting on Gen. 18:21, that the "mystery" here hints at the fact that God (as Aristotle taught) lacks knowledge of particulars; this is an example, Nachmanides deploringly but somewhat cryptically notes, of Ibn Ezra's "pleasing himself with foreign offspring."

3. Jacob suggests that "the motive and purpose of the visit of the three men with Abraham is revealed" to have been to strengthen Abraham's courage for his questioning God: "For this reason God had appeared to him in the shape of men who visit with him, eat at his table, and converse with him in the greatest affability; even some teasing of Sarah is added. All this shall give Abraham courage so he may dare speak to God as man speaks to his fellow" (*The First Book of the Bible* ad 18:21).

4. See Leibowitz, *Studies in the Book of Genesis,* 164–70; Buber, "Abraham the Seer," 40.

5. I believe that an approach such as Thompson's (*The Origin Tradition of Ancient Israel I,* 93)—claiming that "the tone of the tale is wholly at odds with the seriousness of the introduction, which is in awe of both God and Abraham. In the story we have not awe but humor. In comic relief, Abraham, *tongue in cheek,* bargains with God"—altogether misses the import of the passage.

6. See Rashi and Ibn Ezra ad Gen. 26:5; Grotius, *On the Law of War and Peace,* 1.1.10 (also 3.1.4.3), which refers us to Isa. 5:3, Ezek. 18:25, Jer. 2:9, and Mic. 6:2 as well as to Rom. 2:6 and 3:6. Calvin, *Commentary on Genesis* ad 18:25: Abraham "reasons from the nature of God, that it is impossible for Him to intend anything unjust. I grant that, in using the same form of speaking, the impious often murmur against God, but Abraham does far otherwise." He "retains this principle, that it was impossible for God, who is the Judge of the world, and by nature loves equity, and whose will is the law of justice and rectitude, should in the least degree swerve from righteousness." Therefore, Calvin concludes, "whenever some appearance of contradiction presents itself in the works of God, only let our persuasion of His justice remain fixed." "Paul seems to have taken from this place" (Calvin adds) "the answer with which he represses the blasphemy of those who charge God with injustice. 'Is God unrighteous? Far from it, for how could there be injustice with Him who judges the world?' (Rom. 3:5–6)."

7. See also Abimilech's protest to God at Gen. 20:4–5 (on which see Alter, *Genesis* ad loc.). Pascal even declares (on the basis, admittedly, of the somewhat misleading Vulgate translation of Isa. 5:4 as *quod debui*—"in regard to which I was obligated"), "There is a reciprocal duty between God and men. One must excuse this translation, *quod debui;* "accuse me!" says God in Isaiah 1. God is obliged to carry out his promises, etc. . . . God owes it to men not to lead them in any way into error" (*Pensées,* #840 [= Brunschvicg #843]; compare Plato *Euthyphro* 7d–8e, 10d–11b, 11e–15e).

8. Compare Otto, *The Idea of the Holy,* 99–100, 182–83.

9. It seems to me that Otto (ibid., 5; cf. 6, 11, 51, 53, 109–11, 136–40), in his understandable effort to bring out the transcendent, and even transmoral,

elements in our experience of the holy or dreadful in God, overreacts against Kantian or neo-Kantian theology when he asserts, of Abraham's exemplary experience of God as holy or dreadful, that "if the ethical element was present at all, at any rate it was not original." Similar overreaction marks his claim that the scriptural God's wrath in itself "has no concern whatever with moral qualities" (ibid., 18; cf. 19, 107). Otto seems to become trapped in self-contradiction when he asserts (ibid., 52) on the one hand that the holy as applied to God "is originally not a moral category at all," and on the other hand that God's holiness is an object of "praise" and that "the object of such praise is not an absolute might" but "a might that has at the same time the supremest *right* to make the highest claim to service"; for claims of right are claims of justice, of morality, of צדקה (recall Gen. 15:6).

10. When the Lord displays to Moses His knowable attributes, these consist in mercy, love, and retributive justice (Exod. 34:6–7; see similarly Jer. 9:23–24). See also Calvin's account of "the kind of being we know God to be" (*Institutes,* 1.2.3; 1.4.2 and 4; 1.5.7; 1.10.2). Calvin teaches that it is "superstition" ("from which even Augustine was not always free"—Calvin refers to the Saint's *On Predestination and Grace*) to attempt to deny the truth that divine omnipotence necessarily implies that "sins are manifestations not merely of divine permission or patience, but also of divine power"—that God acts in and through human sin—as Augustine rightly teaches in *On Holy Predestination.* But Calvin shows the moral line that must be drawn when he adds, "Nevertheless, in the same work there is always a wide difference between what the Lord does, and what Satan and the ungodly design to do. The wicked instruments which he has under his hand, and can turn as he pleases, he makes subservient to His own justice" (*Institutes,* 2.4.3–5). Or as he puts it in another place, "God, while not willing treachery, with another end in view justly wills the revolt" (ibid., 1.18.4; see the whole of chap. 18; see also 2.5.11).

11. See Calvin's careful spelling out (ibid., 3.2.14–20, 24, 26–27), in light especially of the exemplary experience articulated by David in the Psalms, of the alternation of complete confidence, in knowledge, with fearful uncertainty or doubt that characterizes the experience even or especially of the truly faithful.

12. See Leibowitz, *Studies in the Book of Genesis,* 185, which explains Ibn Ezra's laconic comment ("The reason why the Lord said 'within the city'—'if I find fifty righteous *within the city*'—implies that they fear the Lord *in public;* compare Jeremiah [5:1]") thus: "In other word, the few can turn the scales and save the place, if the righteous individuals concerned are 'within the city,' playing a prominent part in public life and exerting their influence."

13. Contrast the justice of Zeus, as it is characterized (without protest) by Hesiod (*Works and Days* 238–49):

Often an entire city suffers for an evil man,
who sins and devises outrageous deeds.
And upon them from heaven the Son of Cronos lays great trouble,
famine and plague together. And the people waste away.
Nor do the women bear; and the homes diminish,
through the contriving of Olympian Zeus. And sometimes again
the Son of Cronos either destroys their army or their walls
or else does away with their ships in the harbor.
You kings, you too, even you, mark well this Justice.

14. It seems to me that the deepest teaching and challenge in the Scripture is avoided if one reads this crucial passage, as Kass does ("Educating Father Abraham: The Meaning of Fatherhood," 37; "A Genealogy of Justice," 49–50), to the effect that the lesson Abraham is supposed to learn is the need to embrace "political justice," which "is not altogether just"—the lesson that "one must be willing to overlook, at least to some extent," the "demand for absolutely strict justice for each individual"; that "if one is to care for justice of a nation, and especially as its founder, one must be willing not only to moderate . . . the love of strict justice," one "must even be willing to sacrifice" it ("at least in part").

15. Contrast *Al-Qur'an* 11.74 and 29.31–32. The amiable St. Chrysostom in this crucial case misses or obscures the profound moral point: "Since Abraham was not bold enough to speak directly on behalf of his nephew, he made a general entreaty for everyone out of a desire to save his life along with theirs and rescue them along with him" (*Homilies on Genesis* 42.16). The Targum attributed to Jonathan ben Uzziel similarly diminishes the majesty of Abraham's concern for justice by inserting in its rendering of Gen. 18:22, "Abraham was still ⟨*beseeching mercy for Lot, and ministering in prayer*⟩ before the Lord."

16. Ezek. 14:12–23 and 18 entire. See also Zeph. 2. The fact that, in the event, God did save the single just man in Sodom—and that it is incredible that such a possibility could not have occurred to Abraham, in his concern for Lot—renders dubious von Rad's historicist interpretation, which would seem to illustrate the hermeneutic pitfalls into which such "higher criticism" stumbles. Von Rad argues that since this whole section belongs to a "source" that predates the time when, he claims, seventh-century Israel for the first time discovered the principle of individual moral responsibility, it follows that it was a "great misunderstanding" of traditional hermeneutics to see in the present conversation on justice "this individualizing tendency, which was later present (Deut. 24:16; 2 Kgs. 14:6; Ezek. 18:1ff.)." According to von Rad, the author only "dares to replace old collective thinking with new." Abraham is not depicted as "concerned with the release from the city of the guiltless or their special preser-

vation. He is concerned with something quite different and much greater [*sic*], namely from beginning to end with Sodom as a whole!"

17. Luther, LG, *Werke,* 43:36: "If you divide the whole of Scripture, it contains two things, promises and threats, that is, benefits and penalties."

18. See *Mishnah,* Pirke Avoth 6.1 and 6.7; Philo *On Rewards and Punishments* 27–33; St. Chrysostom *Homilies on Genesis* 47.10; Maimonides *Eight Chapters,* chap. 4.

19. See *Mishnah,* Pirke Avoth 5.23 as interpreted by Maimonides *Commentary to Mishnah Abot* ad loc. and *Eight Chapters,* chap. 6. Also Pirke Avoth 1.14 as interpreted by Rashi ad loc.; *The Avot of Rabbi Nathan,* chap. 5 and chap. 11, p. 62 (the dictum of Rabbi Yose); and Matt. 5:10–12, 5:43–6:4, 6:16–18.

20. *Conflict of the Faculties,* in *Akademieausgabe,* 7.63. The full gravity of Kant's rejection, as fallacious, of Abraham's purported experience of God's command for sacrifice is indicated a few pages later (7.66), where Kant remarks that the account of Pentecost in Acts 2–3, esp. 3:25, teaches that the Holy Spirit on that occasion inspired the teaching that non-Jews "could also be regarded as admitted into this [Christian new] covenant, if they were willing to believe in the sacrifice which Abraham was willing with his only son to bring to God (as the symbol of the unique sacrifice of the World-savior); then they would be children of Abraham in faith." Kant adds, "By which, however, it does not at all belong to religion, to have to believe this as a fact and impose this belief on natural human reason." We note that Kant concedes that one *cannot be certain* that it is not God Who thus speaks, issuing commands that do not accord with the strict canon of rational morality. Kant thus seems to leave his position, or his adherence to the absolute sovereignty of reason, without firm rational or empirical ground. But in this same context he points to what he likely regards as a probative dimension of his own *historical* situation (the Enlightenment) and its prospects: "It is not to be expected that, when the Bible that we possess should cease to be believed, another would arise in its place; for public miracles do not occur a second time in the same matter—for the failure of the previous one in respect to endurance would take all belief from the following." "What will happen," Kant pointedly asks, "when church belief must one day do without this great instrument of guiding the people?" (ibid., 7.65 and 68).

21. E.g., Josephus *Antiquities* 1.13.4; *Midrash Rabbah* on Gen. 56; the Palestinian Targums, including "Jonathan" (but not Onqelos), ad Gen. 22:6–10; Jacob, *The First Book of the Bible* ad 22:10. See in a similar vein Calvin, *Commentary on Genesis* ad 22:9; and *Al-Qur'an* 37.102–5, which has Ishmael, the son whom Abraham is commanded, in a dream, to sacrifice, become the interpreter of the dream and thus the announcer of the command.

22. *Commentary on Genesis* ad 22:2; Luther, LG, *Werke,* 43:204. See similarly

St. Ephrem the Syrian's *Commentary on Genesis* ad loc., which insists even more explicitly on Abraham's utter confidence in the corporeal resurrection of Isaac. The fundamental puzzle is sharpened rather than solved by the ancient Midrashim according to which Abraham actually did slaughter and burn Isaac, who was immediately resurrected—thus exemplifying before Abraham's own eyes the fundamental creed of corporeal resurrection and the personal immortality of the just—and *whom Abraham then proceeded to try to slaughter a second time,* being only at this point stopped by the words of the Lord (reinterpreting "second time" in Gen 22:15 and interpreting the term תחת in v. 13 as meaning "after" rather than "instead of"). See Spiegel, *The Last Trial,* esp. chaps. 4 and 6, and ll. 59–64 of the poem "The Akedah" by Rabbi Ephraim ben Jacob of Bonn, on pp. 148–49.

23. Jacob rather characteristically blurs the problem by saying that Abraham went up Mount Moriah in the same spirit that Moses went up Sinai: "Feeling that he will receive a great revelation, one way or the other, he wants to be alone with his sacrifice and with God as Moses was on Mount Sinai (Ex. 19:12 ff.)" (*The First Book of the Bible* ad 22:5).

24. LG, *Werke* 43:202. On Gen. 22:11 Luther says, "Ibi vides, quam secure ludat divina maiestas in morte et omnibus viribus mortis. Colludit hic cum suo Patriarcha et eius filio, qui simul in summa Angustia et maxima victoria mortis constituti sunt."

25. *The First Book of the Bible,* 146–47: "Abraham loved God so much that he gave up his own son *so that all his followers may know the highest good.* . . . Moriah is a *summit* of religious *experience.* . . . Everything stands revealed there; both the *character* of the man who goes there as well as the essence of the divine" (my italics). The contradiction becomes more vivid in Herder's laudation of Abraham as the "Symbol of the entire covenant": "He waited long for the promise and saw it not; when finally he experienced the first fruit of it in Isaac, he had to sacrifice this. Regard all this as Symbol, of how things must be with his God-covenanted people. The friendship of God ought to be the purpose of their being chosen—but a sacrificial, burdensome friendship. The virtue, to which Abraham was educated, is one that is not visible to the eye, an unknown and a retiring—but thereby a nobler and more beautiful—virtue. It is called: Trust in Him, even as regards the most difficult and furthest future—i.e., Faith. A hero in faith, that is, in simple Greatness of Soul, in intimacy of the heart with the purest Being—that was Abraham! Such ought his people to be; and a hero of that kind is a higher being of the human spirit" (*Spirit of Hebrew Poetry,* in *Schriften zum Alten Testament,* 883).

26. Strauss, "Jerusalem and Athens," 161: Abraham's is "the trust that God in His righteousness will not do anything incompatible with His righteousness

and that while or because nothing is too wondrous for the Lord, there are firm boundaries set to Him by His righteousness, by Him. This awareness is deepened and therefore modified by the last and severest test of Abraham's trust. . . . The same concern with God's righteousness that had induced him to plead with God for the preservation of Sodom if ten just men should be found in that city, induced him not to plead for the preservation of Isaac, for God rightfully demands that He alone be loved unqualifiedly."

27. Consider the difficulty in Kass's formulation: "Only if Abraham is willing to do without the covenant (and, indeed, is willing to destroy it himself) out of awe-reverence *for the Covenantor* [my italics], can he demonstrate that he *merits* the covenant and its promised rewards" ("Educating Father Abraham: The Meaning of Fatherhood," 40).

28. See Heb. 6:13. Amos 4:2 and Ps. 89:35–36 report God as having sworn "by My holiness," and at Isa. 62:8 God is reported as having sworn "by His right hand." For other instances of God's swearing, but without indication of "by Myself," see Ps. 95:11 (also Heb. 3:11), 110:4, 132:11, Isa. 14:24–25, Amos 8:7; cf. Luke 1:73.

29. Luther subsequently goes much further: "Now it is to be wondered at, and is impossible for reason to credit, that God can and wishes to abolish death, and change it into life. But this is more wonderful: that Abraham and Isaac were convinced that this whole action is a game, and not death. . . . Death is a game— that is what Abraham was believing and sensing, . . . of this Abraham was very certain. . . . God says to Abraham: 'Kill your son etc.'; In what spirit? Playfully, pretending, joking. A happy and pleasant sport" (LG, *Werke,* 43:203, 205, 218–19, 230; see also 212 and 216: when the fire was laid, Luther suggests, Abraham delivered to his son an "oration" reconciling the apparent contradiction between promise and command through the doctrine of the resurrection of the dead).

30. At the National Gallery of Art, Washington, Rosenwald Collection 1963.11.1979; viewable on the Internet at www.nga.gov/cgi-bin/pimage?46 623+0+0.

31. Auerbach, reading this story in comparison with the Homeric poems, concludes that here the "speech does not serve, as does speech in Homer, to manifest, to externalize thoughts—on the contrary, it serves to indicate thoughts which remain unexpressed . . . [and] are only suggested by the silence and the fragmentary speeches; the whole, permeated with the most unrelieved suspense and directed toward a single goal (and to that extent more of a unity), remains mysterious and 'fraught with background' " (*Mimesis,* 12).

32. The Talmudic Babba Bathra 16a and 100a. See also the *Zohar* 1.103b and Rashi ad Gen. 18:19, as well as *Al-Qur'an* 4.125.

33. See Herder's *Spirit of Hebrew Poetry,* dialogue 7, in *Schriften zum Alten Testament,* 836.

CHAPTER 9. *Kierkegaard's Challenge*

1. *Fear and Trembling,* trans. Lowrie, 79. All references in parentheses in this chapter are to pages of this text, unless otherwise noted.

2. See *Søren Kierkegaard's Journals and Papers,* 1.5, #7 (dated 1850): "Generally it is a basic error to think that there are no negative concepts; the highest principles of all thought or the proofs of them are certainly negative. Human reason has boundaries; that is where the negative concepts are to be found. Boundary disputes are negative, constraining."

3. With a view to Plato's *Euthyphro,* this same thought could easily be reformulated in Platonic language as the priority of the *ideas*—e.g., the *ideas* of piety and justice—over the being and authority of the god or gods; but in contrast to Hegel, the *Euthyphro* also depicts, in the pious Euthyphro's stubborn intransigence, Plato's acute awareness of the believer's experientially based resistance to the philosophic dialectic.

4. See also *Journals and Papers,* 2.9, #1117 (1846): "The believer says to himself: 'The most detestable of all would be for you to allow yourself, in any ever so hidden thought, to insult God by thinking of him as having done wrong.'" Also 2.123, #1406.

5. See also ibid., 2.6, #1107 (1843).

6. Ibid., 1.4, #6 (1844): "N.B. God can appear to man only in the miracle, i.e., as soon as he sees God he sees a miracle. But on his own it is not possible for him to see the miracle, since the miracle is his own annihilation. [In margin: N.B.] The Jews expressed this figuratively by saying that to see God is death. It is more accurate to say that to see God or to see the miracle is by virtue of the absurd, for understanding must step aside."

7. Kierkegaard characterized the book as "the purely personal definition of existential faith" (ibid., 1.8, #11 [1850]).

8. In his journal of 1850 (ibid., 1.6, #9) Kierkegaard speaks self-consciously of the originality of his articulation of the religious experience: "But 'faith' has perhaps never before been represented by someone who is just as dialectical as he is immediate. He alone is continually aware that this immediacy of which he speaks is the new immediacy, and precisely this is assured by the negative sign. Take another relationship. Blessedness—and suffering. Here the true expression is: blessedness is in suffering. But it is rarely presented this way."

9. See also the entry entitled "To Sacrifice" in ibid., 4.4, #3832 (1851): "In order to determine whether this or that is a sacrifice, one must always look at the beginning. Many a man, intending to make a profit by some deal or other, has

failed and suffered a loss. Then he seeks to reinterpret the result (inverted) in terms of his having made a sacrifice—in order to get some profit anyway, that is, honor and esteem for having made a sacrifice." Also 1.154, #374 (1848).

10. Ibid., 1.7, #10 (1850): "I gladly undertake, by way of brief repetition, to emphasize what other pseudonyms have emphasized. The absurd is not the absurd or absurdities without any distinction (wherefore Johannes de Silentio: 'How many of our age understand what the absurd is?' [*Fear and Trembling*, 110–11]). The absurd is a category, and the most developed thought is required to define the Christian absurd accurately and with conceptual correctness. The absurd is a category, the negative criterion, of the divine or of the relationship to the divine. When the believer has faith, the absurd is not the absurd—faith transforms it, but in every weak moment it is again more or less absurd to him. The passion of faith is the only thing which masters the absurd—if not, then faith is not faith in the strictest sense, but a kind of knowledge. The absurd terminates negatively before the sphere of faith, which is a sphere by itself. To a third person the believer relates himself by virtue of the absurd; so must a third person judge, for a third person does not have the passion of faith. Johannes de Silentio has never claimed to be a believer; just the opposite, he has explained that he is not a believer—*in order to illuminate faith negatively*" (my italics).

11. That the retreat we have descried in *Fear and Trembling* is Kierkegaard's own, and not merely a sign of some failing in his pseudonymous voice Johannes de Silentio, is shown by the remarkable entry in his journal entitled "Christianity—Judaism," in *Journals and Papers*, 2.506, #2222 (1852):

Abraham draws the knife—then he gets Isaac again; it was not carried out in earnest; the highest earnestness was "the test," but then once again it became the enjoyment of this life.

It is different in the N.T. The sword did not hang by a horsehair over the Virgin Mary's head in order to "test" her to see if she would keep the obedience of faith in the [crucial] moment—no, it actually did penetrate her heart, stabbed her heart—but then she got a claim upon eternity, which Abraham did not get. The Apostle [Paul] was not brought to the extremity where it was revealed to him that he would come to suffer all things in order to "test" whether he personally would keep the obedience of faith—no, he actually did suffer everything, he actually did come to weep and cry out while the world rejoiced, he actually was crucified—but then he got a claim upon eternity, which Abraham did not get.

The Old Testament "test" is a child's category; God tests the believer to see if he will do it and when he sees that he will, the test is over. Actually to die to the world is not carried out in earnest—but eternity is not manifested either. It is different with Christianity.

Thus in one sense Christianity is infinitely more rigorous than Judaism; letting go, giving up, and losing the things of this earth, sheer suffering, and dying to the world are literally in earnest. In another sense Christianity is infinitely more gentle, for it manifests eternity. But to be molded and transformed so that one is consoled *solely by eternity* [my italics] means to become spirit, but to become spirit is the most agonizing of all the sufferings, even more agonizing than "the test" in the O.T.

See similarly the subsequent remarkable entry, #2223 (1853), entitled "New 'Fear and Trembling,' " as well as #2224, 2225 (both 1854); 4.400, #4666 (1851); and 6.433, #6791, entitled "Abraham—New *Fear and Trembling*" (1852).

Conclusion

1. In "the later history of the patriarchal tradition," Westermann remarks (*Genesis 12–36,* 577), "Jacob and Israel were used side by side as a designation for the people of Israel; the prophets can direct accusations against 'Jacob,' but not against Abraham."

2. See Wildavsky, *The Nursing Father,* chap. 2, "From Slavery to Anarchy: Learning from Pharaoh What Not to Do."

3. Jacob wrestles in fearful seriousness with the divine which he directly experiences in all its unpenetrated mystery and from which he wins not so much illumination as a decisive blessing (Gen. 32:24–32). The god with whom Socrates characterizes himself as having wrestled is Proteus (*Euthyphro* 15d; *Ion* 541e–542a; cf. Homer *Odyssey* 4.382ff. and Plato *Republic* 381d and context). More precisely, Socrates rather playfully suggests that he has wrestled with two avatars of Proteus: Euthyphro and Ion. The deeply ambiguous, and far from clear-cut, outcomes of these contests would seem to have confirmed Socrates in his conviction as to the rightness of his refutational life-activity, directed chiefly at the promising and nobly pious young rather than at the confirmed mature spokesmen of divinity (and still less at divinity itself), and focused chiefly on the investigation of justice and nobility ("the human things") rather than "the divine things." Yet this presupposed on Socrates' part a gripping experience of the challenge presented by the call of divine authority. Besides, Socrates has great rivals—it suffices to mention Aristophanes and Machiavelli—whose insistence on a more direct confrontation Socrates (as we can tell especially from some of his more playful utterances) would not entirely discount. After all, Socrates (or Plato) did enter some wrestling contests. Consider chap. 11 of Strauss's *The Argument and the Action of Plato's Laws* in light of his *Socrates and Aristophanes.* See also Strauss, *Thoughts on Machiavelli,* 165–66: "Bowing to the principle of authority is sterile if it is not followed by surrender to authority

itself, i.e., to this or that authority. If this step is not taken one will remain enmeshed in the religious longing or the religiosity so characteristic of our centuries, and will not be liberated by religion proper." Cf. letter to Karl Löwith of February 23, 1950, in *Gesammelte Schriften*, 3.674: "Heidegger religiös? Vielleicht ist das 'psychologisch' richtig und sicher 'geistesgeschichtlich'—alle 'modernen' Leute sind religiös."

Works Cited

Citations in the text and notes from primary sources are by standard pagination, or section numeration, of recognized critical editions. These editions, except in the case of the Scriptures, are not listed here, except where peculiarities or page numbers of a specific edition are significant. All translations from primary sources not written in English are my own unless otherwise noted, in which case the full bibliographic citation for the translation used is given below.

Primary Sources

SPECIFIC SCRIPTURAL TEXTS AND TRANSLATIONS QUOTED

The Anchor Bible: Genesis. Trans. E. A. Speiser. Garden City, N.Y.: Doubleday, 1982.

Die Bibel, oder Die Ganze Heilige Schrift des Alten und Neuen Testaments nach der Übersetzung Martin Luthers. Stuttgart: Württembergische Bibelanstalt, 1968.

The Bible as Read and Preached in the Old Synagogue: A Study in the Cycles of the Readings from Torah and Prophets, as well as from Psalms, and in the Structure of the Midrashic Homilies. 2 vols. Ed. Jacob Mann. Cincinnati: Hebrew Union College, 1940.

Biblia Hebraica Stuttgartensia. Ed. R. Kittel et al. 4th and rev. ed. Stuttgart: Deutsche Bibelgesellschaft, 1977.

The Book of Enoch. Ed. and trans. R. H. Charles. London: Society for Promoting Christian Knowledge, 1925.

The Book of Jubilees; or the Little Genesis. Trans. from the editor's Ethiopic text by R. H. Charles. London: Adam and Charles Black, 1902.

The Greek New Testament. Ed. Kurt Aland et al. 3rd ed., corrected. Stuttgart: Deutsche Bibelgesellschaft, 1983.

The New Oxford Annotated Apocrypha: The Apocryphal / Deuterocanonical Books of the Old Testament. Ed. Bruce M. Metzger, Roland E. Murphy, et al. New York: Oxford University Press, 1991.

Al-Qur'an. Trans. Ahmed Ali. "Final revised edition." Princeton: Princeton University Press, 2001 [orig. publ. 1994].

Septuaginta, Id est Vetus Testamentum graece iuxta LXX interpretes. Ed. Alfred Rahlfs. Stuttgart: Deutsche Bibelgesellschaft, 1979.

Septuaginta: Vetus Testamentum Auctoritate Academiae Scientarum Gottingensis edi-

tium; I Genesis. Ed. John William Wevers. Gottingen: Academy of Sciences, 1974.

Targum Neofiti 1: Genesis. In *The Aramaic Bible: The Targums,* vol. 1A, trans. and ed. Martin McNamara. Collegeville, Minn.: Liturgical Press, 1992.

The Targum Onqelos to Genesis. In *The Aramaic Bible: The Targums,* vol. 6, trans. and ed. Bernard Grossfeld. Wilmington, Del.: Michael Glazier, 1988.

Targum Pseudo-Jonathan: Genesis. In *The Aramaic Bible: The Targums,* vol. 1B, trans. and ed. Michael Maher. Collegeville, Minn.: Liturgical Press, 1992.

SPECIFIC EDITIONS AND TRANSLATIONS
OF OTHER PRIMARY TEXTS QUOTED

Abravanel, Isaac. *Commentary on the Pentateuch* [brief selections]. Trans. Robert Sacks. In *Medieval Political Philosophy: A Sourcebook,* ed. Ralph Lerner and Muhsin Mahdi. Ithaca, N.Y.: Cornell University Press, 1972.

Albo, Joseph. *Sefer Ha-ʿIkkarim / Book of Principles [Roots].* 4 vols. Ed. and trans. Isaac Husik. Philadelphia: Jewish Publication Society of America, 1929.

Al-Ghazali [Abu Hamid Muhammed Ibn Muhammed al-Tusi al-Ghazali]. *The Incoherence of the Philosophers.* Trans. Michael Marmura. Provo, Utah: Brigham Young University Press, 1997.

Augustine, St. *The Literal Meaning of Genesis.* 2 vols. Trans. John Hammond Taylor. New York: Newman Press, 1982.

Averroës [Abu al-Walid Muhammed ibn Ahmad ibn Muhammed ibn Rushd]. *The Incoherence of the Incoherence.* Trans. Simon Van den Bergh. 2 vols. London: Luzac, 1954.

Babylonian Talmud. Trans. I. Epstein. In Soncino Classics translations. Brooklyn: Judaica Press, 1973.

Barth, Karl. *Church Dogmatics.* Vol. 3, pts. 1 and 2 ("The Doctrine of Creation"). Trans. G. W. Bromiley et al. Edinburgh: T. and T. Clark, 1958 and 1960.

Bayle, Pierre. *Dictionnaire Historique et Critique* [Historical and Critical Dictionary]. 4 vols. 4th ed. "Revue, corrigée, et augmenté, avec la vie de l'auteur, par Mr. Des Maizeaux." Amsterdam: P. Brunel et al., 1730.

Bettenson, Henry, ed. *Documents of the Christian Church.* London: Oxford University Press, 1960.

Calvin, John. *Commentaires de Jean Calvin sur l'ancien testament: Le livre de la Genèse.* Ed. André Malet. Geneva: Labor et Fides, 1962.

———. *Institutio Christianae Religionis.* 2 vols. Ed. A. Tholuck. Edinburgh: T. and T. Clark, 1874.

———. *Institution de la religion chrestienne.* 5 vols. Ed. Jean-Daniel Benoit. Paris: Vrin, 1957.

Churchill, Winston Spencer. *The Gathering Storm.* Boston: Houghton Mifflin, 1948.

Cohen, Hermann. *Jüdische Schriften.* 3 vols. New York: Arno Press, 1980.

Derrida, Jacques. "Comment ne pas parler: Dénégations." In *Psyché: Inventions de l'autre.* Paris: Galilée, 1987. Translated by Ken Frieden as "How to Avoid Speaking: Denials." In *Derrida and Negative Theology,* ed. Harold Coward and Toby Foshay. Albany: State University of New York Press, 1992.

Descartes, René. *Oeuvres.* Vol. 6. Ed. Charles Adam and Paul Tannery. Paris: Vrin, 1965.

Diels, Hermann, and Walther Kranz, eds. *Die Fragmente der Vorsokratiker.* 2 vols. 6th ed. Zurich: Weidmann, 1985.

Edwards, Jonathan. *Notes on Scripture.* Ed. Stephen J. Stein. New Haven: Yale University Press, 1998.

Filmer, Sir Robert. *Patriarcha and Other Writings.* Ed. J. P. Sommerville. Cambridge: Cambridge University Press, 1991.

Gilgamesh, Translated from the Sîn-Leqi-Unninnî Version. Ed. John Gardner and John Maier, with the assistance of Richard A. Henshaw. New York: Alfred A. Knopf, 1984.

Ginzberg, Louis. *The Legends of the Jews.* 7 vols. Trans. Henrietta Szold et al. Philadelphia: Jewish Publication Society of America, 1967.

Grotius, Hugo. *Adamus Exul: Tragoedia* [*The Exile of Adam: A Tragedy*]. Latin text with facing English trans. In *The Celestial Cycle: The Theme of Paradise Lost in World Literature with Translations of the Major Analogues,* ed. and trans. Watson Kirkconnell. Toronto: University of Toronto Press, 1952.

Halevi, Jehudah. *Songs.* In *Three Jewish Philosophers,* ed. Hans Lewy, Alexander Altmann, and Isaak Heinemann. New York: Atheneum, 1972.

Hegel, G. W. F. *Hegels theologische Jugendschriften.* Ed. Herman Nohl. Tübingen: J. C. B. Mohr, 1907. Translated by T. M. Knox as *Early Theological Writings.* Philadelphia: University of Pennsylvania Press, 1971.

———. *Die Vorlesungen über die Philosophie der Religion* [Lectures on the Philosophy of Religion]. 3 vols. Ed. Walter Jaeschke. Hamburg: Felix Meiner, 1993.

Herder, Johann Gottfried. *Schriften zum alten Testament.* Ed. Rudolf Smend. Frankfurt am Main: Deutscher Klassiker, 1995.

Hippolytus of Rome. *Refutatio Omnium Haeresium.* Ed. Miroslav Marcovich. Patristische Text und Studien, vol. 25. Berlin: Walter De Gruyter, 1986.

Hobbes, Thomas. *Leviathan, with Selected Variants from the Latin Edition of 1688.* Ed. Edwin Curley. Indianapolis: Hackett, 1994.

Hooker, Richard. *Works.* 3 vols. Ed. John Keble. 7th ed., rev. by R. W. Church and F. Paget. New York: Burt Franklin, 1970 [reprint of 1887 ed.].

Ibn Ezra, Abraham. *Commentary on the Pentateuch: Genesis.* Trans. H. Norman Strickman and Arthur M. Silver. New York: Menorah Press, 1988.

James, William. *The Varieties of Religious Experience: A Study in Human Nature.* New York: New American Library, 1958.

Jerome, St. *St. Jerome's Hebrew Questions on Genesis.* Trans. with introd. and commentary by C. T. R. Hayward. Oxford: Clarendon Press, 1995.

Kant, Immanuel. *Lectures on Philosophical Theology.* Trans. Allen W. Wood and Gertrude M. Clark. Ithaca: Cornell University Press, 1978.

———. *Werke.* Berlin: Königliche Preussischen Akademie der Wissenschaften, 1902–38. [Referred to as the *Akademieausgabe.*]

Kierkegaard, Søren. *Fear and Trembling: A Dialectical Lyric.* In *Fear and Trembling and the Sickness unto Death,* trans. Walter Lowrie. Princeton: Princeton University Press, 1974.

———. *Søren Kierkegaard's Journals and Papers.* 7 vols. Ed. and trans. Howard and Edna Hong. Bloomington: Indiana University Press, 1967–78.

Kock, T., ed. *Comicorum Atticorum Fragmenta.* 3 vols. Leipzig: B. G. Teubner, 1880–88.

Lewis, C. S. *Perelandra.* New York: Collier-Macmillan, 1965.

Locke, John. *Questions Concerning the Law of Nature.* Ed. and trans. Robert Horwitz, Jenny Strauss Clay, and Diskin Clay. Ithaca: Cornell University Press, 1990.

———. *The Reasonableness of Christianity as Delivered in the Scriptures.* Ed. John C. Higgins-Biddle. Oxford: Clarendon Press, 1999.

———. *Two Treatises of Government.* Rev. ed. Ed. Peter Laslett. New York: New American Library, 1963.

———. *Works.* 10 vols. Aalen, Germany: Scientia Verlag, 1963 [reprint of 10th ed. of 1824].

Lucretius, Titus. *De Rerum Natura* [On the Nature of Things]. Ed., with prolegomena, critical apparatus, trans., and commentary, by Cyril Bailey. 3 vols. Oxford: Clarendon Press, 1947.

Luther, Martin. *Lectures on Genesis, 1–25.* In *Luther's Works,* vols. 1–4, ed. Jaroslav Pelikan. St. Louis: Concordia, 1958–70.

———. *Werke: Kritische Gesamtausgabe.* Weimar: Hermann Böhlaus Nachfolger, 1883–.

Maimonides or Rambam [Moses ben Maimon]. *The Commentary to Mishnah Abot.* Trans. Arthur David. New York: Bloch, 1968.

———. *Eight Chapters.* In *Ethical Writings of Maimonides,* ed. and trans. Raymond L. Weiss and Charles E. Butterworth. New York: New York University Press, 1975.

———. *The Guide of the Perplexed.* Trans. Shlomo Pines. Chicago: University of Chicago Press, 1963.

———. *Maimonides' Introduction to the Talmud.* Trans. Zvi Lampel. Brooklyn: Judaica Press, 1998.

———. *Mishneh Torah: The Book of Knowledge.* Ed. and trans. Moses Hyamson. Jerusalem: Feldheim, 1974.

Midrash Rabbah. In Soncino Classics translations. Brooklyn: Judaica Press, 1973.

Milton, John. *Christian Doctrine*. In *Complete Prose Works,* vol. 6, ed. Maurice Kelley. New Haven: Yale University Press, 1973.

Nachmanides or Ramban [or Nahmanides: Moses ben Nachman]. *Commentary on the Torah: Genesis*. Trans. Charles B. Chavel. New York: Shilo, 1971.

Nathan, Rabbi. *The Avot of Rabbi Nathan*. In *The Fathers According to Rabbi Nathan,* trans. Judah Goldin. Yale Judaica Series, vol. 10. New Haven: Yale University Press, 1955.

Nuovo, Victor, ed. *John Locke and Christianity: Contemporary Responses to The Reasonableness of Christianity*. Bristol: Thoemmes Press, 1997.

Pascal, Blaise. *Pensées*. In *Oeuvres complètes,* 1 vol., ed. Louis Lafuma. Paris: Editions du Seuil, 1963.

Rashi [Rabbi Solomon the Son of Isaac]. *"Rashi" on the Pentateuch: Genesis*. Ed. and trans. James H. Lowe. London: Hebrew Compendium, 1928.

Roberts, Alexander, and James Donaldson, eds. *The Ante-Nicene Fathers*. 9 vols. Buffalo: Christian Literature Co., 1886.

Rosenzweig, Franz. "The Unity of the Bible: A Position Paper vis-à-vis Orthodoxy and Liberalism." In *Scripture and Tradition* by Martin Buber and Franz Rosenzweig, trans. Lawrence Rosenwald with Everett Fox. Bloomington: Indiana University Press, 1994.

Rousseau, J.-J. *Discours sur l'origine et les fondemens de l'inégalité parmi les hommes*. In *Diskurs über die Ungleichheit / Discours sur l'inégalité,* ed. Heinrich Meier. Paderborn, Germany: Schöningh, 1984.

———. *Oeuvres complètes*. 5 vols. Ed. B. Gagnebin et al. Paris: Gallimard, Bibliothèque de la Pléiade, 1959–95.

Soroush, Abdolkarim. "The Sense and Essence of Secularism." In *Reason, Freedom, and Democracy in Islam: Essential Writings of Abdolkarim Soroush,* trans. and ed. Mahmoud and Ahmad Sadri. Oxford: Oxford University Press, 2000.

Spinoza, Benedict de. *The Political Works*. Ed. A. G. Wernham. Oxford: Oxford University Press, 1965.

———. *Spinoza Opera*. 2 vols. Ed. Carl Gebhardt. Heidelberg: Carl Winters Universitäts Buchhandlung, 1925.

Strauss, Leo. *The Argument and the Action of Plato's Laws*. Chicago: University of Chicago Press, 1975.

———. *Gesammelte Schriften*. Ed. Heinrich Meier. 3 vols. to date. Stuttgart: J. B. Metzler, 1996–.

———. "Jerusalem and Athens: Some Preliminary Reflections." In *Studies in Platonic Political Philosophy*. Chicago: University of Chicago Press, 1983.

———. *Natural Right and History*. Chicago: University of Chicago Press, 1953.

———. "On the Interpretation of Genesis." *L'homme: Revue française d'anthropologie* 21 (1981): 5–36.

——. *Persecution and the Art of Writing.* Glencoe, Ill.: Free Press, 1952.

——. *Philosophy and Law: Contributions to the Understanding of Maimonides and His Predecessors.* Trans. Eve Adler. Albany: State University of New York Press, 1995 [orig. publ. 1935].

——. *Socrates and Aristophanes.* New York: Basic Books, 1966.

——. *Spinoza's Critique of Religion.* Trans. Elsa M. Sinclair. New York: Schocken, 1965 [orig. publ. 1930].

——. *Thoughts on Machiavelli.* Glencoe, Ill.: Free Press, 1958.

Thomas Aquinas, St. *Compendium of Theology.* Trans. Cyril Vollert. St. Louis: Herder, 1947.

——. *Summa contra Gentiles.* Trans. English Dominicans. London: Burns, Oates, and Washbourne, 1934.

——. *Summa Theologica.* Trans. English Dominicans. London: Burns, Oates, and Washbourne, 1912–36; repr. New York: Christian Classics, 1981.

Voegelin, Eric. *The New Science of Politics: An Introduction.* Chicago: University of Chicago Press, 1952.

Zohar. In Soncino Classics translations. Brooklyn: Judaica Press, 1973.

Secondary Works and Contemporary Commentaries

Aalen, S. *Die Begriffe "Licht" und "Finsternis" im Alten Testament, im Spätjudentum und im Rabbinisimus.* Oslo: Norske Videnskaps-akademi i Oslo, 1951.

Albright, William Foxwell. "The Biblical Period." In *The Jews: Their History,* ed. Louis Finkelstein. New York: Schocken, 1974.

——. *From the Stone Age to Christianity.* Baltimore: Johns Hopkins Press, 1940.

Alter, Robert. *The Art of Biblical Narrative.* New York: Basic Books, 1981.

——. *Genesis: Translation and Commentary.* New York: W. W. Norton, 1996.

Alter, Robert, and Frank Kermode, eds. *The Literary Guide to the Bible.* Cambridge: Harvard University Press, 1987.

Anbar, M. "Genesis 15: A Conflation of Two Deuteronomic Narratives." *Journal of Biblical Literature* 101 (1982): 39–55.

Auerbach, Erich. *Mimesis.* Trans. Willard Trask. Princeton: Princeton University Press, 1953.

Bainton, Roland. *Here I Stand: A Life of Martin Luther.* New York: New American Library, 1977.

Barr, James. "The Synchronic, the Diachronic, and the Historical: A Triangular Relationship?" In *Synchronic or Diachronic? A Debate on Method in Old Testament Exegesis,* ed. Johannes C. de Moor. Oudtestamentische Studien, vol. 34. Leiden: E. J. Brill, 1995.

Barth, Karl. *Der Römerbrief.* Zürich: Theologischer Verlag, 1989 [orig. publ. 1919; 2nd ed. 1922].

Bartlett, Robert. *The Idea of Enlightenment: A Post-mortem Study.* Toronto: University of Toronto Press, 2000.

Bickerman, Elias J. "The Historical Foundations of Postbiblical Judaism." In *The Jews: Their History,* ed. Louis Finkelstein. New York: Schocken, 1974.

Blenkinsopp, Joseph. *The Pentateuch: An Introduction to the First Five Books of the Bible.* New York: Doubleday, 1992.

Bloom, Harold, and David Rosenberg. *The Book of J.* New York: Grove Weidenfeld, 1990.

Blum, E. *Die Komposition der Vätergeschichte.* Neukirchen-Vluyn: Neukirchener Verlag des Erziehungsvereins, 1984.

Bonhoeffer, Dietrich. *Creation and Fall: A Theological Interpretation of Genesis 1– 3.* Trans. John C. Fletcher et al. London: SCM Press, 1959.

Buber, Martin. "Abraham the Seer." In *On the Bible: Eighteen Studies,* ed. Nahum Glatzer. New York: Schocken, 1968.

Burkert, Walter. *Greek Religion.* Trans. John Raffan. Cambridge: Harvard University Press, 1985.

Caputo, John D. *The Prayers and Tears of Jacques Derrida: Religion without Religion.* Bloomington: Indiana University Press, 1997.

Carr, David M. *Reading the Fractures of Genesis: Historical and Literary Approaches.* Louisville, Ky.: Westminster John Knox Press, 1996.

Cassirer, Ernst. *The Philosophy of the Enlightenment.* Trans. Fritz C. A. Koelln and James P. Pettegrove. Princeton: Princeton University Press, 1951.

Cassuto, Umberto. *A Commentary on the Book of Genesis.* Trans. Israel Abrahams. 2 vols. Jerusalem: Magnes Press, 1961–64.

———. *The Documentary Hypothesis and the Composition of the Pentateuch.* Trans. Israel Abrahams. Jerusalem: Magnes Press, 1961.

Childs, Brevard S. *Biblical Theology of the Old and New Testaments: Theological Reflection on the Christian Bible.* Minneapolis: Fortress Press, 1993.

———. *Introduction to the Old Testament as Scripture.* Philadelphia: Fortress Press, 1979.

Craghan, J. F. "The Elohist in Recent Literature." *Biblical Theological Bulletin* 7 (1977): 23–35.

Cross, Frank M. *Canaanite Myth and Hebrew Epic: Essays in the History of the Religion of Israel.* Cambridge: Harvard University Press, 1973.

Dantinne, E. "Création et séparation." *Le muséon* 74 (1961): 441–51.

Doctorow, E. L. Introduction to *The First Book of Moses, Called Genesis.* New York: Grove Press, 1999.

Eissfeldt, Otto. *The Old Testament: An Introduction, Including Apocrypha and Pseudoepigrapha.* Trans. Peter R. Ackroyd. Rev. ed. New York: Harper and Row, 1965.

Elazar, Daniel J. *Kinship and Consent: The Jewish Political Tradition and Its Contemporary Manifestations.* Ramat-Gan: Turtledove, 1981.

Elazar, Daniel J., and Stuart A. Cohen. *The Jewish Polity: Jewish Political Organization from Biblical Times to the Present.* Bloomington: Indiana University Press, 1985.

Faguet, Emile. *Dix-huitième siècle: Etudes littéraires.* Paris: Boivin, 1898.

Fish, Stanley. *Surprised by Sin: The Reader in Paradise Lost.* London: Macmillan, 1967.

Fokkelman, J. P. *Narrative Art in Genesis: Specimens of Stylistic and Structural Analysis.* Amsterdam: Van Gorcum, Studia Semitica Neerlandica, 1975.

Fortin, Ernest L. "Augustine and the Problem of Human Goodness." In *The Birth of Philosophic Christianity: Studies in Early Christian and Medieval Thought,* vol. 1 of *Collected Essays,* 3 vols., ed. J. Brian Benestad. Lanham, Md.: Rowman and Littlefield, 1996.

Fradkin, Hillel. "Biblical Interpretation and the Art of Writing" [review of Robert Alter's *Art of Biblical Narrative*]. *This World* 1 (1982): 139–45.

———. "God's Politics—Lessons from the Beginning." *This World* 4 (1983): 86–104.

———. "Poet-Kings: A Biblical Perspective on Heroes." In *Political Philosophy and the Human Soul: Essays in Memory of Allan Bloom,* ed. Michael Palmer and T. L. Pangle. Lanham, Md.: Rowman and Littlefield, 1995.

———. "With All Your Heart and with All Your Soul and with All Your Might: Love in the Hebrew Bible." In *Reflections on Love and Friendship,* ed. Nathan Tarcov. Chicago: University of Chicago Press, forthcoming.

Frankfurt, Henri, et al. *Before Philosophy: The Intellectual Adventure of Ancient Man.* Harmondsworth, U.K.: Penguin, 1951.

Frye, Northrop. *The Great Code: The Bible and Literature.* New York: Harcourt Brace Jovanovich, 1982.

Guitton, Jean. *Le temps et l'éternité chez Plotin et Saint Augustin.* Paris: Vrin, 1971.

Gunkel, Hermann. *Genesis.* Trans. Mark E. Biddle. Macon, Ga.: Mercer University Press, 1997. [A translation of the commentary portion of *Genesis / übersetzt und erklärt von Hermann Gunkel,* orig. publ. 1901.]

Hahn, Herbert F. *The Old Testament in Modern Research.* Updated ed. by Horace D. Hummel. Philadelphia: Fortress Press, 1985.

Hess, R. S. "The Genealogies of Genesis 1–11 and Comparative Literature." *Biblica* 70 (1989): 251–53.

Hirsch, Samson Raphael. *The Pentateuch, Translation and Commentary.* Trans. Isaac Levy. 2nd ed. Gateshead, England: Judaica Press, 1973.

Houtman, C. "The Pentateuch." In *The World of the Old Testament,* vol. 2 of *Bible Handbook,* ed. A. S. Van Der Woude, trans. Sierd Woudstra. Grand Rapids, Mich.: Eerdmans, 1989.

Humbert, P. "Emploi et portée bibliques du verbe *yasar* et de ses dérivés substantifs." *Festschrift O. Eissfeldt, Beihefte zur Zeitschrift für die Alttestamentliche Wissenschaft* 77 (1958): 82–88.

———. *Etudes sur le récit du Paradis et de la chute dans la Genèse*. Paris: Mémoires de l'Université de Neuchatel 14, 1940.

Hurvitz, Avi. "The Evidence of Language in Dating the Priestly Code: A Linguistic Study in Technical Idioms and Terminology." *Revue biblique* 81 (1974): 25–46.

Jacob, Benno. *Das erste Buch der Tora, Genesis*. Berlin: Schocken, 1934. Abridged, edited, and translated by Ernest I. Jacob and Walter Jacob as *The First Book of the Bible: Genesis*. New York: KTAV, 1974.

Jonas, Hans. *The Gnostic Religion: The Message of the Alien God and the Beginnings of Christianity*. 2nd ed., rev. Boston: Beacon Press, 1972.

Kass, Leon. "Educating Father Abraham: The Meaning of Fatherhood." *First Things* 48 (December 1994): 32–43.

———. "Educating Father Abraham: The Meaning of Wife." *First Things* 47 (November 1994): 16–26.

———. "Evolution and the Bible: Genesis 1 Revisited." *Commentary* 86 (November 1988): 28–39.

———. "A Genealogy of Justice." *Commentary* 102 (July 1996): 44–51.

———. "Man and Woman: An Old Story." *First Things* 17 (November 1991): 14–26.

———. "Seeing the Nakedness of His Father." *Commentary* 93 (June 1992): 41–47.

———. "What's Wrong with Babel?" *American Scholar* 58 (1989): 41–60.

———. "Why the Dietary Laws?" *Commentary* 97 (June 1994): 42–48.

Katsh, Abraham I. *Judaism in Islam: Biblical and Talmudic Backgrounds of the Koran and Its Commentaries*. 3rd ed. New York: Sepher-Herman, 1980.

Kaufmann, Yehezkel. *The Religion of Israel: From Its Beginnings to the Babylonian Exile*. Trans. and abridged by Moshe Greenberg. New York: Schocken, 1960.

Kittel, G., et al., eds. *Theologisches Wörterbuch zum Neuen Testament*. 10 vols. Stuttgart: W. Kohlhammer, 1932–79.

Knierim, Rolf. "Criticism of Literary Features, Form, Tradition, and Redaction." In *The Hebrew Bible and Its Modern Interpreters,* ed. Douglas A. Knight and Gene M. Tucker. Philadelphia: Fortress, 1985.

Knight, Douglas A. "The Pentateuch." In *The Hebrew Bible and Its Modern Interpreters,* ed. Douglas A. Knight and Gene M. Tucker. Philadelphia: Fortress, 1985.

Kogan, Barry. *Averroës and the Metaphysics of Causation*. Albany: State University of New York Press, 1985.

Leibowitz, Nehama. *Studies in the Book of Genesis, in the Context of Ancient and Modern Jewish Bible Commentary.* Trans. and adapted by Aryeh Newman. Jerusalem: World Zionist Organization, 1972.

Leiman, Sid Z. *The Canonization of Hebrew Scripture: The Talmudic and Midrashic Evidence.* Hamden, Conn.: Archon, Transactions of the Connecticut Academy of Arts and Sciences, 1976.

Licht, Jacob. *Storytelling in the Bible.* Jerusalem: Magnes Press, 1978.

Martin, William J. *Stylistic Criteria and the Analysis of the Pentateuch.* London: Tyndale Press, 1955.

May, Gerhard. *Creatio ex Nihilo: The Doctrine of "Creation out of Nothing" in Early Christian Thought.* Trans. A. S. Worrall. Edinburgh: T. and T. Clark, 1994.

Meier, Heinrich. *Carl Schmitt, Leo Strauss und "Der Begriff des Politischen."* 2nd and enl. ed. Stuttgart: J. B. Metzler, 1998.

Momigliano, Arnaldo. "The Second Book of Maccabees." In *Essays on Ancient and Modern Judaism,* ed. Silvia Berti, trans. Maura Masella-Gayley. Chicago: University of Chicago Press, 1994.

Noth, Martin. *A History of Pentateuchal Traditions.* Trans. B. W. Anderson. Englewood Cliffs, N.J.: Prentice-Hall, 1972.

Nuland, Sherwin B. *How We Die: Reflections on Life's Final Chapter.* New York: Random House, 1993.

O'Donovan, Oliver, and Joan Lockwood O'Donovan, eds. *From Ireneus to Grotius: A Sourcebook in Christian Political Thought.* Grand Rapids, Mich.: Eerdmans, 1999.

Otto, Rudolf. *The Idea of the Holy.* Trans. John W. Harvey. Oxford: Oxford University Press, 1972.

Owen, J. Judd. *Religion and the Demise of Liberal Rationalism: The Foundational Crisis of the Separation of Church and State.* Chicago: University of Chicago Press, 2001.

Pangle, Thomas L. "A Critique of Hobbes's Critique of Biblical and Natural Religion in *Leviathan.*" *Jewish Political Studies Review* 4 (Fall 5753 / 1992): 25–57.

———. *The Ennobling of Democracy: The Challenge of the Postmodern Era.* Baltimore: Johns Hopkins University Press, 1992.

———. "The Hebrew Bible's Challenge to Political Philosophy: Some Preliminary Reflections." In *Political Philosophy and the Human Soul: Essays in Memory of Allan Bloom,* ed. Michael Palmer and T. L. Pangle. Lanham, Md.: Rowman and Littlefield, 1995.

———. *The Spirit of Modern Republicanism: The Moral Vision of the American Founders and the Philosophy of Locke.* Chicago: University of Chicago Press, 1988.

Pelikan, Jaroslav. *The Christian Tradition: A History of the Development of Doctrine.* 5 vols. Chicago: University of Chicago Press, 1971–89.

Rad, Gerhard von. *Das erste Buch Mose: Genesis.* 6th ed. Göttingen: Vandenhoeck und Ruprecht, 1961. Translated by John H. Marks as *Genesis: A Commentary.* Philadelphia: Westminster Press, 1961.

———. "The Form-Critical Problem of the Hexateuch." In *The Problem of the Hexateuch and Other Essays,* trans. E. W. Trueman Dicken. Edinburgh: Oliver and Boyd, 1966 [orig. publ. 1938].

———. *Old Testament Theology.* Trans. D. M. G. Stalker. New York: Harper and Row, 1962.

Rendtorff, Rolf. "Between Historical Criticism and Holistic Interpretation: New Trends in Old Testament Exegesis." *Vetus Testamentum Supplements* 40 (1987): 298–303.

———. *Das überlieferungsgeschichtliche Problem des Pentateuch.* Berlin: Walter de Gruyter, 1977. Translated as *The Problem of the Process of Transmission in the Pentateuch.* Sheffield: *Journal for the Study of the Old Testament* Supplement Series 89, 1990.

———. "The 'Yahwist' as Theologian? The Dilemma of Pentateuchal Criticism." *Journal for the Study of the Old Testament* 3 (1977): 2–10.

Robbins, F. E. "The Influence of Greek Philosophy on the Early Commentaries." *American Journal of Theology* 16 (1912): 218–40.

Rosenberg, Joel. "Meanings, Morals, and Mysteries: Literary Approaches to the Torah." *Response* 9 (1975): 67–94.

Sacks, Robert. "The Lion and the Ass: A Commentary on the Book of Genesis (Chapters 1–10)." *Interpretation: A Journal of Political Philosophy* 8 (1980): 29–101.

Sarna, Nahum M. *The Jewish Publication Society Torah Commentary: Genesis.* Jerusalem: Jewish Publication Society, 1989.

Schmid, Hans Heinrich. *Der sogenannte Jahwist.* Zurich: Theologischer Verlag, 1976.

Schmuttermayr, Georg. " 'Schöpfung aus dem Nichts' in 2 Makk 7,28? Zum Verhältnis von Position und Bedeutung." *Biblische Zeitschrift,* n.s., 17 (1973): 203–28.

Scholem, Gershom. *Major Trends in Jewish Mysticism.* New York: Schocken, 1973.

———. *The Messianic Idea in Judaism and Other Essays on Jewish Spirituality.* New York: Schocken, 1974.

———. *On the Kabbalah and Its Symbolism.* New York: Schocken, 1973.

———. "Schöpfung aus Nichts und Selbstverschränkung Gottes." *Eranos-Jahrbuch* 25 (1956/57): 87–119.

Skinner, John. *A Critical and Exegetical Commentary on Genesis.* New York: Scribners, 1910.

Sorabji, Richard. *Time, Creation, and the Continuum: Theories in Antiquity and the Early Middle Ages.* London: Duckworth, 1983.

Spiegel, Shalom. *The Last Trial: On the Legends and Lore of the Command to Abraham to Offer Isaac as a Sacrifice—the Akedah.* Trans. Judah Goldin. New York: Random House, Pantheon Books, 1967.

Thompson, Thomas L. *The Origin Tradition of Ancient Israel I: The Literary Formation of Genesis and Exodus 1–23.* Sheffield: *Journal for the Study of the Old Testament* Supplement Series 55, 1987.

Van Seters, John. *Abraham in History and Tradition.* New Haven: Yale University Press, 1975.

————. *In Search of History: Historiography in the Ancient World and the Origins of Biblical History.* New Haven: Yale University Press, 1983.

————. "The Primeval Histories of Greece and Israel Compared." *Zeitschrift für die Alttestamentliche Wissenschaft* 100 (1988): 1–22.

————. *Prologue to History: The Yahwist as Historian in Genesis.* Louisville, Ky.: Westminster John Knox Press, 1992.

Vink, J. G. "The Date and Origin of the Priestly Code in the Old Testament." *Oudtestamentische Studiën* 11 (1969): 1–144.

Vriezen, Th. C. *The Religion of Ancient Israel.* Trans. H. Hoskins. Philadelphia: Westminster Press, 1967.

Weiss, H.-F. *Untersuchungen zur Kosmologie des hellenistischen und palästinischen Judentums.* Berlin: Akademie Verlag, 1966.

Wellhausen, Julius. "Die Composition des Hexateuchs," *Jahrbücher für deutsche Theologie* 21 (1876): 392–450, 531–602; and 22 (1877): 407–79.

————. *Prolegomena to the History of Israel; with a Reprint of the Article "Israel" from the Encyclopaedia Britannica.* Trans. W. Robertson Smith. Atlanta: Scholars Press, 1994 [reprint of the 1885 ed.].

Westermann, Claus. *Genesis 1–11: A Commentary.* Trans. John J. Scullion, S. J. Minneapolis: Augsburg, 1984.

————. *Genesis 12–36: A Commentary.* Trans. John J. Scullion, S. J. Minneapolis: Augsburg, 1985.

Wevers, John William. *Notes on the Greek Text of Genesis.* Society of Biblical Literature, Septuagint and Cognate Studies Series, no. 35. Atlanta: Scholars Press, 1993.

Whybray, R. N. *Introduction to the Pentateuch.* Grand Rapids, Mich.: Eerdmans, 1995.

————. *The Making of the Pentateuch: A Methodological Study.* Sheffield: *Journal for the Study of the Old Testament* Supplement Series 53, 1987.

Wildavsky, Aaron. *Assimilation versus Separation: Joseph the Administrator and the Politics of Religion in Biblical Israel*. New Brunswick, N.J.: Transaction, 1993.

———. *The Nursing Father: Moses as a Political Leader*. University: University of Alabama Press, 1984.

Williams, Arnold. *The Common Expositor: An Account of the Commentaries on Genesis, 1527–1633*. Chapel Hill: University of North Carolina Press, 1948.

Winnett, Frederick V. "Re-examining the Foundations." *Journal of Biblical Literature* 84 (1965): 1–19.

Index